Star Wars

Essays Exploring a Galaxy Far, Far Away

Edited by

Emily Strand

Amy H. Sturgis

Series in Cinema and Culture

Vernon Press

www.vernonpress.com

In the Americas:
Vernon Press
1000 N West Street, Suite 1200
Wilmington, Delaware, 19801
United States

In the rest of the world:
Vernon Press
C/Sancti Espiritu 17,
Malaga, 29006
Spain

Series in Cinema and Culture

Library of Congress Control Number: 2023936068

ISBN: 978-1-64889-671-2

Cover design by Vernon Press. Cover image by Emily Austin.

Table of Contents

Foreword

Ian Doescher

It starts with wonder. It's different for everyone; for me, it was the creatures. It was Bossk; it was the Ewoks; it was Jabba the Hutt; it was Hammerhead (only much later did I learn his real name, Momaw Nadon). I saw *Return of the Jedi* at age six, sitting in the theater with my parents, my uncle translating into Japanese for my aunt in the row behind us. I made up stories with action figures. I watched *The Making of a Saga* to learn—and re-learn, after repeated viewings—how the magic was made. I stretched out my hand to see if maybe, this time, I could move an object using the Force. And my story isn't unique. While the details are different, I fell in love with *Star Wars* the way billions of people have since 1977. People just like you. It starts with wonder.

After the wonder, *Star Wars* becomes part of your cultural consciousness. No matter where in the world you go, you notice people of all ages wearing *Star Wars* shirts. You hear the theme music playing in Minnesota's Mall of America. You see a man in a Stormtrooper outfit in Belgrade. You hang out with members of the *Star Wars* fan club in Kuala Lumpur. You encounter life-size R2-D2 replicas at a London comic con. You realize *Star Wars* has a broader reach and has "become more powerful"—as Obi-Wan Kenobi might say—"than you can possibly imagine." You see *Star Wars* everywhere.

Next, you codify your thoughts and opinions. *Star Wars* is the modern mythology; you know its characters as well as you know your friends. If pressed, you could separate them into major gods (e.g., Leia, Luke, Darth Vader), minor gods (e.g., Boba Fett, Qui-Gon Jinn, Maz Kanata), and aetiological myths (e.g., how Han Solo won the *Millennium Falcon*). You form beliefs and take sides in longstanding arguments: Who shot first? Is *The Last Jedi* a work of genius or the worst of the bunch? Where do you stand on the Prequels? In what order should you watch the movies? You realize that in a gathering of 1,138 *Star Wars* fans, there will be 1,139 opinions.

Then, you make connections. You relate *Star Wars* to other important pieces of your life. People who love electronics build droids. People who sew make costumes. People who draw make fan art. People who write create fiction and nonfiction. There are *Star Wars* books about parenting, education, philosophy, religion, cooking, architecture, and the film industry (naturally). The stories have been expanded, explained, and transformed into everything from comics to erotica, paper art to video games, arcana to academic articles, and children's books to, yes, Shakespeare. You make connections because *Star Wars* is part of your identity, and you want it to speak to your other interests.

Eventually—whether you're a scholar or a fan or some combination of the two—you seek out books like this one, which connects *Star Wars* to language, numerology, motherhood, art and artists, identity, and much more. With each page, you smile at familiar references, you grapple with new ideas, you reshape your thoughts and beliefs, and you emerge with a new understanding and appreciation of this thing—this film series, this story machine, this cultural juggernaut, this contemporary collection of legends—called *Star Wars*.

And in the end, you're right back at wonder. Happy reading, and may the Force be with you.

Portland, Oregon, January 2023

Introduction

Emily Strand and Amy H. Sturgis

After more than 45 years since its first release, can there possibly be *more* to say about *Star Wars*?

As the "acafans"[1] we proudly admit we are, we could be biased, but we suspect that even if 1977's *Star Wars* had been the only *Star Wars* film, both fans and academics would still be talking and writing about it today. Of course, there is no need for such speculation. There are no alternate timelines to speak of in *Star Wars* as boggle the imagination in *Star Trek* and other franchises. There is no world in which that 1977 film phenomenon—one that saw audiences wrapping around blocks to see it and cinemas clearing the house between showings, when they'd never had to before[2]—was a stand-alone. George Lucas talked of sequels even as the first film was in production. But with now more than a dozen feature films, hundreds of novels and comics, close to 400 episodes of narrative television (and counting), and a distinctive and desirable brand serving up everything from toys to fashion, from kitchen utensils to cars, *Star Wars* continues to provide rich fodder for conversation from as many angles as there are visible star systems in the night sky over Mos Espa.

One need not be as ambitious as Anakin Skywalker to want to visit them all. But this is no small feat; the universe is still expanding, after all. As *Star Wars* stretches out in space and time, it only gains relevance. An obvious, recent example is the 2022 first season of the television show *Andor*, contextualizing one of the heroes of 2016's critically acclaimed *Rogue One: A Star Wars Story*. Critics have noted real-world parallels to *Andor*'s depiction of unease and dissatisfaction morphing into rebellion in places like Iran, China, and Peru and among global activists concerned with climate change, reproductive rights, and

---

[1] This is a term for an academic who identifies as a fan of what they study, popularized by Matt Hills in his monograph *Fan Cultures* (Oxfordshire, UK: Routledge, 2002), but forerun by Patricia Gillikin's founding of ACAFEN-L, an academic group for the study of fandom. See "Acafan" on Fanlore, accessed January 27, 2023, https://fanlore.org/wiki/Acafan.

[2] Chris Taylor, *How Star Wars Conquered the Universe: The Past, Present, and Future of a Multibillion Dollar Franchise* (New York: Basic Books, 2014), 183.

racial justice.[3] But this amplified relevance of *Star Wars* stretches backwards as well, as previous works in the franchise resonate in new ways for new audiences in new times. For instance, the Prequel films of the 1990s and early 2000s presently enjoy something of a renaissance, as demonstrated by new works that narratively explore those "Dark Times" in which the Prequel films leave off, like the seventh season of *Star Wars: The Clone Wars* (2020), *The Bad Batch* (2022-), and *Obi-Wan Kenobi* (2022-). Indeed, even *Star Wars Episode II: Attack of the Clones* (2002), a film many fans and critics point to as the worst of the franchise, carries a grim, new relevance in a post-COVID-19 pandemic, post-January 6, 2021 world in which American democracy is widely regarded to be backsliding. Turns out, when you look beyond the romance scenes between Padmé and Anakin that made some fans cringe in *Attack of the Clones*, one finds a darkly political film that poses important questions about the nature of fear and how it contributes not just to one man's descent into evil but to the transformation of democracy into tyranny.[4]

This enduring and expanding relevance of *Star Wars* certainly helped bring the editors of this volume together. Our connection began as that of student and teacher; Emily Strand had taken Amy H. Sturgis's courses at Signum University, an online institution for the study of speculative fiction. When Sturgis announced she would offer a course on *Star Wars* in the fall of 2015 in anticipation of the new films soon to be released, Strand eagerly registered. The space afforded by the course for observation, dialogue, investigation, and interpretation led to collaborations by Sturgis and Strand at conferences, in edited collections, and on podcasts. When an opportunity to co-edit scholarly volumes on *Star Wars* and *Star Trek* emerged, Sturgis and Strand came together as an editing team, drawing other scholars into the "larger world" of academic conversation on these franchises' enduring and expanding relevance.

The essays ultimately selected for the present volume (and for its companion volume, *Star Trek: Essays Exploring the Final Frontier*, also published by Vernon Press) represent a broad range of scholarship by an international, highly qualified, and diverse array of scholars. Chapters herein astutely observe and fruitfully reflect on every era of the franchise from *A New Hope* to *Andor*, demonstrating the franchise's continued resonance. Some chapters put the

---

[3] Oli Mould, "Star Wars Andor captures the essence of resistance that is happening in the real world," The Conversation, November 17, 2022, https://theconversation.com/star-wars-andor-captures-the-essence-of-resistance-that-is-happening-in-the-real-world-194566.

[4] Jason T. Eberl and Kevin S. Decker, "Introduction, 'The Circle is Now Complete,'" in *The Ultimate Star Wars and Philosophy: You Must Unlearn What You Have Learned*, ed. Jason T. Eberl and Kevin S. Decker (Chichester, UK: Wiley Blackwell, 2016), 2.

franchise in dialogue, as Ian Doescher describes in the foreword, with the scholar's own academic expertise. Others take the franchise on its own terms, telling the story of some aspect of it in revealing, insightful, and sometimes critical detail. All chapters help readers gain awareness, insight, and appreciation for, as Doescher puts it, the "cultural juggernaut" that is *Star Wars*. (Doescher's own Shakespearean translations of *Star Wars* confront this juggernaut—in both its glories and faults—through his mastery of the clever genre of pastiche, increasing reader's appreciation for both Shakespeare and *Star Wars*. His works are highly recommended.) But *Star Wars* inspires critique as well as admiration, and many observations of the scholars whose writings fill this book are not unqualified. Indeed, one of the many ways in which *Star Wars* continues to assert its relevance is in the observable ways it has evolved and changed over time, often in answer to critique.

Exploring the Series and Films

This dynamic of change is readily observable in our first essay, a broad-ranging and compelling textual analysis of the evolution of Twi'leks from 1977 to today by *Star Wars* non-fiction author Amy Richau. Richau's sharp-eyed look at *Star Wars'* treatment of this iconic species, marked by their long, fleshy head tails and a certain sexual allure, tells another story: how the metaphorical Other has been perceived and presented in *Star Wars*—and how it might be going forward. It's a complicated story that resonates in a #MeToo world. In the next chapter, Vikki Terrile writes about a subtler but no less relevant strain of *Star Wars*: the importance of makers like Rey, Kuiil, Rose Tico, and others in the stories who, through their making, resist tyranny, giving us hope for a more vibrant existence—not just for ourselves as individuals but for our communities, our society. As Rose Tico says, the way we'll win is by saving what we love; Terrile's analysis invites us to consider the role of creative endeavors in fostering a stronger, freer society. Lastly, in this section, in focusing on a bleak, even misogynistic aspect of the franchise, Éloïse Thompson-Tremblay's study of mothers in *Star Wars* performs important work, acknowledging the grim truth that motherhood in the stories makes even strong women disposable, passive, dispossessed. But Thompson-Tremblay's work also points up how essential these sometimes forgotten women are to the stories and their heroes. As *Star Wars* expands into the future, the chapter notes how its message about mothers shifts, as recent *Star Wars* television shows demonstrate. Perhaps motherhood—in *Star Wars* and in real life—need not sap a woman's will to live.

Exploring the Ideas

The powerful ideas that thread through *Star Wars* stories keep viewers coming back to the franchise, offering windows into larger concepts, and such vistas of insight feature in our second section of the volume. Emily Strand's chapter, "*21-87*: Not Just a Number in *Star Wars*," spans the franchise to reveal the depth of influence of Arthur Lipsett's 1963 experimental film *21-87*, not just on Lucas but also on the creators who make *Star Wars* today. No matter what one thinks of the Sequel films, in their overt emphasis on rebelling against the Machine for the sake of self-actualization and—even higher on Maslow's hierarchy of human needs—transcendent connection with others,[5] Strand's essay argues the Sequels are, in at least this sense, of whole cloth with the franchise. In "The Map in the Mirror: Reflections of Time, Self, and Salvation in *Star Wars* and *Harry Potter*," Kathryn N. McDaniel argues that the mirrors both Rey and Harry encounter serve as metaphorical maps, pointing them through past, present, and even future realities to their own heroic destinies. Along this journey, the many striking parallels McDaniel identifies between these two heroes and their stories will fascinate those familiar with both franchises. Finally, in this section, Jennifer Russell-Long takes a creative approach to her argument that paratexts, like the *Star Wars* card game Sabacc, are an important way in which fans create and express cultural memory. Sabacc gameplay, she argues, offers material, ludonarrative experiences that effectively gain players a better appreciation of the many perspectives that make up *Star Wars*—not to mention real-world history and culture. (Russell-Long's chapter may also inspire you to acquire your own deck and give Sabacc, a storied blend of Blackjack and Poker, a try. We receive no commissions.)

Exploring the Multimedia Storytelling

Four chapters in the final section of the volume explore the important narrative and cultural contributions in other forms of *Star Wars* media besides the blockbuster films—or behind the scenes. Aaron Masters's essay on the complex moral perspectives in the video game *Star Wars: Knights of the Old Republic II—The Sith Lords* provides a valuable contribution to both *Star Wars* scholarship and to video game studies. It also gives film-only fans of *Star Wars* a glimpse into the important characters, narratives, and ideas featured in other media. In "This is the Way: *The Mandalorian* and the Evolving Serial Medium," Paul Johnson explores the serial nature and production techniques of *Star Wars*'s first streaming television show, demonstrating how *The Mandalorian* adheres to fundamental aspects of the franchise while innovating new ways for at-home viewers to immerse in its alluring world.

The volume's final two chapters expertly explore behind-the-scenes aspects of *Star Wars* storytelling. Andrew Higgins's chapter, "From 'Utinni!' to 'Aliit

---

[5] Atul Gawande, *Being Mortal: Medicine and What Matters in the End* (New York: Henry Holt and Company, 2013), 127.

Ori'shya Tal'din': The Glossopoeiac Journey of *Star Wars*," gives a fascinating and expansive view into a crucial but sometimes overlooked aspect of *Star Wars* world-building: invented languages. In his comprehensive study, Higgins chronicles the creative and problematic methods that marked the franchise's early approaches to language invention, mostly done through sound-capture. But Higgins also details how the franchise's approach to constructed languages has evolved and complexified over the decades, upping *Star Wars*'s conlang game and bringing opportunities for greater diversity and representation in *Star Wars*. Finally, veteran *Star Wars* fiction author John Jackson Miller expands our minds about the troublesome question of canonicity in the franchise's books and comics. His valuable insider perspective will help long-time readers of tie-in works better understand Disney's 2014 decision to de-canonize the Expanded Universe (or EU, now known as "Legends"). As Miller shows, there will always be a bit of truth in these "legends," as characters, planets, storylines, and other elements from the EU are harvested to feature in new, canonical works of *Star Wars* literature.

Author Chris Taylor says, "the greatest strength of *Star Wars* is what it doesn't tell you."[6] Lucas left much of the world-building and narrative context off-screen in that first *Star Wars* film, inviting viewers to imagine for themselves, as the best stories do. The following chapters aim not only to expand our understanding of the many and multiplying narratives from a galaxy far, far away but also to help us grasp the many ways in which *Star Wars* resonates with our contemporary world. The future is always in motion, as a wise Jedi once said, and these essays provide a fascinating set of coordinates to explore. Shall we make the jump?

Bibliography

"Acafan." Fanlore. Accessed January 27, 2023. https://fanlore.org/wiki/Acafan.

Eberl, Jason T. and Kevin S. Decker. "Introduction, 'The Circle is Now Complete.'" In *The Ultimate Star Wars and Philosophy: You Must Unlearn What You Have Learned*, edited by. Jason T. Eberl and Kevin S. Decker, 1-4. Chichester, UK: Wiley Blackwell, 2016.

Gawande, Atul. *Being Mortal: Medicine and What Matters in the End.* New York: Henry Holt and Company, 2013.

Hills, Matt. *Fan Cultures*. Oxfordshire, UK: Routledge, 2002.

Mould, Oli. "Star Wars Andor captures the essence of resistance that is happening in the real world." The Conversation. November 17, 2022. https://theconversation.com/star-wars-andor-captures-the-essence-of-resistance-that-is-happening-in-the-real-world-194566.

---

[6] Taylor, *How Star Wars Conquered the Universe*, 180.

Taylor, Chris. *How Star Wars Conquered the Universe: The Past, Present, and Future of a Multibillion Dollar Franchise.* New York: Basic Books, 2014.

Part 1:
Exploring the Series and Films

Chapter 1

The Evolution of Twi'leks in the *Star Wars* Universe

Amy Richau

Abstract: From Oola, an enslaved dancer in *Return of the Jedi,* to Rebellion General Hera Syndulla in *Star Wars Rebels* the depictions of the Twi'lek species throughout four decades of *Star Wars* storytelling reflect a central theme of *Star Wars*: underdogs battling an oppressive regime against all odds. The many appearances of female Twi'leks in *Star Wars* also mirror the evolution of the representation of women and the "Other" in *Star Wars* stories, from sexualized background characters with no agency to popular and complex characters in high-stakes storylines. From a textual analysis of *Star Wars* films, television series, books, video games, specials, and comics, this essay traces the history of Twi'leks in *Star Wars,* showing how the depiction of Twi'leks reveals the dynamism of *Star Wars.* From their origins as scantily clad dancers used in the background of male-dominated spaces, Twi'lek characters have progressed to fully formed heroic characters and villains who play a major part in present and future *Star Wars* stories.

Keywords: *Star Wars,* Twi'leks, Other, women, representation, Oola, Bib Fortuna, Garza Fwip, Hera Syndulla, Loden Greatstorm, Lourna Dee, slavery, Aayla Secura, Ryloth, Orn Free Taa

***

As one of the most prominent humanoid alien species in *Star Wars,* Twi'leks are easily identifiable by their head tails (or lekku). Over 800 named Twi'lek characters have appeared in *Star Wars* films, television series, books, comics, and video games.[1] Twi'leks were first seen in the 1983 film *Star Wars Episode VI: Return of the Jedi* as both an enslaved dancer and a criminal agent; more recent Twi'lek characters have been Jedi Masters, rebel heroes, and complicated villains. As the representation of Twi'leks widened, so too did the story of their

---

[1] Category: Twi'leks, Wookieepedia, accessed February 23, 2022, https://starwars.fandom.com/wiki/Category:Twi%27leks.

homeworld, the planet Ryloth. The struggle of the Twi'leks and their homeworld, in many ways, mirrors a recurring theme in *Star Wars*: finding hope in a seemingly winless scenario as characters fight for their freedom.

Twi'lek characters, from their debut in *Return of the Jedi* to appearances in the 2021-2022 live-action television series *The Book of Boba Fett*, began with little agency but have evolved into a more diverse and dynamic species whose characters effect significant narrative consequences. Much of this evolution can be seen in fits and starts, with regressions in between, as not all *Star Wars* creators felt the need to move Twi'leks (especially female Twi'leks) beyond the role of sexualized eye candy for the audience. But significant progress has been made in the depiction of Twi'lek characters; in recent years, *Star Wars* stories have included Twi'lek characters as fully realized heroes and villains whose motivations go beyond the tragic history of their home planet. Examining this progress tracks how *Star Wars* creators have addressed stereotypes and gendered roles within the story-world of the franchise, making intentional choices to move Twi'leks beyond victimhood and into their own diverse and meaningful narratives.[2] Chris Kempshall notes the role such non-human characters like Twi'leks play within science fiction is "to provide an alternative 'other' through which human identity can be measured and compared."[3] As Twi'leks have journeyed from a victimized human-adjacent species or a stand-in for the "Other" in *Star Wars*, their increased representation and more meaningful characterization show how the *Star Wars* galaxy has begun to embrace the Other in its storytelling, making the galaxy a more welcoming space for diverse characters and the creators interested in telling their stories.

1983: Henchmen and the enslaved

Twi'lek characters made their *Star Wars* debut in *Return of the Jedi*, the film that closed out the Original Trilogy. In crime lord Jabba the Hutt's palace on the desert planet Tatooine, we meet Bib Fortuna, a male Twi'lek who serves as Jabba's henchman, and Oola, a female Twi'lek enslaved by Jabba as his dancer. Bib Fortuna, with menacing red eyes and pale white skin, comes across as both comical and scary, speaking broken Basic, the lingua franca (English) of *Star Wars*, and bumbling around as he does Jabba's bidding; he

---

[2] As there is such a high volume of Twi'lek characters in *Star Wars* stories, this essay focuses mainly on their depiction in films and television series, with some attention to notable Twi'lek appearances in books, comics, and video games.

[3] Chris Kempshall, *The History and Politics of* Star Wars: *Death Stars and Democracy* (London and New York: Routledge, 2023), 179.

appears easily mind-tricked by Jedi Luke Skywalker.[4] Oola is a scantily clad, green-skinned female Twi'lek who first appears with a chain around her neck, sitting at the feet of Jabba's throne. When Oola resists dancing for Jabba, he sends her down a trap door to her death in a rancor pit.[5]

There has been much commentary (and rightly so) on how few female characters speak in the original *Star Wars* film trilogy, yet Oola rarely figures in these conversations. In 2017, *Vulture* put together a compilation video that included all the women with lines of dialogue in the Original Trilogy of *Star Wars* films—besides Leia—who spoke in English.[6] This English-only rule excluded both Sy Snootles, who sings in Jabba's palace, and Oola, who begs Jabba for her life in Huttese. Omitting Oola's words from this conversation ignores the pleas of an enslaved character—one notably portrayed by Femi Taylor, the first Black actor in a meaningful role in a *Star Wars* film. W. Travis Shedd notes that Twi'lek characters "are entertainers and objects to be looked at and desired, and like slaves, they are not given their due agency as people but instead are considered disposable property to the point where Oola's barbaric death on Jabba's whim does not visibly enrage anyone."[7] Viewers can't understand exactly what Oola is saying (her lines of dialogue do not include subtitles), but her desperate movements and vocalizations speak for themselves. Ignoring Oola's lines of dialogue is even more problematic as her story ties directly to Leia's time in Jabba's palace. As Lori Maguire notes, after Jabba kills Oola, "Her replacement is Leia, who uses her chain to exact the vengeance Oola couldn't."[8]

1984-1998: History of Ryloth

The idea that female Twi'leks were targets of the slave trade and objects of sexual desire and male Twi'leks were corrupt aides or officials would stay with *Star Wars* storytelling and the world-building around their homeworld, Ryloth, in the years to come. Kempshall observes the tendency of *Star Wars* to fall into the "planet of hats" trope in its depiction of aliens, "where the

---

[4] *Star Wars Episode VI: Return of the Jedi*, directed by Richard Marquand (1983; Beverly Hills, CA: 20th Century Fox/Lucasfilm Ltd.), Disney+, https://www.disneyplus.com/movies/star-wars-return-of-the-jedi-episode-vi/6QGKo5mjDBS8.

[5] Ibid.

[6] Chris Wade and Abraham Riesman, "Every Line from a (Non-Leia) Woman in Star Wars," *Vulture*, December 13, 2017, https://www.vulture.com/2015/12/star-wars-all-female-lines-excluding-leia.html.

[7] W. Travis Shedd, "Tracing the Evolution Nexus of Race, Species, and 'Otherness' in the *Star Wars* Film Franchise," MA thesis (Georgetown University, 2016), 56.

[8] Lori Maguire, "Fear is the Path to the Dark Side," in *Star Wars and History*, ed. Nancy R. Reagin and Janice Liedl (Hoboken, NJ: John Wiley & Sons, 2013), 220-221.

attributes of a single individual come to reflect those of the entire species."[9] In the case of Twi'leks, the "hat" in their early depiction was not only their head tails but their involvement in the galactic slave trade. Diegetically, the Twi'leks' history with slavery explains why Twi'leks were later seen on so many planets, as they were trafficked against their will to serve masters across the galaxy. Much of this Twi'lek content in the late 1980s and early 1990s came from role-playing game (RPG) sourcebooks that contributed basic facts about the Twi'lek species.[10] As the only two Twi'lek characters in *Star Wars* up to this point were Oola and Bib Fortuna, an enslaved female and a male who works for her enslaver, it's not surprising that the history of their species first focused on the subject of slavery. The sourcebook for the original *Star Wars: The Role-Playing Game*, released in 1987, notes that each Twi'lek city is governed by a "head-clan" consisting of five (notably male) Twi'leks.[11] One detail of this early description of the Twi'lek species is essential: they did not have the technology to travel through space, leaving them dependent on neighboring planets to keep in contact with other worlds. This lack of technology made them vulnerable to space pirates, smugglers, and criminal syndicates such as the Hutts, who controlled Tatooine, a planet close to Ryloth, on star maps. The Hutts were just one group interested in the main resource Ryloth had to offer: the mineral ryll. Ryll, known casually as "spice," had medicinal purposes but was trafficked as a highly addictive drug by criminal syndicates. "Slaving vessels often scour the planet to stock their thriving trade, and smugglers regularly raid ryll stockpiles. Certain Twi'lek head-clans have *adapted* to the situation, selling their own people in order to preserve their complexes. . . . Unfortunately, the slave trade grows stronger as Twi'leks—especially females—gain popularity among those who buy and sell intelligent species."[12]

The combination of a secluded world, a valuable drug, and a local population considered sexually attractive to many species across the galaxy was a dangerous combination for many Twi'leks. The 1987 RPG sourcebook describes female Twi'leks as "seductive and captivating" and notes, "Even the Emperor (according to rumors) keeps a harem of Twi'lek dancers for special occasions."[13]

---

[9] Kempshall, *The History and Politics of* Star Wars, 180.

[10] While these sources are no longer considered canonical, they are significant in helping trace Twi'leks' narrative evolution, and as John Jackson Miller notes, many works of the so-called "Expanded Universe" still inform today's canonical *Star Wars* storytelling. See John Jackson Miller's essay in this volume.

[11] Bill Slavicsek and Curtis Smith, *The Star Wars Sourcebook* (New York: West End Games, 1987), 81.

[12] Ibid., 81-82. Emphasis original.

[13] Ibid., 82.

These details about the history of Ryloth serve as an explanation—or excuse—for how Oola ended up trapped in Jabba's Palace and provided a road map for future depictions of Twi'leks as victims of crime lords.

Later role-playing games and their accompanying sourcebooks introduced new Twi'lek characters who were mercenaries, Imperial spies, politicians, and business owners. The 1995 West End games role-playing sourcebook *Platt's Starport Guide* had a section on the Ryloth city Kala'uun that introduced over a dozen new Twi'lek characters, including a mechanic named Seeker, the Starport Master named Koh'shak,[14] and a female Twi'lek named Mal'aa who owned a restaurant.[15] The guide also mentioned the slave lord Voorg the Thandicant, who required Twi'leks to sell their own people to him as tribute and provided "protection and a limited amount of technology to keep the city functioning."[16] This RPG's more in-depth look at a city on Ryloth gave readers their first glimpse of a Twi'lek community, and while many of these characters are clearly struggling with enslavement, it's a mark of Twi'lek progress to see Mal'aa, a female Twi'lek who owns her own business.

The first Twi'lek Force users both had histories of enslavement, but their stories focus more on their Force powers. The 1993 comic series *Star Wars: Tales of the Jedi,* which took place 4000 years before *A New Hope,* debuted the first Twi'lek Jedi, Tott Doneeta. According to the *Tales of the Jedi Guide,* slavers captured Doneeta and his family, but a group of Jedi rescued them. Doneeta convinced one of the Jedi to train him, and he later became highly skilled at communicating with beasts via the Force.[17] The first live-action appearance of a Twi'lek post-*Return of the Jedi* was the Dark Jedi Boc Aseca in the video game *Star Wars Jedi Knight: Dark Forces II.*[18] A now-obsolete (and non-canonical) article from the gaming collective Wizards.com included a backstory for Aseca that involved brutal enslavement, helping lead Aseca on a path to becoming a Dark Jedi, driven to madness.[19] In the game, Aseca cackles maniacally and looks strikingly similar to Bib Fortuna. Some of the first to focus on Twi'lek characters' lives after their enslavement, both stories notably

---

[14] Peter Schweighofer, *Star Wars: Platt's Starpoint Guide* (Honesdale, PA: West End Games, 1995), 145.

[15] Ibid, 154-155.

[16] Ibid, 151.

[17] George R. Strayton, *Tales of the Jedi Companion* (Honesdale, PA: West End Games, 1996), 33.

[18] LucasArts, *Star Wars Jedi Knight: Dark Forces II,* LucasArts, Microsoft Windows, 1997. Boc Aseca was a computer-generated character throughout much of the game but was portrayed by actor Time Winters in cut scenes.

[19] Abel G. Peña and Jason Fry, "The Dark Forces Saga, Part 4," Wizards.com, May 26, 2005, https://web.archive.org/web/20100430201940/http://wizards.com/default.asp?x=starwars/article/sw20050526a.

took place away from the Twi'lek homeworld of Ryloth. While the backstory of Ryloth solidified the Twi'leks' entanglement with slavery during this time period, introducing characters in Jedi and Force user roles hints at a future that will bring Twi'lek characters more to the center of *Star Wars* storytelling.

1999-2007: Aayla Secura, Mission Vao, and Darth Talon

The Prequel films and a celebrated video game brought mixed messages regarding Twi'leks, but overall, this era represents several steps forward in Twi'lek representation, especially for female characters. However, the first Prequel film, 1999's *Star Wars Episode I: The Phantom Menace*, set 36 years before *Return of the Jedi*, reverted to Twi'lek depictions from the past. On Tatooine, twin female Twi'leks serve podracer Sebulba. The twins aren't in chains and appear smiling and happy in the film as they massage Sebulba—a disturbing portrayal of individuals enslaved in both mind and body. Even more disturbing, in *The Phantom Menace*, audiences learn that enslaved individuals can have tracking devices implanted in their bodies that kill them if they try to escape.[20]

Twi'leks are notably not the only species enslaved in *The Phantom Menace*. Anakin Skywalker and his mother Shmi are humans enslaved to junk dealer Watto. But unlike the Skywalkers, there is no suggestion that any character (or the audience) should empathize with the Twi'lek twins. The *Episode I Visual Dictionary* doesn't even bother to give these characters names, referring to them merely as "Twi'lek Twins." Their entry is more about their master than about them; it says Sebulba purchased the twins in part to make his fellow racers jealous.[21] Valerie Frankel notes the twins are "dressed in mesh jumpsuits open to the waist" and suggests they are "clearly eye candy for the audience and the character (Sebulba)."[22] Shedd notes that "Twi'leks are so close to humans . . . yet their marking as the Other makes their enslavement and overt bodily exploitation easier to accept."[23] The audience, many of whom would not have seen the RPG books, comics, or video games with Twi'leks that came between *Return of the Jedi* and *The Phantom Menace*,

---

[20] *Star Wars Episode I: The Phantom Menace*, directed by George Lucas (1999; Beverly Hills, CA: 20th Century Fox/Lucasfilm Ltd.), Disney+, https://www.disneyplus.com/movies/star-wars-the-phantom-menace-episode-i/2ezYynkgW1AH.

[21] David West Reynolds, *Star Wars Episode I: The Visual Dictionary* (New York: DK Publishing, 1999), 53. The twins are eventually named as Ann and Tan Gella in the 2013 mobile card game *Force Collection*. "Ann Gella/Canon," Wookieepedia, accessed January 12, 2023, https://starwars.fandom.com/wiki/Ann_Gella.

[22] Valerie Frankel, *Star Wars Meets the Eras of Feminism: Weighing All the Galaxy's Women Great and Small* (Lanham, MD: Lexington Books, 2018), chap. 2, Kindle.

[23] Shedd, "Tracing the Evolution Nexus of Race, Species, and 'Otherness,'" 75.

might well assume Twi'leks were created purely for the purpose of including scantily clad, subservient female characters in *Star Wars*.

Another new character introduced in the Prequel films continues Bib Fortuna's legacy as a male Twi'lek willing to collaborate with anyone to ensure his own privilege. Orn Free Taa, a rare male Twi'lek with four lekku instead of two, is a senator from Ryloth seen in the background in all three Prequel films. A description of Taa in the *Episode I Visual Dictionary* gives a hint to the more significant, sinister role he will play in future *Star Wars* stories. "[Taa] views galactic government as merely the sport of the mighty like himself. In his excesses, he has grown vile and corpulent, but he is confident that money and power will always make him attractive."[24]

The most prominent role played by a Twi'lek in the Prequels is that of Jedi Knight Aayla Secura, who appears briefly in both *Star Wars Episode II: Attack of the Clones* (2002) and *Star Wars Episode III: Revenge of the Sith* (2005). Aayla Secura debuted in the comic series *Star Wars: Republic*'s story arc "Twilight." In this arc, Aayla and her Jedi Master Quinlan Vos suffer amnesia after being drugged by her uncle during a mission to Ryloth.[25] It is yet another example of a male Twi'lek taking advantage of a female Twi'lek for profit, gain, or protection. While it's certainly a giant step in the right direction to have a female Jedi character, Secura's initial introduction isn't a homerun in terms of advancing female or Twi'lek empowerment. Samantha Kountz says, "all hope is dashed when she (Secura) appears in scanty battle gear and [is] given little to no screen time."[26] Like all female Jedi in the Prequel films, Secura has no lines of dialogue, so the only impression Secura can make on the audience is visual. Despite being one of a few Jedi survivors, Secura is hard to spot in the Battle of Geonosis in *Attack of the Clones*.[27] In *Revenge of the Sith*, during a Jedi Council meeting, Secura appears only as a hologram; in the film's depiction of Order 66, clone troopers easily gun her down.[28] Writing about Secura in the *Star Wars* Prequels, Kountz argues that "despite their sensuality, the Twi'leks have been regarded as little more than disposable sex-slaves."[29]

---

[24] Reynolds, *Star Wars Episode I: The Visual Dictionary*, 63.

[25] John Ostrander, *Star Wars #19* (Milwaukie, WI: Dark Horse Comics), 2000.

[26] Samantha Kountz, "We Come in Peace: Immigration in Post-Cold War Science Fiction Film," *Foundation*, Vol. 43, Issue 119 (Winter 2014): 34.

[27] *Star Wars Episode II: Attack of the Clones*, directed by George Lucas (2002; Beverly Hills, CA: 20th Century Fox/Lucasfilm Ltd.), Disney+, https://www.disneyplus.com/movies/star-wars-attack-of-the-clones-episode-ii/mgpYHGnzZW6N.

[28] *Star Wars Episode III: Revenge of the Sith*, directed by George Lucas (2005; Beverly Hills, CA: 20th Century Fox/Lucasfilm Ltd.), Disney+, https://www.disneyplus.com/movies/star-wars-revenge-of-the-sith-episode-iii/4WvbqLFumNvi.

[29] Kountz, "We Come in Peace," 34.

This is true in many cases, but ignores that Secura, while baring her midriff, is still a Jedi Master, one of the most highly respected roles in the *Star Wars* galaxy. While Secura's role is a small one, and her portrayal falls into a few clichés, it is still a mark of progress that a female Twi'lek appears on screen wielding a lightsaber in battle rather than pulling on the chains of her abductor.

The 2003 role-playing video game *Star Wars: Knights of the Old Republic* (*KotOR*) and its 2004 sequel introduced a flurry of new Twi'lek characters. Many of the Twi'leks had histories of being enslaved, but the most significant Twi'lek from *KotOR* was Mission Vao, a teenaged, street-wise orphan.[30] Vao is arguably one of the first female Twi'leks not overtly sexualized in a *Star Wars* story (certainly a wise idea as Vao was around 14 years old), and *KotOR* discussions regularly mention her as a fan favorite. Journalist Megan Crouse praised *KotOR* for not "dooming all members of their [Twi'lek] species to some form of slavery" by giving fans Vao, "a street-smart thief who would fit in perfectly with the smugglers and scoundrels of the galaxy."[31] John Walker for *Eurogamer* described Vao as "possibly the most notorious character from *KotOR*, famously loved or loathed, simply because BioWare did such a splendid job writing a 14-year-old girl."[32] However, *KotOR* also continued to showcase storylines featuring enslaved Twi'leks, continuing the theme of powerful individuals exploiting Twi'leks across the galaxy. In a room in the crime lord Davik Tang's estate, players can find two female and one male Twi'lek. These Twi'leks offer the player "massages" and beg the player not to tell Davik if they are displeased with their services.[33]

Twi'leks in the Prequels and *KotOR*, in many ways, take two steps forward, one step back in terms of their representation. In 2006, shortly after the last Prequel film was released, one of the most notorious Twi'lek characters debuted: Darth Talon. Created by John Ostrander and Jan Duursema (who also created Aayla Secura), Darth Talon was a red-skinned female Sith Lord who played a significant part in the *Star Wars: Legacy* comic series. Talon's red skin (a rarer shade for Twi'leks) was covered in black tattoos she earned in battle. Many of these tattoos were highly visible as she wore what essentially amounted to a tiny black bikini in many of the *Legacy* comics.[34] Audiences may legitimately critique

---

30 BioWare, Obsidian Entertainment, Aspry Media, *Star Wars: Knights of the Old Republic*, LucasArts, Electronic Arts, Microsoft Windows, 2003.

31 Megan Crouse, "What *Star Wars: The High Republic* Can Learn From *Knights of the Old Republic*," Den of Geek, May 28, 2020, https://www.denofgeek.com/books/star-wars-high-republic-knights-of-the-old-republic-spoilers/.

32 John Walker, "Bastard of the Old Republic," *Eurogamer*, September 21, 2014, https://www.eurogamer.net/articles/2014-09-21-bastard-of-the-old-republic.

33 BioWare, *Knights of the Old Republic*.

34 John Ostrander, *Star Wars: Legacy* series #1-50 (Milwaukie, WI: Dark Horse Comics, 2006-2010).

Talon as yet another female Twi'lek in barely any clothing, but it is also imperative to acknowledge Darth Talon's power and agency, even when it comes to her choice of outfit; a clear difference exists between a character forced to wear a skimpy outfit to please her master and a character who reveals a lot of skin because she wants to, or more accurately, because the woman who drew her, Jan Duursema, wanted her to. Tori Carlo praised Talon's relationship with the Jedi Cade Skywalker in the *Legacy* comics, noting Cade's "love-hate relationship with the dark side is personified through his conflicting relationship with Talon since she simultaneously represents the Sith he hates and the power he desires."[35] Talon was impossible to miss because of her appearance, but her character would not have resonated with fans for so many years had she been nothing more than content for a pin-up poster. The character Darth Talon serves as an example of a character whose ramped-up sexiness may have been more acceptable due to her Otherness as a Twi'lek; however, she is also a strong female character with her own powerful agency in *Star Wars* stories. Even for audiences that may have not cared for her appearance, her storyline stands as an example of progress for Twi'leks—and for the Other—in *Star Wars* storytelling.

2008-2013: The Clone Wars

In 2008, the animated film *Star Wars: The Clone Wars* released in theaters, followed by an animated television series of the same title that would eventually run seven seasons, finishing in 2020.[36] *The Clone Wars* series gave *Star Wars* creators the space and time to develop some already established Twi'lek characters, such as Aayla Secura, and the chance to portray the homeworld of the Twi'leks, Ryloth. A Ryloth-focused story arc in Season One, in particular, gave voice to Twi'lek characters who refused to be victimized.[37] The changes in

---

[35] Tori Carlo, "Star Wars: Darth Talon & Cade Skywalker Are the Best Sith/Jedi Romance—NOT Reylo," *CBR*, March 1, 2021, https://www.cbr.com/darth-talon-cade-skywalker-star-wars-romance/.

[36] While the series *Star Wars: The Clone Wars* began before the Disney purchase of Lucasfilm in 2012 and the reboot of the new *Star Wars* canon, the series is considered canon along with the first six *Star Wars* films. It is not to be confused with the 2003-2005 animated series *Star Wars: Clone Wars* developed and drawn by Genndy Tartakovsky, which is not considered canon.

[37] *Star Wars: The Clone Wars*, season 1, episode 20, "Innocents of Ryloth," directed by Justin Ridge, written by Randy Stradley and Henry Gilroy, aired March 6, 2009, on Cartoon Network, Disney+, https://www.disneyplus.com/video/d4f5abd5-3e71-4cef-9928-6be9527fdb89; *Star Wars: The Clone Wars*, season 1, episode 21, "Liberty on Ryloth," directed by Rob Coleman, written by Henry Gilroy, aired March 13, 2009, on

the depiction of Twi'leks in these episodes was not an accident. In an interview discussing this Ryloth arc, writer Henry Gilroy addressed the sexualized history of the Twi'lek species and how he and his fellow creators at Lucasfilm saw this as an opportunity to change the legacy of the Twi'lek people. Gilroy stated, "we wanted to change the point of view . . . because of the way they [Twi'leks] had been sexualized both in *Return of the Jedi* and even Aayla Secura walking around in her tube top . . . there was this feeling like these are really sexualized characters. And Dave [Filoni] and I had a discussion early on: 'we need to change that, and we need to show that there's a variety of types of people here.'"[38]

Both Senator Orn Free Taa and a new character, Twi'lek freedom fighter Cham Syndulla, figure prominently in these episodes that provide *Star Wars* fans' first look at the Twi'lek homeworld in a television series.[39] As the story unfolds, the Twi'leks are starving under the Separatist droid occupation. The Jedi and clone troopers arrive, intending to drive the Separatists out while helping the local Twi'lek population. Notably, some of the clone troopers don't appear to have much respect for the Twi'leks, referring to them derogatorily as "tail-heads" and expressing frustration that they aren't getting out of the way fast enough for the clones to do their work.[40] But a group of clones comes across a young Twi'lek girl who helps humanize (for lack of a better word) the Twi'leks to the soldiers, who perhaps have only previously seen Twi'leks in sexualized pin-up posters in their barracks, such as those seen in previous episodes.[41] Amy Ratcliffe, in her book *Star Wars: Women of the Galaxy*, notes the importance of the Twi'lek girl, Numa, in this arc as we see her "courageously help Obi-Wan Kenobi and the clone troopers of the Republic stop the invading army, in the process inspiring her fellow captive Twi'leks and making an emotional connection with several of the clones."[42]

Cartoon Network, Disney+, https://www.disneyplus.com/video/0f87705e-7773-4154-8ff8-fdee5671431d.

[38] Henry Gilroy, interview with John Mills and Matthew Rushing, *Aggressive Negotiations: A Star Wars Pod*, podcast audio, October 1, 2019, https://podcasts.apple.com/us/podcast/issue-181-henry-gilroy-the-ryloth-arc/id1079442864?i=1000451875733.

[39] Ryloth has yet to be seen in a live-action television series or film.

[40] *Star Wars: The Clone Wars*, "Innocents of Ryloth."

[41] See *Star Wars: The Clone Wars*, season 1, episode 5, "Rookies," directed by Justin Ridge, written by Steven Melching, aired October 24, 2008, on Cartoon Network, Disney+, https://www.disneyplus.com/video/598d1e7b-f39e-4527-9487-b5e891f5eefa; see also *Star Wars: The Clone Wars*, season 1, episode 16, "Hidden Enemy," directed by Steward Lee, written by Drew Z. Greenberg, aired February 6, 2009, on Cartoon Network, Disney+, https://www.disneyplus.com/video/7c732b05-b90f-4090-a184-5652be228139.

[42] Amy Ratcliffe, *Star Wars: Women of the Galaxy* (San Francisco: Chronicle Books, 2018), 143.

The Jedi know they won't succeed in aiding Ryloth on their own. They need the help of a local—in this case, the Twi'lek leader Cham Syndulla. Cham doesn't trust Senator Orn Free Taa to protect Ryloth's interests, but he also doesn't trust the Jedi, worrying they will, in turn, occupy Ryloth once they drive out the Separatists.[43] These few episodes represent a leap forward in showing a variety of Twi'leks with competing interests and different sets of motives and morals. Cham Syndulla, in particular, is a strong, independent leader who is not looking to be saved by the Jedi and is only willing to work with them on his own terms.

Despite the addition of more fully realized and complex Twi'lek characters during this time period, there are still many examples of female Twi'lek characters who are sexualized or exploited, with some moments of resistance. In a scene from *The Clone Wars* film set in Jabba's palace, female Twi'leks are not in chains but are presumably enslaved and not free to leave as they dance for Jabba and comfort him after his son is kidnapped.[44] Later, in Ziro the Hutt's club on Coruscant, viewers can see the silhouette of a Twi'lek on the wall performing a suggestive, exotic dance.[45] Several episodes in the fourth season of *The Clone Wars* series focus on the slavers of Zygerria. Working undercover in the episode "Slaves of the Republic," Anakin Skywalker sees an enslaved female Twi'lek who chooses to kill herself by jumping off a high balcony to avoid returning to a slave re-education camp.[46] This scene echoes Oola's resistance to Jabba the Hutt in *Return of the Jedi* much more than, for example, the twin Twi'lek servants in *The Phantom Menace*. It is also more reflective of the real-world practice of slavery and the desperate acts many individuals undertake to escape it. Paul Finkelman compares Oola's action to Africans throwing themselves overboard during transatlantic crossings of slave ships and German slave labor prisoners throwing themselves at guards or barbed wire, "knowing their acts would end their lives."[47] Such depictions of enslaved Twi'leks' pain and suffering—or that of any species or group thrust into slavery—allow viewers to recognize such characters as people rather than property.

---

[43] *Star Wars: The Clone Wars*, "Liberty on Ryloth."

[44] *Star Wars: The Clone Wars*, directed by Dave Filoni (2008; Burbank, CA: Warner Brothers/Lucasfilm), Disney+, https://www.disneyplus.com/video/edf47542-e14a-45a6-b56d-ee73c3e8ddb7.

[45] Ibid.

[46] *Star Wars: The Clone Wars*, season 4, episode 12, "Slaves of the Republic," directed by Brian Kalin O'Connell, written by Henry Gilroy, aired December 2, 2011, on Cartoon Network, Disney+, https://www.disneyplus.com/video/22ffd322-9702-403f-93d3-47dc7780e062.

[47] Paul Finkelman, "From Slavery to Freedom in a Galaxy Far, Far Away," in *Star Wars and History*, ed. Nancy R. Reagin and Janice Liedl (Hoboken, NJ: John Wiley & Sons, 2013), 249.

While many of the background Twi'lek characters in *The Clone Wars* are enslaved servants or dancers, from the very first season of the series, Jedi Master Aayla Secura becomes a more fully realized character than in the Prequel films. Still wearing a skimpy, midriff-baring outfit, she's also shown to be a very capable Jedi and finally has a voice with lines of dialogue. In "Jedi Crash," Secura is the wise voice of reason Ahsoka Tano needs when she fears losing her Master, Anakin Skywalker.[48] In "The Zillo Beast Strikes Back," Secura fights alongside Master Yoda as they try to gain control of the beast.[49] Overall, Secura appears in about a dozen episodes of *The Clone Wars* and remains one of the most recognizable Twi'lek characters in *Star Wars* stories. In these later offerings, Secura presents a strong and empowering female Twi'lek character who is much more than what Kempshall calls the "depth-building window dressing"[50] Twi'leks and other aliens represented in the original *Star Wars* films, largely due to tight production budgets—and to which the Prequel films relegate her character, despite their much higher levels of production.

2014-2019: Hera Syndulla

Shortly after Disney purchased Lucasfilm in 2012, the television series *Star Wars Rebels* brought a new Twi'lek hero to *Star Wars* lore, becoming one of the most influential female *Star Wars* characters of the last decade. *Rebels* aired for four seasons, from 2014 to 2018. The series follows the crew members of Hera's ship, the *Ghost*, as they work together to fight against the Galactic Empire at the dawn of a unified Rebel Alliance. The crew includes Hera, a Twi'lek pilot, Jedi in hiding Kanan Jarrus, Mandalorian Sabine Wren, Lasat warrior Garazeb Orrelios, Lothal orphan Ezra Bridger, and Hera's astromech droid, nicknamed Chopper.

Hera, as captain of the *Ghost* and leader of this formidable crew, possesses an immediate and enduring sense of power throughout the series. Frankel describes Hera as "the captain, leader, and planner of the *Star Wars Rebels* team, who recruits most of the members. As such, she is the truest believer in the cause."[51] Stephenie McGucken notes that Hera is also the matriarch of the

---

[48] *Star Wars: The Clone Wars*, season 1, episode 13, "Jedi Crash," directed by Rob Coleman, written by Katie Lucas, aired January 16, 2009, on Cartoon Network, Disney+, https://www.disneyplus.com/video/28c0b907-8efe-4400-af50-c13c66e18468.

[49] *Star Wars: The Clone Wars*, season 2, episode 19, "The Zillo Beast Strikes Back," directed by Steward Lee, written by Steven Melching, aired April 16, 2010, on Cartoon Network, Disney+, https://www.disneyplus.com/video/6f2cd6cf-8e7a-42e6-893a-6465f2683648.

[50] Kempshall, *The History and Politics of* Star Wars, 182.

[51] Valerie Frankel, *Star Wars Meets the Eras of Feminism*, chap. 6, Kindle.

Ghost crew family and appreciates that "the pairing of Hera and Sabine allows them to escape the 'one woman in the galaxy' pattern that too often dominates Leia, Padmé, and Ahsoka stories."[52] In addition to leading the *Ghost* crew on missions, Ratcliffe also notes Hera's caregiving role in many episodes: "Hera's there for her team members with a pep talk, a hard truth, or whatever else they need. It's this caregiver aspect, adjacent to her warrior side, that has led fans to give her the affectionate nickname 'Space Mom.'"[53]

Rebels not only creates a strong female Twi'lek leader but gives her a love interest, Kanan Jarrus, without diminishing Syndulla's authority in the group, with outsiders, or even with the audience. Her romantic feelings toward Kanan never distract from her involvement in dangerous missions in the series; for both of them, the rebellion comes first. McGucken notes, "Whenever Hera is challenged, her rightful place as captain is shortly reaffirmed through an active display of bravery, as well as a general eye roll to the person questioning her—even if it is her partner, Kanan."[54] Hera's appearance is also strikingly different from many Twi'leks we have seen before. Rather than a tight-fitting outfit that reveals a lot of skin, Hera wears a loose-fitting, no-nonsense jumpsuit and the practical accoutrement of a pilot. Kountz described Hera as "the direct antithesis to Oola in *Return of the Jedi* as she is shown as wearing no makeup, practically dressed in rebel military pilot gear, and with complete political and sexual independence."[55]

Slavery is never mentioned in Hera's backstory, but the Season One episode "Idiot's Array" makes clear that Hera and the rest of the characters are aware of the association of Twi'leks with slavery. In this episode, the *Ghost* crew are forced to help Lando Calrissian after Zeb loses their astromech droid Chopper to the smuggler in a game of Sabacc.[56] On the mission, Lando surprises the *Ghost* crew by offering Hera to the criminal Azmorigan in exchange for the cargo he seeks. No one uses the word slave, but everyone knows what's going on. Hera plays along, mockingly thanking "Lord Calrissian" for delivering her to her new master. Azmorigan notes, "her attire is preposterous,"[57] insinuating he would expect his new servant to wear a more revealing outfit than a flight suit. Hera

---

[52] Stephenie McGucken, "Rebelling Heroines: Hera, Sabine, and Ahsoka in *Star Wars Rebels*," in *Fourth Wave Feminism in Science Fiction and Fantasy: Volume 2: Essays on Television Representations, 2013-2019*, ed. Valerie Estelle Frankel (Jefferson, NC: McFarland, 2019), Section IV, Kindle.

[53] Ratcliffe, *Star Wars: Women of the Galaxy*, 77.

[54] McGucken, "Rebelling Heroines," Section IV, Kindle.

[55] Kountz, "We Come in Peace," 38.

[56] *Star Wars Rebels*, season 1, episode 11, "Idiot's Array," directed by Dave Filoni, written by Kevin Hopps, aired January 12, 2015, on the Disney Channel, Disney+, https://www.disneyplus.com/video/edf47542-e14a-45a6-b56d-ee73c3e8ddb7.

[57] Ibid.

engineers her escape by manipulating Azmorigan and one of his guards, knocking them out with—of all things—a serving tray.[58] This episode shows quick-thinking Hera saving herself and demonstrates how tough it must be in the galaxy for female Twi'leks who are clearly still targeted for enslavement.

The episode "Hera's Heroes" adds to both Hera's character development and that of her father, freedom fighter from *The Clone Wars*, Cham Syndulla. It also expands the development of the culture of Twi'lek people. When Hera returns to Ryloth for a reunion with her father, the differences between the two are striking.[59] Cham chose to stay on Ryloth as leader of the Free Ryloth movement. His primary and only goal is keeping Ryloth out of the hands of any occupying forces. Hera broke away from her father and left Ryloth, defying him. She is more focused on defeating the Empire—on helping everyone in the galaxy rather than just her own people. Ratcliffe notes, "Hera witnesses the hope the freedom fighters give the citizens of Ryloth and internalizes it. She imagines what such action could mean on a bigger scale, so when the Empire tightens its grip on the galaxy, and she believes she can help stop them, she takes to the stars to fight back."[60] Hera fights against her troubled past with her family rather than a past as a survivor of enslavement. This character dynamic sets her apart from many female Twi'leks in *Star Wars* and is also highly relatable to the audience. Hera is an undeniably influential character in *Star Wars Rebels* and in the franchise in general. In addition to her role as rebellion hero and ace pilot, Hera also becomes a mother after giving birth to Jacen Syndulla.[61] Hera continues to appear in *Star Wars* books, comics, video games, animated shows, and now with the Disney+ streaming show *Ahsoka* (2023), Hera has made her way to live action television as well. But sadly, Jacen has not yet played a part in these projects, so we have yet to see a story that embraces Hera's role as both rebel hero and literal mother, in addition to her figurative role as "Space Mom."

From 2014 to 2019, Twi'lek characters play more significant roles in books than in films.[62] In many cases, these appearances reveal the effects of past

---

[58] Ibid.

[59] *Star Wars Rebels*, season 3, episode 5, "Hera's Heroes," directed by Justin Ridge, written by Nicole Dubuc, aired October 15, 2016, on the Disney Channel, Disney+, https://www.disneyplus.com/video/77af8e53-d662-4c0c-8eed-7b2c56490308.

[60] Ratcliffe, *Star Wars: Women of the Galaxy*, 77.

[61] *Star Wars Rebels*, season 4, episode 15, "Family Reunion—and Farewell," directed by Dave Filoni, Bosco Ng, and Sergio Páez, written by Dave Filoni, Henry Gilroy, Kiri Hart, Simon Kinberg and Steven Melching, aired March 5, 2018, on the Disney Channel, Disney+, https://www.disneyplus.com/video/abcb0676-0f12-45c7-8a8f-45d80e66e3c3.

[62] Twi'leks are only seen in the background of the films *Rogue One: A Star Wars Story* (including a blink-and-you'll-miss-it appearance by Bib Fortuna's cousin, Beezer, as a

trauma on Twi'lek characters. In the 2015 novel *Lords of the Sith,* one of Cham Syndulla's freedom fighters, Isval, helps save a young female Twi'lek from sex trafficking.[63] Isval reveals she has saved many female Twi'leks over the years as a way to heal the wounds of her own tragic past. Yendor, who appears in Claudia Gray's novels *Lost Stars* and *Bloodline* as well as Rebecca Roanhorses's *Resistance Reborn,* is a Twi'lek leader who expresses to Leia the fear that, now his people have gained independence, their hard-won freedom may be endangered by joining larger movements.

> For centuries, we suffered under the oppression of the Hutts and their criminal enterprises. The Empire's domination doubled our difficulties. Only in the past few decades, in the era of the New Republic, have we been able to assert our own independence and our own rule.[64]

Isval going out of her way to save younger Twi'leks from the abuse she experienced and Yendor setting boundaries, even with his allies, are both empowering storylines, showing that the Twi'leks are more than a species of victims for others to exploit or rescue.

2019-present: Mercenaries and madams

The expansion of the *Star Wars* universe into live-action television expanded the history of Ryloth and included many Twi'leks focused on controlling their own destinies. In 2019's *The Mandalorian,* Season One, Twi'lek twins play significant roles in "The Prisoner," in which Xi'an, a mercenary, helps rescue her brother Qin from a New Republic prison cell.[65] Xi'an wears a form-fitting but not particularly revealing outfit, fitting for a thief or spy on a job requiring quick and easy movements. While her character is a bit eccentric, she also clearly takes care of herself and is highly skilled with her set of blades. There is no mention of Ryloth, slavery, or spice in the episode; Xi'an and her brother Qin just happen to be Twi'leks, which is an important step to freeing all Twi'lek characters from the same motivations and backstories again and again.

---

member of Saw's Partisans) and *Solo: A Star Wars Story.* They do not appear at all in the three Sequel *Star Wars* films *The Force Awakens, The Last Jedi,* and *The Rise of Skywalker,* although Aayla Secura's voice can be heard encouraging Rey near the end of *Rise.*

[63] Paul S. Kemp, *Lords of the Sith* (New York: Del Rey, 2015), 107-113.

[64] Claudia Gray, *Bloodline* (New York: Del Rey, 2016), chap. 2, Kindle.

[65] *The Mandalorian,* season 1, episode 6, "The Prisoner," directed by Rick Famuyiwa, written by Christopher Yost and Rick Famuyiwa, aired December 13, 2019, Disney+, https://www.disneyplus.com/video/37bcdcd3-335d-40e5-abaa-7ca435ab7beb.

2021 brought the introduction of both a Twi'lek hero and villain in stories set during the High Republic Era. *The High Republic: Light of the Jedi* introduced Twi'lek Jedi Master Loden Greatstorm, described on StarWars.com as one of the best teachers in the Jedi Order.[66] Another Twi'lek, Lourna Dee, sits on what appears to be the opposite moral side of the Jedi as a mercenary leader within the evil Nihil syndicate. In *Light of the Jedi* and throughout several High Republic books and comics, Dee is shown as a ruthless, take-no-prisoners-type nemesis to the Jedi. The original audio drama *The High Republic: Tempest Runner*, later released as a book, focused entirely on Dee's character, revealing her backstory. As a youth in the Twi'lek colony Aaloth, where her family was royalty, Dee was manipulated and betrayed by her spice-running boyfriend, leading to the death of her family and Dee's enslavement.[67] While audiences are not expected to root for Dee's actions or forgive her choices, it's a fascinating look into how a character who simply craves freedom can end up working with a criminal organization like the Nihil. Stories set in the High Republic era are fairly recent, and it's notable that Twi'lek characters already appear in leadership positions; the death of one of these characters, Loden Greatstorm, is a significant narrative driver throughout the stories in Phase One of the High Republic publishing project.

The new animated television series *Star Wars: The Bad Batch* (2021-) delves even more into the history of the Twi'lek people. *The Bad Batch* episodes "Devil's Deal" and "Rescue on Ryloth" show Ryloth shortly after Order 66, at the very beginning of Palpatine's Galactic Empire. Unsurprisingly, Orn Free Taa remains a pawn of whatever side appears equipped to keep him in a position of power, while the Syndulla family—including a young Hera and introducing Hera's mother, Elani—fights against the transition to another occupying force.[68] These episodes reveal a diverse Twi'lek populace with varying interests, hopes, and dreams for themselves and for the people of Ryloth. Significantly, these episodes also focus on Twi'lek characters and their actions. Here, *Star Wars* audiences see—more than in any previous story—through Twi'lek eyes, not merely through those of Jedi or clone troopers. Members of the Bad Batch arrive to help them only after Hera cleverly asks for their assistance.[69] *The Bad Batch* also offers a progressive new look for a

---

[66] Charles Soule, *Star Wars: Light of the Jedi* (New York: Del Rey, 2021); "Loden Greatstorm Databank Entry," StarWars.com, accessed April 8, 2022, https://www.starwars.com/databank/loden-greatstorm.

[67] Cavan Scott, *Star Wars: Tempest Runner* (New York: Del Rey, 2022), 194-199.

[68] *Star Wars: The Bad Batch*, season 1, episode 11, "Devil's Deal," directed by Steward Lee, written by Tamara Becher-Wilkinson, aired July 9, 2021, Disney+, https://www.disneyplus.com/video/9e08c288-ba6b-44e1-8369-e5b7e3422592.

[69] *Star Wars: The Bad Batch*, season 1, episode 12, "Rescue on Ryloth," directed by

female Twi'lek character who first debuted in *Star Wars: The Clone Wars.* The episode "Cut and Run" shows an interesting update to female Twi'lek Suu Lawquane's wardrobe from her first appearance in *The Clone Wars*' second season episode, "The Deserter." While Suu's barely-there outfit in *The Clone Wars* bordered on the absurd,[70] Suu's outfit in *The Bad Batch* is much more practical (and considerably less revealing) for a farmer and mother of two.[71] It's encouraging to see a character like Suu dressed in a way that makes her character more believable, and her words and actions stand out—more than her cleavage.

A more recent *Star Wars* television series, *The Book of Boba Fett* (2021-), shows some things change and some stay the same for Twi'leks in Jabba's Palace on Tatooine. The teaser for *The Book of Boba Fett*—a post-credit scene at the end of Season Two of *The Mandalorian*—pays homage to the first time audiences saw Bib Fortuna and Oola in Jabba's Palace in *Return of the Jedi.* Now five years after the events of *Jedi,* bounty hunters Boba Fett and Fennec Shand enter the throne room to discover a bloated Bib Fortuna sitting on Jabba's throne. A blue-skinned female Twi'lek sits chained at the foot of Fortuna's throne, exactly where Oola had been seated in *Return of the Jedi.* After Fennec opens fire on some of Fortuna's minions, the female Twi'lek tries to flee, but she's stopped by her chains. Fennec looks to the enslaved Twi'lek, shoots her chain, and motions for her to leave.[72] This scene shows one female character helping another female character escape enslavement—a powerful image. It also confirms that slavery is still an issue for some Twi'leks in the New Republic.

The Book of Boba Fett's first episode, "Stranger in a Strange Land," introduced audiences to female Twi'lek Garsa Fwip, the owner of a club in Mos Espa called The Sanctuary.[73] The Sanctuary has the elegant look and feel

---

Nathaniel Villanueva, written by Jennifer Corbett, aired July 16, 2021, Disney+, https://www.disneyplus.com/video/1961a670-c7e2-417e-84ff-8fc34322d6ce.

[70] *Star Wars: The Clone Wars,* season 2, episode 10, "The Deserter," directed by Robert Dalva, written by Carl Ellsworth, aired January 1, 2010, on Cartoon Network, Disney+, https://www.disneyplus.com/video/09f9af96-40bd-4e9a-a18d-92fb9f373298.

[71] *Star Wars: The Bad Batch,* season 1, episode 2, "Cut and Run," directed by Steward Lee, written by Gursimran Sandhu, aired May 7, 2021, Disney+, https://www.disneyplus.com/video/382d40ec-932e-4ff5-a7db-e2a949e74a20.

[72] *The Mandalorian,* season 2, episode 8, "The Rescue," directed by Peyton Reed, written by Jon Favreau, aired December 18, 2020, Disney+, https://www.disneyplus.com/video/2b916945-c54e-4dc1-a250-811aa302e07f.

[73] *The Book of Boba Fett,* season 1, episode 1, "Stranger in a Strange Land," directed by Robert Rodriguez, written by Jon Favreau, aired December 29, 2022, Disney+, https://www.disneyplus.com/video/a92bdf06-e51a-462d-919f-3341a9d5e083.

of the casino on Canto Bight from *The Last Jedi* as opposed to shady Mos Eisley Cantina from *A New Hope* or *The Mandalorian*. Fwip's appearance is unmistakably that of a wealthy business owner. Jennifer Beals, who portrayed Fwip, and director Robert Rodriguez discussed how Fwip intentionally recalls the character Rick in *Casablanca* with an unspoken power.[74] Her flowing dress with gold embellishments—very feminine without being very revealing—looks like an outfit the queen of Naboo, Padmé Amidala, might have worn in the Prequel films. Beals described her character in an interview, saying, "it was really important to me that it's clear that she's no one's slave and that she's no one's master. That is why she is a madam. She runs a place called the Sanctuary."[75] Beals's phrasing of "no one's slave and no one's master" as associated with the term "madam" is intriguing since two of Fwip's employees are a female and a male Twi'lek whose appearances provide a comparison to enslaved Twi'leks from previous *Star Wars* stories, such as Sebulba's twins. Interestingly, in *The Book of Boba Fett*, the male Twi'lek's outfit is the more revealing of the two, as he is completely shirtless. Like Sebulba's twins, these two Twi'leks do not appear mistreated. But unlike Sebulba's servants (from what audiences can tell), as the series continues, Fwip treats the female Twi'lek as more aide than servant, dispersing payments when needed; it's possible Fwip has the two dress seductively to disguise their roles as functionaries for her with access to the club's coffers. While Fwip as a character marks an important step forward in the journey to seeing Twi'lek characters in varied positions of power, it's unclear how much of that power extends to other Twi'lek characters in The Sanctuary. As it appears that Garsa and her employees were all killed in a bombing in Season One of *The Book of Boba Fett*, we may never know.

A new male Twi'lek character introduced in *The Book of Boba Fett*, the unnamed majordomo to the mayor of Mos Espa, mirrors Bib Fortuna's role in *Return of the Jedi*, but with a certain polish. While Fortuna growled orders in Huttese, the majordomo speaks in Basic with no hint of a Twi'lek accent, thanks to having attended finishing school on Coruscant.[76] And while Fortuna is an active participant in the enslavement of Oola in Jabba's Palace, relishing his role as Jabba's henchman, the cultured majordomo in *The Book of Boba Fett* wants no role in the fighting; he tells the mechanic Peli Motto, "I am not a

---

[74] Angélique Roché, "Jennifer Beals on *The Book of Boba Fett* and Joining the *Star Wars* Universe," *Harper's Bazaar*, January 4, 2022, https://www.harpersbazaar.com/culture/film-television/a38664138/jennifer-beals-book-of-boba-fett-interview/.

[75] Ibid.

[76] *The Book of Boba Fett*, season 1, episode 7, "In the Name of Honor," directed by Robert Rodriguez, written by Jon Favreau, aired February 9, 2022, Disney+, https://www.disneyplus.com/video/d939789b-dd61-4d5a-926b-28e815fb2617.

threat." This occurs during a battle sequence right before Motto compliments his head tails, calls him "pretty face," and offers him protection.[77] A male Twi'lek seeking aid from a flirty female mechanic shows how current *Star Wars* creators continue to break free from gender- and species-based stereotypes.

A bright future for Twi'leks

From Oola and Bib Fortuna in *Return of the Jedi* to Loden Greatstorm and Lourna Dee in the *High Republic*, from Cham Syndulla to Hera Syndulla, from Sebulba's enslaved twins in *The Phantom Menace* to Garsa Fwip's alluring aides in *The Book of Boba Fett*, Twi'leks represent a close-to-human, Othered species rising from a history of systemic oppression. Like many *Star Wars* characters, Twi'leks are looking for hope in a galaxy full of extraordinary challenges. Further, the evolution of their representation in *Star Wars* reflects the evolution of female and marginalized human characters in the franchise—and beyond. Kempshall notes the Otherness of marginalized character groups within *Star Wars* "serves as a comparison for those who are othered outside of it."[78] Sexualized Twi'lek background characters still appear in *Star Wars* stories, but they are no longer the main representation of Twi'leks—far from it in most cases. Twi'leks are now also the main characters and drivers of narratives in *Star Wars* stories; they are just as likely to be the hero or the villain as they are to be rescued by the hero or terrorized by the villain. Centering Twi'lek characters has helped to center and elevate all Othered characters, showing such stories are just as meaningful and important as those centering human (or racial majority, dominant-culture) characters.

Star Wars creators should not be expected to shy away from the history and effects of Twi'leks' centuries-long abuse by other species, but it's encouraging that few recent Twi'lek characters are defined or motivated only by their current or previous enslavement. If every story centered on Twi'lek pain and suffering, their stories would focus more on their oppressors than their own lives. Rather, observing the way Twi'leks have evolved in *Star Wars* stories shows that fans can expect more dynamic Twi'lek stories in the future, like one in which, for instance, we might see Hera Syndulla juggle her roles as rebellion hero *and* mother. It's a big galaxy out there for *Star Wars* storytellers—with plenty of room to expand on the impact and influence of Twi'leks and other formerly-marginalized characters for many years to come.

---

[77] Ibid.

[78] Kempshall, *The History and Politics of* Star Wars, 193.

Bibliography

"Ann Gella/Canon." Wookieepedia. Accessed January 12, 2023. https://starwars.fandom.com/wiki/Ann_Gella.

Becher-Wilkinson, Tamara, writer. *Star Wars: The Bad Batch.* Season 1, episode 11, "Devil's Deal." Directed by Steward Lee. Aired July 9, 2021. Disney+. https://www.disneyplus.com/video/9e08c288-ba6b-44e1-8369-e5b7e3422592.

BioWare, Obsidian Entertainment, Aspyr Media. *Star Wars: Knights of the Old Republic.* LucasArts, Electronic Arts. Windows. 2003.

Carlo, Tori. "Star Wars: Darth Talon & Cade Skywalker Are the Best Sith/Jedi Romance—NOT Reylo." *CBR.* March 1, 2021. https://www.cbr.com/darth-talon-cade-skywalker-star-wars-romance/.

Category: Twi'lek. Wookieepedia. Accessed February 23, 2022. https://starwars.fandom.com/wiki/Category:Twi%27leks.

Corbett, Jennifer, writer. *Star Wars: The Bad Batch.* Season 1, episode 12, "Rescue on Ryloth." Directed by Nathaniel Villanueva. Aired July 16, 2021. Disney+. https://www.disneyplus.com/video/1961a670-c7e2-417e-84ff-8fc34322d6ce.

Crouse, Megan. "What *Star Wars: The High Republic* Can Learn From *Knights of the Old Republic.*" *Den of Geek.* May 28, 2020. https://www.denofgeek.com/books/star-wars-high-republic-knights-of-the-old-republic-spoilers/.

Dubuc, Nicole, writer. *Star Wars Rebels.* Season 3, episode 5, "Hera's Heroes." Directed by Justin Ridge. Aired October 15, 2016, Disney Channel. Disney+. https://www.disneyplus.com/video/77af8e53-d662-4c0c-8eed-7b2c56490308.

Ellsworth, Carl, writer. *Star Wars: The Clone Wars.* Season 2, episode 10, "The Deserter." Directed by Robert Dalva. Aired January 1, 2010, Cartoon Network. Disney+. https://www.disneyplus.com/video/09f9af96-40bd-4e9a-a18d-92fb9f373298.

Favreau, Jon, writer. *The Mandalorian.* Season 2, episode 8, "The Rescue." Directed by Peyton Reed. Aired December 18, 2020. Disney+. https://www.disneyplus.com/video/2b916945-c54e-4dc1-a250-811aa302e07f.

———, writer. *The Book of Boba Fett.* Season 1, episode 1, "Stranger in a Strange Land." Directed by Robert Rodriguez. Aired December 29, 2022. Disney+. https://www.disneyplus.com/video/a92bdf06-e51a-462d-919f-3341a9d5e083.

———, writer. *The Book of Boba Fett.* Season 1, episode 7, "In the Name of Honor." Directed by Robert Rodriguez. Aired February, 9, 2022. Disney+. https://www.disneyplus.com/video/d939789b-dd61-4d5a-926b-28e815fb2617.

Filoni, Dave, dir. *Star Wars: The Clone Wars.* 2008; Burbank, CA: Warner Brothers/Lucasfilm. Disney+. https://www.disneyplus.com/movies/star-wars-the-clone-wars/AVmv1ulT1nQW.

———, Henry Gilroy, Kiri Hart, Simon Kinberg and Steven Melching, writers. *Star Wars Rebels.* Season 4, episode 15, "Family Reunion—and Farewell." Directed by Dave Filoni, Bosco Ng, and Sergio Páez. Aired March 5, 2018, Disney Channel. Disney+. https://www.disneyplus.com/video/abcb0676-0f12-45c7-8a8f-45d80e66e3c3.

Finkelman, Paul. "From Slavery to Freedom in a Galaxy Far, Far Away." In *Star Wars and History*, edited by Nancy R. Reagin and Janice Liedl, 229-254. Hoboken, NJ: John Wiley & Sons, 2013.

Frankel, Valerie. *Star Wars Meets the Eras of Feminism: Weighing All the Galaxy's Women Great and Small.* Lanham, MD: Lexington Books, 2018.

Gilroy, Henry. Interview with John Mills and Matthew Rushing. *Aggressive Negotiations: A Star Wars Pod.* Podcast audio. October 1, 2019. https://web.archive.org/web/20200709073437/https://www.spreaker.com/user/10684996/an-181#.

_______, writer. *Star Wars: The Clone Wars.* Season 1, episode 21, "Liberty on Ryloth." Directed by Rob Coleman. Aired March 13, 2009, Cartoon Network. Disney+. https://www.disneyplus.com/video/0f87705e-7773-4154-8ff8-fdee5671431d.

_______, writer. *Star Wars: The Clone Wars.* Season 4, episode 12, "Slaves of the Republic." Directed by Brian Kalin O'Connell. Aired December 2, 2011, Cartoon Network. Disney+. https://www.disneyplus.com/video/22ffd322-9702-403f-93d3-47dc7780e062.

Gray, Claudia. *Bloodline.* New York: Del Rey, 2016.

Greenberg, Drew Z., writer. *Star Wars: The Clone Wars.* Season 1, episode 16, "Hidden Enemy." Directed by Steward Lee. Aired February 6, 2009, Cartoon Network. Disney+. https://www.disneyplus.com/video/7c732b05-b90f-4090-a184-5652be228139.

Hopps, Kevin, writer. *Star Wars Rebels.* Season 1, episode 10, "Idiot's Array." Directed by Dave Filoni. Aired January 12, 2015, Disney Channel. Disney+. https://www.disneyplus.com/video/edf47542-e14a-45a6-b56d-ee73c3e8ddb7.

Kemp, Paul S. *Lords of the Sith.* New York: Del Rey, 2015.

Kempshall, Chris. *The History and Politics of* Star Wars: *Death Stars and Democracy.* London and New York: Routledge, 2023.

Kountz, Samantha. "We Come in Peace: Immigration in Post-Cold War Science Fiction Film." *Foundation*, Vol. 43, Issue 119 (Winter 2014): 29-40. https://fanac.org/fanzines/Foundation/Foundation119.pdf.

"Loden Greatstorm Databank Entry." StarWars.com. Accessed April 8, 2022. https://www.starwars.com/databank/loden-greatstorm.

Lucas, George, dir. *Star Wars Episode IV: A New Hope.* 1977; Beverly Hills, CA: 20th Century Fox/Lucasfilm Ltd. Disney+, https://www.disneyplus.com/movies/star-wars-a-new-hope-episode-iv/12fVeZxD2fWJ.

_______, dir. *Star Wars Episode II: Attack of the Clones.* 2002; Beverly Hills, CA: 20th Century Fox/Lucasfilm Ltd. Disney+. https://www.disneyplus.com/movies/star-wars-attack-of-the-clones-episode-ii/mgpYHGnzZW6N.

_______, dir. *Star Wars Episode III: Revenge of the Sith.* 2005; Beverly Hills, CA: 20th Century Fox/Lucasfilm Ltd. Disney+. https://www.disneyplus.com/movies/star-wars-revenge-of-the-sith-episode-iii/4WvbqLFumNvi.

Lucas, Katie, writer. *Star Wars: The Clone Wars.* Season 1, episode 13, "Jedi Crash." Directed by Rob Coleman. Aired January 16, 2009, Cartoon Network. Disney+. https://www.disneyplus.com/video/28c0b907-8efe-4400-af50-c13c66e18468.

LucasArts. *Star Wars: Jedi Knight: Dark Forces II.* LucasArts. Microsoft Windows. 1997.

Maguire, Lori. "Fear is the Path to the Dark Side." In *Star Wars and History,* edited by Nancy R. Reagin and Janice Liedl, 203-226. Hoboken, NJ: John Wiley & Sons, 2013.

Marquand, Richard, dir. *Star Wars: Return of the Jedi.* 1983; Beverly Hills, CA: 20th Century Fox/Lucasfilm Ltd. Disney+. https://www.disneyplus.com/movies/star-wars-return-of-the-jedi-episode-vi/6QGKo5mjDBS8.

McGucken, Stephanie. "Rebelling Heroines: Hera, Sabine, and Ahsoka in *Star Wars Rebels.*" In *Fourth Wave Feminism in Science Fiction and Fantasy Volume 2: Essays on Television Representations, 2013-2019,* edited by Valerie Estelle Frankel, 151-166. Jefferson, NC: McFarland, 2019.

Melching, Steven, writer. *Star Wars: The Clone Wars.* Season 1, episode 5, "Rookies." Directed by Justin Ridge. Aired October 24, 2008, Cartoon Network. Disney+. https://www.disneyplus.com/video/598d1e7b-f39e-4527-9487-b5e891f5eefa.

_______, writer. *Star Wars: The Clone Wars.* Season 1, episode 19, "The Zillo Beast Strikes Back." Directed by Steward Lee. Aired April 16, 2010, Cartoon Network. Disney+. https://www.disneyplus.com/video/6f2cd6cf-8e7a-42e6-893a-6465f2683648.

Ostrander, John. *Star Wars #19.* Milwaukie, WI: Dark Horse Comics, 2000.

_______. *Star Wars: Legacy* series #1-50. Milwaukie, WI: Dark Horse Comics, 2006-2010.

Peña, Abel G. and Jason Fry. "The Dark Forces Saga, Part 4." Wizards. May 26, 2005. https://web.archive.org/web/20100430201940/http://wizards.com/default.asp?x=starwars/article/sw20050526a.

Ratcliffe, Amy. *Star Wars: Women of the Galaxy.* San Francisco: Chronicle Books, 2018.

Reynolds, David West. *Star Wars Episode I: The Visual Dictionary.* New York: DK Publishing, 1999.

Roché, Angélique. "Jennifer Beals on *The Book of Boba Fett* and Joining the *Star Wars* Universe." *Harper's Bazaar.* January 4, 2022. https://www.harpersbazaar.com/culture/film-television/a38664138/jennifer-beals-book-of-boba-fett-interview/.

Sandhu, Gursimran, writer. *Star Wars: The Bad Batch.* Season 1, episode 2, "Cut and Run." Directed by Steward Lee. Aired May 7, 2021. Disney+. https://www.disneyplus.com/video/382d40ec-932e-4ff5-a7db-e2a949e74a20.

Schweighofer, Peter. *Star Wars: Platt's Starpoint Guide.* Honesdale, PA: West End Games, 1995.

Scott, Cavan. *Star Wars: Tempest Runner.* New York: Del Rey, 2022.

Shedd, W. Travis. "Tracing the Evolution Nexus of Race, Species, and 'Otherness' in the *Star Wars* Film Franchise." MA thesis, Georgetown University, 2016.

Slavicsek, Bill and Curtis Smith. *The Star Wars Sourcebook.* New York: West End Games. 1987.

Soule, Charles. Star Wars: *Light of the Jedi.* New York: Del Rey, 2021.

Stradley, Randy and Henry Gilroy, writers. *Star Wars: The Clone Wars.* Season 1, episode 20, "Innocents of Ryloth." Directed by Justin Ridge. Aired March 6, 2009, Cartoon Network. Disney+. https://www.disneyplus.com/video/d4f5abd5-3e71-4cef-9928-6be9527fdb89.

Strayton, George R. *Tales of the Jedi Companion.* Honesdale, PA: West End Games, 1996.

Wade, Chris and Abraham Riesman. "Every Line from a (Non-Leia) Woman in Star Wars." *Vulture.* December 13, 2017. https://www.vulture.com/2015/12/star-wars-all-female-lines-excluding-leia.html.

Walker, John. "Bastard of the Old Republic." *Eurogamer.* September 21, 2014. https://www.eurogamer.net/articles/2014-09-21-bastard-of-the-old-republic.

Yost, Christopher and Rick Famuyiwa, writers. *The Mandalorian.* Season 1, episode 6, "The Prisoner." Directed by Rick Famuyiwa. Aired December 13, 2019. Disney+. https://www.disneyplus.com/video/37bcdcd3-335d-40e5-abaa-7ca435ab7beb.

Chapter 2

Saving What We Love: The Hope and Resistance of Makers and Craftspeople in Disney's *Star Wars*

Vikki C. Terrile

Abstract: While makers and craftspeople have figured throughout the *Star Wars* universe, they have become more prominent in the recent Disney works, particularly in *The Mandalorian* and in the Sequel Trilogy. These makers include Rey, Rose Tico, Babu Frik, Kuiil, and the Armorer. Whereas contemporary making is often situated in notions of community and connectedness, makers within the post-Empire *Star Wars* universe often work alone, reflecting an ethos more in line with traditional mythologies of rugged individualism and homesteading common in Western and science fiction. In *Star Wars*, craftsmanship is about survival but also related to professional identity, differing from contemporary maker activities which are often viewed as hobbies. At the same time, a spirit of love undergirds these making activities, such as Rey's tinkering around her homestead and Kuiil's pride in what he has built for himself. Within the post-Empire *Star Wars* universe, making and tinkering reflect the contemporary understanding of these activities as reclamations of power. In addition to survival and resistance making, these strategic processes include the upholding of persecuted subcultural traditions, in the cases of the Armorer and Albrekh. Artisanship in the Disney *Star Wars* universe also challenges gendered norms around making. This chapter explores how making in its varied forms exists and is celebrated in the Disney *Star Wars* universe and can be interpreted through theories of power and resistance.

Keywords: *Star Wars*, making, craft, resistance, mechanics, homesteading, Rey, Kuiil, Rose Tico, Peli Motto, Trace Martez, Armorer, Boba Fett, Tusken Raiders, Cassian Andor, Karis Nemik, gaderffii, gaffi stick

***

"That's how we're gonna win. Not fighting what we hate; saving what we love."

—Rose Tico, *Star Wars Episode VIII: The Last Jedi*[1]

While makers and craftspeople have been visible throughout the *Star Wars* universe (young Anakin Skywalker is an obvious example), they have become even more prominent in the Disney era. The timing of these newer entries in the saga coincides with the "maker movement"[2] in the United States and other Western cultures, envisioned as both a return to the romance of an idealized preindustrial society and the importance of craftspersons therein[3] and, increasingly, as a site of protest and resistance.[4] Making and crafting became enormously popular in contemporary culture in the first decade of the twenty-first century, as did identity markers around making, creating, and tinkering. It is not surprising, then, that these signifiers are more visible in the Disney *Star Wars* universe.

Tanya Harrod and Catharine Rossi both discuss the role of making in Daniel Defoe's *Robinson Crusoe*, a well-known example of making in English language fiction. In the novel, first published in 1719, Robinson Crusoe survives a storm that destroys his ship. Crusoe is shipwrecked on an island without hope of rescue and uses ingenuity and craftsmanship to eke out his survival.[5] Harrod notes that "Defoe's masterpiece charms us because we are set to wondering how we would manage if everything familiar were stripped away, if craft became a dire necessity."[6] This may be true in both fiction and real life. Paula Guerra describes punk DIY (do-it-yourself) activities in modern-day Portugal as "The need to survive on the fringe of the mainstream, in a self-taught mode that tilts against the capitalist system."[7]

---

[1] To JAMV with love and gratitude for patiently rewatching everything *Star Wars* with me for the umpteenth time. Even though I said it was "for my research," you knew all along I would have done it anyway, so thank you for not calling me on the excuse.

Star Wars Episode VIII: The Last Jedi, directed by Rian Johnson (2017; San Francisco: Disney/Lucasfilm Ltd.), DVD.

[2] Dale Dougherty, "The Maker Movement," *Innovations: Technology, Governance, Globalization* 7, no. 3 (2012), 11.

[3] Kathleen Morris, "You Are Not a Lemming: The Imagined Resistance of Craft Citizenship," *The Journal of Modern Craft* 9, no. 1 (2016), 7-8.

[4] Ibid., 6.

[5] Daniel Defoe, *The Life and Adventures of Robinson Crusoe* (Minneapolis, MN: First Avenue Editions, 2016).

[6] Tanya Harrod, "Classic Take on the Industry of One," *Crafts* 246 (January/February 2014), 92.

[7] Paula Guerra, "Raw Power: Punk, DIY and Underground Cultures as Spaces of Resistance in Contemporary Portugal," *Cultural Sociology* 12, no. 2 (2018), 247.

Rossi argues the themes around making and crafting from *Robinson Crusoe* have made their way through centuries of fiction, as "In each telling the protagonist improvises with their material surroundings to make their survival."[8] She further explains, "Everyday making is central to the survivalist novel because making is central to our survival."[9] For characters in the Disney *Star Wars* universe, craft is born of the challenges of surviving in a complex and war-torn galaxy. Within the *Star Wars* universe, survival is fraught; scraping by and making are the reality for most citizens of the galaxy.

But in *Star Wars*, making also becomes a way to move beyond survival into lives that are more vibrant and hopeful. While the exemplar of Crusoe and makers in other fiction often center making as individual acts of survival or rugged individualism,[10] contemporary making in real life is often situated in notions of community and connectedness.[11] In the Disney *Star Wars* universe, makers typically work alone at first, in line with traditional mythologies of rugged individualism and homesteading common in Western and science fiction.[12] This is also in keeping with Harrod's view of Robinson Crusoe as "an industry of one"[13] and what Rossi describes as "the maker as an individual engaging in productive making."[14] In modern Western cultures, craft and making are understood as essential and rooted in the self. As Peter Korn explains, "we practice contemporary craft as a process of self-transformation."[15] Rossi notes that "the impulse to make, or remake, our environment is universal. Even if Crusoe didn't need to make in order to survive, he would have felt compelled to do so anyway."[16]

---

[8] Catharine Rossi, "The Crusoe Condition: Making Within Limits and the Critical Possibilities of Fiction," *The Journal of Modern Craft* 10, no. 1 (2017), 21-22.

[9] Ibid., 20.

[10] Carl Abbott, "Homesteading on the Extraterrestrial Frontier," *Science Fiction Studies* 32, no. 2 (2005), 242.

[11] Red Chidgey, "Developing Communities of Resistance?: Maker Pedagogies, Do-It-Yourself Feminism, and DIY Citizenship," in *DIY Citizenship: Critical Making and Social Media*, ed. Matt Ratto and Megan Boler (Cambridge, MA: The MIT Press, 2004), 105; Kate Orton-Johnson, "DIY Citizenship, Critical Making, and Community," in *DIY Citizenship: Critical Making and Social Media*, ed. Matt Ratto and Megan Boler (Cambridge, MA: The MIT Press, 2004), 142.

[12] Abbott, "Homesteading on the Extraterrestrial Frontier," 242.

[13] Harrod, "Classic Take on the Industry of One," 92.

[14] Rossi, "The Crusoe Condition," 22.

[15] Peter Korn, *Why We Make Things and Why it Matters: The Education of a Craftsman* (Boston: David R. Godine Publisher, 2013), 7.

[16] Rossi, "The Crusoe Condition," 31.

Korn argues further, "creative effort is a process of challenging embedded narratives of belief in order to think the world into being for oneself, and that the work involved in doing so provides a wellspring of spiritual fulfillment."[17] Thus, as the stories of the makers in the Disney *Star Wars* universe progress, they become part of something bigger, often using their individual skills in service to the communities with which they identify. In this way, making and tinkering reflect the contemporary understanding of these activities as "strategic processes through which people reclaim power in their everyday lives."[18] Making (in its varied forms) is notable and even celebrated in the Disney *Star Wars* universe works. Such activities are often acts of resistance, undergirded by devotion and love. Whether it is a love of the objects and things themselves, the work involved, or the cause the making supports or makes possible, love becomes the strongest motivation for making within the Disney *Star Wars* universe.

The language around making

Elucidation of the vocabulary around making is necessary given shifting trends in the modern understanding of the topic. Contemporarily, making and creating are used interchangeably, covering broad categories of somewhat neutral creative activities. Craft is more complex, with connotations of both craftspeople and traditional domestic handicrafts. While "crafting" may be incorporated within discourses around making and the contemporary maker movement, it is often perceived as gendered and "'more feminine . . . frivolous'"[19] than the work connoted by "making." Craft is also used to describe artists whose work is considered "outsider" or folk art.[20] Tinkering refers to what Dale Dougherty describes as work that "used to be a basic skill . . . you could get a little bit more out of life than the average person if you had good tinkering skills—if you could fix your own car, for example, or improve your home or make your own clothes."[21] Making and craft are understudied in fiction[22] and film.

---

[17] Korn, *Why We Make Things and Why it Matters*, 8.

[18] Chidgey, "Developing Communities of Resistance," 104.

[19] Lauren Britton, "Power, Access, Status: The Discourse of Race, Gender, and Class in the Maker Movement," TASCHA, Technology & Social Change Group, University of Washington Information School, last modified March 18, 2015, archived at https://web.archive.org/web/20220321092425/https://tascha.uw.edu/2015/03/power-access-status-the-discourse-of-race-gender-and-class-in-the-maker-movement/.

[20] Jack Z. Bratich and Heidi M. Brush, "Fabricating Activism: Craft-Work, Popular Culture, Gender," *Utopian Studies* 22, no. 2 (2011), 249.

[21] Dougherty, "The Maker Movement," 11.

[22] Rossi, "The Crusoe Condition," 21-22.

Making a life

The importance, even centrality of themes of the American Western in science fiction, is well-established.[23] Specifically, homesteading imagery features prominently in both science fiction literature and film[24] and is present from the beginning of the *Star Wars* saga.[25] In the Disney-era *Star Wars* universe, two homesteads are noteworthy since they highlight individual lives eked out in harsh circumstances and tended with obvious pride and care. They also juxtapose the economic necessities of making for survival with personal joy in the work or its outcomes.

The audience's introduction to Rey in *Star Wars Episode VII: The Force Awakens* (2015) is through a four-minute, nearly wordless observation, rather like "a day in the life" on Jakku.[26] We watch Rey scavenge for parts in an abandoned Star Destroyer and clean them to trade for food portions. As Amy Ratcliffe notes, "She looks at each item she finds from the perspective of possibility, whether turning lenses from a stormtrooper helmet into goggles, or uncovering a fallen AT-AT walker to make it her home."[27] While audiences soon learn Rey is a self-taught and innovative pilot and mechanic, what we witness in her home setting is her domestic making. Alan Dean Foster's *Star Wars: The Force Awakens* novelization notes that Rey places "her gear and supplies onto . . . homemade cabinets and shelves."[28] In the film, the camera settles on a container of dried (dead) flowers and what is clearly a handmade doll meant to look like a Resistance pilot. Rey scratches a notch onto a wall of notches—another day has gone by since the disappearance of her parents—reminiscent of Robinson Crusoe's own homemade calendar.[29] While Crusoe creates his calendar out of

---

[23] Abbott, "Homesteading on the Extraterrestrial Frontier," 243; Jeremiah B.C. Axelrod, "Mutiny on the Sofa: Historical Patterns of Patriarchy and Family Structure in American Science Fiction, 1945–2018," *Pacific Coast Philology* 53, no. 2 (2018), 312; Lane Roth, "Vraisemblance and the Western Setting in Contemporary Science Fiction Film," *Literature/Film Quarterly* 13, no. 3 (1985), 181; Janice Hocker Rushing, "Evolution of 'the New Frontier' in Alien and Aliens: Patriarchal Co-Optation of the Feminine Archetype," *The Quarterly Journal of Speech* 75, no. 1 (1989), 1.

[24] Abbott, "Homesteading on the Extraterrestrial Frontier," 242; Roth, "Vraisemblance and the Western Setting in Contemporary Science Fiction Film," 182.

[25] *Star Wars Episode IV: A New Hope*, directed by George Lucas (1977; Beverly Hills, CA: 20th Century Fox/Lucasfilm Ltd.), DVD.

[26] *Star Wars Episode VII: The Force Awakens*, directed by J.J. Abrams (2015; San Francisco: Disney/Lucasfilm Ltd.), DVD.

[27] Amy Ratcliffe, *Star Wars: Women of the Galaxy* (San Francisco: Chronicle Books, 2018), 177.

[28] Alan Dean Foster, *Star Wars: The Force Awakens* (New York: Del Rey, 2016), 31.

[29] Defoe, *Robinson Crusoe*, 67.

fear he will lose a sense of time and fail to keep the Sabbath, Rey creates what is the largest visual decoration in her home as a reflection of hope that her parents will one day return.

In *The Force Awakens* novelization, the narrator describes Rey's home this way:

> Bits and pieces of homemade décor ornamented isolated alcoves and corners: here a handmade doll fashioned from reclaimed orange flight suit material, there a cluster of dried desert flowers; on the far end of the bed insert, a pillow that had cost her a day's work. It wasn't much, but where such examples of defiant individuality had been placed, they softened the drabness of their surroundings.[30]

Foster's use here of "defiant individuality" to describe Rey's domestic craft is important to our understanding of making in the context of the Disney *Star Wars* universe. Since the interior of Rey's AT-AT is private,[31] the acts Foster calls defiance are likely unseen by anyone but Rey. This does not negate their power, however. Much of the scholarship and popular discourse around twenty-first-century making is couched in terms related to activism and civic engagement. "Craftivism," a popular portmanteau, is viewed as "the intersections of personal, social, and political engagement and third-wave feminism."[32] In this vein, crafting and making are viewed as ways to resist or boycott consumer capitalism and produce both products and community.[33] However, Kathleen Morris believes that making as economic or political resistance is a false narrative, arguing that the marketing of making and craft as a means of resisting or undermining neoliberal capitalism "offers a convincing illusion of free choice and self-determination, while masking a larger system based on oppression, inequity, and state dereliction of duty."[34] The acts and products of Rey's making may not have much impact on the economic or political structures of the galaxy, yet despite Morris's view, they *are* acts of resistance—a personal and private insistence that love and hope can survive, even on the sands of Jakku. Rey's

---

30 Foster, *Star Wars: The Force Awakens*, 31-32.

31 Rey's chronic alone-ness in her AT-AT is implied in the *Star Wars: The Rise of Skywalker* novelization: "Rey had waited so long on Jakku for her parents to come back for her . . . No one ever did. She had vague memories of Unkar Plutt raising her for a few years in a halfhearted, ham-fisted way, before booting her out into the desert to fend for herself as a little girl. Even he had never bothered to check on her." Rae Carson, *Star Wars: The Rise of Skywalker* (New York: Del Rey, 2020), 156.

32 Orton-Johnson, "DIY Citizenship, Critical Making, and Community," 141.

33 Chidgey, "Developing Communities of Resistance," 104, 142.

34 Morris, "You Are Not a Lemming," 8.

private making is more in line with what Jack Z. Bratich and Heidi M. Brush describe as they note, "The current resurgence of crafting has strong links to the anarchist milieu, especially as a politicized practice of resourcefulness, local knowledge, and nonhierarchical organizational forms."[35] While modern making is often voluntary, situated in privilege (free time) and affluence (disposable income),[36] Rey's making uses the same tools she has honed for her survival: resourcefulness and local knowledge. Yet she subverts them into something that sustains her hope, joy, and the memory of her parents.

Kuiil in *The Mandalorian* (2019-) established a solitary homestead for himself after purchasing his freedom from indentured servitude to the Empire. Like Rey, Kuiil is both a homesteader and a mechanic. In Joe Schreiber's *Star Wars: The Mandalorian Junior Novel*, the narrator notes that for Kuiil, helping the Mandalorian repair his ship after it is stripped by Jawas "was an opportunity to lose himself in something he loved. He had always found deep satisfaction in repairing broken things, listening to what was wrong with a piece of machinery and coaxing it back to life."[37] Schreiber's description of Kuiil's tinkering as something he loves, echoes Lydia DeLyser and Paul Greenstein, who explains that "motorcycle restoration—like other forms of making—must be infused with accrued skill *and* love."[38]

The love infused in Kuiil's making connects him to Rey, for the love that makers have for their work may be situated in the work itself, in the objects they create or maintain, or—as for both these makers—in the role their skills play in supporting the causes in which they believe. This understanding of making as "for the cause" plays an explicit and significant role in Kuiil's characterization. In *The Mandalorian*'s Season One episode, "The Reckoning," Mando is troubled to find the IG droid he had destroyed (because it was programmed to kill the Child) at Kuiil's homestead when he returns there with former Rebel shock trooper Cara Dune. Kuiil explains he rescued what remained of IG-11 and reconstructed him as a service droid, his painstaking efforts emphasized by a cinematic montage of his hard work and the droid's halting but sure progress.[39] When the Mandalorian is still loath to accept the reprogrammed droid, Kuiil asks "Do you trust me? . . . Then

---

[35] Bratich and Brush, "Fabricating Activism," 247.

[36] Britton, "Power, Access, Status."

[37] Joe Schreiber, *Star Wars: The Mandalorian Junior Novel* (Los Angeles: Disney Lucasfilm Press, 2021), 42.

[38] Dydia DeLyser and Paul Greenstein, "The Devotions of Restoration: Materiality, Enthusiasm, and Making Three 'Indian Motocycles' Like New," *Annals of the American Association of Geographers* 107, no. 6 (2017), 1463.

[39] *The Mandalorian*, season 1, episode 7, "The Reckoning," directed by Deborah Chow, written by Jon Favreau, aired December 18, 2019, Disney+, https://www.disneyplus.com/video/defe8509-3e33-45e6-90e1-0a8f0f7917e1.

you will trust my work,"[40] emphasizing the link between maker and that which is made. Kuiil had previously told Mando he had "worked a lifetime to finally be free of servitude," earning his freedom from indentured servitude to the Empire through his own skill.[41] Given Kuiil's past serving the Empire and Cara Dune's as a Rebel shock trooper (or "Dropper": specialized infantry dropped on planets to find and eliminate former Imperial warlords[42]), tension arises when the two meet. To intervene, the Mandalorian appeals to Kuiil as a maker, asking if he can modify the Child's hover pram to make it more comfortable. Kuiil answers, "I shall fabricate a better one, then perhaps this Dropper can see how one can win their freedom with the skill of one's hands,"[43] again highlighting his cause-based making. Kuiil here shows pride in both his skill and its application in securing freedom—both for himself and for others. Though he resists becoming involved with the Mandalorian's cause against the Imperials, in the end, he agrees, sacrificing his own hard-won freedom to protect the Child, telling Mando that "None will be free until the old ways [of Imperial slavery] are gone forever."[44] Although this formidable character is killed by Stormtroopers in the very next episode, his contributions to the cause for freedom live on. IG-11—because of Kuiil's handiwork in reprogramming him to protect and nurse—rescues the Child and preserves his freedom, also saving Mando and friends from the Imperials. Kuiil himself may have been no match for the Imperial remnant, but his handiwork remained to promote the cause of freedom.

For these homesteaders in the *Star Wars* universe, much of their craftsmanship is about survival, in line with Guerra's view that "the DIY ethos is also related to 'doing things' when there is a scarcity of resources or a lack of access to them."[45] At the same time, there is clearly love in these activities, as the novelization accounts of both Rey and Kuiil's making suggest. The romance of making, both in its idealized "romanticizing" of the activities that go into craft, exemplified by Kuiil's IG-11 reform montage, and in the more literal sense of "labors of love,"[46] exemplified by the wallpaper of hash marks Rey makes in her solitary home to mark her parents' absence, traces throughout the entire *Star Wars* saga, but is given bold emphasis in the Disney era.

---

[40] Ibid.

[41] *The Mandalorian*, season 1, episode 2, "The Child," directed by Rick Famiyuwa, written by Jon Favreau, aired November 15, 2019, Disney+, https://www.disneyplus.com/series/the-mandalorian/3jLIGMDYINqD.

[42] "Shock trooper," Wookieepedia, accessed November 30, 2022, https://starwars.fandom.com/wiki/Shock_trooper.

[43] *The Mandalorian*, "The Reckoning."

[44] Ibid.

[45] Guerra, "Raw Power," 248.

[46] DeLyser and Greenstein, "The Devotions of Restoration," 1475.

Working for what matters

Making in *Star Wars* is also, as Chidgey says, about the reclamation of power, and sometimes that power is economic. Explicit illustrations of Imperial economics and production in the "Dark Times" before *Star Wars Episode IV: A New Hope* (1977) emerged in 2022's first season of the *Star Wars* television show *Andor*. A prequel to 2016's *Rogue One: A Star Wars Story* set five years before the Battle of Yavin, the series is unflinching in its depiction of the Empire *as* an empire wielding colonizing and oppressive power. Late in Season One, Cassian Andor is arrested by the Empire for no reason and sentenced to six years in the Narkina 5 prison complex. In this narrative arc, it becomes clear the Empire is using the excuse of the recent Aldhani heist (see below) to expand its power. They now incarcerate at will using the Public Order Resentencing Directive[47] as a way to obtain forced labor. Cassian, gathering allies for an escape attempt, tells fellow inmate Kino Loy, "We are nothing to them. . . . We're cheaper than droids and easier to replace."[48] He also notes, "Whatever we're making here, it's clearly something they need. They can't afford to be surprised again."[49] Cassian's observations are apt; the Narkina prisoners are used for labor as if they *were* droids in a decontextualized production line in which they do not even know what they are making and are almost immediately replaced if they die. There is no power for them as individuals in this work—only power for the Empire, as the prisoners toil to create the products it needs to rule. A hidden scene after the final episode of *Andor*'s first season confirms what audiences already suspect: that Cassian spent 34 shifts on Narkina 5 laboring to produce parts for the weapons array on the first Death Star.[50]

Cassian's background on the planet Ferrix positions his stance of resistance to these economic realities of the Empire. Salvage is a key industry of Ferrix, the

---

[47] *Andor*, season 1, episode 8, "Narkina 5," directed by Toby Haynes, written by Beau Willimon, aired October 26, 2022, Disney+, https://www.disneyplus.com/video/e552dfd3-ec1b-4046-8410-711114a2a4ef.

[48] *Andor*, season 1, episode 9, "Nobody's Listening!" directed by Toby Haynes, written by Beau Willimon, aired November 2, 2022, Disney+, https://www.disneyplus.com/video/c41ac934-18c3-4871-8762-4bf3ac75966b. For more on the Narkina 5 arc in *Andor*, see Emily Strand's chapter in this volume.

[49] *Andor*, season 1, episode 10, "One Way Out," directed by Toby Haynes, written by Beau Willimon, aired November 9, 2022, Disney+, https://www.disneyplus.com/video/93c891d6-35cc-4f0f-9d1e-e16e89506ebc. The surprise Cassian refers to here is the recent Aldhani heist of over 80 million Imperial credits, a heist in which Cassian himself played a key role.

[50] *Andor*, season 1, episode 12, "Rix Road," directed by Benjamin Caron, written by Tony Gilroy, aired November 23, 2022, Disney+, https://www.disneyplus.com/video/78c53cd7-c7c1-40c4-b365-a56fae06799e.

home base of Cassian and his community; its economy rests on salvage and sale—both legitimate and black market—of parts. Ferrix's salvage operations range from large-scale yards where grapplers disassemble starships[51] to small shops, like the one owned by Bix Caleen.[52] The value of parts is proportional to their age and purity; the stolen Imperial N-S9 Starpath Unit Cassian plans to sell to Luthen Rael[53] is of immense value because it is fully intact and unused. It is also untraceable and proprietary.[54] The Starpath unit leads Cassian to the burgeoning Rebellion and an opportunity to reflect more deeply on the role of technology and production in Imperial oppression—and its resistance. On Aldhani, preparing for the heist of the Empire's quarterly payroll, Karis Nemik shows Cassian an old navigational tool, explaining it is "One of the best navigational tools ever built. Can't be jammed or intercepted. Something breaks, you can fix it yourself. . . . once you've mastered it, you're free. We've grown reliant on Imperial tech, and we've made ourselves vulnerable. There's a growing list of things we've known and forgotten, things they've pushed us to forget. Things like freedom."[55] Nemik, a true-believer revolutionary who is writing a manifesto for the Rebellion, understands that the Empire's oppressive reach is extended through these small realities of daily life. Having to rely on the Empire for technology that is proprietary and difficult to repair forces citizens to acquiesce to Imperial power for survival.

Within contemporary Western culture, the "right to repair" movement recognizes as oppressive producers' refusal to provide parts and technical guidance for consumers to repair their own devices. As Makov and Fitzpatrick explain, "The right to repair refers to the campaign advocating for the individual rights of consumers to repair their own electronic devices rather than rely on the services offered by producers."[56] In the United States, calls for

---

[51] "Grappler (profession)," Wookieepedia, accessed December 8, 2022, https://starwars.fandom.com/wiki/Grappler_(profession).

[52] "Caleen Salyard," Wookieepedia, accessed December 8, 2022, https://starwars.fandom.com/wiki/Caleen_Salyard.

[53] *Andor*, season 1, episode 1, "Kassa," directed by Toby Haynes, written by Tony Gilroy, aired September 21, 2022, Disney+, https://www.disneyplus.com/video/81361203-cc00-49dd-b60f-8b9203d165d3.

[54] "Imperial N-S9 Starpath Unit," Wookieepedia, accessed December 16, 2022, https://starwars.fandom.com/wiki/Imperial_N-S9_Starpath_Unit?so=search.

[55] *Andor*, season 1, episode 5, "The Axe Forgets," directed by Susanna White, written by Dan Gilroy, October 5, 2022, Disney+, https://www.disneyplus.com/video/beeb4fda-1bd1-4b2d-ace5-088f51077705.

[56] Tamar Makov and Colin Fitzpatrick, "Is Repairability Enough? Big Data Insights into Smartphone Obsolescence and Consumer Interest in Repair," *Journal of Cleaner Production* 313, 127561 (2021), para. 7.

the right to repair laws began with "traditionally self-reliant farmers"[57] unable to repair their own John Deere tractors. There have been calls for a "fixer movement" to go alongside the contemporary maker movement. Thompson argues that a fixer movement "would be a huge cultural shift. In the 20th century, US firms aggressively promoted planned obsolescence, designing things to break. Buying new was our patriotic duty."[58] This right to repair movement echoes *Andor*'s emphasis on the role of economics and production in the Empire's grip on power. For the Empire, sanctioned production and consumption is required to prove loyalty to the state; fixing and tinkering, repairing and re-using, understood by revolutionaries like Nemik and the citizens of Ferrix as self-reliance, are denounced as disloyalty and rebellion. And as *Andor* shows, indeed, they are.

As noted in *The Economist*, "the 'Star Wars' galaxy is both technologically advanced and economically stagnant,"[59] and these qualities of the galaxy drive the need for both mechanical parts and those who work with them. While there appears to be "relatively free intergalactic trade,"[60] it is mediated by guilds, monopolies, and trade federations, all within a galaxy in which enslaved labor is sometimes used for production. Much of the trade we see at the local level is in used products, often machine parts (consider Watto's junk shop), and exchanged in barter, such as when Rey trades scavenged Imperial parts for food rations. Within this context, transport vehicles and droids often need ongoing repair and restoration by their owners (for example, think of Han Solo and Chewbacca's long battle with the hyperdrive on the *Millennium Falcon* or Mando's emergency repairs to the *Razor Crest* when he crashes on Maldo Kreis).[61] Even more privileged inhabitants of the galaxy require parts for ships, given the demands of intergalactic travel and frequent skirmishes (e.g. the damaged hyperdrive of the ship carrying Obi-Wan, Qui-Gon Jinn, and Padmé Amidala in *Star Wars Episode I: The Phantom Menace* [1999]).

---

[57] Joe Keegan, "Why Are so Many Opposing the Right-to-Repair Laws," HackerNoon, last modified September 11, 2021, accessed December 8, 2022, https://hackernoon.com/why-are-so-many-opposing-the-right-to-repair-laws-2ic432nq.

[58] Clive Thompson, "We Need a Fixer (Not Just a Maker) Movement," *Wired*, last modified June 18, 2013, accessed December 8, 2022, https://www.wired.com/2013/06/qq-thompson/.

[59] "Wookienomics: Free Exchange," *The Economist* 417, no. 8969 (December 19, 2015), 102.

[60] Stephen L. Carter, "'Last Jedi' and Star Wars' Economic Problems," Bloomberg Opinion, Bloomberg, last modified December 11, 2017, https://www.bloomberg.com/opinion/articles/2017-12-08/-last-jedi-and-star-wars-economic-problems.

[61] This is likely why the candy-colored, high gloss speeder bikes of the Mods (referred to by some fans as "space Vespas") in *The Book of Boba Fett* (2021-) feel so viscerally wrong; they just don't appear "used" enough.

Thus in the Disney *Star Wars* universe, characters like Rey and Kuiil continue the *Star Wars* emphasis on amateur mechanics who must fix to survive.

But we are also introduced to professional mechanics and fixers: in particular, Rose Tico in the Sequel Trilogy,[62] Peli Motto in *The Mandalorian*, and Trace Martez in *The Clone Wars* series. While in contemporary Western cultures, there is a "long-standing gendered (male) portrayal of efforts to repair and restore mechanical things,"[63] it is notable that almost all of the mechanics we see in detail in the newer *Star Wars* media are female. Even more notable is the way their making and fixing is driven by love for and loyalty to those close to them.

Rose Tico is a maintenance technician, flight engineer, and eventually, the Resistance's "engineering department,"[64] first introduced in *Star Wars Episode VIII: The Last Jedi* (2017). Rose's backstory is developed in Jason Fry's novelization of that film and in Elizabeth Wein's middle reader novel, *Star Wars The Last Jedi: Cobalt Squadron.* A true tinkerer, "Rose [is] good at coming up with makeshift solutions to technical problems."[65] Like many makers, Rose is eager for excellence and quality[66] in her work. Thinking about a power baffler she was able to assemble, "Rose had mixed feelings about this creation of hers. . . . It annoyed her that she hadn't been able to come up with a way to make it smaller. . . . But Rose was secretly very proud of how the baffler worked."[67] This baffler, like much of the technology available to the Resistance, was built with what Rose "managed to scrape together."[68] It is Rose who figures out how the First Order is tracking the Resistance through lightspeed—something believed impossible.[69] Later, when the surviving members of the Resistance land on Crait, Rose is put in charge of inventorying and repairing the machinery left in the abandoned base.[70] Ratcliffe describes Rose as "an everywoman, a working class member of the Resistance,"[71] whose parents sent her with her sister off their home planet to escape the tyranny of the First Order.

---

62 Babu Frik is a lesser example in the Sequel Trilogy films and the third season of *The Mandalorian.*

63 DeLyser and Greenstein, "The Devotions of Restoration," 1463.

64 Jason Fry, *Star Wars: The Last Jedi* (New York: Del Rey, 2018), 25, 117, 333.

65 Elizabeth Wein, *Star Wars The Last Jedi: Cobalt Squadron* (Los Angeles: Disney Lucasfilm Press, 2017), 9.

66 Korn, *Why We Make Things and Why it Matters,* 11.

67 Wein, *Star Wars: The Last Jedi Cobalt Squadron,* 14.

68 Ibid., 189.

69 *Star Wars Episode VIII: The Last Jedi,* directed by Rian Johnson, 2017.

70 Fry, *Star Wars: The Last Jedi,* 337.

71 Ratcliffe, *Star Wars: Women of the Galaxy,* 182.

For Rose, making and fixing become extensions of her loyalty to the Resistance and to her compatriots and extend beyond the mechanical realm. As William J. Astore notes, "every rebel—should be a 'true believer' and thus an ambassador for the cause."[72] Rose's commitment to the Resistance is intimately entwined with her love and grief for her sister, as well as for the loss of her parents and home planet through the exploitation of the First Order.[73] Ratcliffe's explicit identification of Rose as "working class" ties both to the tendency of people's rebellions to connect to citizens "in inaccessible or impoverished areas where they can draw sustenance from the misery or alienation of the people"[74] and perceptions of members of the working class as being more empathetic and willing to help others than more affluent citizens.[75] At the same time, while the innate mechanical ability of characters in the *Star Wars* universe is often linked to Force-sensitivity,[76] this does not seem to be the case for Rose or the other professional mechanics; "working class" in Ratcliffe's assessment may also be coded language for someone who relies less on magic and more on muscle in the *Star Wars* milieu.

Rose is not a "chosen one," but her role in the Resistance is one of fighting tyranny with her gifts for fixing and making, and sometimes this "fixing" extends beyond the physical realm for Rose, especially in her relationship with Finn. When Finn makes the wrong-headed decision to throw himself at the First Order in a suicidal attempt to stop their assault on Crait, Rose "fixes"

---

[72] William J. Astore, "Why Rebels Triumph: How 'Insignificant' Rebellions Can Change History," in *Star Wars and History*, ed. Nancy R. Reagin and Janice Liedl (Hoboken, NJ: John Wiley and Sons, 2012), 15.

[73] Wein, *Star Wars: The Last Jedi Cobalt Squadron*, 10.

[74] Astore, "Why Rebels Triumph," 15.

[75] Antony S.R. Manstead, "The Psychology of Social Class: How Socioeconomic Status Impacts Thought, Feelings, and Behaviour," *British Journal of Social Psychology* 57, no. 2 (2018), 277, 278.

[76] Daniel José Older, *Star Wars: The High Republic Race to Crashpoint Tower* (Los Angeles: Disney Lucasfilm Press, 2021), 10. The idea of using the Force on mechanical objects is a recent addition to the canon, introduced through Padawan Ram Jomaram in Disney's multimedia project, *Star Wars: The High Republic.* Some believe this is a post-factum explanation for how Anakin was able to build C-3PO and his racers so young and with such skill; See Thomas Bacon, "Star Wars' New Force Power Reveals How Anakin Built Threepio," *ScreenRant*, June 29, 2021, https://screenrant.com/star-wars-anakin-c3po-build-force-power/. As with Force healing, this will likely become more developed going forward in the Disney *Star Wars* universe, but it raises relevant questions about the nature of making in the newer *Star Wars* media. For Ram, his Force sensitivity manifests as an ability to feel individual parts and understand their role in the whole; he can feel when and where something is off. See Older, *Race to Crashpoint Tower*, 11.

his decision by physically knocking him out of the way with her hover craft, resulting in her own injury. When Finn runs to her aid, she sums up both her own philosophy and that of the Resistance when she instructs, "That's how we're gonna win. Not fighting what we hate; saving what we love."[77] The kiss she plants on him after uttering these words emphasizes that love and hope for a better future drive Rose Tico's fixing, whether it is literal or metaphorical.

Peli Motto, a hangar mechanic on Tatooine who becomes an ally to both the Mandalorian and the Child, runs her shop in the Mos Eisley spaceport using pit droids as assistants.[78] When the Mandalorian's ship is badly damaged in a fight, he lands on Tatooine and employs Peli's services. In the junior novelization, she tells Mando, "This is my operation. You're not gonna find a better mechanic on the planet."[79] Because of Mando's distrust of droids, he will not allow them to work on his *Razor Crest*, leaving Peli to do the work herself. Even without droid help, Peli completes the extensive repairs in a day and a half, while also babysitting the Child.[80] When Mando returns to Tatooine to support Boba Fett, Peli finds him an N-1 starfighter they can rebuild to replace his *Razor Crest*. In the face of Mando's opposition, she argues, "You know how hard it is to find all original parts from way back in the Galactic Republic?"[81] What follows is another classic "hard-work montage" or "creation sequence"[82] as Peli, Mando, and the droids rebuild the N-1, transforming it into a ship the Mandalorian calls "wizard."[83]

It is not just this hard work montage that connects Peli's making to Kuiil's; both Peli and Kuiil reinforce the themes of caregiving and nurturing central to *The Mandalorian*, initially through their care and concern for droids, an extension of their making and fixing work that then extends to organic beings, especially the Child. Kuiil, during his making montage, describes how he reprogrammed IG-11: "I spent day after day reinforcing its development with patience and affirmation."[84] This loving, parental nurturance then extends to the Child, as he feeds and protects Grogu. While Peli often complains about

---

77 *Star Wars Episode VIII: The Last Jedi*, directed by Rian Johnson, 2017.

78 *The Mandalorian*, season 1, episode 5, "The Gunslinger," directed by Dave Filoni, written by Dave Filoni and Jon Favreau, aired December 6, 2019, Disney+, https://www.disneyplus.com/video/dced26f5-70cc-47c1-960d-c41b99e98638.

79 Schreiber, *Star Wars: The Mandalorian Junior Novel*, 97.

80 Ibid.

81 *The Book of Boba Fett*, season 1, episode 5, "Return of the Mandalorian," directed by Bryce Dallas Howard, written by Jon Favreau, aired January 26, 2022, Disney+, https://www.disneyplus.com/video/0c9fad98-263c-401b-802d-bd697caccd89.

82 "Hard-Work Montage," TV Tropes, accessed March 22, 2022, https://tvtropes.org/pmwiki/pmwiki.php/Main/HardWorkMontage.

83 *The Book of Boba Fett*, "Return of the Mandalorian."

84 *The Mandalorian*, "The Reckoning."

her droids, she is also fiercely protective of them, even consulting them on repair jobs.[85] Her relationship with them is both collegial and familial, as evidenced by her willingness to accept personal risk to protect her BD unit from attack.[86] And like Kuiil, Peli's nurturance of her droids extends to the Child. Peli is an eager, loving babysitter, happy to spend time with the Child and always offering him food. Indeed, her genuine affection and motherly concern for the Child is juxtaposed with Luke Skywalker's more callous, dispassionate treatment of Grogu when Skywalker sends the Child back to Peli's shop in his X-wing, accompanied only by his droid. Typically for Peli, she greets Grogu with great affection and immediate snacks, which her droids help provide.[87]

Trace Martez is a pilot who owns and runs a repair shop, presumably inherited after her parents' death, on the lower levels of Coruscant in Season Seven of *Star Wars: The Clone Wars* (2008-2014, 2020), into which Ahsoka Tano crashes her speeder bike after leaving the Jedi temple.[88] Trace informs Ahsoka that hers is "one of the best repair shops on [level] 1313"[89] and offers to fix the damaged bike. Like many characters across the *Star Wars* saga, Ahsoka can fix her own transportation, and she asks Trace for tools instead. Despite Ahsoka's lack of credits and Trace's need for them, the mechanic allows Ahsoka to bring her wrecked speeder into the shop and work on it there. When Ahsoka observes a Nebula-class freighter in the bay, Trace explains she "assembled [it] . . . piece by piece."[90] Here again, we see an example of both the secondhand economy

---

[85] Schreiber, *Star Wars: The Mandalorian Junior Novel*, 97.

[86] *The Book of Boba Fett*, "Return of the Mandalorian." Admittedly, the status of droids in the *Star Wars* universe is complicated. While frequently in close relationships with organic characters, they are also subjected to forced labor and often denied bodily agency; see Colleen Etman, "The Droids You're Looking For: On Servitude and Sentience in *Star Wars*," *Popular Culture Studies Journal* 9, no. 1, (2021), 80.

[87] *The Book of Boba Fett*, season 1, episode 7, "In the Name of Honor," directed by Robert Rodriguez, written by Jon Favreau, aired February 9, 2022, Disney+, https://www.disneyplus.com/video/d939789b-dd61-4d5a-926b-28e815fb2617.

[88] *Star Wars: The Clone Wars*, season 7, episode 5, "Gone with a Trace," directed by Kyle Dunlevy and Saul Ruiz, written by Dave Filoni and Charles Murray, aired March 20, 2020, Disney+, https://www.disneyplus.com/video/a1dfba86-2134-41e9-8794-e804089.6bef6. In a later episode, Trace's sister refers to it as "the family business." *Star Wars: The Clone Wars*, season 7, episode 7, "Dangerous Debt" directed by Saul Ruiz and Bosco Ng, written by Dave Filoni and Charles Murray, aired April 3, 2020, Disney+, https://www.disneyplus.com/video/468b341b-4d54-4adf-823f-8934ff05800b.

[89] *Star Wars: The Clone Wars*, "Gone with a Trace."

[90] *Star Wars: The Clone Wars*, season 7, episode 6, "Deal or No Deal," directed by Steward Lee and Nathaniel Villanueva, written by Dave Filoni and Charles Murray, aired March 27, 2020, Disney+, https://www.disneyplus.com/video/7ed29bb0-bfff-462c-ae96-f89a4f3f89e2.

common within the *Star Wars* galaxy and making for survival therein; Trace expects cobbling together a ship will help and support her and her sister, Rafa, with whom she shares a strong bond. Trace's use of her mechanical skills for economic survival is juxtaposed with Rafa, who uses more questionable, even criminal means to support them, leveraging Trace's mechanical skills without her full consent or understanding. Rafa repeatedly reminds Trace, "We can't count on anyone, so we count on ourselves . . . That's how we survive."[91] This echoes comments by the Mandalorian Armorer (see below) and explicitly connects Trace's mechanic work not just with survival but with a commitment to and love for family and heritage, including the memory of their deceased parents.

As professionals, Rose, Peli, and Trace make their living by making and fixing; they exist within typical patterns of professional making in contemporary society, where earning a living through craft, particularly in highly skilled repair or restoration, is often subsumed within specialized organizations or through self-employment.[92] That their work is compensated does not diminish the pride, care, and love that goes into—and motivates—the tasks. In fact, professional mechanics may be more exacting and meticulous than even the most ardent hobby makers.[93] Regardless, while economic necessity undergirds the work of these women, love and care remain the driving factors in their fixing and making. Further, the conspicuous subversion of gender expectations in casting women as professional mechanics in the Disney era of *Star Wars* shines an even brighter light on their fixing and making—and on the love that drives them.

For the love of tradition

There is a long history of ritual making within the *Star Wars* universe. An essential coming-of-age ritual for Jedi younglings is the fabrication of their lightsabers. In Steve Perry's 1996 now-non-canonical novel, *Shadows of the Empire,* we see Luke Skywalker work on his lightsaber using a text he found in Ben Kenobi's home.[94] In Marc Sumerak's book, *Star Wars: The Secrets of the Sith,* we learn both how the Jedi infuse the kyber crystals for their lightsabers and how the Sith pervert that ritual to create their own weapons.[95] In *Star Wars: The Clone Wars,* Ahsoka Tano and Yoda take a group of Jedi younglings

---

91 Ibid.

92 DeLyser and Greenstein, "The Devotions of Restoration," 1464.

93 Ibid.

94 Steve Perry, *Shadows of the Empire* (New York: Del Rey, 1997), 34. For more on what constitutes canon works in the Disney era of *Star Wars,* see John Jackson Miller's chapter in this volume.

95 Marc Sumerak, *Star Wars: The Secrets of the Sith* (Los Angeles: Disney Lucasfilm Press, 2022), 18.

to Illum for the Gathering, their ritual journey to collect kyber crystals for the lightsabers they will craft.[96]

In *The Book of Boba Fett* (2021-), we see a memory of Boba Fett's similar quest to find a branch and craft it into a gaderffii or gaffi stick during his time with the Tusken Raiders on Tatooine. Like many of the making scenes in the Disney *Star Wars* universe, this is depicted in a wordless montage, here lasting less than two minutes. We see the craftsperson use a vice and ax to rough shape the gaffi stick, showing Boba Fett how to use a scraper to remove the bark, a mallet and chisels to shape the club head of the stick, and metal-working tools to fashion and forge the spear end. Once crafted, the ritual is completed through a communal dance around the fire with other members of the tribe.[97] This sequence is more difficult than the others to reduce to a trope,[98] because it functions to highlight the heritage and culture of the Tuskens, portrayed as savages in the Original and Prequel Trilogies but treated with more nuance and compassion here. Both the Jedi and the Tusken Raiders craft tools as rituals of initiation; these tools are both weapons and key symbols of their order or tribe—something common to esoteric orders. The sword and wand are crafted by the initiate and consecrated as a ritual of acceptance into the order; these tools then become symbols of membership and the traditions of the order, used in ritual and practice.[99]

Rituals of making are also central to the upholding of other cultural traditions in recent *Star Wars* stories, particularly in the case of the Mandalorian Armorer, whose metalsmithing is tied to the traditions of her order.[100] As with mechanics, metalsmithing is often gendered male.[101] Steven M. Gelber, in his unpacking of DIY home repair and the construction of masculinity, posits "'a half-pound rule.' That is, women did not use any tool weighing more than a half-pound while men, by and large, avoided most tools

---

[96] *Star Wars: The Clone Wars,* season 5, episode 6, "The Gathering," directed by Kyle Dunlevy, written by Christian Taylor, aired November 3, 2012, Disney+, https://www.disneyplus.com/video/dce32899-0e62-479d-b33a-37ca69ad9565.

[97] *The Book of Boba Fett,* season 1, episode 2, "The Tribes of Tatooine," directed by Steph Green, written by Jon Favreau, aired January 5, 2022, Disney+, https://www.disneyplus.com/video/cb9c66d7-355d-4bf4-9c54-bbafb2bb1be1.

[98] TV Tropes, "Hard-Work Montage."

[99] Éliphaz Lévi, *The Magical Ritual of the Santum Regnum,* ed. W. Wynn Westcott (London: George Redway, 1896), 12-13.

[100] Albrekh, a Sith alchemist and metalsmith, serves a similar role but is featured only briefly in *Star Wars Episode IX: The Rise of Skywalker.*

[101] As a contemporary example, only two women have won US cable television's *Forged in Fire* blacksmithing competition at the time of this writing, out of 198 competitions. *Forged in Fire,* History.com, accessed December 22, 2021, https://www.history.com/shows/forged-in-fire.

weighing less."[102] While Gelber is speaking specifically about home tool use in Victorian America, this gendered distinction has largely held over time, as making is still frequently gendered, with men tending towards technology and work with heavy tools and women towards fiber and other "softer" arts.[103]

Therefore, it is noteworthy that the most visible metalsmith in the Disney *Star Wars* universe is the Armorer, a female Mandalorian who forges the Tribe's armor. We are introduced to the Armorer in the first episode of *The Mandalorian* when Mando visits her hidden underground workshop.[104] The Armorer tells the Mandalorian that the bar of beskar steel he has brought to her "was gathered in the Great Purge . . . It is good that it is back with the tribe."[105] Later, when he returns with a large cache of beskar in payment for retrieving the Child, the Armorer forges a complete set of armor for him.[106] The suit is ultimately appreciated by a surprising source: the Client (the Imperial agent looking for the Child), who tells Mando, "What exquisite craftsmanship . . . It is amazing how beautiful beskar can be when forged by its ancestral artisans."[107] The belief in the sacredness of the material and the understanding that the history and tradition of the order supports the maker in her skill and production also echoes the ritual making of esoteric orders[108] and brings an awareness that making in service to belief and tradition adds layers of value and meaning that cannot be found in other more secular making.

We learn later that Mando and his tribe on Nevarro are considered "Children of the Watch"—a fringe group, a cult of zealots—by other Mandalorians.[109] Hinted at in *The Mandalorian* and confirmed in *The Book of*

---

102 Steven M. Gelber, "Do-It-Yourself: Constructing, Repairing and Maintaining Domestic Masculinity," *American Quarterly* 49, no. 1 (1997): 70.

103 Chandan Bose, "Craft as Everyday Site of Assertion: How Do Artisans Talk About Gender and Skill?" *Women's Studies Journal* 31, no. 1 (2017), 83; Bratich and Brush, "Fabricating Activism," 243; Britton, "Power, Access, Status;" Catharine Rossi, "The Maker 2.0: A Craft-Based Approach to Understanding a New Creative Identity," in *Fashioning Professionals: Identity and Representation at Work in the Creative Industries*, ed. Leah Armstrong and Felice McDowell (London: Bloomsbury Publishing Plc, 2018), 191-193.

104 *The Mandalorian*, season 1, episode 1, "The Mandalorian," directed by Dave Filoni, written by Jon Favreau, aired November 12, 2019, Disney+, https://www.disneyplus.com/video/30ea8a44-797d-4da8-b776-2e3636a2bf5a.

105 Schreiber, *Star Wars: The Mandalorian Junior Novel*, 6.

106 Ibid., 49.

107 *The Mandalorian*, "The Reckoning."

108 Lévi, *The Magical Ritual of the Santum Regnum*, 12-13.

109 *The Mandalorian*, season 2, episode 3, "The Heiress," directed by Bryce Dallas Howard, written by Jon Favreau, aired November 13, 2020, Disney+, https://www.disneyplus.com/video/6af69e26-d6f3-4914-b417-0ceaedec6668.

Boba Fett when the Armorer tells Mando, "Had our sect not been cloistered on the moon of Concordia, we would have not survived the Great Purge,"[110] the Children of the Watch are descendants of the Mandalorian Death Watch,[111] lending further weight to the Armorer's role as the keeper of the tribe's faith. This may also more fully explain why the tribe and their rituals, including the forging of their armor, remain hidden. The Armorer explains, "Our secrecy is our survival. Our survival is our strength."[112] This seemed at the time to serve as a reminder to the covert of why they dwell underground in Nevarro, but in light of revelations about their connection to the Children of the Watch, it also speaks to the tenuousness of their existence more broadly. Again, this echoes esoteric traditions typical of hidden orders.[113] While the beskar armor of the Mandalorians is a visual signifier of belonging to the order, the traditions and beliefs behind it and its making are sacred and concealed. Thus every act of making and forging in which the Armorer engages is an act of loving fidelity to this fundamentalist Mandalorian tradition and hope for a better future.

Labors of love

Given the ambiguity around the economics of the *Star Wars* universe,[114] making takes on a range of functions related to survival, resistance, and heritage. While the makers in *Star Wars* create and tinker to subsist within a flawed economic structure, making in contemporary Western culture has been positioned as a legitimized off-shoot of the knowledge economy,[115] an area for business and military innovation,[116] and is at risk of being subsumed as a neoliberal strategy for privatization and individualization.[117] As Catharine Rossi argues about Robinson Crusoe, his "making, like that of all makers, is implicated in a globally distributed economic structure."[118] This is strikingly different from how making is depicted in the Disney *Star Wars* universe, where the impact of characters' making and tinkering impacts immediate individual survival but is not portrayed as galaxy-altering from an economic perspective.

---

[110] *The Book of Boba Fett*, "Return of the Mandalorian."

[111] Pablo Hidalgo, Cole Horton, and Dan Zehr, *The Star Wars Book* (New York: DK Publishing, 2020), 202.

[112] Schreiber, *Star Wars: The Mandalorian Junior Novel*, 49.

[113] Lévi, *The Magical Ritual of the Santum Regnum*, 37.

[114] Carter, "'Last Jedi' and Star Wars' Economic Problems."

[115] Rossi, "The Maker 2.0," 184.

[116] Dougherty, "The Maker Movement," 12.

[117] Chidgey, "Developing Communities of Resistance," 108.

[118] Rossi, "The Crusoe Condition," 24.

What *is* galaxy-altering about making in Disney's *Star Wars* universe is its use in sustaining love, loyalty, and hope across a range of cultural and political traditions. Often, these acts of love and commitment to heritage are acts of resistance, whether personal, political, or religious. Rey's longing for family and her attempts to create a home for herself are expressed through making; Kuiil's love of his work reflects his commitment to freedom. The same love for personal freedom drives salvage operations on Ferrix and helps Cassian Andor connect and commit to the Rebellion. The mechanic skills Rose Tico uses in support of the Resistance, and Peli Motto and Trace Martez use to support themselves and their families, are situated in love, nurturance, and loyalty. The ritual making depicted in recent shows, especially that of the Tuskens and the Mandalorian Armorer, upholds traditions and hope for cultural survival through the strength of ancestral artisanship. DeLyser and Greenstein posit that "Making is romantic . . . making practices . . . reveal labors of love . . . [they] exact devotion: love, care, loyalty, and attention, all sustained over time."[119] The making depicted in the *Star Wars* universe, particularly in the Disney era, is a celebration of such devotion.

Bibliography

Abbott, Carl. "Homesteading on the Extraterrestrial Frontier." *Science Fiction Studies* 32, no. 2 (2005): 240–264.

Abrams, J.J., dir. *Star Wars Episode VII: The Force Awakens.* 2015; Burbank, CA: Disney/Lucasfilm Ltd., 2016. DVD.

Astore, William J. "Why Rebels Triumph: How 'Insignificant' Rebellions Can Change History." In *Star Wars and History*, edited by Nancy R. Reagin and Janice Liedl, 9-39. Hoboken, NJ: John Wiley and Sons, 2012.

Axelrod, Jeremiah B.C. "Mutiny on the Sofa: Historical Patterns of Patriarchy and Family Structure in American Science Fiction, 1945–2018." *Pacific Coast Philology* 53, no. 2 (2018): 308-334.

Bacon, Thomas. "Star Wars' New Force Power Reveals How Anakin Built Threepio." *ScreenRant.* June 29, 2021. https://screenrant.com/star-wars-anakin-c3po-build-force-power/.

Bose, Chandan. "Craft as Everyday Site of Assertion: How Do Artisans Talk About Gender and Skill?" *Women's Studies Journal* 31, no. 1 (2017): 81–87.

Bratich, Jack Z, and Heidi M Brush. "Fabricating Activism: Craft-Work, Popular Culture, Gender." *Utopian Studies* 22, no. 2 (2011): 233–260.

Britton, Lauren. "Power, Access, Status: The Discourse of Race, Gender, and Class in the Maker Movement." TASCHA, Technology & Social Change Group, University of Washington Information School. Last modified March 18, 2015. Archived at https://web.archive.org/web/20220321092425/ https://tascha.uw.

[119] DeLyser and Greenstein, "The Devotions of Restoration," 1475.

edu/2015/03/power-access-status-the-discourse-of-race-gender-and-class-in-the-maker-movement/.

"Caleen Salyard." Wookieepedia. Accessed December 8, 2022. https://starwars.fandom.com/wiki/Caleen_Salyard.

Carson, Rae. *Star Wars: The Rise of Skywalker.* New York: Del Rey, 2020.

Carter, Stephen L. "'Last Jedi' and Star Wars' Economic Problems." Bloomberg Opinion, Bloomberg. Last modified December 11, 2017. https://www.bloomberg.com/opinion/articles/2017-12-08/-last-jedi-and-star-wars-economic-problems.

Chidgey, Red. "Developing Communities of Resistance?: Maker Pedagogies, Do-It-Yourself Feminism, and DIY Citizenship." In *DIY Citizenship: Critical Making and Social Media*, edited by Matt Ratto and Megan Boler, 101–113. Cambridge, MA: The MIT Press, 2004.

Defoe, Daniel. *The Life and Adventures of Robinson Crusoe.* Minneapolis, MN: First Avenue Editions, 2016.

DeLyser, Dydia, and Paul Greenstein. "The Devotions of Restoration: Materiality, Enthusiasm, and Making Three 'Indian Motocycles' Like New." *Annals of the American Association of Geographers* 107, no. 6 (2017): 1461–1478.

Dougherty, Dale. "The Maker Movement." *Innovations: Technology, Governance, Globalization* 7, no. 3 (2012): 11-14.

Etman, Colleen. "The Droids You're Looking For: On Servitude and Sentience in *Star Wars." Popular Culture Studies Journal* 9, no. 1 (2021): 78-96.

Favreau, Jon, writer. *The Book of Boba Fett.* Season 1, episode 2, "The Tribes of Tatooine." Directed by Steph Green. Aired January 5, 2022. Disney+. https://www.disneyplus.com/video/cb9c66d7-355d-4bf4-9c54-bbafb2bb1be1.

_______, writer. *The Book of Boba Fett.* Season 1, episode 5, "Return of the Mandalorian." Directed by Bryce Dallas Howard. Aired January 26, 2022. Disney+. https://www.disneyplus.com/video/0c9fad98-263c-401b-802d-bd697caccd89.

_______, writer. *The Book of Boba Fett.* Season 1, episode 7, "In the Name of Honor." Directed by Robert Rodriguez. Aired February 9, 2022. Disney+. https://www.disneyplus.com/video/d939789b-dd61-4d5a-926b-28e815fb2617.

_______, writer. *The Mandalorian.* Season 1, episode 1, "The Mandalorian." Directed by Dave Filoni. Aired November 12, 2019. Disney+. https://www.disneyplus.com/video/30ea8a44-797d-4da8-b776-2e3636a2bf5a.

_______, writer. *The Mandalorian.* Season 1, episode 2, "The Child." Directed by Rick Famiyuwa. Aired November 15, 2019. Disney+. https://www.disneyplus.com/series/the-mandalorian/3jLIGMDYINqD.

_______, writer. *The Mandalorian.* Season 1, episode 7, "The Reckoning." Directed by Deborah Chow. Aired December 18, 2019. Disney+. https://www.disneyplus.com/video/defe8509-3e33-45e6-90e1-0a8f0f7917e1.

_______, writer. *The Mandalorian.* Season 2, episode 3, "The Heiress." Directed by Bryce Dallas Howard. Aired November 13, 2020. Disney+. https://www.disneyplus.com/video/6af69e26-d6f3-4914-b417-0ceaedec6668.

Filoni, Dave and Jon Favreau, writers. *The Mandalorian.* Season 1, episode 5, "The Gunslinger." Directed by Dave Filoni. Aired December 6, 2019. Disney+. https://www.disneyplus.com/video/dced26f5-70cc-47c1-960d-c41b99e98638.

_______ and Charles Murray, writers. *Star Wars: The Clone Wars.* Season 7, episode 5, "Gone with a Trace." Directed by Kyle Dunlevy and Saul Ruiz. Aired March 20, 2020. Disney+. https://www.disneyplus.com/video/a1dfba86-2134-41e9-8794-e8040896bef6.

_______ and Charles Murray, writers. *Star Wars: The Clone Wars.* Season 7, episode 6, "Deal or No Deal." Directed by Steward Lee and Nathaniel Villanueva. Aired March 27, 2020. Disney+. https://www.disneyplus.com/video/7ed29bb0-bfff-462c-ae96-f89a4f3f89e2.

_______ and Charles Murray, writers. *Star Wars: The Clone Wars.* Season 7, episode 7, "Dangerous Debt." Directed by Saul Ruiz and Bosco Ng. Aired April 3, 2020, Disney+. https://www.disneyplus.com/video/468b341b-4d54-4adf-823f-8934ff05800b.

Forged in Fire. History.com. Accessed December 22, 2021. https://www.history.com/shows/forged-in-fire.

Foster, Alan Dean. *Star Wars: The Force Awakens.* New York: Del Rey, 2016.

Fry, Jason. *Star Wars: The Last Jedi.* New York: Del Rey, 2018.

Gelber, Steven M. "Do-It-Yourself: Constructing, Repairing and Maintaining Domestic Masculinity." *American Quarterly* 49, no. 1 (1997): 66–112.

Gilroy, Dan, writer. *Andor.* Season 1, episode 5, "The Axe Forgets." Directed by Susanna White. Aired October 5, 2022. Disney+. https://www.disneyplus.com/video/beeb4fda-1bd1-4b2d-ace5-088f51077705.

Gilroy, Tony, writer. *Andor.* Season 1, episode 1, "Kassa." Directed by Toby Haynes. Aired September 21, 2022. Disney+. https://www.disneyplus.com/video/81361203-cc00-49dd-b60f-8b9203d165d3.

_______, writer. *Andor.* Season 1, episode 12, "Rix Road." Directed by Benjamin Caron. Aired November 23, 2022. Disney+. https://www.disneyplus.com/video/78c53cd7-c7c1-40c4-b365-a56fae06799e.

"Grappler (profession)." Wookieepedia. Accessed December 8, 2022. https://starwars.fandom.com/wiki/Grappler_(profession).

Guerra, Paula. "Raw Power: Punk, DIY and Underground Cultures as Spaces of Resistance in Contemporary Portugal." *Cultural Sociology* 12, no. 2 (2018): 241-259.

"Hard-Work Montage." TV Tropes. Accessed March 22, 2022. https://tvtropes.org/pmwiki/pmwiki.php/Main/HardWorkMontage.

Harrod, Tanya. "Classic Take on the Industry of One." *Crafts* 246 (January/February 2014): 92.

Hidalgo, Pablo, Cole Horton, and Dan Zehr. *The Star Wars Book.* New York: DK Publishing, 2020.

"Imperial N-S9 Starpath Unit." Wookieepedia. Accessed December 16, 2022. https://starwars.fandom.com/wiki/Imperial_N-S9_Starpath_Unit.

Johnson, Rian, dir. *Star Wars: The Last Jedi.* 2017; Burbank, CA: Lucasfilm Ltd., 2018. DVD.

Keegan, Joe. "Why Are So Many Opposing the Right-to-Repair Laws." HackerNoon. Last modified September 11, 2021. https://hackernoon.com/why-are-so-many-opposing-the-right-to-repair-laws-2ic432nq.

Korn, Peter. *Why We Make Things and Why it Matters: The Education of a Craftsman.* Boston: David R. Godine Publisher, 2013.

Lévi, Éliphaz. *The Magical Ritual of the Santum Regnum*, edited by W. Wynn Westcott. London: George Redway, 1896.

Lucas, George, dir. *Star Wars: A New Hope.* 1977; Burbank, CA: Lucasfilm Ltd., 2004. DVD.

Makov, Tamar and Colin Fitzpatrick. "Is Repairability Enough? Big Data Insights into Smartphone Obsolescence and Consumer Interest in Repair." *Journal of Cleaner Production, 313,* 127561 (2021). https://doi.org/10.1016/j.jclepro.2021.127561.

Manstead, Antony S.R. "The Psychology of Social Class: How Socioeconomic Status Impacts Thought, Feelings, and Behaviour." *British Journal of Social Psychology* 57, no. 2 (2018): 267–291.

Morris, Kathleen. "You Are Not a Lemming: The Imagined Resistance of Craft Citizenship." *The Journal of Modern Craft* 9, no. 1 (2016). 5-14.

Older, Daniel José, *The High Republic: Race to Crashpoint Tower.* Los Angeles: Disney Lucasfilm Press, 2021.

Orton-Johnson, Kate. "DIY Citizenship, Critical Making, and Community." In *DIY Citizenship: Critical Making and Social Media,* edited by Matt Ratto and Megan Boler, 141-155. Cambridge, MA: The MIT Press, 2004.

Perry, Steve. *Star Wars: Shadows of the Empire.* New York: Del Rey, 1997.

Ratcliffe, Amy. *Star Wars: Women of the Galaxy.* San Francisco: Chronicle Books, 2018.

Rossi, Catharine. "The Crusoe Condition: Making Within Limits and the Critical Possibilities of Fiction." *The Journal of Modern Craft* 10, no. 1 (2017): 19–35.

_______. "The Maker 2.0: A Craft-Based Approach to Understanding a New Creative Identity." In *Fashioning Professionals: Identity and Representation at Work in the Creative Industries,* edited by Leah Armstrong and Felice McDowell, 181-201. London: Bloomsbury Publishing Plc, 2018.

Roth, Lane. "Vraisemblance and the Western Setting in Contemporary Science Fiction Film." *Literature/Film Quarterly* 13, no. 3 (1985), 180-186.

Rushing, Janice Hocker. "Evolution of 'the New Frontier' in Alien and Aliens: Patriarchal Co-Optation of the Feminine Archetype." *The Quarterly Journal of Speech* 75, no. 1 (1989): 1–24.

Schreiber, Joe. *Star Wars: The Mandalorian Junior Novel.* Los Angeles: Disney Lucasfilm Press, 2021.

"Shock trooper." Wookieepedia. Accessed November 30, 2022. https://starwars.fandom.com/wiki/Shock_trooper.

Sumerak, Marc. *Star Wars: The Secrets of the Jedi.* Los Angeles: Disney Lucasfilm Press, 2019.

_______. *Star Wars: The Secrets of the Sith.* Los Angeles: Disney Lucasfilm Press, 2021.

Taylor, Christian, writer. *Star Wars: The Clone Wars.* Season 5, episode 6, "The Gathering." Directed by Kyle Dunlevy. Aired November 3, 2012. Disney+. https://www.disneyplus.com/video/dce32899-0e62-479d-b33a-37ca69ad9565.

Thompson, Clive. “We Need a Fixer (Not Just a Maker) Movement.” *Wired*. Last modified June 18, 2013. https://www.wired.com/2013/06/qq-thompson/.

Wein, Elizabeth. *Star Wars: The Last Jedi: Cobalt Squadron*. Los Angeles: Disney Lucasfilm Press, 2017.

Willimon, Beau, writer. *Andor.* Season 1, episode 8, “Narkina 5.” Directed by Toby Haynes. Aired October 26, 2022. Disney+. https://www.disneyplus.com/video/e552dfd3-ec1b-4046-8410-711114a2a4ef.

———, writer. *Andor.* Season 1, episode 9, “Nobody’s Listening!” Directed by Toby Haynes. Aired November 2, 2022. Disney+. https://www.disneyplus.com/video/c41ac934-18c3-4871-8762-4bf3ac75966b.

———, writer. *Andor.* Season 1, episode 10, “One Way Out.” Directed by Toby Haynes. Aired November 9, 2022. Disney+. https://www.disneyplus.com/video/93c891d6-35cc-4f0f-9d1e-e16e89506ebc.

Chapter 3

The Dead Mom's Peril: *Star Wars* and the Dispossession of the Mother Figure

Éloïse Thompson-Tremblay

Abstract: Major texts in popular fiction have a problem keeping parents alive for very long. The death of a parent is often an impetus for the hero's growth in popular culture. Examples abound in the *Star Wars* universe, especially as it pertains to mothers. Through the course of the three trilogies of the Skywalker saga, dead mothers mark the paths of the heroes' journeys and development, forming a matrilinear procession of dead women, passing the torch to one another. Shmi Skywalker, Anakin's mother, is framed as a device for Anakin's character development within the Prequels story. Having to leave her causes trauma in Anakin's young life, and the young Jedi finds comfort in the arms of another woman, Padmé Amidala. Shmi's death marks a shift in Anakin's faith in the Force and the Jedi Order, ultimately pushing Anakin to become Darth Vader. This essay analyzes how Shmi, Padmé, and Leia are framed as tools for the advancement of their children's narratives and character arcs when they become mothers, losing agency and self-determination to the profit of their children, most evident with sons. The essay explores how the Mother figure is treated within the structure of the monomyth, using the work of Joseph Campbell as a framework to discuss their place in *Star Wars,* as well as popular tropes expressed by the mothers of *Star Wars,* for example, Gail Simone's discussion of "Women in the Refrigerators." Recent mothers depicted in newer *Star Wars* shows are also highlighted as a hopeful path for the future of mothers in the franchise.

Keywords: *Star Wars,* agency, motherhood, mythic structure, passivity, personhood, power, relationships, trauma, Shmi Skywalker, Padmé Amidala, Leia Organa, Maarva Andor, Beru Lars

***

"She has lost the will to live."[1] With these words, a medical droid announced to the last remnants of a fallen Republic that Padmé Amidala of Naboo was dying. Throughout the Prequel films that had introduced her to *Star Wars* fans, she survived trade wars, political conspiracies, assassination attempts, and assault, yet Padmé Amidala was wasting away from heartbreak. Meanwhile, in another corner of the galaxy, her husband, Anakin Skywalker, was saved from certain death by his transformation into the famed villain, Darth Vader. As the Queen's screams and whimpers end, the Sith Lord's hissing and mechanical breathing begin; she dies while he is resuscitated into the shadow of his former self.

Then, life: newborn twins thrust into a fractured galaxy as their mother dies. These children, Luke and Leia, are separated for their safety. The boy will become the ward of his aunt and uncle on his father's home planet of Tatooine, while his sister will be raised as a Princess of Alderaan, the daughter of a Queen and a Senator. Only when the twins reunite can they save the galaxy, defeat evil . . . and maybe even talk about their mother.

More than forty years after his introduction, the name Darth Vader invokes his status as a cultural icon: the emblematic villain of George Lucas's *Star Wars* saga. The original saga chronicled Vader's and Luke's constant struggles as father and son, mirroring the fight between light and darkness, rebellion and empire. Across the three original films, audiences were also introduced to Leia, Luke's sister and a lauded rebel leader, who made her mark on the saga with her iconic looks, repartee, and overall fierceness, breaking barriers of female representation in science fiction; Cole Bowman calls her "as dynamic as you can get."[2] In this family portrait of epic proportions, the father, the son, and the daughter are never joined by a mother.[3] Indeed, after remaining nameless for the entirety of

---

[1] This essay would be but half what it is were it not for the guidance of the friends who read and reread my drafts and argued with me about my opinions, which shaped this piece, and gave me countless words of encouragement while I was writing. To them I say a thousand thanks. Thank you to Emily Strand and Amy H. Sturgis who gave me this wonderful opportunity and whose advice took my thought process, and of course this essay, to a whole other level.

Star Wars Episode III: Revenge of the Sith, directed by George Lucas (2005; Beverly Hills, CA: 20th Century Fox/Lucasfilm Ltd.), Disney+, https://www.disneyplus.com/movies/star-wars-revenge-of-the-sith-episode-iii/4WvbqLFumNvi.

[2] Cole Bowman, "Pregnant Padmé and Slave Leia: *Star Wars*' Female Role Models," in *The Ultimate Star Wars and Philosophy: You Must Unlearn What You Have Learned*, ed. Jason T. Eberl and Kevin S. Decker; series editor William Irwin (Chichester, West Sussex, UK: John Wiley & Sons Ltd., 2016), 163.

[3] Indeed, in a thematically important series of episodes in the animated television series *Star Wars: The Clone Wars* (2008-2014, 2020), a mythic trinity of archetypal figures

the Original Trilogy, Padmé Amidala was finally introduced in 1999, with the release of the first Prequel film, *Star Wars Episode I: The Phantom Menace.*

Her portrayal in this trilogy—as she leads, loves, and dies—is paradigmatic of the treatment of other mother figures in the *Star Wars* trilogies. The lives and deaths of mothers in a galaxy far, far away are too often situated solely as relevant to male characters' advancements within the story; Padmé is a prime example of this tendency. Throughout the Skywalker saga, many women—and mothers in particular—are written as though to prove right Dan Rubey's bleak 1978 observation that they "exist primarily to provide motivations for male activity, to act as a spectator, or to serve as mediators between different levels in the male hierarchy."[4] In the nine-film saga, mother figures such as Padmé, Shmi Skywalker, and even Leia (to a lesser degree) are often de-powered and stripped of agency. In death, they serve the storylines of their male children or lovers in situations analogous to those described by Gail Simone as "Women in Refrigerators," whose senseless suffering spurs male self-actualization and heroism.

Moreover, women like Padmé and Shmi find their roots in the female archetypes of mythic stories, as described by Joseph Cambell. An admitted, avid reader of Campbell's work,[5] George Lucas appears to have been inspired by the archetypes of mythic mothers chronicled in Campbell's seminal book, *The Hero with a Thousand Faces.* Shaped by these archetypes, their lives and deaths are overwhelmingly oriented towards the male characters of the narrative, rendering the mothers of *Star Wars* disposable, passive, and dispossessed in the stories they shape behind the scenes. In the process, they often lose their voices, their selves, and their lives.[6]

Shmi Skywalker

The original de-powered mother of the *Star Wars* saga lives on Tatooine. Like her son Anakin, she is a slave on this desert planet. Together, they live as

---

includes Father, Son, and Daughter—no mention of a mother. See the three-episode arc, which begins with *Star Wars: The Clone Wars,* season 3, episode 15, "Overlords," directed by Steward Lee, written by Christian Taylor, aired January 28, 2011, on Cartoon Network, Disney+, https://www.disneyplus.com/video/48c78dd1-73f6-40ef-9e0d-d469ea00ada8.

[4] Dan Rubey, "*Star Wars*: Not So Long Ago, Not So Far Away," *Jump Cut: A Review of Contemporary Media,* no. 18 (August 1978): 10.

[5] Joseph Campbell, *The Hero's Journey: Joseph Campbell on His Life and Work,* ed. Phil Cousineau (Novato: New World Library, 2003), 208.

[6] Diana Dominguez, "Feminism and the Force: Empowerment and Disillusionment in a Galaxy Far, Far Away," in *Culture, Identities and Technology in the* Star Wars *Films,* ed. Carl Silvio and Tony M. Vinci (Jefferson, NC: McFarland, 2007), 128.

peaceful an existence as they can afford, loving each other dearly. Shmi Skywalker—for this is her name, although she is not actually named by another character until *Star Wars Episode II: Attack of the Clones* (2002)—dreams of a life of freedom for her son, the possibility for which is one day escorted into her home by Anakin himself.

When they welcome Qui-Gon Jinn, Padmé, R2-D2, and Jar Jar Binks into their home, the mother appears mostly silent while her exuberant child is eager to show his robot to his new friend. During a meal she prepares for Anakin and their guests, Shmi is a source of information about Tatooine, explaining the slavery and gambling practices common on the planet, outside the purview of the Republic.[7] Later in the story, Shmi again provides crucial information as she reveals to Jedi master Qui-Gon Jinn that Anakin was conceived not out of her union with a man but in a rather more miraculous manner. "There was no father. I carried him, I gave birth, I raised him. I can't explain what happened,"[8] she tells a rather stunned Qui-Gon. This revelation is crucial to Anakin's progression within the story because it frames Shmi's overarching role in the narrative, establishing her within the Virgin Mother archetype. In *The Hero with a Thousand Faces*, Joseph Campbell discusses occurrences in different mythological tales of virgin births brought upon a female, akin to the creator, originating life despite her virginity, becoming the spouse of the "Invisible Unknown."[9] This rationally inexplicable birth marks an aspect of the hero's "miraculous childhood, by which it is shown that a special manifestation of the immanent divine principle has become incarnate in the world."[10]

Although Shmi is unable to explain what has happened to bring Anakin into this world, Qui-Gon's reaction and actions following her confession hint at his belief that this Invisible Unknown of which Anakin was born is in fact the Force itself, operating via the midi-chlorians. Qui-Gon eventually tells Anakin these midi-chlorians are microscopic life forms that serve as conductors of the Force's will.[11] As such, Anakin was essentially conceived out of the

---

[7] *Star Wars Episode I: The Phantom Menace*, directed by George Lucas (1999; Beverly Hills, CA: 20th Century Fox/Lucasfilm Ltd.), Disney+, https://www.disneyplus.com/movies/star-wars-the-phantom-menace-episode-i/2ezYynkgW1AH.

[8] Ibid. While Shmi cannot explain what happened, a 2018 comic gives more insight, strongly implying Palpatine manipulated the Force to impregnate Anakin's mother. This also carries stronger implications of sexual assault against Shmi than the original, more nebulous explanation of his conception in *The Phantom Menace*. See Charles Soule, Giuseppe Camuncoli, *Darth Vader #25* (New York: Marvel Comics, 2018).

[9] Joseph Campbell, *The Hero with a Thousand Faces*, Third Edition (Novato: New World Library, 2008), 255.

[10] Ibid., 276.

[11] *Star Wars Episode I: The Phantom Menace*, directed by George Lucas, 1999.

"union" of Shmi with the Force itself, marking him as unique among the Jedi: a chosen one. In *Star Wars on Trial*, John C. Wright argues the plot of *The Phantom Menace* "required that Qui-Gon have a means to confirm that young Anakin was Destined To Be Big Stuff."[12] The fact that Shmi is understood to have been impregnated by midi-chlorians to create Anakin—giving him the highest count of these Force-conducting microorganisms ever recorded—reinforces his own status in the story as an inherently special being.

The myriad questions viewers may have about what this experience of impregnation by midi-chlorians was like for Shmi—how it affected her or what it gained her over and above the usual method of bringing children into the world—is left unanswered by the narrative. In his book *The* Star Wars *Heresies*, Paul F. McDonald describes Shmi as "the mother of the Force itself,"[13] due to her status as Anakin's mother, invoking Joseph Campbell's characterization of the goddess as the essence of life itself.[14] According to McDonald, Shmi could be considered on an equal standing with the "chosen one." However, Anakin is required by the narrative to be unique and extraordinary, and Shmi is not. His virgin birth underlines his mother's lack of agency by framing her as a spectator rather than a participant in the conception of her child.

Shmi's passivity is an integral part of Anakin's characterization. Her portrayal as a vessel for Anakin's life carries through the rest of her story arc; she serves as a passive conduit for the major turning points in her son's life. As a slave herself, Shmi has very few personal liberties. She cannot leave Tatooine or move to another part of the planet, nor can she work where she chooses. The only aspect of life she controls is who she loves, and she loves her son dearly. Bowman notes the love that women of *Star Wars* have and show is a source of strength for them.[15] Indeed, Shmi's love for her son attunes her to intuition (or perhaps to the Force; the narrative does not say); she often refers to events that were meant to be, such as Anakin helping Qui-Gon and Padmé, or in the matter-of-fact way she describes becoming Anakin's mother.[16] These qualities suggest her certainty that Anakin will eventually leave Tatooine and his condition as a slave.

---

[12] John C. Wright, "May the Midichlorians Be with You," in *Star Wars on Trial*, ed. David Brin and Matthew Woodring Stover (Dallas: BenBella Books, 2015), 111.

[13] Paul F. McDonald, *The* Star Wars *Heresies* (Jefferson, NC: McFarland, 2013), chap. 8, loc. 1081, Kindle.

[14] Campbell, *Hero with a Thousand Faces*, 94.

[15] Bowman, "Pregnant Padmé and Slave Leia," 167.

[16] *Star Wars Episode I: The Phantom Menace*, directed by George Lucas, 1999.

To make this hope and belief a reality, she does have moments of agency in her plight to help Anakin escape slavery, but even these are passive in nature and serve to de-power her. Although she does not have the power to free him herself, she uses what little control she has to ensure he has a better life, even if this means her own de-powering through his separation from her. To that end, when Qui-Gon notices how special Anakin is, Shmi asks him for help, although she does not specify what help she expects or offer specific suggestions. When Qui-Gon subsequently announces that Anakin has been freed, she quietly rejoices for her son, telling him he can now "make his dreams come true."[17] Both characters are, in fact, accomplishing their dreams, with Anakin on his path to becoming a Jedi and Shmi having secured a better future for her son, who will now leave her. When Anakin seeks her approval to go, she tells him that the choice is his alone,[18] implying that she, too, has made a choice: to put her son's life before her own happiness. Then, in a heartbreaking moment, Shmi bids her son to "be brave, and don't look back,"[19] as he leaves Tatooine, potentially forever. Shmi says this, on one hand, to soothe her scared boy, but her advice shows her desire for him to live a truly good life—as opposed to one filled with regret. She tells him to not look back, to let her sacrifice be worthy, to rid himself of doubt, ensuring he will become the good man she believes he can be. In telling her son to essentially forget about her, to not consider her, she displays a bittersweet, passive agency, emphasizing that she has led her life for him.

Their sad separation ripples through the film to push Anakin's storyline forward while leaving hers behind. Ironically, despite Shmi's best intentions, Anakin's departure from his home planet and detachment from his mother marks the first milestone in his transition from a jovial, talented, and imaginative child to a grim, nefarious, and corrupt villain. But this turn has virtually nothing to do with Shmi's parenting or sacrifice and much to do with his experience of love from her and the Jedi philosophy of non-attachment. *Star Wars* repeatedly underscores that a Jedi's training must begin at an early age. When Qui-Gon brings Anakin in front of the Jedi council, Mace Windu cites Anakin's age as a reason not to train him.[20] But the

---

[17] Ibid.

[18] Ibid.

[19] Ibid.

[20] Ibid. Also in *The Phantom Menace*, when Shmi and Qui-Gon discuss Anakin's powers, the Jedi tells her that if her child had been born in the Republic, he would have been identified from a much younger age. Similarly, in *Star Wars Episode V: The Empire Strikes Back* (1980), as Luke Skywalker reaches Dagobah in the hopes of being trained by Yoda, the Jedi master mentions that Luke is too old to train. *Star Wars Episode V: The Empire Strikes Back*, directed by Irvin Kerschner (1980; Beverly Hills, CA: 20th Century Fox/Lucasfilm Ltd.), Disney+, https://www.disneyplus.com/movies/star-wars-the-empire-strikes-back-episode-v/iqtDTZAewwYl.

emphasis on the future Jedi's age is related to Jedi teachings that forbid attachments because the Order follows what John C. Wright refers to as a "doctrine of utter renunciation and detachment."[21] Indeed, attachment must be renounced, for it distracts the Jedi from the study of the Force and their duties to the entire Republic. This detached existence was modeled for Anakin by his mother in her willingness to let her son go out of love for him and parallels Joseph Campbell's descriptions of ascetic heroes such as Siddartha Gautama or Saint Bernard, who became hermits for the good of their moral missions, forsaking or attempting to forsake earthly goods, lust, or relationships for the sanctity of their quests.[22] In this fashion, Jedi initiates learn from a young age how to live in detachment and are chosen for the strength of their minds, allowing them to bear this burden. In addition to their strength, however, the very young age at which younglings enter training would permit them to endure the lack of personal connections in their lives, for they would hardly have experienced it before the start of their training.

Therefore, the focus on Anakin's age in the matter of his training is a red herring, a distraction. The real problem, it seems, is that Anakin has known love, unlike the other pupils, and this narrative judgment against his experience of motherly love places Shmi and motherhood in general in a rather harsh light. It again sets him apart from the others, as Anakin has spent the first nine years of his life forming bonds with the people of his home planet, chief among them his mother. Under the rules of his Jedi training, Anakin should forgo his need for connections, an inheritance from his time with his mother, which proves impossible for the young apprentice. Instead, over the course of the next two episodes, he develops a close, though also discouraged, relationship with his childhood crush Padmé. Anakin, because of this first connection, is both stunted by being cut off from his mother's love and, at the same time, determined to love and be loved again. This perceived weakness then opens him to exploitation by the Sith Lord Darth Sidious, who uses Anakin's attachments to tempt him to the Dark Side. Despite Shmi's best intentions, Anakin's love for and separation from his mother pushes him towards his dark destiny.

Despite having played such an important role in her son's early life, Shmi is left behind, virtually dead to him for a decade, until she is on the brink of her actual death in *Star Wars Episode II: Attack of the Clones* (2002). At the beginning of the film, Anakin has been training as a Jedi for ten years. He has not seen his mother in all this time until he starts having nightmare-visions showing Shmi suffering, begging for help. He first seems to dismiss the dreams, eager to reunite with Padmé instead. Yet when the dreams become more vivid, he leaves Naboo with Padmé to attempt to rescue Shmi.

---

[21] Wright, *Star Wars on Trial,* 108.

[22] Campbell, *Hero with a Thousand Faces,* 103-104.

Returning to Tatooine, he discovers that his mother has married a man, Cliegg Lars, who bought and then freed her. This man informs Anakin that Shmi has been missing for a month after having been abducted by Tusken Raiders. Despite having been freed of the shackles of slavery under Watto, Shmi again finds herself in a captive state at the hands of the "vicious, mindless monsters,"[23] as the Tuskens are described by Lars. Moments after being reunited with her son, Shmi dies—martyr-like after a month of torture, fully dispossessed, in pain—in Anakin's arms. Enraged by her loss, Anakin massacres the whole population of the Tusken camp, where Shmi was kept prisoner. "I killed them . . . not just the men, but the women and the children too,"[24] Anakin confides in Padmé. Following his mother's death, Anakin is firmly set on his path to becoming Vader; Shmi's pain, dispossession, and death advances Anakin's narrative.

Akin to their earlier separation, Shmi suffers in the dark so that Anakin's story may progress, even for the worse. On Naboo, Anakin explains to Padmé that he understands he is shirking his responsibility to protect her, but that he does not have a choice, he *must* go to his mother.[25] His insistence on his lack of choice and his acknowledgment that he is ignoring his duty points to his detachment not only from Jedi teachings, which emphasize duty, but also from his mother's wisdom. By believing he has no choice but to go to Tatooine, Anakin ignores the final pieces of wisdom Shmi imparted to him. First, Shmi gave Anakin her blessing to leave by telling him, "[a] path has been placed before you, the choice is yours alone."[26] By saying this, Shmi declared Anakin's agency and power, reassuring him that he would always have options, even when things seem inevitable. She had given over what little agency she herself possessed so that he would use his powers for the greater good. Secondly, Shmi also asked Anakin not to look back. By ignoring his choice and not only looking but going back to his mother, Anakin drifts from the future Shmi wanted for him, choosing his personal interest over the greater good, further de-powering Shmi and nullifying her sacrifices.

After his massacre of the Tuskens, he confides in Padmé that he wishes to become the most powerful Jedi in the galaxy, so strong he will stop people from dying.[27] This first manifestation of his obsession with preventing the death of those he loves marks a second major milestone on his path to

---

[23] *Star Wars Episode II: Attack of the Clones*, directed by George Lucas (2002; Beverly Hills, CA: 20th Century Fox/Lucasfilm Ltd.), Disney+, https://www.disneyplus.com/movies/star-wars-attack-of-the-clones-episode-ii/mgpYHGnzZW6N.

[24] Ibid.

[25] Ibid.

[26] *Star Wars Episode I: The Phantom Menace*, directed by George Lucas, 1999.

[27] *Star Wars Episode II: Attack of the Clones*, directed by George Lucas, 2002.

becoming Vader. Shmi's excruciating death serves Anakin's advancement in the story, accentuating the idea that women, especially mothers, must suffer in order for the men in their lives to evolve.

The way in which Shmi's pain (and Padmé's, as will be discussed next) facilitate Anakin's evolution towards the Dark Side and drive the plot of the three Prequels is strongly reminiscent of the trope of "Women in Refrigerators," coined by comic book writer Gail Simone in 1999. The metaphor refers to Alexandra DeWitt, a character from the *Green Lantern* comic book series. DeWitt is the girlfriend of Kyle Rayner, the titular hero, until she is killed by one of her boyfriend's antagonists, Major Force, who strangles her and stuffs her in a refrigerator for Rayner to find.[28] Her violent death pushes her boyfriend to attack her killer, leading to a breakthrough in the use of his powers. DeWitt's demise is but one of the many examples Simone lists of comic book women who have been "killed, raped, depowered, crippled, turned evil, maimed, tortured, contracted a disease or had other life-derailing tragedies befall [them],"[29] as a plot device to further a male character's story arc.

This overwhelming tendency to have women suffer—to "fridge" them—can be found in other narratives besides comic books, as the extended pain, de-powering, and gruesome death of Shmi Skywalker in *Star Wars* displays. Green Lantern, after the death of Alex, grows motivated to become the best hero he can be, to honor his late girlfriend's memory, her death acting as a catalyst for his greater advancement. In a similar fashion, Shmi's repeated pains—her condition as a slave, her separation from her beloved son, her torture by the Tuskens, and finally, her death—serve not her own characterization, but Anakin's trajectory within the story. The Prequels explain Vader's origin story, and Shmi's suffering and sacrifice are plot devices that explain how a young slave boy growing up outside the realm of the Republic could have grown to become the galaxy's most feared figure. Furthermore, Shmi's death becomes a tool used by others, namely Chancellor Palpatine, to bait Anakin to the Dark Side. On one occasion, the secret Sith Lord goads Anakin into killing Count Dooku against the principles of the Jedi, then reminds him that he has killed before for revenge, referencing the Tuskens.[30] Later, Palpatine uses Anakin's trauma, caused by Shmi's death, to tempt him to renounce the Jedi in order to save Padmé.[31]

---

[28] Ron Marz, *Forced Entry: Green Lantern*, volume 3, issue 54 (Burbank, CA: DC Comics, 1994).

[29] Gail Simone, "The List," Women in Refrigerators, accessed December 15, 2021, https://lby3.com/wir/women.html.

[30] *Star Wars Episode III: Revenge of the Sith*, directed by George Lucas, 2005.

[31] Ibid.

Indeed, once Shmi has passed, Anakin moves to obsessively caring for the well-being of his wife, Padmé. As he fears for his mother after dreaming of her pain, Anakin starts to experience similar nightmares depicting Padmé dying. Possessed by a desperate will to not lose the only other woman he's ever loved, Anakin is prepared to do anything to save her.

Padmé Amidala

Ray Merlock and Kathy Merlock Jackson describe Padmé's role in the Prequel Trilogy as a "political figure, queen, figurehead, policy maker, compromise seeker, diplomat, senator . . . as well as a woman in love."[32] This description captures the multi-dimensionality Padmé displays as the main female character throughout the first two episodes. But the thread that runs through her various roles is that of mother, both figurative and literal. The more literal Padmé's mothering becomes, the more she goes from a capable, gentle, yet assertive politician, to de-powered and passive, until the narrative "fridges" her as it did Shmi, sacrificing her to further her husband's narrative.

As Queen of Naboo, she is a decisive and courageous leader who is loved by her people, the well-being of whom she consistently puts above any other concerns, including her own safety or standing. When Qui-Gon Jinn and his Padawan learner Obi-Wan Kenobi are dispatched to her home planet, Amidala, speaking through her decoy, initially declines to leave for Coruscant. Bent on staying with her people despite the danger, she eventually agrees to leave only when convinced that her presence before the Senate is the best way to help them.[33] Her fierce determination to protect her people casts her in the role of the Mother of all Naboo. Exemplifying the good mother archetype described by Joseph Campbell, she is "the comforting, the

---

[32] Ray Merlock and Kathy Merlock Jackson, "Lightsabers, Political Arenas, and Marriage for Princess Leia and Queen Amidala," in *Sex, Politics, and Religion in Star Wars,* ed. Douglas Brode and Leah Deyneka (Lanham: The Scarecrow Press, 2012), 79.

[33] *Star Wars Episode I: The Phantom Menace,* directed by George Lucas, 1999. However, her determination to serve her subjects is sometimes used to manipulate her. When the Trade Federation invades Naboo, for example, Nute Gunray knows to exploit the certainty of the Naboo's affliction as leverage to convince Padmé to cooperate with them: "In time, the suffering of your people will persuade you to see our point of view," he tells her. Later on in the film, Senator Palpatine manipulates her into calling for a vote of no-confidence in Chancellor Valorum, insisting that this would be Naboo's best chance at avoiding Federation control. Although doubtful, Padmé eventually agrees, as the fate of her people comes first. In this context, it could be argued that her devotion to Naboo and to democracy contributes to advancing Palpatine's—and by extension Anakin's—narrative arc forward.

nourishing . . . young and beautiful"[34] mother of the people. In motherly fashion, Queen Amidala repeatedly prioritizes others' safety before her own, as when she reveals herself as the Queen to Gungan leader Boss Nass, humbling herself to persuade him to join in their fight. Risking great danger, she knows she must expose herself to save the planet's people. McDonald further describes Amidala as the archetype of the "nurturing earth mother,"[35] comparing her to an incarnation of the fertility goddess on the lush and fruitful paradise that is Naboo.

As the decoy handmaiden Padmé, her motherly qualities are established in *Episode I* as she takes on the role of friend and surrogate mother to young Anakin. Her warm attitude towards him reinforces their bond throughout the film. On the ship to Coruscant, for example, Padmé extends motherly comforts and affection to the boy, listening to his fears and sharing his apprehensions while she wraps him in a robe.[36] This is a gesture McDonald likens to a legal symbol that "means that one will accord parental care and protection to the other."[37] Furthermore, Padmé steadily uses the nickname "Ani" when talking to Anakin, as Shmi did, highlighting her role as a mother substitute in his life in *Episode I.*

In *Attack of the Clones,* Padmé, now a Senator, overwhelmingly retains her stance as a public servant and figurative mother dedicated to the well-being of others, prioritizing duty to them above all else. This is exemplified by her fight against the creation of an Army of the Republic, which she deems anti-democratic. Later on, when Chancellor Palpatine orders that she leave for Naboo, she is frustrated at having to leave the capital during these vital negotiations. Her continued care and concern for the people of Naboo preserve her role as a figurative mother in her senatorial career.

Yet if her motherly demeanor as a politician remains relatively unchanged from that of the Queen, her relationship with Anakin evolves drastically during *Episode II.* When they meet again after a decade at the beginning of the episode, Anakin has never forgotten her. The young knight has clearly moved past their once familial friendship, rather wanting to embark on a romance. For her part, Padmé resists this change. Both his intentions and Padmé's contrasting ones are expressed through the way they address each other during their first interaction. Padmé, on one hand, tells Anakin he will "always be that little boy [she] knew on Tatooine"[38] and consistently calls him "Ani"

---

[34] Campbell, *Hero with a Thousand Faces,* 92.

[35] McDonald, *The* Star Wars *Heresies,* chap, 3, loc. 564.

[36] *Star Wars Episode I: The Phantom Menace,* directed by George Lucas, 1999.

[37] McDonald, *The* Star Wars *Heresies,* chap, 3, loc. 564.

[38] *Star Wars Episode II: Attack of the Clones,* directed by George Lucas, 2002.

during the exchange, demonstrating her maternal love and caring for him. The use of the nickname is less and less frequent as their relationship evolves towards romance. Padmé only uses Shmi's nickname for him on rare occasions for the remainder of the film, on specific occasions when she is acting as mother rather than lover.[39] This approach contrasts with Anakin's, who, in their first scene together, calls Padmé by her first name throughout the conversation; the others in the room address her as "M'lady" or "Senator."[40] Anakin also adopts a rather flirty attitude, revealing a willingness to forgo his Jedi duty for personal benefit—or to benefit those he loves.[41] In the early part of *Episode II*, a shift from Shmi to Padmé as the main woman in Anakin's life is starting to occur. This shift, however, is not complete until Shmi dies. At that moment, according to McDonald, Padmé is "inevitably on her way to becoming the divine mother of the saga,"[42] a role previously occupied by Shmi, the Madonna archetype.

Further on in the film, Padmé begins to change from a figurative to a literal mother. Padmé's literal motherhood eventually becomes Anakin's motivation to become invincible, and as a consequence, she takes on the mantle of pain Shmi has endured for her son. The theme of pain, as relevant to Padmé's storyline, is foreshadowed in the way she and Anakin discuss their love throughout *Attack of the Clones*. Alone together on Naboo, Anakin describes his love for her in terms related to pain and death, such as "agony," "scar," "torment," and "suffering," even implying that he cannot breathe.[43] Although Padmé rebukes his advances at this moment, she later confesses her love for him in quite a similar manner, telling him that she is not afraid to die because she has been "dying a little bit more each day since [he's] come back into [her] life."[44] Their shared use of pain and death imagery to refer to their love indicates the consequences they will face for acting upon this love. Indeed, at

---

[39] She calls him "Ani" on three occasions for the rest of the film: first, when he falls off a Shaak on Naboo and fakes an injury, she is worried and runs to his side asking him "Ani, Ani, are you alright?" (*Star Wars Episode II: Attack of the Clones*, directed by George Lucas, 2002; 0:53:03). She calls him "Ani" again when trying to comfort him after his mother's death (1:24:34-1:25:06). Finally, she calls him "Ani" before leaving for Geonosis, while arguing with him about the morality of going to save Obi-Wan (1:29:28), adopting a rather motherly resolve in the situation.

[40] Ibid.

[41] Ibid. For example, when Padmé wonders who is attempting to kill her, he answers that they will find the culprit, despite Obi-Wan clearly establishing that this is not their mandate.

[42] McDonald, *The* Star Wars *Heresies*, chap 13, loc. 1821.

[43] *Star Wars Episode II: Attack of the Clones*, directed by George Lucas, 2002.

[44] Ibid.

the close of the Prequel Trilogy, Anakin, in fact, cannot breathe on his own; his body is tortured by burns and scars, and he endures agony as a result of his quest to keep Padmé alive. Similarly, Padmé's confession of love is apt; she is, in fact, closer and closer to the moment of her death ever since she began this dalliance with Anakin. At the end of *Episode II*, they marry in secret.

Merlock and Merlock Jackson are not wrong to emphasize Padmé's multi-dimensionality as a character when she is introduced; yet from the beginning of the final Prequel film, she is framed solely as a woman in love, as she is now married to Anakin and carrying his child. The closer she gets to becoming a literal mother, the greater her loss of power and agency becomes; as her passivity grows, her storyline increasingly serves only to advance Anakin's arc. From the scene at the beginning of *Star Wars Episode III: Revenge of the Sith* (2005), in which Padmé announces she is pregnant, she becomes a shadow of her former self. No longer the brave, passionate politician, she has transformed into a fearful woman,[45] defined by the man she loves. As Diana Dominguez points out, she becomes "disturbingly symbolic of the rising statistics of domestic and relationship abuse among young women in [the United States]."[46] Once she becomes the wife of the young Jedi—who himself becomes increasingly unreasonable and paranoid in his obsession with keeping Padmé alive—she loses most of her former interests and concerns with the politics of the Republic, becoming progressively more passive under Anakin's influence. Throughout *Episode III*, Padmé rarely speaks about anything other than her husband and their future child. Remarkably, deleted scenes of the film reveal that she, together with Senator Mon Mothma and a handful of others, was attempting to thwart Palpatine.[47] The choice to delete these scenes and to confine Padmé to her lavish apartments for most of the film is indicative of the saga's de-powering attitude towards mothers, as her anguish and pain become more essential to the plot of the film than her politics. This creates a narrative situation in which, as Jeanne Cavelos writes, "pain heightens the heroism of the males while undercutting the heroism of the female."[48]

---

[45] *Star Wars Episode III: Revenge of the Sith*, directed by George Lucas, 2005. Padmé trembles as she tells Anakin she's pregnant; he pointedly notices her fear and worry.
[46] Dominguez, "Feminism and the Force," 124-125.
[47] Keith A. DeCandido, "The Madness of King George," in *Star Wars on Trial*, ed. David Brin and Matthew Woodring Stover (Dallas: BenBella Books, 2015), 88.
[48] Jeanne Cavelos, "Stop Her, She's Got a Gun! How the Rebel Princess and the Virgin Queen Became Marginalized and Powerless in George Lucas's Fairy Tale," in *Star Wars on Trial*, ed. David Brin and Matthew Woodring Stover (Dallas: BenBella Books, 2015), 312.

Her story comes to an end when she dies following a particularly violent interaction with her husband, reinforcing Dominguez's claim that Padmé is comparable to a victim of domestic abuse. Although she does not directly die from Anakin Force-choking her, she nevertheless goes into labor with the twins and fades away not long after, proclaiming her lover's goodness until the very end, like an abused woman who eventually loses her life remaining loyal to the man she thinks loves her. In a particularly striking passage, Dominguez writes that letting herself die in such a way is "both a supreme form of martyrdom . . . and a supreme form of selfishness."[49] Indeed, by letting herself die from heartbreak, Padmé appears somewhat selfish, as she will not live for the sake of her children. Both her martyrdom and selfishness appear out of character for a woman defined throughout the Prequel Trilogy as a thoroughly selfless leader, putting the needs of the people ahead of her own. This change in her characterization, culminating in her death is telling; as Shmi did before her, Padmé dies because, like Simone's refrigerator women, she can only bring more to the story through her death. Indeed, Bowman suggests Padmé's problem is inherent in the plot's design: "her importance in the film can be seen as being reduced to the births."[50] Now that her character has resolved the question of Luke and Leia's parentage and advanced Anakin's dark destiny, she is no longer necessary, and as Cavelos writes, "the sooner she dies, the more convenient it is for a story that has no interest in her."[51]

In a scene between the twins in *Star Wars Episode VI: Return of the Jedi* (1983), Luke asks Leia whether she remembers her real mother. The young princess answers that though her mother died when she was very young, she does remember images and feelings from her: her beauty and her air of sadness.[52] Although Leia cannot remember specific moments from her time with Padmé, even recalling her appearance is too specific for a mother she knew for mere seconds. This line of the Original Trilogy could have spurred Lucas to have Padmé die later in the Prequels, at least late enough to impress herself upon Leia's memories. But as Cavelos argues, she died at a convenient moment in the narrative, for in death, she is more interesting, pushing forward others' stories.

And not just Anakin's; Paul McDonald contends that with Padmé's pain "comes the possibility of the new hope which will drive the next trilogy,"[53]

---

49 Dominguez, "Feminism and the Force," 127.
50 Bowman, "Pregnant Padmé and Slave Leia," 165.
51 Cavelos, "Stop Her," 316.
52 *Star Wars Episode VI: Return of the Jedi,* directed by Richard Marquand (1983; Beverly Hills, CA: 20th Century Fox/Lucasfilm Ltd.), Disney+, https://www.disneyplus.com/movies/star-wars-return-of-the-jedi-episode-vi/6QGKo5mjDBS8.
53 McDonald, *The* Star Wars *Heresies,* chap 19, loc. 2561.

exemplified through the title retroactively given to the very first *Star Wars* film. Indeed, not only does Padmé's death cement Anakin's new status as a Sith lord by suppressing the strongest motivation he had to return to the good, but it also brings forward hope for his eventual redemption, as her death is linked with Luke's birth. In this manner, her death pushes forward both Anakin's and Luke's storylines. Padmé's death so early in Luke's life eliminates her from the picture, crystallizing a sense of filiation between Luke and Vader. Anakin's and Luke's stories become analogous as would-be heroes deprived of their biological parents from a young age, driving their quest for meaning. Yet if Vader's looming shadow marks Luke's progression through the original saga, the latter exhibits an almost complete lack of interest towards his mother. As the hero looks for information concerning his father at every detour, besides his brief inquiry as to Leia's memories, he remains wholly incurious about his mother: her name, her life, her death. This omission emphasizes Padmé's role in the Prequels as oriented towards the male figures of her life, present and future. But this is the dead mom's peril as one who lives, loves, and dies solely for the benefit of others; like Shmi, Padmé's suffering and eventual death are merely a narrative catalyst for the men she loves.

Leia Organa

As cruel as Padmé's death is, it is softened and partially redeemed by the life and death of her daughter Leia. Two decades before *Star Wars* fans would be introduced to Padmé Amidala, Princess Leia of Alderaan graced theater screens in 1977 with her particular brand of wit and bravery. A Senator and a figurehead of the Rebel Alliance, Leia was a fierce leader with a distinct personality who displayed agency without compromising her femininity. Later, when she falls in love with Han Solo, she remains both a politician and an influential figure in the rebellion against the Empire. When she decides to join Han and fight on Endor, he reacts very positively, indicating that "he is not overly protective of her nor [does he feel] it would be more appropriate that she be safe and out of the way."[54] Contrary to her mother, she falls in love without being effectively cloistered to her chambers.

Leia's situation and character evolve, however, in the more recent Sequel Trilogy. In these films, Leia is now a General in the newly formed Resistance, fighting against the evil First Order. Dan Golding describes her characterization as consistent with a tendency re-booted series have to present female legacy characters such as Leia as "absent, nonexistent, sacrificial homebodies unable

---

[54] Merlock and Merlock Jackson, "Lightsabers, Political Arenas, and Marriage," 84.

to join men, young and old, on their adventures."[55] Indeed, Leia is mostly absent from battle in the Sequels, appearing regularly in the command center wearing intricate gowns quite unsuited to the battlefield. Although it was common to see Leia in command rooms, ordering offensives in the Original Trilogy, she generally wore more practical outfits, reserving her elaborate dresses for other occasions. Furthermore, General Leia spends most of *Star Wars Episode VIII: The Last Jedi* (2017) in a coma, rendered inert by an attack ordered by her own son.

The latter plays a major role in Leia's characterization, for unlike in the Original Trilogy, in the Sequels, she is now a mother. Although she leads the Resistance, she is also mourning her son Ben, who, like her own father, has turned to the Dark Side. But she also acts as a figurative mother to some of the Resistance fighters serving under her. She guides the cocky pilot Poe Dameron, mentoring him as a Resistance leader, but the more significant subject of her motherly attention is Rey, the Jedi trainee she welcomes into the movement. Leia tasks Rey—not Poe—to find Luke, for example, emphasizing a certain familial connection. The General also protectively carries a beacon to guide Rey home and mentors her as a Jedi after Luke dies.

But Leia's agency is reduced by her insistence on needing Luke to bolster support for the Resistance, a conviction she seems to have imparted on others, especially Rey. For example, as Luke refuses to leave the planet Ahch-To to fight alongside his sister, he insists he is not the legend people consider him to be, only for Rey to retort, seeming to ignore him, "The Galaxy may need a legend."[56] Although Luke is rightfully deemed a legend to the Resistance and a threat to the First Order, the fact that Leia does not consider herself equal to the challenge devalues her character. As Emily Strand has noted, "the plot driving need, born in *The Force Awakens* and continuing through [*The Last Jedi*], to 'get Luke back,' as if he is the magic-man antidote to all their problems, is not exactly empowering for the female leadership of the Resistance."[57]

Like Shmi and Padmé, Leia's death is related to her motherhood and serves to advance the character arc of her literal son and figurative daughter. In *Star Wars Episode IX: The Rise of Skywalker* (2019), Leia sacrifices the last of her strength to reach Ben through the Force in a final attempt to bring him back

---

[55] Dan Golding, Star Wars *After Lucas: A Critical Guide to the Future of the Galaxy* (Minneapolis: University of Minneapolis Press, 2019), 188.

[56] *Star Wars Episode VIII: The Last Jedi*, directed by Rian Johnson (2017; San Francisco: Disney/Lucasfilm Ltd.), Disney+, https://www.disneyplus.com/movies/star-wars-the-last-jedi-episode-viii/1nCWFK1pmAI0.

[57] Emily Strand, "Attack of the Last Jedi," *Hogwarts Professor* (blog), January 5, 2018, https://www.hogwartsprofessor.com/attack-of-the-last-jedi/.

into the light. As she communes with her son, she stops him from killing Rey, who in turn realizes she will not strike him down, opting instead to use her gifts to heal him.[58] At that moment, both of them are brought into the light. As a result of Leia's sacrifice, Ben finds the strength to turn back to the good while Rey turns away from the reflexes of a Sith to kill in anger.

In this sequence of events, Leia's role as a mother dispossesses her but not to the same degree as mothers like Shmi and Padmé. Leia's passing, faithful to Golding's description of legacy mother characters' portrayal, is a sacrifice for the benefit of the next generation. However, unlike Shmi or Padmé, Leia seems more in control of her fate, choosing to give her life-force to call her son Ben back to the light. In the peaceful and proactive nature of her death, she redeems those of her mother and grandmother. Indeed, although their three deaths are similar in the way they all die to advance other characters' arcs, Leia's more peaceful death soothes the scar of Padmé's and Shmi's. Leia is thus framed as a powerful figure whose death had meaning in itself, marking a break from the senseless deaths of the women who came before her. If Shmi's death undoubtedly pushes Anakin on his way to the Dark Side, Leia's bolsters Rey's position within the light and wins Ben away from Palpatine's grasp. Moreover, Leia does not only die for Ben and Rey, she also dies for the Resistance, elevating her mentee Poe to leadership and inspiring the next generation of rebels with her selfless act. Finally, as opposed to Shmi and Padmé, Leia dies a peaceful death after having led a relatively long life. Like the actor who gave her likeness to the Princess of Alderaan, Carrie Fisher, Leia dies loved, remembered, and in power.

A less perilous future for mothers?

At the end of *Return of the Jedi*, as Luke celebrates the fall of the Empire surrounded by friends, departed figures join him as Force ghosts. Obi-Wan, Yoda, and the redeemed Anakin smile at him, marking him as a Jedi hero like themselves, united by a bond that death cannot destroy. In this manner, one could imagine Leia joining the women of her past, known and unknown, forming a narrative kinship of the dispossessed mothers of *Star Wars*, even as she opens the way for new attitudes towards women and mothers. Indeed, the powerful portrayal of Beru Lars in the recent television series *Obi-Wan Kenobi* (2022), who springs into decisive action when her adopted son Luke is

---

[58] *Star Wars Episode IX: The Rise of Skywalker*, J.J. Abrams, dir. (2019; San Francisco: Disney/Lucasfilm Ltd.), Disney+, https://www.disneyplus.com/movies/star-wars-the-rise-of-skywalker-episode-ix/5e8JThYwCYgw.

threatened,[59] and the Rebellion-inspiring figure of Maarva Carassi Andor in the 2022 first season of *Andor* (not to mention her narrative counterpart, Lyra Erso in 2016's *Rogue One: A Star Wars Story*) are women who promise a bright, empowered future for the mothers of *Star Wars* and perhaps even indicate that motherhood, as Bowman argues, need not be an oppressive role for women—an impediment to their feminism.[60] Although mothers in *Star Wars* have sometimes been voiceless, sometimes powerless, sometimes nameless, and usually dispossessed, perhaps through Leia's, Beru's, and Maarva's examples, they can unite together amid the sea of male figures whose stories they shape by their suffering. Joining together across four decades of storytelling, perhaps these mothers will regain and retain the will to live—and live boldly—for the next mother to come.

Bibliography

Abrams, J.J., dir. *Star Wars Episode IX: The Rise of Skywalker.* 2019; San Francisco: Disney/Lucasfilm Ltd. Disney+. https://www.disneyplus.com/movies/star-wars-the-rise-of-skywalker-episode-ix/5e8JThYwCYgw.

Bowman, Cole. "Pregnant Padmé and Slave Leia: *Star Wars*' Female Role Models." In *The Ultimate Star Wars and Philosophy: You Must Unlearn What You Have Learned,* edited by Jason T. Eberl and Kevin S. Decker; series editor William Irwin, 161-171. Chichester, West Sussex, UK: John Wiley & Sons Ltd., 2016.

Campbell, Joseph. *The Hero's Journey: Joseph Campbell on His Life and Work,* edited by Phil Cousineau. Novato, California: New World Library, 2003.

_______. *The Hero With a Thousand Faces.* Third Edition. Novato, California: New World Press, 2008.

Cavelos, Jeanne. "Stop Her, She's Got a Gun! How the Rebel Princess and the Virgin Queen Became Marginalized and Powerless in George Lucas's Fairy Tale." In *Star Wars On Trial, The Force Awakens* edition, edited by David Brin and Matthew Woodring Stover, 305-327. Dallas, TX: BenBella Books, 2015.

DeCandido, Keith. "The Madness of King George." In *Star Wars On Trial, The Force Awakens* edition, edited by David Brin and Matthew Woodring Stover, 83-95. Dallas, TX: BenBella Books, 2015.

Dominguez, Diana. "Feminism and the Force: Empowerment and Disillusionment in a Galaxy Far, Far Away." In *Culture, Identities and Technology in the* Star Wars *Films: Essays of the Two Trilogies,* edited by Carl Silvio and Tony M. Vinci, 109-133. Jefferson, NC: McFarland, 2007.

Golding, Dan. *Star Wars After Lucas: A Critical Guide to the Future of the Galaxy.* Minneapolis, MN: University of Minnesota Press, 2019.

---

59 *Obi-Wan Kenobi,* season 1, episode 6, "Part VI," directed by Deborah Chow, written by Joby Harold, Andrew Stanton, and Hossein Amini, aired June 22, 2022, Disney+, https://www.disneyplus.com/video/37ebe960-682b-4de2-b032-d2ae7dcf468b.

60 Bowman, "Pregnant Padmé and Slave Leia," 165.

Harold, Joby, Andrew Stanton, and Hossein Amini, writers. *Obi-Wan Kenobi.* Season 1, episode 6, "Part VI." Directed by Deborah Chow. Aired June 22, 2022. Disney+. https://www.disneyplus.com/video/37ebe960-682b-4de2-b032-d2ae7dcf468b.

Johnson, Rian, dir. *Star Wars Episode VIII: The Last Jedi.* 2017; San Francisco: Disney/Lucasfilm, Ltd. Disney+. https://www.disneyplus.com/movies/star-wars-the-last-jedi-episode-viii/1nCWFK1pmAI0.

Kerschner, Irvin, dir. *Star Wars Episode V: The Empire Strikes Back.* 1980; Beverly Hills, CA: 20th Century Fox/Lucasfilm Ltd. Disney+. https://www.disneyplus.com/movies/star-wars-the-empire-strikes-back-episode-v/iqtDTZAewwYl.

Lucas, George, dir. *Star Wars Episode I: The Phantom Menace.* 1999; Beverly Hills, CA: 20th Century Fox/Lucasfilm Ltd. Disney+. https://www.disneyplus.com/movies/star-wars-the-phantom-menace-episode-i/2ezYynkgW1AH.

_______, dir. *Star Wars Episode II: Attack of the Clones.* 2002; Beverly Hills, CA: 20th Century Fox/Lucasfilm Ltd. Disney+. https://www.disneyplus.com/movies/star-wars-attack-of-the-clones-episode-ii/mgpYHGnzZW6N.

_______, dir. *Star Wars Episode III: Revenge of the Sith.* 2005; Beverly Hills, CA: 20th Century Fox/Lucasfilm Ltd. Disney+. https://www.disneyplus.com/movies/star-wars-revenge-of-the-sith-episode-iii/4WvbqLFumNvi.

Marquand, Richard, dir. *Return of the Jedi.* 1983; Beverly Hills, CA: 20th Century Fox/Lucasfilm Ltd. Disney+. https://www.disneyplus.com/movies/star-wars-return-of-the-jedi-episode-vi/6QGKo5mjDBS8.

Marz, Ron. *Forced Entry: Green Lantern.* Volume 3, Issue number 54. Burbank, CA: DC Comics, 1994.

McDonald, Paul F. *The* Star Wars *Heresies: Interpreting the Themes, Symbols and Philosophies of Episodes I, II and III.* Jefferson, NC: McFarland, 2013. Kindle.

Merlock, Ray and Kathy Merlock Jackson. "Lightsabers, Political Arenas, and Marriage for Princess Leia and Queen Amidala." In *Sex, Politics, and Religion in Star Wars: An Anthology,* edited by Douglas Brode and Leah Deyneka, 77-88. Lanham, MD: The Scarecrow Press, 2012.

Rubey, Dan. "*Star Wars*: Not So Long Ago, Not So Far Away." *Jump Cut,* no. 18 (August 1978): 9-14.

Simone, Gail. "The List." Women in the Refrigerators. Accessed December 15, 2021. https://lby3.com/wir/women.html.

Soule, Charles and Giuseppe Camuncoli. *Darth Vader #25.* New York: Marvel Comics, 2018.

Strand, Emily. "Attack of The Last Jedi." *Hogwarts Professor* (blog). January 5, 2018. https://www.hogwartsprofessor.com/attack-of-the-last-jedi/.

Taylor, Christian, writer. *Star Wars: The Clone Wars.* Season 3, episode 15, "Overlords." Directed by Steward Lee. Aired January 28, 2011. Cartoon Network. Disney+. https://www.disneyplus.com/video/48c78dd1-73f6-40ef-9e0d-d469ea00ada8.

Wright, John C. "May the Midichlorians Be with You." In *Star Wars On Trial, The Force Awakens* edition, edited by David Brin and Matthew Woodring Stover, 99-119. Dallas, TX: BenBella Books, 2015.

Part 2:
Exploring the Ideas

Chapter 4

21-87: Not Just a Number in *Star Wars*

Emily Strand

Abstract: This chapter investigates an obscure art-house film that inspired George Lucas: Arthur Lipsett's 1963 short for the National Film Board of Canada, *21-87*. This film helped Lucas give form and shape to his own long-held interest in the "larger world" of transcendent reality, especially as it relates to human connection. However, Lucas transformed Lipsett's bleak thesis in *21-87* into a much-needed message of hope and optimism. This hopeful, humanistic message, inspired by Lipsett's film, appears throughout the Prequel films, which in part tell the story of Obi-Wan Kenobi's survival against his ultimate antithesis, General Grievous, and of the hopeful survivals of Luke and Leia, pointing to Lipsett's thesis that appreciation of nature and the possibility of shared, transcendent reality are humanity's best hope against a machine-based future. This theme is also carried forward in more recent *Star Wars* animated shows like *The Clone Wars* and *The Bad Batch*, and their indirect but meaningful allusions to Lipsett's work are analyzed in the chapter. Further, the Disney-era Sequel Trilogy makes overt reference to Lipsett's film in reluctant Stormtrooper FN-2187, pointing to Finn's journey from the heart of the Machine into the heart of the Resistance, even into the new Jedi Order. Finally, the Narkina 5 arc in the recent show *Andor* makes overt reference to Lipsett's film and its ideas, revealing *21-87*'s lasting influence on *Star Wars* and insisting that while humans may always fight against the Machine, in embracing one another, they have the power to create a shared, transcendent reality. In *Star Wars*, such a transcendent human community always adds up to victory.

Keywords: film, *Star Wars*, Arthur Lipsett, George Lucas, the Force, machine, the Machine, Machine Age, technology, Jedi, Jedi Order, Luke Skywalker, number, *21-87*, cyborg, General Grievous, Darth Vader, Obi-Wan Kenobi, transcendent reality, Finn, First Order, nature, clone, hope, influence, National Film Board of Canada, Prequel, Sequel, *Andor*, Cassian Andor, Narkina 5, George Lucas

***

With twenty-eight words in the 1977 film *Star Wars* (later known as *Star Wars Episode IV: A New Hope*), Ben Kenobi tells Luke Skywalker of a mysterious Force that gives power to the Jedi and binds, connects, and penetrates all the living. "Other than that," says author Chris Taylor, "the Force is largely a mystery"[1]—one that lends *Star Wars* a gravitas to complement the film's levity. When Lucas gave the Force a real-life, biological aspect in the later Prequel films—those dreaded "midi-chlorians"—fans wanted none of it.[2] This may be because, as Taylor says, "if we want to see the Force of the movies manifest in real life, [we] have to look to religion and art, not biology."[3] Particularly, we must look to an obscure art-house film that inspired Lucas's storytelling and has continued to inspire *Star Wars* creators ever since: Arthur Lipsett's 1963 short for the National Film Board of Canada, *21-87.* This less-than-ten-minute, abstract film helped Lucas give form and shape to his own long-held interest in the "larger world" of transcendent reality, especially as it relates to human connection. Lucas calls the Force (originally "the Force of Others"[4]) of *Star Wars* an "echo" of Lipsett's film,[5] even dropping an allusion to *21-87* in 1977's *Star Wars.* But *21-87*'s influence over *Star Wars* goes beyond the Force to include a dire warning about the dangers of the Machine Age to natural man and his ability to connect to others and to the realm of the spirit. Further, Lucas transforms Lipsett's work into a much-needed message of hope and optimism, particularly through the outcome of the opposition between machine-man Vader and his organic, spiritual son, Luke Skywalker.

This hopeful, humanistic message, inspired significantly by Lucas's interest in Lipsett's film,[6] lingers long in the *Star Wars* franchise, certainly through the

---

[1] Many thanks to early readers of this chapter: Dr. Sara Brown, Jude Cooper (who also served as research assistant), Andrew Rouhier, Dr. Amy H. Sturgis, and Amelia Does. All provided valuable suggestions and encouragement, for which I am grateful.

Chris Taylor, *How Star Wars Conquered the Universe* (New York: Basic Books, 2014), 58.

[2] Try a Google search for "why midi-chlorians ruined *Star Wars*," and behold the many and varied results. See also John Wright, "May the Midi-chlorians Be With You," in *Star Wars on Trial: The Force Awakens Edition*, ed. David Brin and Matthew Woodring Stover (Dallas, TX: BenBella Books, 2015), 99-114.

[3] Taylor, *How Star Wars Conquered the Universe*, 59.

[4] Ibid., 112. The 2016 film *Rogue One: A Star Wars Story* brought back this original phrasing of the most famous *Star Wars* greeting: "May the Force of Others be with you." Directed by Gareth Edwards (2016; San Francisco: Lucasfilm Ltd.), Disney+, https://www.disneyplus.com/movies/rogue-one-a-star-wars-story/14CV6eSbygOA.

[5] Taylor, *How Star Wars Conquered the Universe*, 44.

[6] Another source of inspiration for Lucas's interest in the theme of humanity versus the war machine is, of course, the works of J.R.R. Tolkien, which Lucas clearly admired, from what Taylor and others report of his heavy borrowing of parts of *The Hobbit* to

Prequel era, even if its representative works do not directly reference Lipsett's film. Particularly, the opposition between Obi-Wan Kenobi and General Grievous illustrates Lipsett's thesis about the threat of the Machine Age to natural man and his spiritual connection with others. Further, Lipsett's ideas animate aspects of *Star Wars: The Clone Wars* television show and its descendants, especially in the superiority of the Republic's organic (if mass-produced) clone soldiers over the droid army of the Separatists; *21-87* echoes especially clearly in the clones' insistence on their own personal, human identities through names over numbers.

Viewers might expect Lipsett's obscure influence over *Star Wars* to end with Lucas's involvement in the franchise. However, in the opening scenes of the Disney-era Sequel Trilogy, watchful fans are treated to another overt reference to Lipsett's film in the form of a reluctant Stormtrooper who seems unable (or unwilling) to cope within the First Order machine: FN-2187, later known as "Finn." This calculated designation and its quick evolution into a name foreshadows a character arc that takes Finn from the heart of the Machine into the heart of the Resistance, and even, the final film strongly hints, into the shared, numinous reality of the new Jedi Order. Indeed, many themes of the Sequel Trilogy, but especially its hopeful outcome in the triumph of "just people" over the Final Order, reveal *21-87*'s lasting influence on *Star Wars*. More recently, *Star Wars* television has shown profound influence from Lipsett's filmic ideas, particularly in the Narkina 5 arc of the critically-acclaimed show *Andor*. But *Star Wars* perpetually responds to and transforms Lipsett's bleak ideas, insisting that while humans may always fight against the Machine, in embracing one another, they have the power to create a shared, spiritual reality no Machine can destroy. In *Star Wars*, such a transcendent human community always adds up to victory.

Arthur Lipsett: high priest of sight and sound

Taylor suggests that from a young age, George Lucas showed interest in existential questions, asking his mother at age ten, "How come there's only one God, but so many religions?"[7] As he grew, he became interested in anthropology and social systems, calling mythology "the cornerstone of society."[8] These interests prepared Lucas to encounter and appropriate the work of a particularly existential filmmaker. Arthur Lipsett was the eccentric, experimental artist

---

draft early scripts of the original *Star Wars* film. See Taylor, *How Star Wars Conquered the Universe*, 122-123.

[7] Ibid., 18.

[8] George Lucas, quoted in Randall Frakes, et al., *James Cameron's The Story of Science Fiction*, (San Rafael, CA: Insight Editions, 2018), 91-92.

behind a handful of mid-twentieth-century art-house films for the National Film Board of Canada, such as *Very Nice, Very Nice,* nominated for an Academy Award in 1961, when Lipsett was only 25.[9] Amelia Does writes that Lipsett "was a shaman working in the arts . . . drawn to the spiritual and poetic aspects of life," who often repurposed discarded film and audio, creating collages of sounds and images in order to "explore and reveal what was inside, underneath and around the visual and audio materials used in his collages, to take the viewer into [a] state of imagination."[10] Lipsett was a trail-blazer, constructing non-narrative films from both still and moving images, accompanied by a collage of sound that often sharply contrasts the visual.[11] In her 2012 biography of Lipsett, *Do Not Look Away,* Does says Lipsett "was driven by curiosity, and expressed particular interest in biology, mysticism, and human behaviour;" his films, she says, "touch on the ineffable," making them difficult to categorize or even critique effectively.[12]

Lipsett's 1963 film *21-87* particularly fascinated Lucas. Taylor calls *21-87* "by far the most influential short Lucas ever saw,"[13] and Silberman reports Lucas screened the film two dozen times during his student days.[14] Lucas seemed to respond particularly to Lipsett's signature collagist style; Lipsett "made visual poetry out of film that others threw away,"[15] literally scavenging in trash bins for disused clips of other filmmaker's documentaries. The effect of the sound and images Lipsett chose, rubbing against each other through his careful, innovative editing, created a subversive and imaginative response in the viewer that especially intrigued Lucas. Lipsett once described his approach this way in response to an admirer of *21-87*: "by joining many obviously isolated shots each having their own reality, a multi-reality situation tends to emerge which has the ability to symbolically represent a larger multi-reality situation such as the collective consciousness . . . ."[16] Lucas commented, in Martin Lauvet's 2006 documentary *Remembering Arthur,* that "In terms of understanding the power of sound and picture relationships, there's no one

---

[9] Lois Siegel, "A Clown Outside the Circus," *Cinema Canada,* 134 (October 1986), 12.

[10] Amelia Does, "*Free Fall*: Lipsett is the Shaman, Film is the Ritual," *Senses of Cinema,* August 2013, http://www.sensesofcinema.com/2013/cteq/free-fall-lipsett-is-the-shaman-film-is-the-ritual/.

[11] Amelia Does, *Do Not Look Away: The Life of Arthur Lipsett* (self-pub., Amelia Does, 2012), 15.

[12] Ibid., 16-17.

[13] Taylor, *How Star Wars Conquered the Universe,* 43.

[14] Steve Silberman, "Life After Darth," *Wired,* May 1, 2005, https://www.wired.com/2005/05/lucas-2/.

[15] Ibid.

[16] Arthur Lipsett, letter to Kit Carson, quoted in Does, *Do Not Look Away,* 62.

better than Arthur Lipsett. In the relationship of understanding the editing, cutting from dark to light, light to dark, moving from one side to the other, going from pastoral to shocking, there's no better example than his films."[17]

Among Lipsett's films, there is no better example of what Lucas is describing than *21-87*. Chris Gehman and Brett Kashmere, in their introduction to a forthcoming anthology on Lipsett's canon of work, surmise that *21-87* brings into sharper focus many of the principle traits and themes that concerned Lipsett throughout his career as a filmmaker.[18] The ten-minute film opens with loud machine noise. Then the film's title appears over a photo of a human skull; from its first moments, *21-87* juxtaposes the problem of human mortality with technological advancement in the Machine Age. Images of acrobatic human feats intersperse with those of decaying corpses, hacked apart by scientists (at least, one hopes such gore was prompted by scientific research). Images of humans acting like machines and machines doing the work of humans are overlaid with old-time Gospel music and scripture readings; "I don't believe in mortality," a woman says. In the next breath, a voice implores people to put their faith in "the plain, simple, ordinary facts of life."[19] Then, as disturbing images of human suffering and stupidity transition to more pastoral scenes, a gentle voice breaks in:

> Many people feel that in, sort of, the contemplation of nature and in communication with other living things, they become aware of some kind of a . . . force . . . or something . . . behind this apparent mask which we see in front of us. And they call it God or they . . . you know, depending on their particular disposition.[20]

Further explanation of this intriguing "force" is interrupted by another man's voice: "And somebody walks up, and you say, 'Your number's 21-87, isn't it?'

---

[17] *Remembering Arthur*, directed by Martin Lauvet (2006; Montreal: Public Pictures/NFBC), https://www.nfb.ca/film/remembering_arthur/.

[18] Chris Gehman and Brett Kashmere, "Introduction" to *Strange Codes:* [*an anthology of Arthur Lipsett*]. Forthcoming. Shared via personal communication with Brett Kashmere, January 5, 2022.

[19] *21-87*, directed by Arthur Lipsett, (1963; Montreal: National Film Board of Canada), https://www.nfb.ca/film/21-87/.

[20] Ibid. Also, see Williams for more on this audio's source: a discarded, recorded conversation between Warren S. McCulloch, the artificial intelligence pioneer, and documentarian Roman Kroitor. The clip is Kroitor's response to McCulloch's materialist belief that living things are merely sophisticated machines. Rohan Williams, "21-87: A Star Wars Odyssey," on *Force Material* (blog), September 18, [no year]), accessed January 7, 2022, http://www.forcematerial.com/home/2016/8/28/2187-a-star-wars-odyssey. See also Silberman.

Boy, does that person really, uh, smile."[21] Lipsett's film is relentless and grotesque in its combination of image and sound, depicting technology, machines, suffering, and transcendence. By the film's end, the machine noise becomes indistinguishable from a human moan—of pleasure or pain, it's hard to say. Flashing images, cries, and gunshots mark the film's end, with a repetition of the eponymous audio, "'Your number's 21-87, isn't it?' Boy, does that person really, uh, smile." The film leaves the viewer with the distinct impression that the Machine Age, in which people are numbers without reference to any non-material reality, has the last say, and this triumph of technology and conformity should make us "smile."

Albert Ohayon notes, as many have, that Lucas was "so impressed by Lipsett and this film that he would refer to the film's title in the first *Star Wars* film."[22] Lucas said, "*21-87* had a very powerful effect on me. It was very much the kind of thing that I wanted to do."[23] And it was the kind of thing Lucas *did* do. His original short *Electronic Labyrinth THX 1138 4EB* nods to Lipsett in its moments of audio-visual disconnect, in its Machine-Age-inspired title and in its setting in the year 2187, an intentional allusion to Lipsett.[24] Famously, Lucas would allude to Lipsett again in 1977's *Star Wars,* assigning Princess Leia Organa the prison cell number 2187 on Tarkin's Imperial Star Destroyer—a fitting number to represent the way humanity's organic inclination toward transcendence can be imprisoned by the technology-aided will to dominate others.

21-87 in the Original Trilogy

So much more than the source of passing allusions, however profound, the influence of *21-87* on Lucas's work is particularly notable in the way it helped Lucas articulate what Paul McDonald calls "the most unique character in *Star Wars,* the one that permeates, guides, and flows through the complete saga. . . Its ineffable presence is what truly makes *Star Wars* mythic": the Force.[25] McDonald describes the Force—particularly the Living Force—in *Star Wars* as "grounded in the present moment, the 'here and now,' the only reality we can truly know . . . steeped in flashes of intuition and focused spontaneity, as well as an empathy with and deep connection to all beings."[26] McDonald's

---

[21] *21-87,* directed by Arthur Lipsett, 1963.

[22] Albert Ohayon, "Point of View: *21-87,*" National Film Board of Canada website, accessed January 4, 2022, https://www.nfb.ca/film/21-87/.

[23] George Lucas, quoted in Silberman, "Life After Darth."

[24] Silberman, "Life After Darth."

[25] Paul F. McDonald, *The* Star Wars *Heresies: Interpreting the Themes, Symbols and Philosophies of Episodes I, II and III* (Jefferson, NC: McFarland, 2013), 7.

[26] Ibid., 8.

description could have been lifted straight from the reels of Lipsett's *21-87*, which described a "force," a divine presence, beheld through contemplation of nature and connection with other beings, with the power to create a "larger multi-reality situation such as the collective consciousness . . . ."[27] Such a shared consciousness is a familiar and beloved concept to *Star Wars* fans, whose response to the Force has made it one of the most inviting, inclusive, and enduring features of the franchise.

Yet Lipsett's film sets this benign force of connection and transcendence against its opposite: a reliance on technology that dehumanizes, making false connections, as in the film's eponymous audio clip. It is not a new dilemma, but one that has intrigued philosophers for millenia, treated even in the ancient Hindu text the *Bhagavad Gita*. According to Steven J. Rosen, the *Gita* teaches the proper approach to the material world, including technology, is a selfless employment of it, in service of God.[28] Lucas reports that his own studies of such themes from world religions—and, we can assume, the influence of Lipsett—convinced him that this juxtaposition of the transcendent with the machine-dependent is a

> . . . battle between selfishness and selflessness . . . that being selfish is based on fear—the battle is between fear and no fear. You're afraid of everything and everybody, so you mask it with all this other stuff. But if you can be brave enough to be compassionate to other people, regardless of the consequence, then you will have a happy life.[29]

Two characters in Lucas's original saga express this juxtaposition, inspired by *21-87*, most clearly: Darth Vader and Luke Skywalker. When Vader appears in the opening scenes of *A New Hope*, he presents a disturbing contradiction. Aesthetically stunning, with flowing black capes, a sweeping, Samurai-style helmet[30] and technology-enhanced strength,[31] at once, Vader is clearly

---

[27] Arthur Lipsett, letter to Kit Carson, quoted in Does, *Do Not Look Away*, 62.

[28] Steven J. Rosen, *The Jedi in the Lotus: Star Wars and the Hindu Tradition* (London: Arktos Media, 2010), 127.

[29] Lucas, quoted in Frakes et al., *James Cameron's The Story of Science Fiction*, 99.

[30] *Star Wars Episode IV: A New Hope*, directed by George Lucas (1977; Beverly Hills, CA: 20th Century Fox/Lucasfilm Ltd.), Disney+, https://www.disneyplus.com/movies/star-wars-a-new-hope-episode-iv/12fVeZxD2fWJ. For photo comparisons and discussion of Vader's samurai roots, see Terrance MacMullan, "Elegant Weapons For Civilized Ages," in *Star Wars and History*, ed. Nancy R. Reagin and Janice Liedl (Hoboken, NJ: John Wiley & Sons, Inc., 2013), 78-83.

[31] *Star Wars Tech*, directed by Rick Hill (2007; San Francisco: Lucasfilm Ltd.). According to Wookieepedia, "The one-hour program (46 minutes without commercials) debuted on

unnatural, despotic, and cruel in his manipulation of this mysterious "Force." His rasping breath tells audiences that his suit is a technological contingency plan against death; as the saga unfolds, viewers understand this figure as one who has succumbed to the machine-dependent world of self-preservation, imprisoned as Darth Vader. Rosen says Vader, with his "callous hatred," shows us, "how vicious technology could be."[32]

Luke is his opposite: young, whole, and duty-bound to his family, then to Obi-Wan and his friends. He resolutely and bravely sees the best in people—like Leia, to whom his good instincts draw him. In an obvious nod to Lipsett's ideas (not just his film title), Luke rescues his Force-sensitive counterpart from cell number "21-87," where she has been imprisoned by evil machine-man Vader.[33] Vader, ironically, is the principal figure on whom Luke bestows his signature, self-sacrificing compassion. This is because, as he grows in knowledge of the all-connecting Force, Luke recognizes that part of him *is* Darth Vader, as symbolized in the cave scene in *Star Wars Episode V: The Empire Strikes Back* (1980).[34] This realization foreshadows the revelation in *Empire* that Vader is Luke's father. Even after Vader cuts off Luke's hand, forcing him to become part-machine himself,[35] even after Force-ghost Obi-Wan Kenobi tells Luke, in *Star Wars Episode VI: Return of the Jedi* (1983), that Vader is "more machine, now, than man . . . twisted and evil,"[36] still Luke refuses to break his connection to his father through violence. Luke, with his lightsaber, his mechanical hand, and his very different-from-Vader choices, shows audiences that technology "is as good or bad as the person who uses it."[37] In the end, Luke, who uses technology in the service of good (represented by the light side of the Force), saves Vader from the twin prisons of his selfishness and his suit, inspiring Anakin Skywalker to once again view the world through the prism of his own, human eyes, instead of through the machine.

The History Channel on May 28, 2007, coinciding roughly with the 30-year anniversary of *Star Wars*. The program was later released on DVD and was included in the *Star Wars* saga Blu-Ray box set" (https://starwars.fandom.com/wiki/Star_Wars_Tech, accessed May 5, 2022). It had been available Disney+ but is no longer listed there.

[32] Rosen, *The Jedi in the Lotus*, 117.

[33] *Star Wars Episode IV: A New Hope*, directed by George Lucas, 1977.

[34] *Star Wars Episode V: The Empire Strikes Back*, directed by Irvin Kerschner (1980; Beverly Hills, CA: 20th Century Fox/Lucasfilm Ltd.), Disney+, https://www.disneyplus.com/movies/star-wars-the-empire-strikes-back-episode-v/iqtDTZAewwYl.

[35] Ibid.

[36] *Star Wars Episode VI: Return of the Jedi*, directed by Richard Marquand (1983; Beverly Hills, CA: 20th Century Fox/Lucasfilm Ltd.), Disney+, https://www.disneyplus.com/movies/star-wars-return-of-the-jedi-episode-vi/6QGKo5mjDBS8.

[37] Rosen, *The Jedi in the Lotus*, 123.

"How's Arthur Lipsett? He's a very important guy." Lucas reportedly made such an inquiry to Derek Lamb of the National Film Board of Canada after an NFB screening in California.[38] *Star Wars* shows Lucas's regard for Lipsett's work, and Lucas seems to have shared Lipsett's view that technology is far less essential to what it means to be human than our connection to one another and to a shared, transcendent reality. But Lucas, in *Star Wars*, comes to a different ultimate conclusion than Lipsett, whose film ends bleakly with the "21-87" audio, representing the triumph of the Machine Age. Lucas's original *Star Wars* trilogy takes a decidedly more hopeful tack. "The film industry," says Taylor, "would produce a slate of sour science fiction futures in the 1970s," but Lucas ended that trend with his wildly-popular *Star Wars* trilogy and its signature happy endings.[39] Through the triumph of selfless Luke Skywalker, the transcendent hero, over Darth Vader, the selfish machine-man, *Star Wars* allows that "force . . . or something" of Arthur Lipsett's *21-87* to triumph over the Machine Age as well.

21-87 in the Prequel era

The Prequel Trilogy, on the other hand, is not famous for its happy endings. Despite its lack of direct allusions to Lipsett's film, viewers can clearly observe, in subtle and not-so-subtle ways, the lasting influence of Lipsett's ideas on the storytelling of the Prequel era. Though the ending of *Star Wars Episode III: Revenge of the Sith* (2005) appears bleak, woven into the story are the hopeful ideas, first gleaned from Lipsett but transformed by Lucas's signature optimism, that natural man and the transcendent realm will ultimately endure.

The Prequel Trilogy is often considered the story of Anakin Skywalker's fall, but the films also tell the story of Obi-Wan Kenobi's survival and, through him, that of Luke Skywalker and the Jedi Order itself. In *Star Wars Episode I: The Phantom Menace* (1999), Obi-Wan defeats Sith Lord Darth Maul when his far more experienced Master, Qui-Gon Jinn, perishes on Maul's blade.[40] In *Star Wars Episode II: Attack of the Clones* (2002), Obi-Wan survives an encounter with Jango Fett, the galaxy's baddest bounty hunter; Obi-Wan is captured by the Separatists, attacked by arena beasts, and even survives the ire of another Sith Lord, Count Dooku.[41] The audience's foreknowledge that

---

[38] Seigel, "A Clown Outside the Circus," 13.

[39] Taylor, *How Star Wars Conquered the Universe*, 53.

[40] *Star Wars Episode I: The Phantom Menace*, directed by George Lucas (1999; Beverly Hills, CA: 20th Century Fox/Lucasfilm Ltd.), Disney+, https://www.disneyplus.com/movies/star-wars-the-phantom-menace-episode-i/2ezYynkgW1AH.

[41] *Star Wars Episode II: Attack of the Clones*, directed by George Lucas (2002; Beverly Hills, CA: 20th Century Fox/Lucasfilm Ltd.), Disney+, https://www.disneyplus.com/movies/star-wars-

Obi-Wan must survive each deadly challenge of the Prequels and someday become "old Ben" of *A New Hope* does nothing to cut the suspense of his many survivals but only enhances the hopeful, unbeatable quality of his character as the quintessential Jedi Knight.

In *Revenge of the Sith,* Obi-Wan clashes with his ultimate nemesis: General Grievous, the "fiendish droid leader."[42] Grievous is a cruel, conspicuously congested, cyborg general who, though not Force-sensitive, collects lightsabers as trophies of the Jedi he has defeated.[43] The beginning of the film cleverly foreshadows the film-long clash between these two very different generals and, as McDonald notes, the larger theme their conflict conveys: that of "encroaching mechanization that increasingly threatens the galaxy."[44] This foreshadowing comes when Obi-Wan is nearly killed as buzz droids attack his starfighter in the film's first scenes. He must survive this first trial against machines, with Anakin's help, in order to make it to Grievous's ship, where Chancellor Palpatine is held captive. When Grievous first appears on screen, he is cloaked and coughing, a grim giant whose status—machine or man?—is not entirely clear. Fleshly eyes peer out from behind a skeletal mask, yet whatever kind of organic being he once was is now encased in a mechanized form.[45] Grievous particularly repulses audiences as a cyborg, who function in stories to play into our dangerous human desire for perfection and our anxiety about how that desire threatens to replace "a thoughtful mind with a mechanical brain, a creative intellect with information processing, love with heartless programming."[46]

Lucas has said that Grievous's main role was as an echo of Anakin's transformation to machine-man.[47] But just as significant is Grievous's

---

attack-of-the-clones-episode-ii/mgpYHGnzZW6N. Count Dooku was the Master of Obi-Wan's Master, Qui-Gon Jinn.

[42] Opening crawl from *Star Wars Episode III: Revenge of the Sith,* directed by George Lucas (2005; Beverly Hills, CA: 20th Century Fox/Lucasfilm Ltd.), Disney+, https://www.disneyplus.com/movies/star-wars-revenge-of-the-sith-episode-iii/4WvbqLFumNvi.

[43] Laura Gilbert (for DK) and Jonathan W. Rinzler (for Lucasfilm), ed., *Star Wars Revenge of the Sith: The Visual Dictionary* (London: DK, 2005), 23.

[44] McDonald, *The* Star Wars *Heresies,* 145.

[45] According to the *Revenge of the Sith Visual Dictionary,* Grievous had been a Kaleesh warlord who was rebuilt as a cyborg "On the brink of death following a shuttle crash" (23). The text implies that Sidious/Palpatine himself arranged the crash and oversaw this cybernetic reconstruction (24), which preserved only Grievous's eyes, brain, spinal cord and internal organs. Apparently, "the General is secretly humiliated at having been resurrected as a cyborg" (22). Gilbert and Rinzler, ed., *Star Wars Revenge of the Sith: The Visual Dictionary,* 22-24.

[46] Rosen, *The Jedi in the Lotus,* 117.

[47] J.W. Rinzler, *The Art of Star Wars Episode III: Revenge of the Sith* (New York: Del Rey Books, 2005), 213.

narrative function as a foil to Kenobi, evidenced by their repeated face-offs and by Grievous's ultimate defeat at Kenobi's hand. Compare Grievous with Obi-Wan Kenobi, who is "old Ben": the sole vessel of knowledge of the Force, of transcendent reality, to Luke Skywalker (and viewers) in Lucas's original film. He represents the Jedi, an order all but extinct in the Imperial age of Luke's youth, who are "spiritual beings *in* the mundane world of matter, technology, politics, and desires, who are not *of* this world."[48] Ben is the wise old monk who knows one must *feel* the Force, that unifying connection between all living things, before one can use it—and then only for a higher purpose.[49] Obi-Wan is the sole representative of the power and possibility of the transcendent realm in 1977's *Star Wars*; it is his voice from beyond the grave that encourages Luke to make his "one-in-a-million" shot, bringing down the ultimate emblem of the Imperial war machine: the Death Star.[50] Grievous mocks Kenobi when they meet on the big screen, calling him "The Negotiator," highlighting a major difference between the two; whereas Grievous is always spoiling for a fight, Kenobi "prefers negotiation to conflict," and has historically had "an affinity for deflection" in his lightsaber technique.[51]

Grievous, by contrast, is an aggressive, ghoulish emblem of the larger, diseased, genocidal machine of the Empire, who wishes for a world in which there are no Jedi, no limits on the use of power, no real meaning except for that which comes from the material existence of those physically strong enough to dominate. The *Star Wars: The Clone Wars* (2008-2014, 2020) episode "Grievous Intrigue" explores these motivations, in contrast to Kenobi's, more closely, showing Grievous as motivated not by political ideology but by the will to dominate through machines by being "the leader of the most powerful droid army the galaxy has ever seen,"[52] as he tells Kenobi in the heat of battle. Kenobi responds to this boast by pointing out, in phrasing that echoes Rosen's observations, that Grievous and the Separatist army have "no loyalty, no spirit, just programming. What have you to show for all your power, what have you to gain?" he asks Grievous, who responds, "A future . . . a future where there are no Jedi." Pinning Kenobi to the ground, Grievous declares, "the story of Obi-Wan Kenobi ends here,"[53] implying that through Kenobi's end at Grievous's many hands, so too ends honor, friendship, and the life of

---

[48] MacMullan, "Elegant Weapons For Civilized Ages," 70.

[49] Ibid.

[50] *Star Wars Episode IV: A New Hope*, directed by George Lucas, 1977.

[51] Gilbert and Rinzler, *Star Wars Revenge of the Sith: The Visual Dictionary*, 10.

[52] *Star Wars: The Clone Wars*, season 2, episode 9, "Grievous Intrigue," directed by Giancarlo Volpe, written by Ben Edlund, aired January 1, 2010, on Cartoon Network, Disney+, https://www.disneyplus.com/video/83357ef1-f768-4f3b-8b03-2f0c2e4617e7.

[53] Ibid.

the spirit. In fact, Kenobi gets the best of Grievous in that battle by using the Force to throw one of Grievous's own felled battle droids at him, but Grievous escapes when Kenobi spares his life, whatever is left of it, allowing the existential rivalry between them to continue.[54] It's a rivalry Arthur Lipsett might well have recognized as inspired by his own film *21-87* and its uncomfortable juxtaposition of transcendent human connection with the will to violence and domination through technology.

Grievous greets Obi-Wan with familiarity in the opening scenes of *Revenge of the Sith*, because these two have clashed, as exampled above, throughout the Clone War that has diegetically preceded *Episode III* (though this "prequel to the prequel" material was released after *Episode III*). Grievous escapes his first filmic clash with Obi-Wan by shattering the windscreen of his own ship (an old trick of Grievous's, for those who've watched *The Clone Wars*), allowing his pressurized self to be sucked out into the vacuum of space, knowing his fully-organic opponents cannot survive such exposure.[55] "You lose, General Kenobi!" he cries. Only strength and quick thinking by the Jedi save the good guys,[56] for now. From this point, the Clone War itself seems tied to the continuing existence of Grievous, and he becomes the target of Republic forces.

When the general's whereabouts are later determined, Obi-Wan is deliberately chosen over Anakin to lead the campaign against him, again highlighting this rivalry of opposites. Kenobi rides into battle with Grievous not in his starfighter, but mounted on a varactyl—a giant, organic beast—taking time to lovingly pet the beautiful creature before jumping into battle on his own against Grievous and innumerable battle droids.[57] This hopeless outnumbering recalls Kenobi's lone representation of the Jedi amid the machine of the Galactic Empire in Lucas's original 1977 film. Another clash ensues, this one to the death. A close-up of Grievous's diseased-looking eyes is followed immediately by a parallel close-up of Obi-Wan's clear, blue gaze as he defies the machine general's threats. Grievous, soon partially dismembered by Kenobi, resorts to machine assistance, hopping into an armed wheel bike speeder to flee. Kenobi, his parallel opposite, summons his organic mount to pursue. Having dropped his lightsaber, Obi-Wan uses his bare hands to expose Grievous's organic heart center. Then, hanging precariously from a landing platform, Kenobi uses the Force to summon a nearby weapon, finishing the general with a few well-aimed

---

54 Ibid.

55 From the *Episode III Visual Dictionary*: Grievous's "Gut sack is pressurized synthskin, allowing Grievous to survive in a vacuum." Gilbert and Rinzler, *Star Wars Revenge of the Sith: The Visual Dictionary*, 24.

56 *Star Wars Episode III: Revenge of the Sith*, directed by George Lucas, 2005.

57 Ibid.

blaster bolts to the cyborg's exposed chest. Tossing the blaster aside, Kenobi mutters, "so uncivilized,"[58] humorously recalling old Ben's line from *A New Hope* describing the lightsaber ("an elegant weapon for a more civilized age"[59]). This is more than a gag; it functions to keep viewers cognizant of a recurring theme bridging all eras of *Star Wars*, one inspired by Lipsett's *21-87*: the moral superiority of the organic, transcendent life, over and above a violent, machine-dependent existence.

Another aspect of *Star Wars*'s Prequel era storytelling shows Lipsett's profound and lasting influence as well: the fact that the army of the Republic and the Jedi are not droids like the Separatist soldiers but organic—if mass-produced—human clones. Setting aside the myriad moral dilemmas of utilizing cloned humans for warfare, Lipsett's influence can be read in the way these cloned soldiers, especially as depicted in *The Clone Wars* television show, insist upon their own identities, emblematized in their preference for names over numbers. In "The Deserter," Obi-Wan's continued hunt for Grievous forms a frame narrative for a story about a clone trooper who defected and now leads a civilian life, with a farm and a family, on the planet Saleucemi: Cut Lawquane. Clone Captain Rex takes shelter on his farm after an injury, and when the two clones meet, Rex asks for Cut's "number and rank;" Cut responds with his name.[60] When Rex calls him a "deserter," Lawquane responds that he is "merely exercising my freedom to choose, choose not to kill for a living."[61] Over a meal, the discussion continues, with Cut reminding Rex, "you and I may be clones, but we're still individuals," and asking why Rex goes by a name instead of a number. Rex seems unprepared for the question, giving an illogical answer about efficiency and admitting to never having thought about these issues. Cut clearly has, articulating that "a name has to make you feel unique, especially in an army where everyone looks like you and talks like you." Cut and Rex's debate about individuality and personal choice ends in a lesson for Cut's children on the meaning of the phrase "to each his own" and the importance of being able to choose what to do with one's own life.[62] Especially in the way numbers versus names symbolize a machine-dictated, conformist existence versus the freedom of personal choice and expression in this episode, one can hear the echoing influence of Lipsett's thesis warning against a machine-based future,

---

[58] Ibid.

[59] *Star Wars Episode IV: A New Hope*, directed by George Lucas, 1977.

[60] *Star Wars: The Clone Wars*, season 2, episode 10, "The Deserter," directed by Robert Dalva, written by Carl Ellsworth, aired January 1, 2010, on Cartoon Network, Disney+, https://www.disneyplus.com/video/09f9af96-40bd-4e9a-a18d-92fb9f373298.

[61] Ibid.

[62] Ibid.

expressed in his repeated use of the audio that became eponymous for his film: "'Your number's 21-87, isn't it?' Boy, does that person really, uh, smile."

This theme threads throughout *The Clone Wars*. In Season 1, Episode 1, "Ambush," Yoda requests his clone troopers remove their helmets so he can see their faces. When they remind him they all have the same face, he tells them, "In the Force, very different each one of you are. . . . Clones you may be," he says. "But the Force resides in all life-forms."[63] This certainly cannot be said of the Separatist droid army, indicating both the greater effectiveness and moral superiority of the Jedi's clone army. In Season 4, Episode 9, when the clones question their Jedi general's orders to march into a slaughter, they are tempted to defy orders. In the debate that ensues, Captain Rex reminds trooper Fives to trust in the system, and Fives retorts that while he does believe in the Republic, he insists he is "not just another number."[64] Even more pervasively, *The Clone Wars* expresses this theme of the clones' ironic individuality and moral refusal to be seen as mere "numbers" in the wide visual variety with which it depicts the clones; they tattoo their faces, dye or shave their hair, and decorate their armor, all for the implied purpose of individuating themselves. This overarching theme in *The Clone Wars* is summed up retrospectively in the post-Lucas *Star Wars* television show, *The Bad Batch* (2021-), which explores the immediate aftermath of Order 66 and the transition of clone troopers into Stormtroopers. After discovering the new Galactic requirement that all citizens be issued chain codes to obtain rights such as travel, Echo remarks: "It's ironic. Clones wanted names instead of numbers, yet now people are signing up to be given numbers."[65] This desire to "be" a number is judged by the show's sympathetic characters as a social regression or devolution. Indeed, even the name "*chain* code" suggests that this biometric identifier, instituted by the new Galactic Empire for the ostensible purpose of efficiency, also serves to curb the freedoms of those who bear them. This is a clear reflection of *21-87*, which Gehman and Kashmere say expresses Lipsett's belief that social conformity will create mindless masses who only appear happy and free.[66]

---

[63] *Star Wars: The Clone Wars*, season 1, episode 1, "Ambush," directed by Dave Bullock, written by Steven Melching, aired October 3, 2008, on Cartoon Network, Disney+, https://www.disneyplus.com/video/0bf87f10-d9a1-44ca-8371-f38543eb3706.

[64] *Star Wars: The Clone Wars*, season 4, episode 9, "Plan of Dissent," directed by Kyle Dunlevy, written by Matt Michnovetz, aired November 11, 2011, on Cartoon Network, Disney+, https://www.disneyplus.com/video/5dfa03d3-ec0c-462e-96b9-9995bb5b7e1d.

[65] *Star Wars: The Bad Batch*, season 1, episode 2, "Cut and Run," directed by Steward Lee, written by Gursimran Sandhu, aired May 7, 2021, Disney+, https://www.disneyplus.com/video/382d40ec-932e-4ff5-a7db-e2a949e74a20.

[66] Chris Gehman and Brett Kashmere, "Introduction" to *Strange Codes*, forthcoming.

Before moving to other post-Lucas works that reflect Lipsett's ideas, we must return to *Episode III: Revenge of the Sith* for two more key pointers to Lipsett's influence. The conclusion of the Clone War is achieved tragically through Order 66 and the destruction of the Jedi, which *Episode III* depicts in grim detail. Kenobi—almost alone among the Jedi—evades the Imperial machine in its genocide of his Order, secreting away the hope of the Jedi, baby Luke Skywalker.[67] At the same time, Luke's twin sister Leia (who will eventually become "Prisoner 2187" in *A New Hope*[68]) is preserved by the Organa family. Both these hopeful survivals point to the lingering influence of Lipsett's ideas on *Star Wars*: that appreciation of the natural, organic world (symbolized by the family name "Organa") and the possibility of shared, transcendent reality (represented by Obi-Wan and Luke's survivals) are humanity's best hope against the horrific possibilities of a machine-based future.

21-87 in a new era of *Star Wars*

In the post-Lucas era, *Star Wars* creators are arguably most successful when they rely for inspiration less on *Star Wars* itself and more on that which inspired *Star Wars* from its origins. This helps explain the success of *The Mandalorian* (2019-), in its emulation of the same Japanese samurai films and classic Westerns that inspired George Lucas. The filmic ideas of Arthur Lipsett are certainly at work in the Sequel Trilogy, lending these modern installments of the Skywalker saga a depth of meaning that helps to overcome some of their faults. Primarily, Lipsett's thesis about humanity's power in embracing a shared, transcendent reality to overcome the evils of the Machine Age are on display in the reluctant First Order Stormtrooper who bears the designation FN-2187.

Star Wars The Force Awakens: The Visual Dictionary gives some helpful background about Tuanul Village, the setting of the first Sequel film's opening scenes, and why, despite that FN-2187 was there with "more than sixty stormtroopers to pacify" the village,[69] it had a pacifying effect on him instead. Lor San Tekka, the old man sought by Poe Dameron and the Resistance for

---

[67] *Star Wars Episode III: Revenge of the Sith*, directed by George Lucas, 2005.

[68] Alexandra Bracken, *A New Hope: The Princess, the Scoundrel, and the Farm Boy* (Glendale, CA: Disney Lucasfilm Press, 2015), 54. In this middle-reader novel re-telling the story of *Star Wars Episode IV: A New Hope*, when Leia is referred to as "prisoner two-one-eight-seven" by a Stormtrooper, she briefly considers what this designation means, concluding that to the Empire, "She was a low enough life form that she no longer deserved a name," 55.

[69] Sadie Smith (for DK) and Jonathan W. Rinzler (for Lucasfilm), ed., *Star Wars The Force Awakens: The Visual Dictionary* (New York: DK Publishing, 2015), 15.

information on the whereabouts of Luke Skywalker, is a spiritual leader among a colony of Church of the Force followers who have created "an oasis of life in the otherwise empty Kelvin Ravine" on Jakku and "who praise the virtues of the Force without being graced by the ability to wield it."[70] These religionists "reject the trappings of warfare, especially . . . profit-driven conflicts that have polluted much of the galaxy," defending their village and way of life against the First Order with hand-made weapons.[71] The *Visual Dictionary* does what the film didn't spare time for in painting San Tekka and his village as the flickering light of the Jedi way of life, keeping the flame of transcendent reality alive in a galaxy now ruled by the First Order, a machine of warfare and dominance. FN-2187 is described in the *Visual Dictionary* as "a product of the First Order's methodical, systemized military training programs" yet lacking "the combat zeal or submission to authority evident in his squadmates" and as "more concerned with protecting his squadmates than bringing order to the galaxy."[72] Though FN-2187 hides his misgivings with the First Order during his training, his "spotless profile does not survive a brutal night assault on a sacred village on Jakku."[73] This is because, the Sequels strongly imply as they unfold, FN-2187 is an inherently sacred and spiritual being himself, and destroying Tuanul village, by the light of the Force worshiped there that also resides in him, is an act of self-destruction. This reluctant Stormtrooper, whose moniker FN-2187 is drawn more from Lipsett's film than from Lucas's allusion to it in *Star Wars: A New Hope*, strongly rebuts the same claim Lipsett warns against; that anyone can be truly happy as a nameless servant of the Machine.

Finn, as he becomes known in *Star Wars Episode VII: The Force Awakens* (2015), literally sheds the machine that was his prison, dropping pieces of his Stormtrooper armor all over the wild sands of Jakku.[74] Soon, he meets Rey, who lives alone in the ruins of the Galactic Empire, in one of its more famous machines of death, an AT-AT walker. She is—interestingly, in light of what we know about Arthur Lipsett's filmmaking process—a scavenger who, like Lipsett, cobbles together others' cast-offs to make a living and to maintain her independence. Together, she and Finn help BB-8 (a droid who carries information about Skywalker, the last Jedi, and whose roundness implies

---

[70] Ibid.

[71] Ibid.

[72] Ibid., 20.

[73] Ibid.

[74] *Star Wars Episode VII: The Force Awakens*, directed by J.J. Abrams (2015; San Francisco: Disney/Lucasfilm Ltd.), Disney+, https://www.disneyplus.com/movies/star-wars-the-force-awakens-episode-vii/1LEKJPDPeMr7.

spirituality[75]) escape the First Order. If Rey allegorically stands in for the scavenger-visionary Lipsett, then Finn, formerly of the Machine, does best when he allows Rey to take the lead, symbolized in their humorous squabble over whose hand should be taken as they escape the First Order.[76] Though Rey is pegged early in the film as having Force-sensitivity, Finn is the first character in the Sequels to ignite a lightsaber,[77] implying his natural affinity for the Jedi way of life.

Like Obi-Wan Kenobi in the Prequels, Finn has a foil in the Sequels: Captain Phasma, who never removes her helmet on screen, criticizing Finn for removing his and for his weakness at Tuanul village.[78] Her orders that he be reconditioned spur him to escape with Resistance fighter Poe.[79] Finn bests Phasma more than once in the films, at one point in *The Force Awakens,* depositing her in a trash compactor,[80] but Finn's defeat of Phasma in *Star Wars Episode VIII: The Last Jedi* (2017) is a monumental event in his character arc. Her line to him, "You are a bug in the system,"[81] shows the opposite has become true—lowly FN-2187 has indeed disturbed the First Order. With a mighty whack, Finn cracks her chrome helmet, exposing one terrified blue eye before she falls to a fiery death, calling him scum. But Finn is now "rebel scum,"[82] so even her insult acts as a confirmation of his new life, in which he rebels against the Machine to embrace his own individuality and his transcendent connection with others.

But Finn's destiny in the Sequels is not merely to join the Resistance, however much of an improvement it represents for the former FN-2187. Finn experiences the painful realization on Canto Bight in *The Last Jedi* that the perpetual conflict between Bad Guys and Good Guys fuels a culture of war profiteering that lines the pockets of the already-rich and keeps the oppressed pinned down. Criminal DJ assures Finn that "it's all a machine, partner. Live free, don't join."[83] Finn's own near-death experience fighting the

---

[75] Emily Strand, "Keep your Eye on the Ball!" *Hogwarts Professor* (blog), December 27, 2015, https://www.hogwartsprofessor.com/guest-post-keep-your-eye-on-the-ball-circular-imagery-in-new-force-awakens-echoes-the-rings-in-harry-potter/.

[76] *Star Wars Episode VII: The Force Awakens,* directed by J.J. Abrams, 2015.

[77] Ibid.

[78] Ibid.

[79] Ibid.

[80] Ibid.

[81] *Star Wars Episode VIII: The Last Jedi,* directed by Rian Johnson (2017; San Francisco: Disney/Lucasfilm Ltd.), Disney+, https://www.disneyplus.com/movies/star-wars-the-last-jedi-episode-viii/1nCWFK1pmAI0.

[82] Ibid.

[83] Ibid.

First Order at the end of the film[84] cements this realization of the futility of a materialist perspective, pushing Finn's three-film character arc beyond the First Order, beyond the Resistance. The final Sequel film implies he belongs in the shared, transcendent reality of Rey's new Jedi Order.

Star Wars Episode IX: The Rise of Skywalker (2019)'s first clue that Finn is Jedi material comes when Finn, Rey, Poe, and the others are sinking in a sand pit on Pasana, and Finn calls out to Rey that there's something he never told her.[85] Though viewers never hear what Finn wanted to share, the nature of his revelation slowly becomes clear, in part through Finn's conversation with Jannah, another Stormtrooper deserter. Significantly, Finn and Jannah share their former numeric designations (one more overt allusion to Lipsett). When Jannah marvels at what could have possibly caused her and her fellow troopers to desert, Finn, with great certainty, identifies it as "an instinct . . . a feeling . . . The Force,"[86] which, he says, brought him to Rey, Poe, and now Jannah. In the film's conclusion, Finn and Jannah team up to bring down the command ship of the Final Order, the ultimate war machine, just as Poe and the Resistance are ready to give up. Here the Final Order fleet, in neat rows and with a planet-killing weapon on every ship, is contrasted with the hodge-podge, unorganized, individual but abundant fleet of "just people,"[87] whom Lando Calrissian has brought to stand up to them. In the end, it is Finn's and Jannah's actions, just as much as Rey's and Ben's, that bring an end to the threat of the Final Order war machine in the Sequel Trilogy.[88] The final confirmation of Finn's strong connection to the Force is his ability to sense Rey's death after her confrontation with Palpatine.[89] Fortunately, her death is reversed by the self-sacrifice of Ben Solo, and the possibility that she and Finn will serve together to rebuild the Jedi Order glows brightly in the viewer's imagination. When Finn, Poe, and Rey embrace at the film's end (also the Sequel Trilogy's end), it is a symbolic and harmonious joining of the three main forces that create conflict in *Star Wars*: Jedi (Rey), Empire (Finn), and Rebellion (Poe). This harmonious union hints at the hope and possibility of a future in which all people can live in the dignity, peace, and freedom that comes from embracing a shared, transcendent reality.

---

[84] Ibid.

[85] *Star Wars Episode IX: The Rise of Skywalker*, directed by J.J. Abrams (2019; San Francisco: Disney/Lucasfilm Ltd.), Disney+, https://www.disneyplus.com/movies/star-wars-the-rise-of-skywalker-episode-ix/5e8JThYwCYgw.

[86] Ibid.

[87] Ibid.

[88] Ibid.

[89] Ibid.

Lipsett lives on

The Sequel Trilogy may be complete, but *Star Wars*'s obsession with Lipsett—and with the challenge to our humanity from the Machine Age, so compellingly captured in his *21-87*—lives on in a new era of *Star Wars* streaming television. A multi-episode narrative arc in the 2022 first season of *Andor* captures Lipsett's thesis with devastating clarity and poignancy. Observant viewers will even notice, in these episodes treating Cassian Andor's brief stint in an Imperial prison facility on Narkina 5, another overt reference to Lipsett's film title (from a certain point of view), and other elements of the arc point to Lipsett's filmic ideas and even to aspects of his filmmaking style.

The arc begins in the seventh episode, "Announcement," when Cassian is arrested by shore troopers on the planet Niamos for literally nothing. Because of the Public Order Resentencing Directive, a repercussion of the successful rebel heist on Aldhani (in which Cassian himself played a role), he is sentenced to six years (rather than six months) of hard labor in an Imperial factory.[90] Eventually, audiences learn, from a hidden scene at the end of the season, that the machine part Cassian spends 34 twelve-hour shifts making on Narkina 5 is a component of the Death Star's weapons array,[91] but this information is hardly needed to invoke our dread; the audience can sense, from the moment the prisoners are told to take off their shoes, that Andor now faces a grim prospect on Narkina 5, becoming, as an article on StarWars.com describes, a "faceless servant of the Empire."[92]

This description of Cassian's predicament invokes Lipsett's thesis in *21-87*, as did Finn's predicament at the beginning of *The Force Awakens*. And just as with Finn's trooper designation and character arc, there are several strong pointers to Lipsett in the Narkina 5 arc. First, when Cassian steps out of the transport onto the prison facility platform, a fellow captive says to him, "Breathe deep, brother. This may be the last fresh air we ever taste."[93] Both his

---

[90] *Andor*, season 1, episode 7, "Announcement," directed by Benjamin Caron, written by Stephen Schiff, aired October 19, 2022, Disney+, https://www.disneyplus.com/video/a6963fa0-eb41-4ba8-a923-cb4e24946d90.

[91] *Andor*, season 1, episode 12, "Rix Road," directed by Benjamin Caron, written by Tony Gilroy, aired November 23, 2022, Disney+, https://www.disneyplus.com/video/78c53cd7-c7c1-40c4-b365-a56fae06799e. For more on the economic significance of this knowledge, see Vikki Terrile's chapter in this volume.

[92] Kristen Baver, "*Andor* Analyzed: 5 Highlights from Episode 8, 'Narkina 5,'" StarWars.com, November 1, 2022, https://www.starwars.com/news/andor-episode-8-narkina-5-highlights.

[93] *Andor*, season 1, episode 8, "Narkina 5," directed by Toby Haynes, written by Beau Willimon, aired October 26, 2022, Disney+, https://www.disneyplus.com/video/e552dfd3-ec1b-4046-8410-711114a2a4ef.

familial address and his urging of Cassian to appreciate nature while he can ring of Lipsett's film. Then Cassian and the others get a taste of the "minimally invasive"[94] disciplinary measures the rubber-booted guard explains are employed by the facility: electrifiable steel floors used to shock prisoners into submission through their bare feet. As a demonstration, Cassian and his fellows are shocked on the spot, and the jerky, stop-start editing here recalls the macabre style of Lipsett's film; Cassian and the others writhe in absurd-looking spasms of pain, and their gruesome postures and expressions recall a moment about seven minutes into Lipsett's film when young people are depicted flapping their hands and dancing in jerky, frenzied, disturbing ways while audio of heavy breathing overlays the images.[95] The way the film editing enhances the grotesquery and the lack of human dignity of these images in both films creates a striking parallel.

Another aspect of the arc creates a striking parallel with Lipsett's film. The prison staff on Narkina 5 employs a particular verbal command for obedience. The prisoners are routinely ordered "On Program," which indicates a mandatory posture of "hands on head, eyes front, feet on the floor."[96] This posture renders them inert, submissive, individual, and vulnerable to electric shock through the feet. The peculiar and consistent way in which this posture is referenced in the prison facility, "On *Program*," suggests—as Arthur Lipsett did with his footage of humans acting like machines and machines doing human work— that these men are programmed like droids for instant submission to their captors. When the order is given, compliance must be immediate—automatic, even—or electrocution will follow. To be "On Program" is to be a fully automated component of the Machine that is the Empire.

What's more, the rubber-booted guard's orientation speech to Cassian and the others upon their arrival at the facility indicates its methods, including "On Program," represent improvement and innovation compared to other Imperial detention facilities.[97] Indeed, Gerald Petschk calls it "one of the most ingenious prisons in the Empire."[98] The facility uses hydroelectric energy,[99]

---

[94] Ibid.

[95] *21-87*, directed by Arthur Lipsett, 1963.

[96] *Andor*, "Narkina 5."

[97] Ibid.

[98] Gerald Petschk, "Narkina 5 is One of the Most Ingenious Prisons in the Empire and This is Why," Culture Slate, November 17, 2022, https://www.cultureslate.com/explained/narkina-5-is-one-of-the-most-ingenious-prisons-in-the-empire-and-this-is-why.

[99] *Andor*, season 1, episode 10, "One Way Out," directed by Toby Haynes, written by Beau Willimon, aired November 9, 2023, Disney+, https://www.disneyplus.com/video/93c891d6-35cc-4f0f-9d1e-e16e89506ebc. In the following episode, we also learn there have been devastating environmental effects on local species due to the pollution of the moon's

levying nature's awesome power to create an unnatural, de-humanizing, mundane life of machine labor for its residents, many of whom, like Cassian, are unjustly imprisoned. In one scene, prisoners are shown walking together, naked, into a chamber in the facility; gas is released from the ceiling, presumably to clean them. This disturbing imagery references the gas chambers of the Nazis, in which Jews and those who would not conform were murdered en masse with machinic efficiency. In this allusion to gas chambers with its implication that human innovation can lead to our destruction as easily as our elevation, in the exploitation of nature for the Machine's desires, and in the ironic expectation that prisoners should be grateful for Narkina 5's innovative methods of evacuating their dignity, we hear echoes of *21-87* and especially its eponymous audio suggesting that the gruesome efficiency of the Machine should make us "smile."[100]

These similarities are compelling, but don't add up to a direct reference to Lipsett's work in *Andor*. To spot the very clever but somewhat shrouded direct reference to Lipsett in this arc, a bit of fun with numbers is in order. In Episode 7, Cassian is sentenced to six years hard labor. On Earth, a year consists of 365 days (roughly),[101] and 365 multiplied by six equals 2,190. The following day, after arriving on Narkina 5 and working a partial shift with his new table mates, Cassian is shown to his cell that displays his "tab,"[102] or the number of shifts he has left to work before his sentence is (supposedly) fully served. The number displayed is 2189, a number too close to *21-87* to ignore. Further, this number is given emphasis in the way it hovers above Cassian while he anxiously contemplates his predicament during his first night in his cell and in the way the camera focuses on the number to indicate the passage of time and a new scene, 30 shifts later.[103]

2,189 is two more than 2,187 ordinally, but from another perspective, it is simply one digit off from Lipsett's film's title: ending with a nine instead of a seven. So where's the seven? The answer is: everywhere. In this narrative arc, the number seven, contrary to its traditional representation of perfection or divinity,

---

waters by the Empire's prison facilities. *Andor*, season 1, episode 11, "Daughter of Ferrix," directed by Benjamin Caron, written by Tony Gilroy, aired November 16, 2022, Disney+, https://www.disneyplus.com/video/14b00711-9480-47e5-992e-592ddab074f5.

[100] *21-87*, directed by Arthur Lipsett, 1963.

[101] Of course, different planets may experience different lengths of days and years, but the length of a standard Earth year is a safe frame of reference, because it enables the audience to comprehend the severity of the sentence and charges against Cassian in the story-world. It is also consistent with the well acknowledged real-world approach to *Star Wars* employed by the creators of *Andor*.

[102] *Andor*, "Narkina 5."

[103] Ibid.

represents the Empire's labor-hungry, nature-exploiting system of subjugation and incarceration. On approach to Narkina 5, seven of the seven-sided Imperial prisons can be seen in the waters below. While orienting Cassian to his new life, floor manager Kino Loy explains that in each of these facilities there are "Seven levels of factory, seven rooms per level, seven tables per room, seven men each table."[104] That's a lot of sevens. Indeed, the place seems built on the number seven, which is also the number of seconds they have, once the floor lights begin to blink, to get to their separate cells before being fried. The repetitive use of this divinely associated number points to the hubris of the Empire, as Cassian's comments to Luthen Rael in the third episode express: "They're so proud of themselves, they don't even care. They're so fat and satisfied, they can't imagine . . . that someone like me would ever get inside their house."[105] This arrogance perhaps inspired, diegetically, the design of a prison system around the number for godly perfection. But from the perspective of directly referencing Lipsett's film, we might say we've found our missing number seven.

In fact, numbers crowd the Narkina 5 arc generally; numeric references (whether in dialogue or imagery) in the arc total over 140, with a concentration in the episode "Narkina 5," the title of which itself contains a numeric reference. And that number, five, plays an important balancing role to that of seven in the arc. Cassian is assigned to table five on level five of the complex. A large number five (as well as a two) feature prominently on sliding doors in the background as Cassian finally convinces Kino Loy to help lead an escape. The whole story takes place on the fifth moon in a star system, and more than once the prison population is numbered at 5,000.[106] The repetitive use of five could be related to the number five's symbolism of humanity. Humans have five extremities (two arms, two legs, and a head), and five digits on both hands and feet, and our outstretched bodies form the shape of a five-point star or pentagon.[107] Five is a sacred number in Islam; there are five foundational pillars of action that unite believers, and one of these is to pray five times daily. It is also the number of books in the Torah of Moses, that very human prophet of God, and it is the number of Christ's wounds inflicted in his human suffering and death. Ian

---

[104] Ibid.

[105] *Andor*, season 1, episode 3, "Reckoning," directed by Toby Haynes, written by Tony Gilroy, aired September 21, 2022, Disney+, https://www.disneyplus.com/video/76c8bb56-7cf6-4950-ae78-4fc998329ac7.

[106] The numbers Kino gives Cassian (seven men to a table, seven tables to a room, seven rooms to a level, seven levels to each complex) indicates a total for each complex of 4,802. To call it 5,000 is a significant rounding but proves symbolically effective.

[107] Ian Stewart, "number symbolism," Britannica.com, accessed January 26, 2023, https://www.britannica.com/topic/number-symbolism.

Stewart notes, perhaps because of its association with humanity, that five is also associated with rebelliousness.[108]

The Narkina 5 arc comes to its climax when the men of table five on level five, under Cassian's influence, rebel against the Machine. A convergence of events—Ulaf's pitiful death so close to his release, a report that prisoners are not actually released when their sentences are up but rather reassigned, the reported deaths of an entire floor of inmates who'd figured this out—finally convinces the reluctant Kino to help lead the escape. But Cassian plays a key role in convincing Kino to lead the charge in Episode 9, "Nobody's Listening!" Returning to the theme of the Empire's arrogance and lack of humanity, Cassian tells Kino that the Imperials who run the prison "don't need to care. All they need to do is turn their floor on twice a day and keep their numbers rolling . . . we are nothing to them. We're cheaper than droids and easier to replace."[109] When they overpower the command center on level eight, Cassian pushes Kino to instruct the prisoners over the loudspeakers, and from this point, a new number dominates the arc: one. Kino tells them there is "one way out" of the facility, and they must help each other to escape as one.[110]

This phrase becomes a chant of liberation for the escaping men. The number one has long symbolized unity and solidarity across many cultures, and here the prisoners' cries of "One Way Out!" (which forms Episode 10's title, too) affirm that solidarity of the oppressed is the only way to break the Machine. The phrase is not literal; there are multiple exits to the Imperial prison on Narkina 5 (at least three can be seen as they flee), but the "one way" they will escape is together, as *one*. This loudly echoes Lipsett's central thesis that transcendent power—a "force or something"—can be found in nature and in connection with others. Still chanting the arc's final, triumphant numeric formula, the men—full of the force of their own solidarity and freedom—leap into the waters surrounding the prison. The transcendent aerial shot that closes the prison break sequence is so high above them, the liberated prisoners could well be so many fish escaping their seven-sided tank to swim for freedom.

Perhaps with less of the optimistic twist on Lipsett's ideas that marks previous *Star Wars* stories, the Narkina 5 arc does not end without tragedy. Kino Loy reaches the edge of the prison platform only to realize that he cannot swim, and Cassian is pushed off the platform before he can help. Like

---

108 Ibid.

109 *Andor*, season 1, episode 9, "Nobody's Listening!" directed by Toby Haynes, written by Beau Willimon, aired November 2, 2022, Disney+, https://www.disneyplus.com/video/c41ac934-18c3-4871-8762-4bf3ac75966b.

110 *Andor*, "One Way Out."

Lipsett's *21-87,* the story ends bleakly, leaving audiences with the reminder that rebellions create wounds as well as heal them—a reminder in keeping with *21-87*'s stark ending and with the new show's dark, realistic tone.

"How's Arthur Lipsett? He's a very important guy."

Arthur Lipsett, that high priest of sight and sound who so impressed George Lucas as a student filmmaker, did not live to fully appreciate his own profound influence over *Star Wars,* either under its original creator or in the post-Lucas age. While 1977's *Star Wars* swept the globe in the years that followed its release, Lipsett lived a marginal existence. At ten years old, he had survived his mother's suicide,[111] and he suffered throughout his life from depression, anxiety,[112] and post-traumatic stress; he heard voices, had diagnosed over-sensitivity to sound,[113] paranoid schizophrenia,[114] and after 1970, when his time at the National Film Board of Canada ended, he fell into poverty and creative block, possibly caused by drugs, both prescribed and recreational.[115] Lois Seigel interviewed Lipsett in 1978, noting the difficulty of this endeavor, "because after a brief encounter with him, it becomes obvious that he rejects the standard, ready-made, machine-oriented, artificial way of life upon which most people pattern and pride themselves."[116] Friend and fellow filmmaker Tanya Tree summed up the isolated position in which Lipsett's own prophetic vision placed him: "He was trying to find universals in human culture, like an anthropologist. It was as if he, himself, were from another planet, looking at us all—as he did in his films."[117] Another filmmaker friend, Derek May, said Lipsett's temperament was one of "flirting dangerously with extreme marginality,"[118] and wondered callously whether suicide wasn't simply the outcome of that type of temperament. After many suicide attempts, Lipsett died by hanging himself in his home in 1986, just before his fiftieth birthday.[119]

Another friend of Lipsett, John Max, said, "Something is lacking in the group energy of our community that would permit to let happen what happened to Arthur."[120] In light of what Lipsett inspired in *Star Wars*—namely, Lucas's

---

[111] Does, *Do Not Look Away,* 26.
[112] Seigel, "A Clown Outside the Circus," 12.
[113] Does, *Do Not Look Away,* 93.
[114] Ibid., 100.
[115] Ibid., 86.
[116] Seigel quoted in Does, *Do Not Look Away,* 89.
[117] Seigel, "A Clown Outside the Circus," 14.
[118] Ibid, 14.
[119] Does, *Do Not Look Away,* 101.
[120] Ibid.

"Force of Others" that forms both the numinous power of the saga and its (arguably) most attractive feature—Max's observation seems tragically on point. Amelia Does suggests that the best way to remember Arthur Lipsett, however, is not for how he died but "for his contributions to film as an attempt to understand the self and the role of that self in the world."[121] Viewers can see Lipsett's particular take on this question reflected in how the original *Star Wars* films juxtapose Luke Skywalker with Darth Vader, and in the Prequels, Obi-Wan Kenobi with General Grievous to warn viewers about the threat of the Machine Age to natural man and his spiritual connection with others. Viewers can see Lipsett's influence in the way organic forces are portrayed as morally superior to battle droids in the Prequel era and in the way numbers versus names symbolize a machine-dictated existence versus the freedom of personal choice and expression in *The Clone Wars* and *The Bad Batch*. And perhaps most pointedly, one can see, in the Disney-era Sequels' character Finn, former Stormtrooper FN-2187, and in Cassian Andor's very numeric prison rebellion, Lipsett's thesis that no one can be truly happy as a nameless servant of the Machine—that we are all, deep within, transcendent beings.

Bibliography

Abrams, J.J., dir. *Star Wars Episode VII: The Force Awakens.* 2015; San Francisco: Disney/Lucasfilm, Ltd. Disney+. https://www.disneyplus.com/movies/star-wars-the-force-awakens-episode-vii/1LEKJPDPeMr7.

———, dir. *Star Wars Episode IX: The Rise of Skywalker.* 2019; San Francisco: Disney/Lucasfilm Ltd. Disney+. https://www.disneyplus.com/movies/star-wars-the-rise-of-skywalker-episode-ix/5e8JThYwCYgw.

Baver, Kristen. "*Andor* Analyzed: 5 Highlights from Episode 8, 'Narkina 5.'" StarWars.com. November 1, 2022. https://www.starwars.com/news/andor-episode-8-narkina-5-highlights.

Bracken, Alexandra. *A New Hope: The Prisoner, the Scoundrel, and the Farmboy.* Glendale, CA: Disney Lucasfilm Press, 2015.

Does, Amelia. *Do Not Look Away: The Life of Arthur Lipsett.* Self-pub., Amelia Does, 2012.

———. "Free Fall: Lipsett is the Shaman, Film is the Ritual." *Senses of Cinema.* August 2013. http://www.sensesofcinema.com/2013/cteq/free-fall-lipsett-is-the-shaman-film-is-the-ritual/.

Edlund, Ben, writer. *Star Wars: The Clone Wars.* Season 2, episode 9, "Grievous Intrigue." Directed by Giancarlo Volpe. Aired January 1, 2010, on Cartoon Network. Disney+. https://www.disneyplus.com/video/83357ef1-f768-4f3b-8b03-2f0c2e4617e7.

[121] Ibid., 108.

Edwards, Gareth, dir. *Rogue One: A Star Wars Story.* 2016; San Francisco: Lucasfilm Ltd. Disney+. https://www.disneyplus.com/movies/rogue-one-a-star-wars-story/14CV6eSbygOA.

Ellsworth, Carl, writer. *Star Wars: The Clone Wars.* Season 2, episode 10, "The Deserter." Directed by Robert Dalva. Aired January 1, 2010, on Cartoon Network. Disney+. https://www.disneyplus.com/video/09f9af96-40bd-4e9a-a18d-92fb9f373298.

Frakes, Randall, Brooks Peck, Sidney Perkowitz, Matt Singer, Gary K. Wolfe and Lisa Yaszek. *James Cameron's The Story of Science Fiction.* San Rafael, CA: Insight Editions, 2018.

Gehman, Chris and Brett Kashmere. Forthcoming. "Introduction." In *Strange Codes: [an anthology of Arthur Lipsett]*. Via personal communication with Brett Kashmere, January 5, 2022.

Gilbert, Laura (for DK) and Jonathan W. Rinzler (for Lucasfilm), eds. *Star Wars Revenge of the Sith: The Visual Dictionary.* London: DK, 2005.

Gilroy, Tony, writer. *Andor.* Season 1, episode 3, "Reckoning." Directed by Toby Haynes. Aired September 21, 2022. Disney+. https://www.disneyplus.com/video/76c8bb56-7cf6-4950-ae78-4fc998329ac7.

_______, writer. *Andor.* Season 1, episode 11, "Daughter of Ferrix." Directed by Benjamin Caron. Aired November 16, 2022. Disney+. https://www.disneyplus.com/video/14b00711-9480-47e5-992e-592ddab074f5.

_______, writer. *Andor.* Season 1, episode 12, "Rix Road." Directed by Benjamin Caron. Aired November 23, 2022. Disney+. https://www.disneyplus.com/video/78c53cd7-c7c1-40c4-b365-a56fae06799e.

Hill, Rick, dir. *Star Wars Tech.* 2007; San Francisco: Lucasfilm Ltd. Disney+ (no longer listed).

Johnson, Rian, dir. *Star Wars Episode VIII: The Last Jedi.* 2017; San Francisco: Disney/Lucasfilm, Ltd. Disney+. https://www.disneyplus.com/movies/star-wars-the-last-jedi-episode-viii/1nCWFK1pmAI0.

Kerschner, Irvin, dir. *Star Wars Episode V: The Empire Strikes Back.* 1980; Beverly Hills, CA: 20th Century Fox/Lucasfilm Ltd. Disney+. https://www.disneyplus.com/movies/star-wars-the-empire-strikes-back-episode-v/iqtDTZAewwYl.

Lauvet, Martin, dir. *Remembering Arthur.* 2006; Montreal: Public Pictures/NFBC. Accessed January 4, 2022. https://www.nfb.ca/film/remembering_arthur/.

Lipsett, Arthur, dir. *21-87.* 1963; Montreal: National Film Board of Canada. Accessed May 18, 2020. https://www.nfb.ca/film/21-87/.

Lucas, George, dir. *Star Wars Episode IV: A New Hope.* 1977; Beverly Hills, CA: 20th Century Fox/Lucasfilm Ltd. Disney+. https://www.disneyplus.com/movies/star-wars-a-new-hope-episode-iv/12fVeZxD2fWJ.

_______, dir. *Star Wars Episode I: The Phantom Menace.* 1999; Beverly Hills, CA: 20th Century Fox/Lucasfilm Ltd. Disney+. https://www.disneyplus.com/movies/star-wars-the-phantom-menace-episode-i/2ezYynkgW1AH.

_______, dir. *Star Wars Episode II: Attack of the Clones.* 2002; Beverly Hills, CA: 20th Century Fox/Lucasfilm Ltd. Disney+. https://www.disneyplus.com/movies/star-wars-attack-of-the-clones-episode-ii/mgpYHGnzZW6N.

______, dir. *Star Wars Episode III: Revenge of the Sith.* 2005; Beverly Hills, CA: 20th Century Fox/Lucasfilm Ltd. Disney+. https://www.disneyplus.com/movies/star-wars-revenge-of-the-sith-episode-iii/4WvbqLFumNvi.

MacMullan, Terrance. "Elegant Weapons For Civilized Ages." In *Star Wars and History,* edited by Nancy R. Reagin and Janice Liedl, 66-97. Hoboken, NJ: John Wiley & Sons, Inc., 2013.

Marquand, Richard, dir. *Return of the Jedi.* 1983; Beverly Hills, CA: 20th Century Fox/Lucasfilm Ltd. Disney+. https://www.disneyplus.com/movies/star-wars-return-of-the-jedi-episode-vi/6QGKo5mjDBS8.

McDonald, Paul F. *The* Star Wars *Heresies: Interpreting the Themes, Symbols and Philosophies of Episodes I, II and III.* Jefferson, NC: McFarland, 2013.

Melching, Steven, writer. *Star Wars: The Clone Wars.* Season 1, episode 1, "Ambush." Directed by Dave Bullock. Aired October 3, 2008, on Cartoon Network. Disney+. https://www.disneyplus.com/video/0bf87f10-d9a1-44ca-8371-f38543eb3706.

Michnovetz, Matt, writer. *Star Wars: The Clone Wars.* Season 4, episode 9, "Plan of Dissent." Directed by Kyle Dunlevy. Aired November 11, 2011, on Cartoon Network. Disney+. https://www.disneyplus.com/video/5dfa03d3-ec0c-462e-96b9-9995bb5b7e1d.

Ohayon, Albert. "*21-87*: Point of View." National Film Board of Canada. Accessed January 4, 2022. https://www.nfb.ca/playlists/albert_ohayon/1960s-explosion-creativity/.

Petschk, Gerald. "Narkina 5 is One of the Most Ingenious Prisons in the Empire and This is Why." Culture Slate. November 17, 2022. https://www.cultureslate.com/explained/narkina-5-is-one-of-the-most-ingenious-prisons-in-the-empire-and-this-is-why.

Rinzler, J.W. *The Art of Star Wars Episode III: Revenge of the Sith.* New York: Del Rey Books, 2005.

Rosen, Steven J. *The Jedi in the Lotus: Star Wars and the Hindu Tradition.* London: Arktos Media, 2010.

Sandhu, Gursimran, writer. *Star Wars: The Bad Batch.* Season 1, episode 2, "Cut and Run." Directed by Steward Lee. Aired May 7, 2021. Disney+. https://www.disneyplus.com/video/382d40ec-932e-4ff5-a7db-e2a949e74a20.

Schiff, Stephen, writer. *Andor.* Season 1, episode 7, "Announcement." Directed by Benjamin Caron. Aired October 19, 2022. Disney+. https://www.disneyplus.com/video/a6963fa0-eb41-4ba8-a923-cb4e24946d90.

Siegel, Lois. "A Clown Outside the Circus." *Cinema Canada,* 134 (October 1986): 10–14.

Silberman, Steve. "Life After Darth." *Wired,* May 1, 2005. https://www.wired.com/2005/05/lucas-2/.

Smith, Sadie (for DK) and Jonathan W. Rinzler (for Lucasfilm), eds. *Star Wars The Force Awakens: The Visual Dictionary.* New York: DK Publishing, 2015.

"*Star Wars Tech.*" Wookieepeedia. Accessed May 5, 2022. https://starwars.fandom.com/wiki/Star_Wars_Tech.

Stewart, Ian. "number symbolism." Britannica.com. Accessed January 26, 2023. https://www.britannica.com/topic/number-symbolism.

Strand, Emily. “Keep your Eye on the Ball!” *Hogwarts Professor* (blog). December 27, 2015. https://www.hogwartsprofessor.com/guest-post-keep-your-eye-on-the-ball-circular-imagery-in-new-force-awakens-echoes-the-rings-in-harry-potter/.

Taylor, Chris. *How Star Wars Conquered the Universe.* New York: Basic Books, 2014.

Williams, Rohan. “21-87: A Star Wars Odyssey.” *Force Material* (blog). September 18, [no year]. Accessed January 7, 2022. http://www.forcematerial.com/home/2016/8/28/2187-a-star-wars-odyssey.

Willimon, Beau, writer. *Andor.* Season 1, episode 8, “Narkina 5.” Directed by Toby Haynes. Aired October 26, 2022. Disney+. https://www.disneyplus.com/video/e552dfd3-ec1b-4046-8410-711114a2a4ef.

———, writer. *Andor.* Season 1, episode 9, “Nobody’s Listening!” Directed by Toby Haynes. Aired November 2, 2022. Disney+. https://www.disneyplus.com/video/c41ac934-18c3-4871-8762-4bf3ac75966b.

———, writer. *Andor.* Season 1, episode 10, “One Way Out.” Directed by Toby Haynes. Aired November 9, 2023. Disney+. https://www.disneyplus.com/video/93c891d6-35cc-4f0f-9d1e-e16e89506ebc.

Wright, John C. “May the Midichlorians Be with You.” In *Star Wars On Trial, The Force Awakens* edition, edited by David Brin and Matthew Woodring Stover, 99-119. Dallas, TX: BenBella Books, 2015.

Chapter 5

The Map in the Mirror: Reflections of Time, Self, and Salvation in *Star Wars* and *Harry Potter*

Kathryn N. McDaniel

Abstract: In both *Star Wars* and the *Harry Potter* series, young heroes-in-training face their reflections in a school setting and learn vital truths from that experience. In her training in *The Last Jedi*, Rey confronts the mysterious repeating images of herself in the cave mirrors on Ahch-To. In *Harry Potter and the Sorcerer's Stone*, Harry finds the Mirror of Erised in an unused classroom at Hogwarts and sees his heart's desire: his dead family restored to him. Not only Rey, but also Luke and Kylo Ren confront mirror realities during their educations, just as Harry also sees himself reflected in mirror-like surfaces across the series. These magical and mysterious reflections not only point to crucial information about these young protagonists, but also provide direction for their journeys in the battle between light and dark in each story. In this sense, these mirrors perform the role of maps; they are two-dimensional, space-time compasses necessary for the orientation of both hero and anti-hero. Reflected images prove a source of strength, empathy, and spiritual knowledge. Vitally educational, the maps in the mirrors allow Rey and Harry to withstand tests of their heroism and direct their steps toward defeating and even redeeming sources of evil.

Keywords: *Star Wars, Harry Potter,* mirror, map, Sequel Trilogy, Rey, Harry, Hogwarts, Luke Skywalker, Ahch-To, Joseph Campbell, hero, Hero's Journey, Ben Solo/Kylo Ren, mappa mundi, dyad, Exegol, Marauders' Map, Jedi

***

"Let me see them. My parents. Please."[1]
—Rey, *Star Wars Episode VIII: The Last Jedi*

"It does not do to dwell on dreams and forget to live, remember that."[2]
—Albus Dumbledore, *Harry Potter and the Sorcerer's Stone*

The central protagonists of the *Star Wars* Sequel Trilogy and *Harry Potter* have much in common. As orphans who did not know their parents and who were physically isolated from their own origins, Rey and Harry each have a special destiny to search out and destroy tyrannical evil on the rise in their generation. To fulfill that destiny, they require knowledge about the world they have been thrust into, about how to develop their unique talents, and most importantly, about themselves: who they are, at their very core. The "schools" in which Rey and Harry develop that knowledge exist in unmapped, isolated settings (Ahch-To and Hogwarts), led by aged, flawed mentors who possess ancient wisdom (Luke Skywalker and Albus Dumbledore). Within those educational settings, both Rey and Harry experience profound moments of reflection, literally looking at themselves in powerful mirrors. The insights they gain about their identity from those experiences—who they come from, who they are, and who they will become—prove vital to their larger journey to defeat dark, authoritarian powers. Whether their travels lead them through faraway galaxies or wizard Britain, Rey and Harry each use the visions they see in mirrors as a map to the ultimate destination in their quest and thus a map to the salvation of their world and themselves.

The *Star Wars* franchise has dynamic intersections with the *Harry Potter* stories. The two series share a common literary language, drawing from Joseph Campbell's hero's journey concept, literary alchemy, and ring theory.[3] Not only are there signs of *Star Wars* influencing *Harry Potter*,[4] but the Sequel Trilogy,

---

[1] *Star Wars Episode VIII: The Last Jedi*, directed by Rian Johnson (2017; San Francisco: Disney/Lucasfilm Ltd.), Disney+, https://www.disneyplus.com/movies/star-wars-the-last-jedi-episode-viii/1nCWFK1pmAI0.

[2] J.K. Rowling, *Harry Potter and the Sorcerer's Stone* (New York: Scholastic Books, 1997), 214.

[3] Emily Strand, "Kylo Snape? Is 'The Force Awakens' the Eighth Harry Potter Novel?" *Hogwarts Professor* (blog), December 22, 2015, https://www.hogwartsprofessor.com/guest-post-kylo-snape-is-the-force-awakens-the-eighth-harry-potter-story/.

[4] Discussions of the interconnections between *Star Wars* and *Harry Potter* occur on the following podcasts: Keith Hawk and John Granger, "Lesson 41: Light Sabres and Wands," *MuggleNet Academia*, January 5, 2016, https://mugglenetacademia.libsyn.com/mugglenet-academia-lesson-41-light-sabres-and-wands and Katy McDaniel and John Granger, "Episode 12: Galaxies Not So Far Away," *Reading, Writing, Rowling*, July 9, 2018, https://

coming out after the Potter phenomenon was well-established, shows influences from J.K. Rowling's fantasy series in return.[5] The two series invite comparisons between similar characters and themes. Most significantly, *Star Wars* and *Harry Potter* share a larger story arc in which orphaned protagonists, who contain both light and dark aspects within themselves, go on perilous journeys to find what they need to defeat evil powers and come to terms with their own identities. To succeed, these heroes-in-training need maps to guide them not only to locations where evil resides and may be defeated or redeemed but also toward their own personal histories, which play covert roles in shaping their paths.

Although it may seem surprising, the mirrors Rey and Harry encounter in their educations as Jedi and wizard, respectively, serve as such maps. Several mirror moments in the two series point the protagonists toward the next steps in their journey or warn them away from dark temptations. Like Harry at Hogwarts, who finds the Mirror of Erised in his nighttime wanderings, Rey encounters a mysterious dark mirror in the cave on Ahch-To. But while Harry's mirror shows him his family as a reflection of that which his heart most desires, Rey's mirror remains stubbornly enigmatic when she asks to see her parents. Harry and Rey must puzzle out the meaning of these mirrored reflections, which speak to them in two-dimensional, symbolic language to show their origins—one clear but illusory, the other murky and occluded. Decoding these images proves more useful in directing Rey and Harry to their own present needs and future destinies than to truths about their families.

Beyond these two magical mirrors, Rey and Harry experience additional mirror-like moments in which they see reflections that show their allies, their opposites, or their (potential) futures. Other *Star Wars* stories have also played on the idea of mirror images, particularly in the cave on Dagobah, where opposite reflections test Luke (in *Star Wars Episode V: The Empire Strikes Back* [1980]) and Kylo Ren (in the graphic novel *Star Wars: Age of Resistance—Supreme Leader Snoke #1*).[6] Mirror moments serve as space-time compasses necessary for the orientation of both hero and anti-hero. Unlike Luke and Kylo Ren, Rey and Harry successfully decode the symbolic images provided by their mirror

---

www.mugglenet.com/2018/07/reading-writing-rowling-episode-12-galaxies-not-so-far-away-harry-potter-and-star-wars/.

[5] Ibid.

[6] *Star Wars Episode V: The Empire Strikes Back*, directed by Irvin Kerschner (1980; Beverly Hills, CA: 20th Century Fox/Lucasfilm Ltd.), Disney+, https://www.disneyplus.com/movies/star-wars-the-empire-strikes-back-episode-v/iqtDTZAewwYl. Tom Taylor, *Star Wars: Age of Resistance—Supreme Leader Snoke #1* (New York: Marvel, 2019), Kindle edition.

experiences, discovering truths about themselves, about their past, present, and future, and about the direction for their quest. Seeing themselves clearly, particularly the light and dark that abide within them, Rey and Harry come to understand their ability to make choices independent of their family heritage. Vitally educational, the maps in the mirrors allow Rey and Harry to withstand tests of their heroism and direct their steps toward defeating and even redeeming sources of evil.

Mirrors, maps, and metaphors

Seen as sources of concealed information but also as objects of trickery and deceit, mirrors have a magical history.[7] They appear to collapse three-dimensional space into two dimensions[8] and are commonly depicted in literature and film collapsing time—fusing past, present, and future into one. Mark Pendergrast notes that mirrors reveal "whence we have come, what we imagine, how we think, and what we yearn for."[9] Since their ancient origins, they have been viewed as devices that not only appeal to vanity but reveal hidden truths about individuals and places in all times. Scrying, or catoptromancy, the ancient art of fortune-telling through mirrors, similarly has a long, global history. Various cultures have believed that mirrors can contain one's spiritual energy or one's opposite essence, and they have often been feared for their seemingly magical ability to create powerful, convincing illusions or serve as portals between the worlds of the living and the dead.[10]

Mirrors also have a long history of use as literary metaphors, which Miranda Anderson attributes to the similarities between mirrors and metaphors: "the physical properties of a mirror relate to the figurative properties of a metaphor," she says, in that they both communicate ideas via transference, i.e., analogy.[11] The confusing, multifaceted nature of mirror imagery allows artists to relay sophisticated ideas about the self in relation to the exterior world. Anderson argues, "The complexity of the mirror as a literary motif arises from the liminal space which it inhabits, being neither entirely subject

---

[7] Mark Pendergrast, *Mirror Mirror: A History of the Human Love Affair with Reflection* (New York: Basic Books, 2003).

[8] Some renaissance artists, like Giotto, appear to have used mirrors for this practical purpose of making three-dimensional spaces appear two-dimensional so that they were easier to capture on canvas. Ibid., 131.

[9] Ibid., ix.

[10] Lynn Holden, "Reflections on the Double," in *The Book of the Mirror*, ed. Miranda Anderson (Newcastle: Cambridge Scholars Publishing, 2007), 122.

[11] Miranda Anderson, "Chaucer and the Subject of the Mirror," in *The Book of the Mirror*, ed. Miranda Anderson (Newcastle: Cambridge Scholars Publishing, 2007), 70.

nor entirely object"; in other words, the mirror may reveal the self as subject (producing self-consciousness) but also the self as an object (replicating the other's gaze).[12] Mirror metaphors are thus often employed to illustrate the construction of the self and the "blurring between outer and inner."[13] The literary use of doppelgängers, or mirrored twins, performs a similar function in merging the familiar (self) with the strange (other) in ways that may produce psychological or spiritual revelations.[14]

In this ability to orient the viewer, blending the interior with the exterior on a two-dimensional plane, mirrors can be likened to maps, which perform a similar function. As Peter Turchi explains, the map is also a metaphor "for recording who we are, where we are, what is, and what might be."[15] As a result, maps like mirrors also allow the viewing of all times in a single glance. Medieval mappa mundi, for example, distilled "geographical, historical and religious knowledge" such that "all history is here, happening at the same time."[16] Turchi declares, "To ask for a map is to say, 'Tell me a story.'"[17] Such map-stories invite exploration of possibility, of far-flung destinations (or destinies); at the same time, they show the location of the person doing the exploring—not only where they are now, but where they have been and where they might go. Simon Garfield notes that the Hereford mappa mundi, which has hung on a church wall in Hereford, England, for centuries, shows the greatest wear from curious fingers at the point of Hereford itself: what people most wanted to touch on this map was their own location, the reflection of their own place in the world.[18]

Thus, maps and mirrors serve similar purposes in allowing a compressed view of self and other, present-day as well as past and future. They speak symbolically, in two dimensions, and in story. Their revelations may puzzle or enlighten, but the viewer's interpretation of what they see in these two-dimensional objects will point them in a particular direction and show how they relate to the past and future, here and there. Sensitive to the power of maps and mirrors as metaphors, the creators of *Star Wars* and *Harry Potter* use them as space-time compasses in the spiritual development of their

---

[12] Ibid.

[13] Ibid., 73.

[14] Holden, "Reflections on the Double," 127.

[15] Peter Turchi, *Maps of the Imagination: The Writer as Cartographer* (San Antonio, TX: Trinity University Press, 2004), 11.

[16] Simon Garfield, *On the Map: Why the World Looks the Way It Does* (London: Profile Books, 2012), 46.

[17] Turchi, *Maps of the Imagination,* 11.

[18] Garfield, *On the Map,* 56.

protagonists as these heroes-in-training orient themselves to their worlds and toward that which is spiritually good.

Place, orientation, and journey

Both *Star Wars* and *Harry Potter* depict their heroes undertaking travel through vast spaces, wilderness, and even underground as they seek to understand themselves, their origins, and their destinies (present, past, and future). Rey and Harry begin their journeys from mundane, barren, and stifling circumstances: Rey in the desert junkyard of Jakku ("pretty much nowhere," Luke acknowledges[19]) and Harry in the imagination-phobic, "perfectly normal," suburban home of the Dursleys at number four Privet Drive.[20] These places are dead-ends where the orphans were intentionally shielded by the obscurity and isolation of their surroundings. But as evil becomes ascendant, Jakku and Privet Drive become launch points for adventurous voyages into marvelous realms previously unimagined. Far from straightforward, the journey itself plays a central role in cultivating heroic values in the protagonists. The quest motif is common to the hero's journey, and significantly, Rey and Harry will need special devices to orient themselves toward their quests' ultimate destinations.[21] These devices appear strikingly similar to each other and lead to very similar moments of heroic self-sacrifice.

These orienting objects do not always appear in an obvious map-like form. Although Harry has a literal map in the Marauder's Map, for example, this map does not help him much in pointing him toward how to defeat Voldemort—in fact, it often distracts him from that mission by allowing him to fixate (negatively) on Draco in Book Six or (longingly) on Ginny in Book Seven.[22] Harry is only able to orient himself, after long rambles in the wilderness in the seventh book, by decoding the imagery and significance of the Deathly Hallows: the Elder Wand, the Resurrection Stone, and the Invisibility Cloak. These three objects are represented symbolically by a bisected circle enclosed in a triangle, which Hermione discovers sketched in a book of fairy stories written in Ancient

---

[19] *Star Wars Episode VIII: The Last Jedi*, directed by Rian Johnson, 2017.

[20] Rowling, *Sorcerer's Stone*, 1.

[21] We might also note the similarity between Rey's "cloaked binary beacon . . . to light her way home" (*Star Wars Episode VIII: The Last Jedi*, directed by Rian Johnson, 2017) and the Deluminator in *Harry Potter*, which Ron uses to find his way back to Harry and Hermione in *Deathly Hallows*. These devices are not maps but rather serve as anchors or leading strings to help keep the heroes connected to their base.

[22] Like the Mirror of Erised, the Marauder's Map poses the danger of allowing Harry a fantasy of connection, encouraging him to "dwell on dreams," instead of completing the tasks Dumbledore has set for him, namely the elimination of Voldemort's Horcruxes that allow him to stave off death.

Runes.[23] Once he interprets the meaning of the Hallows symbol, Harry understands the Hallows themselves to be devices staving off death, each of which has limitations and temptations. This orienting knowledge—nourished by his grief at Dobby's death—allows Harry to focus on the quest to defeat Voldemort not by claiming the Hallows but by eliminating his Horcruxes. Instead of trying to find the Elder Wand (the object of Voldemort's quest), Harry searches out the remaining objects (and living beings) into which Voldemort has encased pieces of his soul. Interestingly, the Hallows appear to be part of Harry's family heritage as a descendent of the Peverell brothers, who first gained them as a prize won from Death. Harry will eschew his family legacy to pursue the destruction of Voldemort's and the Gaunt family's death-defying creations instead.

In his travels to seek out Horcruxes, Harry comes to realize that a piece of Voldemort exists within himself—this is the evil that whispers to him, that tempts him. He must make a choice to defeat that evil within himself as a means to end Voldemort's malevolent tyranny, even if that means sacrificing his own life. He must be willing to die at the hands of his enemy in order to ensure his enemy's defeat. Because of the journey he has undertaken and its many twists and turns, Harry has the judgment to make this choice in the Forbidden Forest at Hogwarts where, deliberately without the Hallows, he allows Voldemort to kill him and thereby kill the piece of the Dark Lord residing in Harry.[24] Paradoxically, Harry's self-sacrifice allows him to live on so that he can defeat Voldemort in the final Battle of Hogwarts, bringing victory to the side of good and saving the wizarding world from Death-Eater tyranny.

Star Wars similarly highlights a perilous search that will end in the hero's willingness to meet death—the key to defeating evil. Each film in the *Star Wars* Sequel Trilogy is built around Rey traveling across space to find either someone important (Luke, Kylo Ren, and Emperor Palpatine) or a map that shows where they are. *Star Wars Episode VII: The Force Awakens* (2015) centers on the Resistance's search for a lost piece of "an ancient map"[25] that will show them where to find Luke, who they believe is the key to defeating the authoritarian First Order. BB-8 has a piece of this digital map, which in a sense, becomes part of Rey's mind once she sees it. Ren believes that if he has

---

[23] This is the "original" runic version of *The Tales of Beedle the Bard*, specifically "The Tale of the Three Brothers." Hermione also finds the symbol on the old Peverell tombstone in Godric's Hollow, a letter written by Albus Dumbledore to Gellert Grindelwald, and a necklace worn by Xenophilius Lovegood. J.K. Rowling, *Harry Potter and the Deathly Hallows* (New York: Scholastic Books, 2007), 406, 394, 326.

[24] Rowling, *Deathly Hallows*, 691-704.

[25] Jason Fry, *Star Wars: The Last Jedi*, expanded edition (New York: Del Rey, 2018), 111.

Rey, he does not need the map itself because he will be able to take its image from her mind; she, in this way, has become the embodied map to Luke Skywalker. Ren fails in his attempt to pull the map from her mind and instead awakens the power of the Force within her, allowing her to see into his mind.[26]

At the end of *The Force Awakens*, Rey uses her knowledge of the digital map to find Luke in the Unknown Regions on the isolated island of Ahch-To, "the most unfindable place in the galaxy"[27] and the origin point of the Jedi Order. In the wake of Han Solo's death, she hopes Luke will take up his lightsaber again. Instead, he begins (reluctantly) to train her as a Jedi, showing her where he keeps the ancient Jedi texts, even as he scoffs at the failures of Jedi wisdom. On Ahch-To, Rey experiences not only the cryptic mirror reflection in the cave, but four related interactions with her mirror opposite in the story, Kylo Ren, with whom she now shares a psychic connection that positions them as doubles for each other, with Rey and Ren referred to jointly as a dyad.[28] When it becomes clear that Luke will not be the galaxy's savior, Rey leaves Ahch-To. This time she seeks out Ren, believing that her dyad partner's redemption will rescue the galaxy from First Order tyranny. Her presence helps to turn him against his evil mentor Snoke, but she resists Ren's offer to share the imperial throne with him and, in *Star Wars Episode IX: The Rise of Skywalker* (2019), sets off to find Emperor Palpatine, who in Voldemort-like fashion has risen from the grave.

To find the Emperor, Rey searches for a map in the form of a Sith wayfinder. Kylo Ren has one, and she sets off on a quest to find the other in preparation for meeting with and defeating the source of evil. Like the Deathly Hallows symbol, the wayfinder is in a triangular shape, a pyramid that acts as a map—a "hyperspatial lodestone," as C-3PO says[29]—that shows the way to hidden domains of the Sith.[30] Finding the wayfinder depends on translating ancient

---

[26] This unmistakably echoes the scene in *Harry Potter and the Order of the Phoenix* where Snape, "teaching" Harry mind-shielding (Occlumency) by forcibly reading his mind (Legilimency), ends up on the receiving end when Harry reads Snape's mind and finds his "worst memory." J.K. Rowling, *Harry Potter and the Order of the Phoenix* (New York: Scholastic Books, 2003), 638-650.

[27] Fry, *The Last Jedi*, 85.

[28] "Emperor Palpatine/Darth Sidious," StarWars.com, accessed September 30, 2022, https://www.starwars.com/databank/emperor-palpatine-darth-sidious.

[29] *Star Wars Episode IX: The Rise of Skywalker*, directed by J.J. Abrams (2019; San Francisco: Lucasfilm Ltd.), Disney+, https://www.disneyplus.com/movies/star-wars-the-rise-of-skywalker-episode-ix/5e8JThYwCYgw.

[30] Note that the filmmakers of the Sequel Trilogy opted to develop the wayfinder device instead of using holocrons—educational devices that could be used by either the Jedi or the Sith—perhaps to emphasize the specific triangular shape (holocrons could be created

runes from an old Sith dagger discovered in underground tunnels on Pasaana.[31] Although Rey is eventually able to use the runes to find Palpatine's wayfinder on the old Death Star, she battles an evil image of herself and then Kylo Ren, during which the wayfinder is destroyed. She later uses the wayfinder Ren had appropriated from the ruined estate of his grandfather, Darth Vader, to find Palpatine on Exegol.[32] There she will resist his appeal to join the Dark Side in pursuit of power and eternal life. Much like Harry's decision to chase Horcruxes instead of Hallows, Rey's use of the wayfinder descended from the Skywalker line, not the Palpatine line, to find the place where she meets her destiny reveals her following the Light Side of the Force in the final confrontation, no matter her family legacy.[33] Her grandfather, the Emperor, creates an impossible choice for Rey: she may join him and live, but if she dies, he will claim her power and rule eternally himself. Contrary to his claims, the choices she subsequently makes lead to her death and his—but then also, like Harry, her resurrection, in which the evil within her has been tamed, and her mirror opposite Ren (Ben Solo) has been redeemed.

The Hallows and the Sith wayfinder thus both point to the goal of cheating death in order to have eternal life, which is the aim of Voldemort and Emperor Palpatine. Their locations are concealed in ancient runes and symbolic code but appear to pass down as inheritance to succeeding generations. In the wrong hands, these devices may lead to temptation and, ultimately, submission to the Dark Side. Although guided to locations of dark forces and the final showdown between good and evil, Rey and Harry are nevertheless able to withstand the tempting appeals of ambition, fame, power, and eternal life. They instead embrace, in mirror contrast, the values of humility, self-sacrifice, friendship, and heroic death. Their ability to retain these values amid both grief and temptation is the result of a different set of maps that show them not where to go but rather

---

in a variety of shapes) and the wayfinder's specific connection to death and the Dark Side. "Holocron," Wookieepedia, accessed April 14, 2022, https://starwars.fandom.com/wiki/Holocron.

[31] This weapon is called "Ochi's Blade" and is used, much like the Elder Wand, to defeat all other weapons, including lightsabers. Like the First Brother in "The Tale of the Three Brothers," Ochi bragged about his unbeatable weapon in a tavern (cantina), which allowed Luke to track him to Pasaana where he died (though the blade would remain with him instead of passing to others, as happens in "The Tale of the Three Brothers"). "Ochi," Wookieepedia, accessed April 8, 2022, https://starwars.fandom.com/wiki/Ochi.

[32] "Sith Wayfinder," Wookieepedia, accessed April 8, 2022, https://starwars.fandom.com/wiki/Sith_wayfinder.

[33] I am indebted to Amy H. Sturgis for this insight. Although circumstances prevent Rey from using the Palpatine wayfinder (unlike Harry's deliberate choice to pursue Horcruxes), the symbolic parallel still resonates strongly.

who they are and how they can balance the good and bad within them to save their worlds. These maps are the ones they find in the mirrors.

Finding heritage, self, and direction in the mirror

The mirrors in *Star Wars* and *Harry Potter* exist in literal and embodied forms. Harry's literal mirrors are the Mirror of Erised and the mirror Sirius gave him as a gift,[34] while Rey's most obvious mirror appears in the reflective surface of the underground cave on Ahch-To. Both series also explore heroic development through interaction with mirrored characters. Harry thinks he sees his father across the Great Lake at Hogwarts but later discovers he was seeing himself in the future, and throughout the series, he struggles with his mirror similarities and mental connection to his nemesis, Voldemort.[35] Rey, meanwhile, battles against her Dark Side reverse image on the old Death Star as well as with Kylo Ren as her embodied opposite in the Force. In the past, Luke Skywalker and Kylo Ren each experienced their own mirror moments during training on Dagobah, where in the Dark Side cave, they confronted enemies who turned out to be themselves. All of these questing characters reveal important aspects of themselves through their engagement with mirror images and find opportunities to understand their future choices. Their ability to learn through self-reflection in these educational settings will shape their destined paths. These two series, then, emphasize the educational power of mirrors as a source of knowledge—about the relation between past, present, and future, as well as about the individual's role in shaping events.

When Harry Potter first receives his Invisibility Cloak—which he does not yet know is one of the Deathly Hallows—he uses it to explore Hogwarts at night, aiming to investigate the Hogwarts library's Restricted Section for clues to the identity of Nicholas Flamel, whom we later discover created the "Sorcerer's Stone" that grants eternal life. Creeping down from Gryffindor Tower under the Cloak, Harry searches the Restricted Section until he is interrupted by the "bloodcurdling shriek" of the first book he opens.[36] As he runs away from the

---

[34] There are other mirrors in the *Harry Potter* books, too, used for different purposes. For example, Hermione's use of a mirror to avoid looking directly at the basilisk in *Chamber of Secrets* is a classic use of mirror-as-shield. J.K. Rowling, *Harry Potter and the Chamber of Secrets* (New York: Scholastic Books, 1999).

[35] For more on twins or doubles in the *Harry Potter* series, see Carol Eshleman, "Twin Core: An Exploration of Twins in the Wizarding World," in *Harry Potter for Nerds II*, ed. Kathryn McDaniel and Travis Prinzi (Oklahoma City: Unlocking Press, 2015), 45-62. See also Shira Wolosky, *The Riddles of Harry Potter: Secret Passages and Interpretive Quests* (New York: Palgrave Macmillan, 2010), 99-126.

[36] Rowling, *Sorcerer's Stone*, 206.

library and from Snape and Filch, he stumbles into an empty, "unused" classroom where he finds "a magnificent mirror, as high as the ceiling."[37] Amid the shadowy gloom of this space, Harry is shocked to see himself, visible despite the cloak, surrounded by people who look like him: "Harry was looking at his family, for the very first time in his life."[38] He returns to the classroom, first with Ron and then alone, becoming obsessed with viewing this reflection of himself with the family from whom he had been separated for so long.

On the third night, however, Harry finds his headmaster Albus Dumbledore in the room. Dumbledore tells him that this mirror "shows us nothing more or less than the deepest, most desperate desire of our hearts" and that people "have wasted away before it, entranced by what they have seen, or been driven mad, not knowing if what it shows is real or even possible."[39] He tells Harry that the mirror is going to be moved, and he should not go looking for it: "If you ever *do* run across it, you will now be prepared. It does not do to dwell on dreams and forget to live, remember that."[40] This has been a lesson for Harry, one that he will learn well. The fantasy of connection with his parents and the Potters is a tantalizing illusion, but it cannot be allowed to distract him from his present life or his future.[41]

When Harry finds the mirror again at the end of the book, he will remember this lesson to good effect. Professor Quirrell, Voldemort's agent, pronounces the Mirror of Erised "the key to finding the Stone"[42]—thus, it is a kind of map. Harry realizes that when looking at his reflection, he must wish to see himself finding the Stone. This is a desire for the present and not for the past, seeking something tangible and immediate, not eternal life. And so this time, upon seeing his reflection in the mirror, the Stone manifests as a real object in his pocket. As Dumbledore explains, "only one who wanted to find the Stone—find it, but not use it—would be able to get it, otherwise, they'd just see themselves making gold or drinking the Elixir of Life."[43] Harry has learned to separate what is necessary to defeat Voldemort from both his desire for identity and connection through his parents[44] and from his ambition for future personal achievement or eternal physical life.

---

37 Ibid., 207.

38 Ibid., 209.

39 Ibid., 213.

40 Ibid., 214.

41 Shawn E. Klein, "The Mirror of Erised: Why We Should Heed Dumbledore's Warning," in *Harry Potter and Philosophy: If Aristotle Ran Hogwarts*, ed. David Baggett and Shawn E. Klein (Chicago: Open Court, 2004), 92-104.

42 Rowling, *Sorcerer's Stone*, 289.

43 Ibid., 300.

44 Anne Parker-Perkola discusses how the Mirror of Erised helps Harry to name and also

Harry's next mirror-moment occurs not with a literal mirror but across Hogwarts's Great Lake. In *Prisoner of Azkaban*, Harry, Hermione, and wounded Sirius Black face a flood of Dementors aiming to suck out their souls with the Dementor's Kiss. Although Harry attempts to cast a Patronus spell, it is not powerful enough to drive them away. As his consciousness fades and the Dementors advance, Harry sees across the reflective pool a man who looks like his father, James Potter, casting a stag Patronus. This magical spell repulses the Dementors, saving the three from annihilation. When Harry and Hermione travel backwards in time in the last part of the novel, however, and Harry awaits a reunion with his father by the lake, he suddenly realizes that this reflection was not of the deceased James but of his lookalike in this generation: Harry himself. As Shira Wolosky notes, Harry has accepted "the memory of his father as part of his own sense of self."[45] Seeing his reflection successfully fend off Dementors inspires Harry with the confidence to cast the spell successfully: he knows he can do it because he has already seen himself do it in a reflected image across the water of the Great Lake.[46] This time-travel experience suggests the tension between destiny (it was always Harry who cast the Patronus to save them) and choice (Harry must at that moment take charge of that which he knows was destined)—a tension that pervades Harry's conflict with Voldemort. In this case, Harry realizes that the mirror image shows him the future instead of the past, himself and not his father, his own achievement and not a legacy.

Harry must learn these lessons again when in the last book in the series he finds the broken piece of the magical two-way mirror his godfather Sirius had given him in *Order of the Phoenix*. Harry does not unwrap this gift until after Sirius's death, at which time he finally reads his godfather's instructions explaining that he could say Sirius's name into the mirror in order to communicate with him. Had Harry opened his gift and used it earlier, this communication device could have prevented the tragedy that led to Sirius's death. When Harry tries to speak to Sirius from "beyond the veil" of death at the end of this book, he will see only his own reflection staring back at him, which provokes him to break the mirror in frustration.[47] This mirror is not a portal to the world of the dead. Nevertheless, he keeps the mirror fragment among his possessions.

---

redirect his desire for family in "Harry Potter and the Transfiguration of Desire," in *The Alchemical Harry Potter: Essays on Transfiguration in J.K. Rowling's Novels*, ed. Anne Mamary (Jefferson, NC: McFarland, 2021), 46-62.

[45] Wolosky, *The Riddles of Harry Potter*, 83.

[46] Harry's Patronus appears in the form of his father's Animagus, a stag, reinforcing that his father lives within him.

[47] Rowling, *Order of the Phoenix*, 857-859.

In the last book, *Deathly Hallows*, Harry will rediscover the two-way mirror when it cuts him, drawing blood, just as he is reading information about Dumbledore that makes him question his mentor's goodness. The mirror shard calls forth in Harry emotions of bitterness, regret, and longing. As Harry packs his trunk and ponders Dumbledore's death, the mirror's significance shifts from a reminder of Harry's role in his godfather's death to doubts about his greatest teacher, doubts surfacing as he confronts the Hogwarts headmaster's moral failures. Harry has to decide whether Dumbledore's cause was good and whether to claim the prophecy—that neither he nor Voldemort can live "while the other survives"—as his own destiny.[48] When Harry had initially looked into the fragment, he saw only his own green eye reflected. But at the end of this chapter, he catches a flash of blue in the glass. He wants to believe this is Albus Dumbledore's eye, peering at him from beyond the grave, and he will use the mirror to call for help when Harry, Ron, Hermione, and Luna are imprisoned at Malfoy Manor.

It is, however, Dobby who comes to their rescue at the behest, not of the deceased Albus, but rather his brother Aberforth Dumbledore, who now holds the other half of Sirius's mirror. In the chapter called "The Missing Mirror," Aberforth shelters Harry, Ron, and Hermione and not only reveals that he possesses this other mirror but also relays even more troubling information about Albus's past. As Albus's "missing" mirror—missing in the sense of having been absent for almost the entirety of the book series—this man who looks so much like Harry's headmaster encourages Harry to abandon the quest to defeat Voldemort. When Aberforth asks, "How can you be sure you aren't dispensable, just like my little sister?," Harry, in an echo of his rediscovery of the mirror fragment, feels as if "a shard of ice" pierced his heart.[49]

However, by this point in the story, Harry is able to distinguish the truth, and the value of his quest, from its mirror image. Sirius's magical mirror has led Harry to his teacher's embodied mirror who, as Albus's opposite, gives Harry inverse advice: run away, don't participate. As the Mirror of Erised taught Harry in the very first book, he does not find in this embodied mirror a lost, longed-for past, nor a glorious future—both of which would be illusions. Instead, he stays focused on the need of the moment: finding the dangerous death-defying objects that allow evil to persist, no longer the Sorcerer's Stone but now Voldemort's Horcruxes. Harry has learned from these mirror-moments that the imperfection of one's heroes is no reason to abandon the side of good, that focusing on the immediate needs of the present can advance the cause of justice, and that he himself has the power to save the

---

[48] Ibid., 841.

[49] Rowling, *Deathly Hallows*, 568.

day. Only after he asserts this self-knowledge to Aberforth ("I'm going to keep going until I succeed—or I die"[50]) does Albus's embodied mirror show him the hidden tunnel into Hogwarts that Harry, Ron, and Hermione will use to join their friends in the final battle against Voldemort.[51] Harry's insight into the balance of good and evil within himself, the flawed nature of mentors and heroes (including himself), and his own ability to choose his destiny allows him to rise heroically to the point of self-sacrifice for the true "greater good."

Rey's experiences with both literal and embodied mirrors likewise help her to understand herself and her choices in relation to her muddled past, precarious present, and destined future. In *The Last Jedi*, whispers from the Dark Side of the Force appear to call Rey to the cave on Ahch-To, a place she had seen "only in dreams,"[52] much like the whispers of the Restricted Section called to Harry in the Hogwarts library before he found the Mirror of Erised. A wet world, Ahch-To is also the origin place of the first Jedi Temple and thus training grounds.[53] Here Rey has several mental encounters with Kylo Ren, whose mind is now linked to hers (as Harry's is to Voldemort's), though he remains physically distant. Unlike Harry, Rey engages in conversations with her opposite on the Dark Side, conversations in which the two reveal themselves to each other—both physically, in that they actually see each other,[54] and psychologically—in order to persuade each to the other's side. Rey tells Ren that she is lost: "I need someone to show me my place in all this."[55] In response, Ren explains Rey's lack of heritage. "Your parents threw you away like garbage," he says, pointing out that her search for father figures,

---

[50] Ibid., 569.

[51] Tolonda Henderson and Amy M. Von Lintel discuss the properties of a variety of images in the *Harry Potter* series in their chapter "More than Moving Images: The Visual Culture of *Harry Potter*." They, too, emphasize the ability of moving images to bring the dead back into the world of the living—at least in an illusory way—and to "collapse the 'here-now' with the 'there-then.'" In discussing this scene with Aberforth, they focus on the painting of Ariana and how (real) Neville emerges from it: "In this scene, we are taken on a complex space-time journey between the 2d and the 3d, the screenic and the physical, the visual and the embodied, the illusionary and the 'real.'" I would add that this same journey is reinforced in this scene by their encounter with Aberforth as an embodied mirror. In *From Here to Hogwarts: Essays on Harry Potter Fandom and Fiction*, ed. Christopher E. Bell (Jefferson, NC: McFarland, 2016), 145.

[52] *Star Wars Episode VIII: The Last Jedi*, directed by Rian Johnson, 2017.

[53] Similarly, damp Scotland is the site of the original Hogwarts School of Witchcraft and Wizardry.

[54] In fact, Rey seems discomfited by seeing Ren's naked chest and asks him to put on a cowl, which he ignores.

[55] *Star Wars Episode VIII: The Last Jedi*, directed by Rian Johnson, 2017.

in Han and then Luke, is her "greatest weakness."[56] Instead, he urges her to "Let the past die. Kill it if you have to. That's the only way to become who you're meant to be."[57] Rey thinks the solution to her disorientation is finding her "place" and finding who her parents were; Ren thinks the solution is to erase the past and "become" in isolation. Neither is entirely correct; they will instead need each other, their mirror doubles, to fulfill their destinies.[58]

Shortly after this conversation, Rey follows the whispers into the cave, falling in a dark, shimmering pool. She pulls herself out of the water and walks toward polished cave walls that act as a mirror to reveal her form. Stretching out her hand toward the reflective surface, she looks first forward then backward over her shoulder, seeing herself replicated in a seemingly infinite circle. The actions of each reflected Rey cycle domino-like through the chain and circle back, the clicking of her snapped fingers from one Rey to the next suggesting the passage of time from past to future and then back to the present. The film audience hears her later relaying her thoughts to another person; she says, "I should have felt trapped or panicked, but I didn't. This didn't go on forever. I knew it was leading somewhere, that at the end it would show me what I came to see."[59] She steps toward the wall again, this time seeing shadows on the surface, and pleads to see her parents. But disappointingly the shadows merge into her solitary reflection staring back. "I never felt so alone," she says.[60] Viewers then realize she has been talking not to Luke but to Kylo Ren, not to her heroic mentor but to her nemesis.

Surprisingly, Ren comforts her by telling her "You're not alone," and she snaps back, "Neither are you. It's not too late."[61] The two reach out their hands to each other, a meeting of opposites through their mental and visual connection that becomes physical, and in this moment both think they see the other coming around to their own side in the future. But Luke interrupts them, destroys Rey's stone room, and orders her to leave, frightened by her link to darkness. Rey's experience of these mirrors—the literal one in the cave and the embodied one in Ren—has shown her the future and strengthened her resolve that, regardless of her past, she has the ability to act in the present to create a chain of events

---

56 Ibid.

57 Ibid.

58 The important twins in the Sequel Trilogy will therefore be Rey and Ren, not Rey and Snoke or Rey and Palpatine, which would more closely parallel the twinning of Harry with Voldemort. This choice in *Star Wars* is more like forging a mirror relationship between Harry and Snape (see Strand, "Kylo Snape?") or perhaps Harry and Draco.

59 *Star Wars Episode VIII: The Last Jedi*, directed by Rian Johnson, 2017.

60 Ibid.

61 Ibid.

that will lead to Ren's redemption and the triumph of the Light Side of the Force, not only within him but throughout the galaxy. Although Ren had believed Rey was a map to Luke, Ren has now become Rey's map—showing where he is and her path to salvation.

This scene has been a lynchpin in recent analyses of the Sequel Trilogy that point to the importance of reconciling past (heritage), present (self), and future (destiny). Matthew Bortolin, in *The Zen of R2-D2*, reads the scene in the mirrored cave as an example of the Buddhist concept of karma: "the string of choices you make that lead you from one action to the next, and the consequences of those choices."[62] As a result, Rey's experience with this dark mirror teaches her that her "actions and choices—one after another after another—were what defined her, not her parents, not some wished-for Jedi lineage. Her actions and choices were what would make or break the fate of the galaxy."[63] In *Star Wars After Lucas*, Dan Golding argues that *The Last Jedi* film as a whole plays with questions of how much the past matters to the present (including past *Star Wars* movies). Ren's nihilist rejection of the past and Luke's bitter judgment of its (and his) failures are balanced by Rey's more measured understanding that the past, and past heroes like Luke, cannot be counted on to save the galaxy now or in the future.[64]

Significantly, both Luke and Ren have had their own experiences with mirror reflections in their training on Dagobah, and they each failed to learn these lessons from their encounters. Like Ahch-To, Dagobah is a wet planet on which a failed Jedi master resides in self-imposed exile and on which a Dark Side cave, surrounded by a pool of water, will test the trainees' connection to light and dark aspects of the Force. The cave contains, Yoda explains, nothing that the trainee does not bring in with him: it is, thus, a reflection of the self and only that.[65] In *Empire Strikes Back*, Luke enters the cave with his lightsaber, though Yoda had told him he would not need it, and finds himself face-to-face with an image of his nemesis, Darth Vader. Failing to compose his response, he lashes out in battle and strikes down the figure, only to find his own face reflected back at him from under the heavy mask. In

---

[62] Matthew Bortolin, *The Zen of R2-D2: Ancient Wisdom from a Galaxy Far, Far Away* (Sommerville, MA: Wisdom Publications, 2019), 60.

[63] Ibid.

[64] Dan Golding, *Star Wars After Lucas: A Critical Guide to the Future of the Galaxy* (Minneapolis, MN: University of Minnesota Press, 2019), 195-196. Yoda tries to explain this point to Luke after Rey leaves Ahch-To: "We are what they grow beyond." *Star Wars Episode VIII: The Last Jedi*, directed by Rian Johnson, 2017.

[65] Water images abound in the novelization's version of this scene in *Empire Strikes Back*, emphasizing the reflective nature of the cave. Donald F. Glut, *Star Wars: The Empire Strikes Back* (New York: Del Rey, 1980), 141-144.

destroying Vader, he has killed himself and revealed his dark impulses. Luke thinks this is some kind of trick, but this moment prefigures the revelation of Luke's past ties to Vader and his future role in Vader's destruction. It also suggests Luke's intolerance of the Dark Side within himself, a flaw that will lead to an impulsive reflex to kill his nephew Ben Solo when he sees the darkness within him, thus setting in motion a chain of disastrous events that will lead to Luke's self-exile.

Kylo Ren's own experience of the Dark Side cave appears in the graphic novel *Star Wars: Age of Resistance—Supreme Leader Snoke #1*. Training Ren as his apprentice, Snoke takes him to the cave on Dagobah and, inverting Yoda's advice, tells him that the cave contains "only what you've been too weak to bury."[66] In the cave Ren confronts the image of Luke (which Snoke refers to as the "light within" him). Despite this Luke's reluctance to fight, Ren kills him with his lightsaber. However, the test continues when Ren's parents Leia and Han appear, calling him Ben to remind him of who he is and that he is loved. They are there to show him himself, in the light. Ren's response surprises Snoke; instead of striking down this image, Ren obliterates the cave. "The past is the past," Ren tells Snoke amid the ruins.[67] He then promises that the cave is no longer necessary because Snoke will not need any other apprentices than himself.[68] Like Luke, Ren has failed to interpret the significance of this mirror that shows his past, present, and future at once; unlike Luke, his reaction was not to dismiss but to destroy. As Luke did not accept the darkness in himself, as revealed by his father's image, Ren has failed to accept the light that remains within him, displayed in his parents' pleas. Both men are out of balance with the Force, and this will affect their ability to control future events.

Despite Luke's fear of another Dark Side trick on Ahch-To, the remote island's dark mirror successfully points Rey to her true self and to her efficacy in creating change, regardless of her parentage. When Rey leaves Ahch-To, she sets in motion a chain reaction by seeking out her mirrored twin, Ren, thus choosing the present and herself over the past and Luke Skywalker. She chooses what she sees in the mirror: herself and a redeemable Ren. She sees the light within him as well as the dark. This choice becomes her direction and, consequently, her destiny. It is important that she seeks out Ren instead of vice versa because the choices and vision of the future then remain under

---

[66] Taylor, *Star Wars: Age of Resistance—Supreme Leader Snoke* #1.

[67] Ibid.

[68] Ibid. This will turn out to be true, not because Ren will be his loyal apprentice for eternity, but because Ren will destroy Snoke as thoroughly as he did the Dark Side cave.

her control instead of his. Indeed, this is the point at which Ren appears to lose control of the way the story proceeds: Rey now controls the narrative.

Both Rey and Harry Potter thus learn how to see themselves in literal mirrors (the Mirror of Erised and the cave walls on Ahch-To) and embodied mirror images (Harry's future self at the Great Lake and Rey's opposite self Ren on board the *Supremacy*). These educational experiences play a critical role in helping them understand the limitations of the past to determine their present. When Harry needs to see the Stone instead of his family, he will. When Rey needs to resist Ren's twisted lure of their togetherness on the Imperial throne, she will. Their heroic development requires that they see themselves clearly and also that they understand that the significant failures of past heroes (and their mentors) Albus Dumbledore and Luke Skywalker do not tarnish the continuing quest for good over evil, for love and friendship over individual glory, for self-sacrifice over eternal physical life. The mirrors they encounter compress time so that past, present, and future can be seen at once. These mirrors thereby become maps for both heroic travelers, showing them the true object of their quest and where to find it, as well as how to reach their ultimate destination, the scene of their self-sacrifice—for Harry, the Forbidden Forest and for Rey, Exegol. The mirror-maps reveal who the protagonists are and the route to salvation for themselves and their world.

Destiny and destination

Following their exterior and interior maps to the point of the ultimate battle between dark and light, Rey and Harry will effectively use their self-knowledge to forge a new notion of heritage and destiny. Their knowledge, obtained through dynamic encounters with mirror images, will enable their victory over evil tyranny and death itself. Despite their fears, Harry and Rey will not face darkness alone. At the climax, both protagonists will find community in lost heroes to give them strength for their battle, and both will claim those communities as part of their identities at the end of each series.

Understanding that a piece of Voldemort's dark soul lives within him, Harry walks into the Forbidden Forest to allow Voldemort to kill him without a fight. On his way, he puts away his wand and the Invisibility Cloak so that he is entirely vulnerable to the Dark Lord's killing curse. However, he uses the other Hallow in his possession, the Resurrection Stone, to call forth the images of the dead heroes of his parents' generation: his mother and father and their friends Sirius and Lupin. He does not call them to bring them back to life but in anticipation of joining them in death: "He was not really fetching them: They were fetching him."[69] They offer reassuring words, but more importantly, they provide him company on this journey toward death. "Stay close to me," he requests of them: "their presence was his courage, and the reason he was able to keep putting one foot in front of the other."[70] Voldemort delivers the killing spell but destroys only the piece of himself within Harry; in the liminal space of an imagined King's Cross station, Harry decides to rejoin the living to continue the fight against Voldemort. When Harry later duels with this evil twin, the connection now severed, he urges the Dark Lord's true self, Tom Riddle, to find remorse for his actions. Unable to do that, Voldemort is killed by his own rebounding curse and thereafter, readers are assured, "All was well."[71]

By the end of the Sequel Trilogy, Luke, Ren, and Rey all find a balance within the Force, balance obtained through acknowledgement of the past and their own deliberate self-sacrifice. The climax of *The Last Jedi* occurs when Luke reaches an understanding of himself and his role in the present-day conflict with the First Order. Overcoming his self-recriminations and feelings of powerlessness after Rey leaves Ahch-To, Luke mentally projects, in mirror-like fashion, a younger image of himself to stand squarely in front of Kylo Ren and the massively destructive weapons of the First Order. Infuriated, Ren is unable to destroy him in this form because this Luke is an illusion, a mere reflection. When Luke vanishes, he has not been vanquished but rather transformed into a legend.[72]

The journey from the *Supremacy* to Endor and finally to Exegol in *Rise of Skywalker* leads to Ren's redemption, not as a legend but as a human being. Ren witnesses Rey—his inverse mirror image—consistently resist the lures of limitless power and limitless life offered first by him and then by Emperor Palpatine. He sees the strength in her that results from this determination and also begins to recognize that possibility within himself. Rey holds an unshakeable confidence that he may still be turned to the Light Side, which proves more tempting to him than his appeals to the Dark Side were to her. Although Rey fatally injures Ren with his own lightsaber when they duel on the watery moon Endor, she quickly extends her own life force to heal him, telling him that she wanted to join him, to take his hand—not Kylo Ren's hand, but Ben's. She thus projects to him a vision of himself, his true self, that yet remains within him. In a scene reminiscent of Harry's in King's Cross, and a mirrored reversal of their confrontation in *The Force Awakens,* Ren converses with his father, Han. This time he successfully rejects the Dark Side, throwing away his

---

[69] Rowling, *Deathly Hallows*, 698.
[70] Ibid., 700.
[71] Ibid., 759.
[72] Golding, *Star Wars After Lucas*, 197-198.

lightsaber when Han reminds him, "Kylo Ren is dead. My son is alive."[73] When he meets up with Rey on Exegol in the final confrontation with the Emperor, he is Ben Solo again and will fight as Rey's double against the Emperor's evil tyranny.

Although his presence helps Rey, she will nevertheless be pushed to the brink in this confrontation with her grandfather, Emperor Palpatine, who orders her to allow her death to be "the final word in the rebellion."[74] To find the strength she needs to challenge him, she will, like Harry, need the assistance of a hall of lost heroes—in this case, former Jedi. Earlier attempts to call on the Jedi had failed, but at this pivotal moment, when Rey calls, "Be with me," the voices of former Jedi surround her to encourage her at the point of her self-sacrifice.[75] Past Jedi like Obi-Wan, Yoda, Qui-Gon Jinn, and Luke Skywalker chorus: "These are your final steps, Rey. Rise and take them"; "Alone, you have never been"; "Every Jedi who has ever lived lives in you now"; and "Rey, the Force will be with you. Always."[76] No longer the mere "scavenger girl" the Emperor calls her, Rey declares, "I'm all the Jedi."[77] No matter who her parents were, or her kinship to the Emperor, she has found her true lineage in the Jedi Order. She has seen herself amid her family.

Having found her place in the story, understanding her identity and heritage, Rey raises the lightsaber in her hand, and sacrifices her life to obliterate the Emperor's temple and the Sith Order. Like Harry in the Forbidden Forest, Rey appears to have died. However, in a significant departure, the man she had seen in the mirror, Ben Solo, crawls to her side out of the hole into which he had fallen, breathes life into her as she had done for him on Exegol, and then perishes, fading into the Force. This final redeeming act leaves Rey to reestablish the balance in the Force. Unlike Harry's twin Voldemort, in the Sequel Trilogy Rey's Dark Side twin Ren sees himself clearly, expresses remorse, and acts with self-sacrificial heroism in the end. There is no suggestion that Rey is purely good, that darkness has been excised from her as it was from Harry. Rather, her choices have led her to balance the pull she feels between light and dark. Acknowledging that both exist within her, she knows she can choose to fight for the light. In that sense, despite the differences, the theme of choosing one's heroic fate unites these two stories.

These choices are made possible by the "seeking" in these heroes' journeys—the search for knowledge about their family heritage, their self-identity, and

---

[73] *Star Wars Episode IX: The Rise of Skywalker*, directed by J.J. Abrams, 2019.
[74] Ibid.
[75] This request "Be with me," echoes Harry's request "Stay close to me."
[76] *Star Wars Episode IX: The Rise of Skywalker*, directed by J.J. Abrams, 2019.
[77] Ibid.

their destiny. Rey's and Harry's quests are enabled by the maps they discover and their confrontation with enigmatic but revelatory mirrors, literal and embodied, that show them how past, present, and future create one unified whole. Their mirror experiences test the heroes' ability to separate illusion from reality and provide knowledge of their own capacities. Seeing clearly, they know how to assert control over their own stories, how to plot out their own life journeys: the map is in them now. In the end, Rey and Harry have learned not to "dwell on dreams" of the past but to live in the present.

The dénouements of these two epic stories reveal that Harry and Rey continue to choose their relation to the past in order to influence the future, even after the epic battles have been won. In the final scenes, both protagonists have forged new identities, illustrated in symbolic naming that connects past with present and points to a different future. Lynn Holden argues that "knowledge of a person's name conveys power," in the same way as seeing them in a mirror, because name, like image, is linked to an individual's essence.[78] Harry names one of his children "Albus Severus," forming a familial link with two flawed but redeemed heroes in his conflict with Voldemort, while "Rey from Nowhere" chooses her own last name: Skywalker.[79] These names carry forward a new heritage that acknowledges that heroes may be flawed, families may be broken, and yet accurately seeing oneself and one's true relation to the past can lead to choices that facilitate the victory of light over dark. Salvation, both individual and galactic, does not require perfection but does require insight about the influence of the past, self-efficacy in the present, and vision of the future. Decoding the complex, metaphorical language of the maps in the mirrors provides Rey and Harry the self-knowledge they need to stand against and even redeem evil, tyrannical forces. In saving their worlds, they will find themselves and redefine the future.

Bibliography

Abrams, J.J., dir. *Star Wars Episode IX: The Rise of Skywalker.* 2019; San Francisco: Disney/Lucasfilm Ltd. Disney+. https://www.disneyplus.com/movies/star-wars-the-rise-of-skywalker-episode-ix/5e8JThYwCYgw.

---

[78] Holden, "Reflections on the Double," 121. Consider how Rey's use of Ben's name in *Rise of Skywalker* recalls him to himself. Harry also calls Voldemort "Tom" in a similar attempt, though Voldemort is too far gone at this point to respond to the invocation of his earlier self.

[79] It's also worth noting that Harry only uses the Elder Wand to restore his original phoenix-feather wand and then returns the Elder Wand to Dumbledore's tomb. Similarly, Rey buries Luke's and Leia's lightsabers and uses instead her own golden one, formed from the staff she used on Jakku. These choices reflect their (respectful) rejection of certain parts of their heritage in favor of creating something new going forward that belongs uniquely to them.

Anderson, Miranda. "Chaucer and the Subject of the Mirror." In *The Book of the Mirror,* edited by Miranda Anderson, 70-79. Newcastle: Cambridge Scholars Publishing, 2007.

Bortolin, Matthew. *The Zen of R2-D2: Ancient Wisdom from a Galaxy Far, Far Away.* Sommerville, MA: Wisdom Publications, 2019.

"Emperor Palpatine/Darth Sidious." StarWars.com. Accessed September 30, 2022. https://www.starwars.com/databank/emperor-palpatine-darth-sidious.

Eshleman, Carol. "Twin Core: An Exploration of Twins in the Wizarding World." In *Harry Potter for Nerds II,* edited by Kathryn McDaniel and Travis Prinzi, 45-62. Oklahoma City, OK: Unlocking Press, 2015.

Fry, Jason. *Star Wars: The Last Jedi,* expanded edition. New York: Del Rey, 2018.

Garfield, Simon. *On the Map: Why the World Looks the Way It Does.* London: Profile Books, 2012.

Glut, Donald F. *Star Wars: The Empire Strikes Back.* New York: Del Rey, 1980.

Golding, Dan. *Star Wars After Lucas: A Critical Guide to the Future of the Galaxy.* Minneapolis, MN: University of Minnesota Press, 2019.

Hawk, Keith and John Granger. "Lesson 41: Light Sabres and Wands." *MuggleNet Academia.* January 5, 2016. Podcast, MP3, 1:53. https://podcasts.apple.com/us/podcast/mugglenet-academia-lesson-41-light-sabres-and-wands/id523481044?i=1000360146193.

Henderson, Tolonda and Amy M. Von Lintel. "More than Moving Images: The Visual Culture of *Harry Potter.*" In *From Here to Hogwarts: Essays on Harry Potter Fandom and Fiction,* edited by Christopher E. Bell, 140-158. Jefferson, NC: McFarland, 2016.

Holden, Lynn. "Reflections on the Double." In *The Book of the Mirror,* edited by Miranda Anderson, 121-131. Newcastle: Cambridge Scholars Publishing, 2007.

"Holocron." Wookieepedia. Accessed April 14, 2022. https://starwars.fandom.com/wiki/Holocron.

Johnson, Rian, dir. *Star Wars Episode VIII: The Last Jedi.* 2017; San Francisco: Disney/Lucasfilm, Ltd. Disney+. https://www.disneyplus.com/movies/star-wars-the-last-jedi-episode-viii/1nCWFK1pmAI0.

Kerschner, Irvin, dir. *Star Wars Episode V: The Empire Strikes Back.* 1980; Beverly Hills, CA: 20th Century Fox/Lucasfilm Ltd. Disney+. https://www.disneyplus.com/movies/star-wars-the-empire-strikes-back-episode-v/iqtDTZAewwYl.

Klein, Shawn E. "The Mirror of Erised: Why We Should Heed Dumbledore's Warning." In *Harry Potter and Philosophy: If Aristotle Ran Hogwarts,* edited by David Baggett and Shawn E. Klein, 92-104. Chicago: Open Court, 2004.

McDaniel, Katy and John Granger. "Episode 12: Galaxies Not So Far Away: Harry Potter and Star Wars." *Reading, Writing, Rowling.* July 9, 2018. Podcast, MP3 audio, 1:22:54. https://www.mugglenet.com/2018/07/reading-writing-rowling-episode-12-galaxies-not-so-far-away-harry-potter-and-star-wars/.

"Ochi." Wookieepedia. Accessed April 8, 2022. https://starwars.fandom.com/wiki/Ochi.

Parker-Perkola, Anne. "Harry Potter and the Transfiguration of Desire." In *The Alchemical Harry Potter: Essays on Transfiguration in J.K. Rowling's Novels,* edited by Anne Mamary, 46-62. Jefferson, NC: McFarland, 2021.

Pendergrast, Mark. *Mirror Mirror: A History of the Human Love Affair with Reflection.* New York: Basic Books, 2003.

Rowling, J.K. *Harry Potter and the Chamber of Secrets.* New York: Scholastic Books, 1999.

_______. *Harry Potter and the Deathly Hallows.* New York: Scholastic Books, 2007.

_______. *Harry Potter and the Order of the Phoenix.* New York: Scholastic Books, 2003.

_______. *Harry Potter and the Sorcerer's Stone.* New York: Scholastic Books, 1997.

"Sith Wayfinder." Wookieepedia. Accessed April 8, 2022. https://starwars.fandom.com/wiki/Sith_wayfinder.

Strand, Emily. "Kylo Snape? Is 'The Force Awakens' the Eighth Harry Potter Novel?" *Hogwarts Professor* (blog), December 22, 2015, https://www.hogwartsprofessor.com/guest-post-kylo-snape-is-the-force-awakens-the-eighth-harry-potter-story/.

Taylor, Tom. *Star Wars: Age of Resistance—Supreme Leader Snoke #1.* New York: Marvel, 2019. Kindle edition.

Turchi, Peter. *Maps of the Imagination: The Writer as Cartographer.* San Antonio, TX: Trinity University Press, 2004.

Wolosky, Shira. *The Riddles of Harry Potter: Secret Passages and Interpretive Quests.* New York: Palgrave Macmillan, 2010.

Chapter 6

Sabacc Fans' Playable Representations of *Star Wars* Cultural Memory

Jennifer Russell-Long

Abstract: The culturally-selected card game of Sabacc has long been revered in *Star Wars* culture, evolving each time it enters the household of fans. With scholar Richard Dawkins's concept of cultural memes in mind, the game has been replicated and variated over time within both literature and real-life. Adaptation scholar Linda Hutcheon's postulation of the cultural selection of traveling stories helps explain how Sabacc has been chosen by both fans and writers around the world to replicate a beloved fictional universe. The game is played on over ten different *Star Wars* planets with more than eighty variations in the *Star Wars* universe within comic books, graphic novels, and a variety of animation and film series. But Sabacc is also a game fans play on our planet; communities within *Star Wars* and real-life communities of players converge to form literary cultural memories. Just as the villain Q, from *Star Trek: The Next Generation,* repeatedly sets up historiographical games to expose the psychological, social, and cultural depths of their participants, a similar dynamic helps explain Sabacc fans' interest in playable representations of the *Star Wars* game. Wide-ranging narrative representation and community experience powerfully generate a particular kind of cultural memory; the interplay between *Star Wars* universe knowledge, Sabacc rule materiality, and each new game situation works to reinvigorate the adapting narratives.

Keywords: *Star Wars*, cultural memory, Game Studies, meta-cultural, metagame, Play Studies, Sabacc, cultural literacy, Leia

***

> *Glancing out of the corner of my eye towards my "Corellian Spike" Sabacc opponents, I threw down my newly-bought 2021 Han Solo replica gold spike dice to roll doubles, which meant all my cards and my fellow players' cards were going to be replaced. This could have been lucky or tragic, just like the things that life throws at us from time to*

> *time. But luck and the Force were on my side, as my new hand revealed a winning Prime Sabacc hand of +10, -10 and sylop 0.*

The card game of Sabacc is revered in a galaxy far, far away. In the *Star Wars* universe, the most famous Sabacc game—the Corellian Spike variation—won Han Solo the *Millennium Falcon* from Lando Calrissian on the planet Numidian Prime.[1] Sabacc conversation entered the *Star Wars* universe early; cut dialogue from *Star Wars Episode V: The Empire Strikes Back* (1980) had Han Solo blurting out that Lando Calrissian won Cloud City in a Sabacc game.[2] Three years later, the game found its way into a Lando Calrissian novel[3] and has peppered the *Star Wars* universe ever since. Dynamic variations of the game continue to diversify across multiple formats, from comic books to cartoons to novels,[4] and the game has been played on many different *Star Wars* planets with more than eighty variations in the *Star Wars* universe.[5]

But Sabacc is also a game played on our planet. Sabacc card decks contain 76 cards, but variants such as Corellian Spike involve a 62-card deck and two six-sided dice called spike dice. Sabacc has features of both Blackjack and Poker and centers around gambling for the hand pot in individual card hands; the Sabacc pot goes to the overall winner of a full set of games. The game's two to eight players must rely equally on skill and chance during play. Sabacc

---

[1] *Solo: A Star Wars Story*, directed by Ron Howard (2018; San Francisco, CA: Disney/Lucasfilm Ltd.), Disney+, https://www.disneyplus.com/video/e42a76aa-2805-43bf-81ec-d5a853b498d0.

[2] Lauren Bouzereau, *Star Wars the Annotated Screenplays: Star Wars A New Hope, The Empire Strikes Back, Return of the Jedi* (New York: Ballantine Books, 1997), 191.

[3] Neil L. Smith, *Lando Calrissian and the Mindharp of Sharu: A Novel* (New York: Del Rey, 1983).

[4] Some key examples of *Star Wars* comics and novels that feature Sabacc in the narrative, besides Smith's *Lando Calrissian and the Mindharp of Sharu* (1983), include John Jackson Miller's *Star Wars: A New Dawn* (New York: Del Rey, 2014), Marvel Comics' *Solo: A Star Wars Story 3* by Robbie Thompson and Will Sliney (New York: Marvel, 2019), and *Beckett 1* by Gerry Duggan and Marc Laming (New York: Marvel, 2018). Disney produced an episode of the animated series *Star Wars Rebels* titled "Idiot's Array" in 2015 that also heavily featured Sabacc (season 1, episode 11, directed by Steward Lee, written by Kevin Hopps, aired January 19, 2015 on Cartoon Network, Disney+, https://www.disneyplus.com/video/edf47542-e14a-45a6-b56d-ee73c3e8ddb7). This essay aims not to provide a close reading of these texts in its study of Sabacc, but rather seeks to use gaming theory to show the significance of Sabacc as a cultural aspect of *Star Wars* that generates cultural memory among those who play and the potential of games and gaming to enhance cultural literacy.

[5] Pablo Hidalgo, *Solo: A Star Wars Story, The Official Guide* (New York: DK Publishing, 2018), 89. This source reveals Calrissian "has studied more than 80 variant forms" of Sabacc, implying more than 80 variants of the game exist.

has complex rules and is notorious for unpredictability.[6] The fascination and interest in Sabacc within *Star Wars* media is evident from the more than 230,000 fandom websites, critical reviews, and YouTube "how to play" videos that pop up after a quick Google search.

Commercially produced Sabacc card decks now allow for more real life gameplay in the twenty-first century, but for years, dedicated fans made their own decks. This dynamic combination of narrative representation and community experience powerfully generates a particular kind of cultural memory. Gameplay performance with physical items such as cards and dice—and the re-creation of *Star Wars* cultural understanding inherent in each game—dynamically deepens both the canon and fans' decades-long engagement with it. The interplay of *Star Wars* universe knowledge, Sabacc rule materiality, and each new game situation works to reinvigorate adapting cultural narratives, both in the fictional universe and outside of it. Cultural memory is both newly created and *re*-created simultaneously through *Star Wars* Sabacc.

Cultural memory studies and *Star Wars* Sabacc

Cultural memory is a concept first defined by German Egyptologist Jan Assmann, who termed the historical consciousness of group memory as "the textuality of the past."[7] Games have been used as historical texts,[8] but analyzing games as constructions of cultural memory provides distinct insight. Scholar Jason Begy describes the difference, explaining that cultural memory studies aid interaction with and construction of the past, while avoiding two main difficulties of historical studies: problems of historical accuracy and representation of past people. Instead, cultural memory studies center around how the past is constructed and why people construct it in specific ways.[9]

---

[6] Reilly Blanton, "How to Play Sabacc," *The Star Wars Report* (blog), November 19, 2019, https://www.starwarsreport.com/2019/11/20/how-to-play-sabacc/; Joel Cross, "Rules of Sabacc," accessed January 1, 2022, http://sabacc.sourceforge.net/rules; "Sabacc," Wookieepedia, accessed December 10, 2022, https://starwars.fandom.com/wiki/Sabacc.

[7] Roland Alexander Ißler, "Cultural Memory," in *The Bonn Handbook of Globality*, ed. Kühnhardt Ludger and Mayer Tilman (New York: Springer, 2019), 807.

[8] Jason Begy, "Board games and the construction of cultural memory," *Games and Culture* 12, no. 7-8 (2017): 718-738; Adam Chapman, "Is Sid Meier's civilization history?" *Rethinking History* 17, no. 3 (2013): 312-332; and see also Matthew Wilhelm Kapell and Andrew B.R. Elliott, eds., *Playing with the Past* (New York: Bloomsbury, 2013).

[9] Begy, "Board games and the construction of cultural memory," 719.

This concept relates to the study of games, because people desire to play games in specific ways that often depend on cultural influences. In this line of analysis, the past is a human construct of the present. For example, people playing Sabacc in 2023 reconstruct "history" in the *Star Wars* universe in ways particular to their present circumstance. Since cultural memory is innately shared, Begy says it depends on communicative and interactive acts.[10] Sabacc requires complex styles of communication, including bluffing and the navigation of varying social and economic statuses between players. Begy outlines how "one unique way games as a medium can participate in constructing cultural memory is by simulating historically situated structural metaphors."[11] Such simulations encourage counterfactuals, changing historical detail through interactivity and allowing for in-depth conceptualization of history, not tied down to the re-creation of purely factual events and people.[12] Instead of focusing on fact and accuracy, cultural memory-focused analysis of games and gaming can uncover ideologies, constructed social rules of interaction, or socio-economic implications of Sabacc.

Sabacc paratexts: repurposing through gameplay

The definition of paratexts originated in 1987 with Gérard Genette as he used it to describe all the physical and conceptual features deriving from a text. Jonathan Gray began playing with the word years later, aiming to discuss how "paratexts are intrinsic parts of text as social and cultural units."[13] Gray delineates how the paratextual *Star Wars* action figures from the late 1970s and early 1980s helped sustain fan interest in the film series even through long periods of time between episodes. As Gray explains, the *Star Wars* action figures helped invigorate the "never-ending series of grand and cosmic battles of mythic proportions."[14] His research delves into the myriad of ways these paratextual toys represent childhood memories of happily playing with friends or siblings, of gifts at holidays from family or others close to us, and of ways to endlessly recreate the *Star Wars* narrative.[15]

Sabacc similarly represents a *Star Wars* paratext intrinsically linked to its narrative, easily played, and recreated among friends and family. However, rather than focus on the nostalgic feelings Sabacc may invite, this card game

---

[10] Ibid., 720.
[11] Ibid., 718.
[12] Ibid., 720.
[13] Robert Brookey and Jonathan Gray, "'Not merely para': continuing steps in paratextual research," *Critical Studies in Media Communication* 34, no. 2 (2017): 101-110.
[14] Jonathan Gray, *Show Sold Separately: Promos, Spoilers, and Other Media Paratexts* (New York: NYU Press, 2010), 180.
[15] Ibid., 184.

enables players into enjoyable mindfulness of the present duality of being here in the real world yet always a part of the *Star Wars* universe—a universe enriched, cherished, and sparked to life daily by its players. Each new game of Sabacc draws in players to experience new chances to make decisions that help them win or lose, just as *Star Wars* characters have, but with an adapted cultural narrative all their own. Rather than look to the past, Sabacc brings its players into the present moment with the hope of future winnings. Gameplay brings a unique sense of connectedness to the *Star Wars* universe.

Sabacc gameplay: uncovering *Star Wars* culture

Star Wars cultural narratives powerfully reveal themselves through Sabacc gameplay. There is a backstory—a multi-dimensional narrative—behind why Lando Calrissian cheats and Han Solo risks everything for the *Millennium Falcon* in their fateful Sabacc game. A player makes gaming choices charged with the energy of their existence as a cultural being. This power of choice within game narratives is not lost upon the character Q in *Star Trek: The Next Generation's* Season One episode, "Hide and Q." After nodding to eighteenth-century English philosopher David Hartley's famous quote about games revealing humanity, Q revises the reflection to "You reveal yourself best in *how* you play."[16] Q repeatedly sets up historiographical games to expose the psychological, social, and cultural orientations of his games' participants, the *Enterprise* crew.

In an analogous way, *Star Wars* fans' playable representations of *Star Wars* through Sabacc gameplay also expose aspects of the game's participants and thus create cultural memory. The physical elements of the game—cards, cheating devices, and dice—combine with nonphysical elements—verbal bluffing, purposeful delays of gameplay through conversation, and the unique socio-economic background each player brings to the Sabacc table—to create meaningful interactions with *Star Wars* history and culture for players. Begy notes how cultural memory is embedded within objects;[17] *Star Wars* narrative memories are thus embedded within Sabacc's objects. Sabacc is not just a physically re-creatable card game from the *Star Wars* world. The act of playing Sabacc presents and represents *Star Wars* "history" in real life, giving meaning and understanding to physical artifacts and paratexts such as the gold dice

---

[16] *Star Trek: The Next Generation*, season 1, episode 10, "Hide and Q," directed by Cliff Bole, written by Maurice Hurley and Gene Roddenberry, aired November 23, 1987, on Paramount, Paramount+, https://www.amazon.com/gp/video/detail/B00BZC1RB8/ref=atv_hm_hom_1_c_lZOsi7_2_3.

[17] Begy, "Board games and the construction of cultural memory," 735.

and the characters who used them in past stories.[18] Game variations such as Cloud City Casino, Empress Teta Preferred, and Corellian Gambit represent specific planetary cultures and key people from *Star Wars*. Even the Galactic Empire had a Sabacc variation called Trooper Sabacc, where the goal is to take more time with the game to alleviate the boredom between work assignments,[19] revealing insights into Stormtrooper lifestyle to those who play, embedding players and their choices in a lived, diverse experience of *Star Wars*, and creating cultural memory.

Researcher Anthony Pickles studies card games as representations of specific regional or spatial cultural memory within Pacific anthropology. He found that "card games become overwritten with local value narratives in ways that make them important clues to cultural perceptions and everyday economic thinking."[20] Pickles believes gambling within card games is tied to socio-economic forces. These forces become apparent in *Star Wars* narratives in which Sabacc plays a direct role in the plot. In such narratives, players must buy into the game, and this requires money or valuable items, such as in *Star Wars Rebels* when Zeb bets Hera's faithful droid, Chopper, subsequently losing him to Lando Calrissian.[21] Selling everything you own—or your crew captain's beloved droid—to buy into a Sabacc game is risky, but success could give an impoverished player the kind of life they desire. For hard-luck-prone Han Solo, buying into Sabacc won him the *Millennium Falcon*, which brilliantly navigates the *Star Wars* galaxy, occasioning the ship's meaningful lore, like the record-breaking Kessel Run, the rescue of Princess Leia Organa, and the escape of Rey, Finn, and BB-8 from the clutches of the First Order. It even occasions Han's own heroism as, because of the ship, he becomes involved in the Rebellion. As such, the cultural memory of Han Solo winning the *Millennium Falcon* during a Sabacc game has deep anthropological significance to *Star Wars* history. Gambling within Sabacc, like gambling in the card games studied by Pickles, represents years of embedded cultural memory. *Star Wars* fans know one hand of Sabacc can forever change the course of history. The possibility for a new life and desire for change are

---

[18] Additionally, players' own Earth culture echoes in Sabacc. With its Blackjack and Poker influences, the 76-card Sabacc deck has 60 numbered cards divided into four suits and two sets of eight special cards. Each player initially receives two cards from the dealer, followed by four hands with phases that involve betting, calling, shifting, and drawing. See Blanton, "How to Play Sabacc" and Cross, "Rules of Sabacc."

[19] Trooper Sabacc: Fixed-Dark Side, *Star Wars*: Special Edition Limited *Star Wars* Customizable Card Game (Fresno, CA: Decipher, Inc., 1998).

[20] Anthony J. Pickles, *Money Games: Gambling in a Papua New Guinea Town: ASAO Studies in Pacific Anthropology, Vol. 10* (New York: Berghahn Books, 2019), 97.

[21] *Star Wars Rebels*, "Idiot's Array."

culturally written into Sabacc cards, as Pickles' Pacific regional card games contained years of local narratives. Further, Sabacc mirrors the values of the narrative universe from which it springs; gambling on a hand of Sabacc implies hope for a big win, and hope drives narratives across diegetic *Star Wars* history.

Throughout the *Star Wars* saga, rules innate to the fictional world play out within the rules of Sabacc gameplay. Paul Booth utilizes paratextual board games to emphasize the merging of board game rules with fictional cult world rules. Booth describes how cult worlds establish their own rules with "character relationships, fictional cultures, natural laws, history of the world," and more.[22] Players of the paratextual board games fill in contextual details through gameplay. One of Booth's examples includes several *Star Trek*-based games and the fans who repeatedly reinterpret the classic and sequel series. Using Axel Bruns' term produsage,[23] Booth explains how all of the *Star Trek* universe is in a kind of process that remains incomplete, like Gray's description of *Star Wars* action figures and their affordance of those endless battles. The board games are paratexts of their fictional world, but in a different way than Sabacc. These "ludic extensions to the Star Trek franchise develop deeper, more rich integrations of the complexities of the narrative world for fans to investigate."[24] Since Sabacc is an actual game within the fictional world, it is more than a ludic extension. Sabacc is a fictional *Star Wars* game that gained traction in real world ludic replications.

Sabacc replicates and travels across time, location, and peoples, carrying cultural insight. From the first mention of Sabacc, *Star Wars* fans have attempted to design their own game, bringing *Star Wars* culture into their social gaming circles. Sabacc evolves each time it enters the household of fans and each time it is written into a *Star Wars* narrative. With Richard Dawkins's concept of cultural memes in mind, the game—like a meme—has been replicated and iterated over time within both literature and real life. Dawkins's memes are self-replicating units of culture that humans acknowledge as possessing an existence all their own. Like Dawkins's description of a single phrase from Beethoven's Ninth Symphony abstracting into its own particular memory, Sabacc has abstracted from the *Star Wars* universe.[25] Adaptation scholar Linda Hutcheon's postulation of the cultural selection of traveling stories also helps express how Sabacc has been

---

[22] Paul Booth, *Game Play: Paratextuality in Contemporary Board Games* (New York: Bloomsbury Academic, 2015), 22.

[23] Produsage means "nothing is ever finished," "everything is always in process." Ibid., 15.

[24] Ibid., 15.

[25] Richard Dawkins, *The Selfish Gene*, 30th Anniversary Edition (New York and Oxford: Oxford U. Press, 2006), Google ebook, 216-217, 220.

chosen by both fans and writers around the world to replicate a beloved fictional universe.[26] Hutcheon explores why "adults are . . . addicted to what have been called 'sagas'—narratives like *Star Wars* or *Star Trek* that span several media (film, television, comics, novels) and both retell and extend popular stories," explaining that each adaptation involves "memory and change, persistence and variation."[27]

Sabacc gameplay immersion: reenacting and reshaping *Star Wars* history

> *I glance down at the glitter and fancy marker writing of my homemade Sabacc cards during this 1984 game. My friends and I sip drinks inspired from the Cantina bar scenes and make up probable game rules as we go. My free hand smooths out the Princess Leia costume I sewed from old sheets, and I hope for a winning hand to facilitate my desire to buy new ships for the Rebel Alliance.*

This vignette of cultural construction demonstrates how counterfactual influences are acceptable in studying cultural memory, as opposed to history—even diegetic history. The homemade Sabacc cards relate to mimetic fan replication described by Matt Hills as a conceptual link from text to reality.[28] However, since branding and copyright of Sabacc were not in existence at this point, there was a lot of room for interpretation of the textual sources. With the lack of clear visual models and rules, early Sabacc replications were loyal to *Star Wars* culture rather than replicating physical card details. Princess Leia did not have scenes playing Sabacc in the films, but through the imaginative interactivity of Sabacc, a faithful character portrayal of Princess Leia is created and expressed through Sabacc gameplay. It is not strictly accurate to the fictional *Star Wars* universe, but these acts of gameplay faithfully represent *Star Wars* culture and Princess Leia's particular values. Roleplaying as Leia winning money at Sabacc to spend on buying the Rebel Alliance new ships fits the *Star Wars* cultural profile. In these powerful moments, Hutcheon writes, the "conservative comfort of familiarity is countered by the unpredictable pleasure in difference."[29] Sabacc players become part of the known *Star Wars* universe through Sabacc gameplay, but they also bring novel characterizations flecked with their own hopes and

---

[26] Linda Hutcheon, *A Theory of Adaptation*, second edition (Oxfordshire, UK: Routledge, 2013), 197-199.
[27] Ibid., 173.
[28] Matt Hills, "From Dalek half balls to Daft Punk helmets: Mimetic fandom and the crafting of replicas," *Transformative Works and Culture* 16 (2014): 1-20.
[29] Hutcheon, *A Theory of Adaptation*, 176-177.

desires, whether for characters such as Princess Leia or for their own artistic ideas, expressed in costuming and creatively adapted cards.

Hutcheon's concept of familiarity-in-difference parallels Kurt Lancaster's "cathartic moment" discussion of the "textual performer" in cosplay, who participates to experience the deep feelings gained from the story's first showing.[30] But the role-playing enjoyment of becoming Princess Leia in the vignette went beyond familiarity and opportunities for catharsis. The performance did not just center around the text of *Star Wars* but rather the cultural significance of *Star Wars* and the characterization of someone who, just like a real person, was subject to changes and different reactions during Sabacc gameplay, depending on the day and ludic differences. Abigail De Kosnik utilizes Lancaster's application of Schechner's theory that "memories of . . . actors' performances of characters reside within the fan text."[31] In this way, past behaviors are placed into new situations.[32] With Sabacc, representations of Princess Leia are more closely related to her values than her behaviors. Fan performance of Sabacc gameplay seeks out and venerates the heart of *Star Wars* culture.

Star Wars Sabacc players seek this aesthetic, immersive quality of gameplay that puts them into a revered alternate universe. Sabacc gameplay prompts players to act out new narratives ranging from roleplaying *Star Wars* characters in innovative ways to formulating new stories based on the game's results. Thus there is an interplay between *Star Wars* universe knowledge, Sabacc rule materiality, and each new game situation. Depending on the background of the players, dialogue can range from basic rule formation to dramatic fantasy role play representative of the *Star Wars* universe. Scholars Holger Pötzsch and Vít Šisler researched representations of the past in history-based simulated game worlds.[33] They stress that all historical versions of a narrative are unattainable as pure fact; reenactment and reshaping of history are inevitable across all types of literature.[34] However, in contrast to such forms as novel and film, games present a way to represent history negotiated by the players and influenced by the game designers' variables.[35]

---

[30] Kurt Lancaster, *Interacting with Babylon 5: Fan Performance in a Media Universe* (Austin, TX: University of Texas Press, 2001), 131-132.

[31] Abigail De Kosnik, "What is global theater? or, What does new media studies have to do with performance studies?" *Transformative Works and Culture*, special edition on Performance and Performativity in Fandom, 18 (2015), 2.3.

[32] Ibid.

[33] Holger Pötzsch and Vít Šisler, "Playing Cultural Memory: Framing History in Call of Duty: Black Ops and Czechoslovakia 38-89: Assassination," *Games and Culture* 14, no. 1 (2019): 4.

[34] Ibid., 5.

[35] Ibid., 7.

Card games such as Sabacc, video games, and board games all provide opportunities for critical analysis of past fictional or nonfictional culture, linking to theoretical approaches that consider literature as abstraction; embracing such abstraction through gameplay offers a deeper glimpse into past culture.

Embracing abstraction can also pull players into the kinds of gaming decisions and elements of play "historical" characters face, facilitating cultural immersion and creating cultural memory. Han Solo benefits from the unexpected shift in cards between players, so when modern players experience similar gameplay, they feel the frustration or thrill of pure chance and its effect on their success in the game, like Solo. A player with immense skill can be taken out at the last moment in Sabacc. This game threat further immerses players in the world by paralleling the looming threat of the Galactic Empire in the saga, which randomly wipes out people and planets depending on its leadership's whims for power and control. Successful Sabacc players not only win money or ships, but can even gain their freedom from the clutches of the Empire, buying their way out of the Imperial war machine.[36] The game results have the power to change lives forever in *Star Wars*, and its potential to immerse real world players in stakes of this scale and importance drives cultural understanding. In a 2020 comic, *Star Wars Adventures: Driving Force*, a pirate attempts to sum up the cultural significance of this game, saying, "But everyone loves Sabacc. It's . . . like . . . the game of the galaxy."[37] Sabacc is the game of the galaxy because it shapes the galaxy, and immersing in such a galaxy-shaping game has the power to create cultural memory in those who play.

With a game so pervasive across the different planets and cultures of the *Star Wars* universe, it is surprising the franchise took so long to officially trademark the game of Sabacc. In 2017, a lawsuit arose over infringement in the use of Sabacc between Lucasfilm and Ren Ventures. Ren Ventures had used the game concepts in a mobile application, and in the absence of a trademark by Lucasfilm, it had subsequently trademarked "Sabacc" in 2016.[38] With the release of *Solo: A Star Wars Story* (which heavily features the game) looming, both Disney and Ren wanted to market the game more intensively. Lucasfilm won

---

[36] For example, Han Solo winning the *Millennium Falcon* in a game of Sabacc helps him escape a life of persecution and subjugation by the Empire, from which he has deserted; eventually he becomes a legendary helper of the Rebellion. *Solo: A Star Wars Story*, directed by Ron Howard, 2018.

[37] Ian Flynn, *Star Wars Adventures: Driving Force* 10 (San Diego, CA: IDW Publishing, 2020), 8.

[38] "Sabaac," Wookieepedia.

with a 2018 trademark of "Sabacc."[39] Working with Disney, Hasbro Gaming released a children's version of Sabacc called the "Han Solo Card Game" on April 12, 2018, and a Disney Theme Park Merchandise adult version was originally sold from Disney's Galaxy's Edge, and can be purchased from sellers like Amazon and Walmart. When the present author visited Disney World's Galaxy's Edge in December of 2020 and August of 2021, Sabacc sold out on the shelf every day. Clearly, visitors want to take a piece of the *Star Wars* universe home with them—one that can be enjoyed through the act of gameplay.

Scholars Marie-Laure Ryan and Jan-Noël Thon present the components of a story-world as a series of repeating elements with characters, objects, social rules, values, and character reactions.[40] The construction of the *Star Wars* story-world occurs within Sabacc with the imagination, performance, and embodiment seen and described by Ryan and Thon. *Star Wars* story-worlds have been recreated since the fictional universe began as representations of Dawkins's concept of cultural memes that travel across Earth, adapting thousands of times through Hutcheon's descriptions of familiarity and difference.[41] In light of its history of fan-inspired play that led to the game reaching a larger audience through official licensing as a *Star Wars* product, there is a flow of real and fictional cultural past and present that enters Sabacc games.

Adapting the magic gaming circle: Sabacc and metagaming

This flow of the real and fictional in Sabacc contrasts with the static concept of the traditional magic circle of gaming, the usefulness of which is a source of ongoing debate among scholars of games and gaming—a debate that provides insight into how cultural influences affect gameplay. Johan Huizinga first coined the term magic circle in 1938, and Katie Salen Tekinbaş and Eric Zimmerman's 2004 writing evolves this definition. Huizinga defines the magic circle as a space for play that self-contains a kind of material or conceptual world,[42] while Tekinbaş and Zimmerman see the magic circle more as a voluntary, independent circle of gameplay potentially creating meaning through player actions and resulting outcomes.[43] Scholar Jaakko

---

[39] Madhavi Sunder, "Intellectual Property in Experience," *Michigan Law Review* 117, no. 2 (2018): 197.

[40] Marie-Laure Ryan and Jan-Noël Thon, eds., *Storyworlds Across Media: Toward a Media-Conscious Narratology* (Lincoln, NE: U of Nebraska Press, 2014), 31-33, 129.

[41] Dawkins, *The Selfish Gene*, ebook, 216-217, 220; Hutcheon, *A Theory of Adaptation*, 197-199.

[42] Johan Huizinga, *Homo Ludens* (Boston, MA: Beacon Press, 1955), 10.

[43] Katie Tekinbaş and Eric Zimmerman, *Rules of Play* (Cambridge, MA: MIT Press, 2004), Google ebook, 48.

Stenros defends the magic circle from scholars who posit there is no separation of play from ordinary life because play is and always has been a natural, normal part of life.[44] Stenros argues the magic circle is useful in understanding the border of play,[45] explaining that the playful mindset, social negotiations, and game spaces represent the magic circle notion in part due to the special gaming rules' separation from real life and the special time and space of game creation.[46] Stenros develops the idea of a game's social negotiations as driven by cultural norms with culturally coded rules.[47]

Stenros's concept of a game's cultural borders within an evolved magic circle provides insight toward Sabacc's role within *Star Wars* literature and real-life play, and evolving definitions of metagaming and metagame provide more diverse tools for analysis. In 2017, Stephanie Boluk and Patrick LeMieux authored a book about metagaming, noting how the combination of "attitude, affinity, experience, achievement, status, community, competition, strategy, spectatorship, statistics, history, economy, and politics"[48] all influence the way humans make games out of games. In 2021, Kokkinakis and fourteen other authors jointly published "Metagaming and Metagames in Esports," concluding that metagames invoked "optimized strategy based on the game and the game's surrounding structure," which can include events occurring during the game that do not affect the game itself, such as trash talking or social status.[49] The authors note that the verb "metagaming" indicates that players actively influence gaming outcomes, utilizing factors outside the gaming environment.[50]

These various authors contribute to the viewpoint of games and gaming as ongoing cultural productions, with Sabacc elements as vigorously paratextual.

---

[44] Jaakko Stenros, "In defense of a magic circle: the social, mental and cultural boundaries of play," *Transactions of the Digital Games Research Association* 1, no. 2 (2014): 148-150.

[45] Ibid., 147-185, 148-150.

[46] Ibid., 148-150.

[47] Ibid., 174. Mia Consalva argues that game theorists should not be blocked by structural thinking or conceptions of gameplay as inside and outside circles, and she even argues that "cheating can be an excellent path into studying the gameplay situation." Mia Consalvo, "There is no magic circle," *Games and culture*, no. 4 (2009): 408, 415.

[48] Stephanie Boluk and Patrick LeMieux, *Metagaming: Playing, Competing, Spectating, Cheating, Trading, Making, and Breaking Videogames*, (Minneapolis, MN: U. of Minnesota Press, 2017), 9-10.

[49] Athanasios Kokkinakis, Peter York, Moni Patra, Justus Robertson, Ben Kirman, Alistair Coates, Alan Pedrassoli Chitayat et al., "Metagaming and metagames in Esports," *International Journal of Esports* (2021): 4, 18.

[50] Ibid., 3-5.

Their dynamic definitions can be applied to a gaming circle that diffuses culture like a process of osmosis in circular membranes. In analyzing playable literature such as Sabacc, the metagaming concept might be adapted to apply the more fluid concept of a cultural inner and outer game circle. Within *Star Wars,* the cultural outer circle represents the planet or regional location of the game. The inner game circle concept expands prior notions of a traditional, self-contained magic circle by focusing on the cultural impact on gaming behaviors and rules that occur as gameplay unfolds in real time. Cultural outer and inner circles exchange information through passive transfer of ideology. An open flow of culture does not require extra energy because of the active political, economic, and social systems already creating the society. Changing the circle's focus to the players' roles of perpetuating cultural influence, production, and memories through gameplay increases gaming and thus cultural literacy, shedding light on how the parts of Sabacc gameplay fit into the system of *Star Wars* culture. Nonverbal communication, dialogue patterns, cheating methods, socio-economic status of the players, and spatial-temporal specifics are all parts of the inner game circle of Sabacc and prove valuable to comprehending the cultural outer circle system. When players understand the cultural inner circle of Sabacc, they have the potential to reflect meta-culturally.

Solo: A Star Wars Story: meta-cultural gameplay

In *Solo: A Star Wars Story,* young Han Solo is first defeated by Lando Calrissian in a game of Sabacc, with his own ship and the *Millennium Falcon* in the pot.[51] Solo's strong card playing skills combine with a desperate energy to escape his current socio-economic circumstances, but he is thwarted by Lando's cheating, which delivers to Calrissian a winning Full Sabacc hand. When Han plays Lando a second time at the end of the film, the audience now possesses a history with Sabacc. Han enthusiastically hugs Lando, presumably to be friendly, but actually to remove the cheating card inside the mechanical device up Lando's sleeve.[52]

This maneuver occurs outside the game, yet strategically sets Han up to win inside the game. When the pot includes the *Millennium Falcon* in the last hand, Han employs his typical delay and bluff tactic; his new sidekick Chewie helps by acting as if Han's hand were not that good.[53] There is much to gain; the *Falcon* is not just a ship in a game of cards but represents a chance for Han to escape his past life and improve his social, economic, and personal

---

[51] *Solo: A Star Wars Story,* directed by Ron Howard, 2018.

[52] Ibid.

[53] Ibid.

status. Han is playing at life within "the game of the galaxy," drawing upon history, physically manipulating gameplay prior to the game, actively following gaming rules, and throwing his own verbal forms of delay into the mix. When Lando tries to distract everyone with taunts, then realizes that his cheating card is missing, Han smirks.[54] The characters do not realize it, but the audience knows everyone's lives are going to take new directions now. Light and shadows dance around the Sabacc card table representing the constant flux of good and bad luck. The physical artifacts of Sabacc—the cards, credit chips, and other betting pieces—glint with the same light that shines on Han's infectious grin as he finally triumphs over Lando, winning the *Millennium Falcon.*

Here audiences can observe the way the design of both narrative and game converge in Sabacc. Besides the interplay of light and dark that reflects Solo's down-and-up luck in the film and in this iconic scene, Sabacc itself contains positive and negative numbered cards symbolic of the light and dark in everyone. Some variations require the winner to be as close to zero as possible in their card hand, representing the desirable balance of light and dark prominent in *Star Wars* narratives. Scholars Anne Sullivan and Anastasia Salter took a closer look at card and board games that are narrative-centric, noting that variations of Monopoly have nothing to do with gaming mechanics. For example, the *Star Wars* version of Monopoly does not represent the *Star Wars* universe or incorporate its narratives. It is simply Monopoly with a superficial, aesthetic veneer of *Star Wars* on the outside and *Star Wars* locations, figures, and cards used in the game. But in both its light and dark cards, its emphasis on balance, and as discussed earlier, in the way the game's capricious turns recall the Galactic Empire's violent whims, Sabacc physically and symbolically relates to *Star Wars*, pointing to the larger narrative, akin to how Quidditch in the *Harry Potter* saga acts as a symbol set for that saga's larger narrative.[55]

Sullivan and Salter point out how card and board games have been ignored for their narrative design principles, citing games that build narrative through the gameplay.[56] While Sabacc does not build a narrative, it is intricately reflective of a narrative, yet suffers from the same lack of scholarly attention

---

[54] Ibid.

[55] Emily Strand, "The Second War Was Won on the Quidditch Pitch of Hogwarts: Quidditch as a Symbol Set in the Harry Potter Narrative," in *Harry Potter for Nerds II*, ed. Kathryn N. McDaniel and Travis Prinzi (Oklahoma City, OK: Unlocking Press, 2015), 115-138.

[56] Anne Sullivan and Anastasia Salter, "A taxonomy of narrative-centric board and card games," *Proceedings of the 12th International Conference on the Foundations of Digital Games* (New York: Association for Computing Machinery, 2017), 1-10.

Sullivan and Salter bemoan. The emerging design of narrative and play within physical games as exemplified by Sabacc deserves additional study.

Ludonarrative formulations of Sabacc

Sabacc also works in ludonarrative ways—ways that acknowledge the interplay between gameplay and narrative—to formulate cultural memory of *Star Wars* philosophies with each new gaming situation. First, Sabacc offers opportunities for meta-cultural analysis applicable to games in other forms of narrative literature and in real life. Its meta-culturalism demonstrates the dynamic ability of games and gameplay to cross-communicate with culture. Zimmerman's "Manifesto for a Ludic Century" describes a second ludonarrative function that can be applied to Sabacc: developing game literacy, as demonstrated earlier.[57] Playfulness drives innovation, and understanding game components helps players see the entire system. This assemblage of imagery, text, physical artifacts, narrative, and ritualistic actions in gameplay has the power to help players piece together a holistic culture; cultural memory playfully constructs within Sabacc. The *Star Wars* universe game of Sabacc presents personal backgrounds of unique cultures, but vast backgrounds of societal culture flow together with these individual viewpoints. Everyone becomes more aware of their own and other's cultural influences around the Sabacc table, and the game brings out possibilities for changes in circumstance and narrative. Such reflections are meta-cultural and meta-historical within each metagame.

Holger Pötzsch and Vít Šisler's meta-historical analysis of games helps direct a meta-cultural analysis of Sabacc. Pötzsch and Šisler contrast the videogames *Call of Duty: Black Ops* with *Czechoslovakia 38-39: Assassination*, noting the limited ability to explore historical settings and a primary focus on battle-related choices in *Call of Duty: Black Ops*. By contrast, *Czechoslovakia 38-39: Assassination* offers a wide variety of characters from many socio-economic and political backgrounds. The latter videogame "enables playful exploration of contradictions in constant collective negotiation of a shared past."[58] This way of exploring alternate memories of the past from different perspectives equates to meta-historical reflection, defined as historical reflection that lies "beyond the scope of historical narrative or inquiry; transcending history."[59] The card game

---

[57] Eric Zimmerman, "Manifesto for a Ludic Century," in *The Gameful World: Approaches, Issues, Applications*, ed. Steffen P. Walz and Sebastian Deterding (Cambridge, MA: The MIT Press, 2015), 21.

[58] Pötzsch and Šisler, "Playing Cultural Memory," 5.

[59] "metahistorical," OED Online, Oxford University Press, accessed June 15, 2021, web (paywall).

Sabacc's great variety of interplanetary and interspecies gameplay as representative of the *Star Wars* cultural universe can assist in understanding the value of meta-cultural mentality, defined as "that which transcends any particular culture, or exists across cultures."[60]

Sabacc and cultural immersion

Scholar Michael Marek highlights how "effective communicators today must be able to quickly identify commonalities across cultures" and remember that "all cultures have value."[61] Meta-cultural perspective, said Marek, signifies the ways we communicate, understand, and gain the competence that allows us to navigate diverse cultures over time. While designing a chart of four levels of cultural understanding, Marek found the highest level was achieved through cultural immersion.[62] Playing the game of Sabacc immerses players within the *Star Wars* cultural world, and all the different variations speak to the variety of planets, regions, and people from which they originate. Recognizing and respecting the different rules, nuances of behavior, communication, viewpoints on game cheating, and spatial-temporal considerations inside a Sabacc game can create meta-cultural competency in the real world. Sabacc provides experiences that allow players to rehearse respect for diversity in various facets of life across the real world.

The *Star Wars* game Sabacc actively re-creates cultural memory with an immersive, comprehensive set of game rules, with materiality, and with ludonarrative elements. Its applications to game studies, English literature, history, sociology, psychology, and more are clear. The production of cultural memory during Sabacc play and in other forms of gaming is not tied to issues of historical accuracy or factual representation of people. As a result, Sabacc cultural memory game production has the potential to free players to engage with the past as a dynamic system of perspectives. History is made up of the perspectives of millions of individuals experiencing varieties of events in diverse ways. It is virtually impossible to represent every person's perspective properly and accurately on what happened at one point in time. Therefore, engagement with culturally created parts of a game could go further to promote comprehension of an entire system of culture than more stagnant forms of literature such as written words or static images.

---

[60] "metacultural," OED Online, Oxford University Press, accessed June 15, 2021, web (paywall).

[61] Michael W. Marek, "The Meta-Cultural Perspective: Communication, Understanding, Engagement, Appreciation, and Competence," Wayne State College, Wayne, Nebraska, based on an Invited Presentation at the Asia University in Taichung, Taiwan, June 12, 2019, 7.

[62] Ibid., 3.

Beyond the meta-game

Recreation is an activity done purely for enjoyment, such as a game of cards with friends. But such an activity can also re-create—can, in other words, prove generative. By engaging in the recreation of physical gaming media, scholars, students, and fans engage in a re-creation of cultural memory to understand how "ideas about the past are constructed, circulated, and preserved."[63] Sabacc offers scholars of gaming studies and related disciplines a lesser-explored iteration of this important effect of gaming. However, scholar Andrei Zanescu studied another story-world-based card game—Gwent, the *Witcher* card game—stating, "Gwent is an oddity, because . . . the card game exists both as a metagame representing the characters from that universe, and as a game internal to that universe."[64] Similarly, Sabacc not only exists as a metagame, but as a dynamic re-creation and performance of *Star Wars* cultural memory reflecting the story-world's philosophy on life and giving old and new meaning to physical artifacts of the game. Modern Sabacc players can immerse themselves in the *Star Wars* universe with both materiality and imagination, "playing" not only inside established plots but also outside them, creating new scenarios in the same fictional world.

In addition to the value of cultural memory production through gameplay, Sabacc contains the components of what Zimmerman calls a "playful system," or a "human system and a social system rife with contradictions and with possibility."[65] Since Sabacc is a card game open to constant interpretation and variation, it has more possibilities for its players to actively design the game through play than many other forms of gaming. For example, video game players are sometimes limited by the game designers in terms of input, resulting in constraints on output (cheat codes have their limits as well), but in a game like Sabacc, players have more choices within the game due to different rules, methods of communication, and interpretive choices in role-playing characters; this in turn creates a greater variety of outcomes. By playfully engaging with the literature of the *Star Wars* universe, players gain insight into how the game parts fit together to produce a memory of cultures. Zimmerman declares in his manifesto that people must be ready for the Ludic Century by being able to play with all kinds of information. Linear media, he notes, is being replaced, and video games present opportunities for inhabitation, manipulation, and exploration—the same skills needed in day-

---

63 Begy, "Board games and the construction of cultural memory," 719.
64 Andrei Zanescu, "Counter-Balkanism in The Witcher & Gwent: A Historical Reinvention Beyond the Balkan Paradigm," (Master's thesis, Concordia University, 2018), 7.
65 Zimmerman, "Manifesto for a Ludic Century," 2.

to-day life in the twenty-first century.[66] Games such as *Star Wars* Sabacc offer additional and more fluid exploration.

This potential for more dynamic experiences stems in part from how cultural memory construction within card games differs from historical construction; it does not have the same problems of representation or accuracy. For *Star Wars* fans, the range of narrative representations are endless within the Sabacc card game. Fictional communities within *Star Wars* and real-life communities of players converge to form literary cultural memories; understanding this process could significantly enhance the critical tools scholars possess for analysis of both games and culture. Game studies and playful literature should not forget to include the importance of card games such as Sabacc within *Star Wars* in research and pedagogical plans. Convergence of inner and outer realities and osmosis-like cultural circles of gameplay position *Star Wars* Sabacc as a paratextual metagame that enhances our understanding of cultural memory both in real-life scenarios and in literary analysis.

> *I threw down my Prime Sabacc hand of +10, -10 and sylop 0 and lifted my head in triumph. In yet another variation, I had made homemade betting cards with* Star Wars *cultural references on one side and real-life consequences on the other. This meant that, in addition to fantasizing about my new purple Star Cruiser, I would not have to do laundry for a month! As part of our adapted Sabacc rules, I ended the game by giving a dramatic soliloquy about boarding my newly-won ship, what it looked like on the inside, and which planets I intended to visit. By any accounting, it certainly beat laundry.*

Bibliography

Begy, Jason. "Board games and the construction of cultural memory." *Games and Culture* 12, no. 7-8 (2017): 718-738.

Blanton, Reilly. "How to Play Sabacc." *The Star Wars Report* (blog), November 19, 2019. https://www.starwarsreport.com/2019/11/20/how-to-play-sabacc/.

Boluk, Stephanie and Patrick LeMieux. *Metagaming: Playing, Competing, Spectating, Cheating, Trading, Making, and Breaking Videogames.* Vol. 53. Minneapolis, MN: U. of Minnesota Press, 2017.

Booth, Paul. *Game Play: Paratextuality in Contemporary Board Games.* New York: Bloomsbury Academic, 2015.

Bouzereau, Lauren. *Star Wars The Annotated Screenplays: Star Wars A New Hope, The Empire Strikes Back, Return of the Jedi.* New York: Ballantine Books, 1997.

[66] Ibid., 1-2.

Brookey, Robert and Jonathan Gray. "'Not merely para': continuing steps in paratextual research." *Critical studies in media communication* 34, no. 2 (2017): 101-110.

Chapman, Adam. "Is Sid Meier's civilization history?" *Rethinking History* 17, no. 3 (2013): 312-332.

Consalvo, Mia. "There is no magic circle." *Games and culture* 4, no. 4 (2009): 408-417.

Cross, Joel. "Rules of Sabacc." Accessed January 1, 2022. http://sabacc.sourceforge.net/rules.

Dawkins, Richard. *The Selfish Gene.* Second Edition. New York and Oxford: Oxford University Press, 1989. Google e-book.

De Kosnik, Abigail. "What is global theater? or, What does new media studies have to do with performance studies?" *Transformative Works and Culture,* special edition on Performance and Performativity in Fandom, 18 (2015).

Duggan, Gerry and Mark Laming. *Beckett 1, Volume 1.* New York: Marvel Comics, 2018.

Flynn, Ian. *Star Wars Adventures: Driving Force 10.* San Diego, CA: IDW Publishing, 2020.

Gray, Jonathan. *Show Sold Separately: Promos, Spoilers, and Other Media Paratexts.* New York: NYU Press, 2010.

Hidalgo, Pablo. *Solo: A Star Wars Story, The Official Guide.* New York: DK Publishing, 2018.

Hills, Matt. "From Dalek half balls to Daft Punk helmets: Mimetic fandom and the crafting of replicas." *Transformative Works and Cultures* 16 (2014): 1-20.

Hopps, Kevin, writer. *Star Wars Rebels.* Season 1, episode 11, "Idiot's Array." Directed by Steward Lee. Aired January 19, 2015, on Cartoon Network. Disney+. https://www.disneyplus.com/video/edf47542-e14a-45a6-b56d-ee73c3e8ddb7.

Howard, Ron, dir. *Solo: A Star Wars Story.* 2018; San Francisco, CA: Disney/Lucasfilm Ltd. Disney+. https://www.disneyplus.com/video/e42a76aa-2805-43bf-81ec-d5a853b498d0.

Huizinga, Johan. *Homo Ludens.* Boston, MA: Beacon Press, 1955.

Hurley, Maurice and Gene Roddenberry, writers. *Star Trek: The Next Generation.* Season 1, episode 10, "Hide and Q." Directed by Cliff Bole. Aired November 23, 1987, on Paramount. Paramount+. https://www.amazon.com/gp/video/detail/B00BZC1RB8/ref=atv_hm_hom_1_c_lZOsi7_2_3.

Hutcheon, Linda. *A Theory of Adaptation,* Second Edition. Oxfordshire, UK: Routledge, 2013.

Ißler, Roland Alexander. "Cultural Memory." In *The Bonn Handbook of Globality,* edited by Kühnhardt Ludger and Mayer Tilman. New York: Springer, 2019.

Kapell, Matthew Wilhelm and Andrew B.R. Elliott, eds. *Playing With the Past.* New York: Bloomsbury, 2013.

Kokkinakis, Athanasios, Peter York, Moni Patra, Justus Robertson, Ben Kirman, Alistair Coates, Alan Pedrassoli Chitayat et al. "Metagaming and metagames in Esports." *International Journal of Esports.* September 13, 2021. https://www.ijesports.org/article/51/html.

Lancaster, Kurt. *Interacting with Babylon 5: Fan Performance in a Media Universe.* Austin, TX: University of Texas Press, 2001.

Marek, Michael W. "The Meta-Cultural Perspective: Communication, Understanding, Engagement, Appreciation, & Competence." Wayne State College, Wayne, Nebraska. Based on an Invited Presentation at Asia University, Taichung, Taiwan, June 12, 2019.

"metacultural." OED Online. Oxford University Press. Accessed June 15, 2021. Web (paywall).

"metahistorical." OED Online. Oxford University Press. Accessed June 15, 2021. Web (paywall).

Miller, John Jackson. *Star Wars: A New Dawn.* New York: Del Rey, 2015.

Pickles, Anthony J. *Money Games: Gambling in a Papua New Guinea Town: ASAO Studies in Pacific Anthropology, Vol. 10.* New York: Berghahn Books, 2019.

Pötzsch, Holger and Vít Šisler. "Playing Cultural Memory: Framing History in Call of Duty: Black Ops and Czechoslovakia 38-89: Assassination." *Games and Culture* 14, no. 1 (2019): 3-25.

Ryan, Marie-Laure and Jan-Noël Thon, eds. *Storyworlds Across Media: Toward A Media-Conscious Narratology.* Lincoln, NE: U. of Nebraska Press, 2014.

"Sabacc." Wookieepedia. Accessed December 10, 2022. https://starwars.fandom.com/wiki/Sabacc.

Smith, L. Neil. *Lando Calrissian and the Mindharp of Sharu: A Novel.* New York: Del Rey, 1983.

Stenros, Jaakko. "In Defense Of A Magic Circle: The Social, Mental and Cultural Boundaries of Play." *Transactions of the Digital Games Research Association* 1, no. 2 (2014): 147-185.

Strand, Emily. "The Second War Was Won on the Quidditch Pitch of Hogwarts: Quidditch as a Symbol Set in the Harry Potter Narrative." In *Harry Potter for Nerds II,* edited by Kathryn N. McDaniel and Travis Prinzi, 115-138. Oklahoma City, OK: Unlocking Press, 2015.

Sullivan, Anne and Anastasia Salter. "A taxonomy of narrative-centric board and card games." *Proceedings of the 12th International Conference on the Foundations of Digital Games* (2017).

Sunder, Madhavi. "Intellectual Property in Experience." *Michigan Law Review* 117, no. 2 (2018): 197.

Tekinbaş, Katie Salen and Eric Zimmerman. *Rules of Play.* Cambridge, MA: The MIT Press, 2004.

Thompson, Robbie and Will Sliney. *Solo: A Star Wars Story 3.* New York: Marvel, 2018.

Trooper Sabacc-Fixed-Dark Side, Special Edition Limited *Star Wars* Customizable Card Game. Fresno, CA: Decipher, Inc., 1998.

Zanescu, Andrei. "Counter-Balkanism in The Witcher & Gwent: A Historical Reinvention Beyond the Balkan Paradigm." Master's thesis. Concordia University, 2018.

Zimmerman, Eric. "Manifesto for a Ludic Century." In *The Gameful World: Approaches, Issues, Applications,* edited by Steffen P. Walz and Sebastian Deterding, 21. Cambridge, MA: The MIT Press, 2015.

Part 3:
Exploring the Multimedia Storytelling

Chapter 7

Choice and Consequence in *Star Wars*: *Knights of the Old Republic II—The Sith Lords*

Aaron Masters

Abstract: Video games have been part of the *Star Wars* franchise since 1982; since then, more than a hundred have been produced and have subsequently shown themselves capable of significant narrative contributions. Arguably the most important example of the narrative power of *Star Wars* RPGs prior to Disney's acquisition of the franchise was Bioware's *Star Wars: Knights of the Old Republic* (*KotOR*), released in 2003. Having received multiple re-releases on a variety of platforms in the years since and even the prospect of a full remake in development, *KotOR* remains one of the most successful examples of *Star Wars* narrative. This chapter analyzes the game's unique and philosophically complex commentary on the moral ambiguities of the *Star Wars* setting. Moreover, it details how, in presenting this commentary as an interactive RPG, *Knights of the Old Republic II—The Sith Lords* uses the conventions and interactivity of its medium to allow players to metatextually explore the consequences of the conclusions it draws.

Keywords: character, choice, consequence, game studies, ludonarrative, morality, narrative, role-playing, *Star Wars*, video games, *Knights of the Old Republic*, *Knights of the Old Republic II—The Sith Lords*

***

Video games have been part of the *Star Wars* franchise ever since Parker Brothers released *Star Wars: The Empire Strikes Back* in 1982 for the Atari 2600.[1]

---

[1] Ian Bogost and Nick Montford, *Racing the Beam: The Atari Video Computer System* (Cambridge, MA: MIT Press, 2009), 119.

Since then, more than a hundred have been produced.[2] The fact that Parker Brothers was able to do this under their existing license for "toys and games" suggests the initial conception of *Star Wars* video games was primarily as merchandise rather than as a medium for narrative. Yet *Star Wars* video games have subsequently shown themselves capable of significant narrative contributions; recent releases such as 2019's action role-playing game (RPG) *Star Wars Jedi: Fallen Order* expanded on the known history of the "Dark Times" between *Episodes III* and *IV* within the new Disney canon. Arguably the most important example of the narrative power of *Star Wars* RPGs prior to Disney's acquisition of the franchise was Bioware's *Star Wars: Knights of the Old Republic* (*KotOR*), released in 2003.[3] Having received multiple re-releases on a variety of platforms in the years since and even the prospect of a full remake in development,[4] *KotOR* remains both well-known and well-respected, often regarded as one of the most successful examples of *Star Wars* narrative.[5] 2004's *Star Wars: Knights of the Old Republic II—The Sith Lords* (*KotOR2*) was undoubtedly imperfect as a game, but among its imperfections lies unique and philosophically complex commentary on the moral ambiguities of the *Star Wars* setting. Moreover, in presenting this commentary as an interactive RPG, *KotOR2* uses the conventions and interactivity of its medium to allow players to metatextually explore the consequences of the conclusions it draws.

In the shadow of Revan and The Nameless

When LucasArts, the subsidiary tasked with overseeing and licensing computer games for Lucasfilm, announced in July 2000 that they were working with the Canadian developer Bioware to create an RPG, they could hardly have been in better hands. The release that year of Bioware's *Baldur's*

---

[2] Ibid.

[3] Kieron Gillen described it in his contemporary review as "the first successful Western-style console Role-Playing Game of the modern age." "Star Wars: Knights of the Old Republic," *Eurogamer*, September 17, 2003, https://www.eurogamer.net/r-starwarskotor-x. *Cf.* also Matthew Barr's discussion of the game in "The Force Is Strong with This One (but Not That One): What Makes a Successful Star Wars Video Game Adaptation?," *Arts*, 2020; 9(4): 131.

[4] Dan Brooks, "Star Wars: Knights Of The Old Republic Strikes Back With New Remake," StarWars.com, September 9, 2021, https://www.starwars.com/news/knights-of-the-old-republic-remake.

[5] For example, Rob Gordon in "Star Wars: Knights Of The Old Republic Switch Review—A Fantastic RPG" says, "Even though times have changed, the story beats and plot twists still hit home today, and it's undoubtedly one of the best *Star Wars* narratives ever written." *ScreenRant*, November 17, 2021, https://screenrant.com/star-wars-knights-old-republic-switch-review.

Gate II: Shadows of Amn was lauded by gaming magazine *IGN* as "the culmination of the powerful RPG renaissance that's been driving the genre over the last several years; a rebirth that originally started with its predecessor, *Baldur's Gate*."[6] Building on the design principles of the *Dungeons & Dragons* tabletop game from which many of their gameplay mechanics were derived,[7] these games pioneered the capacity of their players to influence the stories themselves. Plots were segregated into sets of discrete "quests," the order of which the player usually had some control over by means of multiple explorable locations and static secondary characters. Largely by offering multiple dialogue options, they also allowed players to define the personalities and moral tone of their characters.

KotOR is an obvious heir to these design concepts and uses them to encapsulate the tropes of its *Star Wars* setting. Though it takes place 4,000 years prior to *Star Wars Episode I: The Phantom Menace* (1999), its plot (written by Bioware staff writer Drew Karpyshyn) is familiar: the Galactic Republic is at war with the Sith, led by the part-cyborg Darth Malak. The protagonist, a former Sith Lord called Revan who was betrayed by Malak, begins the game as an amnesiac allied by circumstance to the Jedi.[8] This mechanism allows the player the freedom to define the character's morality for themselves during the main body of the game, but also affords a revelation that evokes, when it comes, the "Luke, I am your father" moment in *Star Wars Episode V: The Empire Strikes Back* (1980).[9]

The multiple dialogue choices of the *Baldur's Gate* games carry over into *KotOR*, but link to a morality spectrum that tracks the player's position in relation to the canonical "Light" and "Dark" sides of the Force. Friendly and altruistic actions or opinions generally move them toward the "Light Side"—selfish or sadistic, the reverse. The game's cast of companion characters are placed at various points on this spectrum, and thus the player's relationships with those characters can vary depending on their relative positions within it. There are points in the story at which certain characters might shift their alignment on the spectrum (the classic *Star Wars* trope of "falling to the Dark

---

[6] IGN Staff, "*Baldur's Gate II: Shadows of Amn*: Review," *IGN*, October 11, 2000, https://www.ign.com/articles/2000/10/10/baldurs-gate-ii-shadows-of-amn.

[7] See Jason Wilson, "The Dungeons & Dragons Effect," Game Spy, August 24, 2010, http://www.gamespy.com/articles/111/1115803p1.html; see also Brad King and John Borland, *Dungeons and Dreamers: The Rise of Computer Game Culture from Geek to Chic* (Emeryville, CA: Mc-Graw-Hill, 2003), 27.

[8] Drew Karpyshyn, *Star Wars: Knights of the Old Republic*, LucasArts, various platforms, 2003.

[9] *Star Wars Episode V: The Empire Strikes Back*, directed by Irvin Kerschner (1980; Beverly Hills, CA: 20th Century Fox/Lucasfilm Ltd.), Disney+, https://www.disneyplus.com/movies/star-wars-the-empire-strikes-back-episode-v/iqtDTZAewwYl.

Side"), but at a basic level, all actions and opinions are depicted as relative to this fixed and largely unexamined philosophical framework. This extends to the game's climax, which—though the final fight with Malak occurs whether the player has chosen to push their character to the "Light" or "Dark" end of the alignment spectrum—is given different context by the events immediately leading up to it and produces a different ending: either saving the Republic as a redeemed Jedi or conquering it as a restored Sith Lord.[10] The choices are simplistic, but their consequences are consistent both with the inherited philosophy of the game's setting and—crucially—with the game's mechanics. As Richard Dees admits, "the moral universe of *Star Wars* has two colors: black and white. . . . Every identifiable character in the six movies works either for the Light Side of the Force or for the Dark Side."[11] Thus, *KotOR* satisfactorily avoids what Clint Hocking has described as "ludonarrative dissonance,"[12] subsequently defined by Frédéric Seraphine as "a state of emersion [or pulling a player out of the game experience] that is triggered by a semiotic mismatch between play and narration."[13] The binary nature of *Star Wars* excuses the game developers from having to create a truly emergent narrative free from an imposed structure without robbing the player of their ability to affect that narrative; the circumscription of their choice as a binary opposition is implied by the universe in which the game is set.

Such was LucasArts's faith in *KotOR* that they started pushing for a sequel before the game was even released.[14] When Bioware, already in pre-production for their own IP project *Jade Empire*, turned down this sequel, they recommended the newly founded Obsidian Entertainment. Though Obsidian had no previous titles under its belt, it was made up of several prominent members of Black Isle Studios, the team responsible for sophisticated and well-received RPGs such as *Planescape: Torment* (1999) and *Icewind Dale* (2000). *Planescape* was especially

---

[10] Chris Kempshall also makes this point in *The History and Politics of* Star Wars: *Death Stars and Democracy* (London and New York: Routledge, 2023), 161.

[11] Richard H. Dees, "Moral Ambiguity in a Black-and-White Universe," in *Star Wars and Philosophy*, ed. Kevin S. Decker and Jason T. Eberl (Chicago & La Salle, IL: Open Court, 2005), 39.

[12] Clint Hocking, "Ludonarrative Dissonance in *Bioshock*," Clicknothing Typepad, October 7, 2007, https://clicknothing.typepad.com/click_nothing/2007/10/ludonarrative-d.html; Frédéric Seraphine, "Ludonarrative Dissonance: Is Storytelling About Reaching Harmony?," Academia.edu, accessed June 8, 2022, https://www.academia.edu/28205876/Ludonarrative_Dissonance_Is_Storytelling_About_Reaching_Harmony, 2.

[13] Ibid., 3.

[14] Jordan Maison, "Knights of the Old Republic II Developer Chris Avellone Discusses the Game's Impact 15 Years Later," *cinelin*, June 12, 2019, https://web.archive.org/web/20200611214227/https://www.cinelinx.com/news/culture/knights-of-the-old-republic-ii-developer-chris-avellone-discusses-the-games-impact-15-years-later/.

notable for the degree to which it pushed the boundaries of player choice and self-determination; a contemporary review by Greg Kasavin notes, "the game lets you perceive small details if your character is intelligent, understand philosophical implications if he's wise, and intimidate or charm if he's strong or charismatic. Your character's moral alignment and his affiliation with Sigil's different factions are openly flexible and have a noticeable impact on the course of the game."[15] It also anticipated *KotOR*'s use of a protagonist whose history weighs heavily on the narrative of the game as it plays out; as Chris Dahlen observes, "*Planescape* neatly balances a rich protagonist with an emergent narrative: although you wake up as a blank slate and you can roleplay any way you choose, you're just the latest in a series of personalities that have controlled this beaten-up body. The Nameless One has also been wild and savage, cold and calculating, and an obnoxious do-gooder—and you have to deal with the fallout."[16] Though he goes on to remark that "*Star Wars: Knights of the Old Republic* pulled a similar trick, but the reveal was far more straightforward,"[17] the options for choice-based characterization in *KotOR* are much more fundamentally limited by the franchise's own moral landscape, as described above. In *Planescape*, your in-game choices do not decide which of two incarnations of a pre-set character you become; they are the embodiment and summation of the narrative itself.

There is only you

The story of *KotOR2*'s development is an unhappy one, beset both with technical problems and a punishingly tight release schedule.[18] The final product, on release, was plagued by bugs and broken quests, with a great deal of narrative material cut at the last minute, particularly from its final act.[19]

---

[15] Greg Kasavin, "*Planescape: Torment*: Review," *GameSpot*, December 21, 1999, https://www.gamespot.com/reviews/planescape-torment-review/1900-2535119/.

[16] Dahlen, Chris. "*Planescape: Torment*," *The Escapist*, August 23, 2005, https://www.escapistmagazine.com/planescape-torment/.

[17] Ibid.

[18] See Maison, "Chris Avellone Discusses the Game's Impact 15 Years Later," and Emperor Devon, "Interview with Chris Avellone, Obsidian Entertainment," *Star Wars Knights*, 2007, accessed June 12, 2023, archived at http://web.archive.org/web/20150924105808/http://www.starwarsknights.com/interview20070924.php.

[19] A dedicated fan community has unofficially managed to fix a lot of these bugs in the PC release, with one particularly impressive undertaking, known as "The Sith Lords Restoration Project," using discarded files still present in the game data to "complete" much of the cut content. In 2022, Lucasfilm licensed developer Aspyr announced that this content would be officially released as a free update for *KotOR2*'s re-release on the Nintendo Switch console, effectively canonizing the changes. In June 2023, however, Aspyr announced without explanation that the update "will not be moving forward for release." See Demi Williams, "Star Wars KOTOR 2 Restored Content DLC Canceled on

Nevertheless, the game—imperfect though it was—managed to fuse the precedent of its direct predecessor with Obsidian's more nuanced take on ludonarrative consistency in such a way as to provide a unique perspective from which to view the *Star Wars* franchise.

Set five years after the first game, *KotOR2*'s plot moves away from the Republic-against-Sith struggle that dominates its predecessor (and to which the series would eventually return in its latest incarnation: the 2008 online multiplayer RPG *Star Wars: The Old Republic*). The Jedi have been all but killed off, the Sith are in hiding, and both are viewed by most characters in the game as aloof and largely indistinguishable factions of the same group.[20] The Republic is portrayed less as the "hapless, hopeless, clueless mélange of bickering futility" it appears to be in the Prequel films;[21] it is shown to be making efforts to restore planets devastated by war, such as Telos for instance. Nevertheless, the Republic is an ailing and largely impotent background player, crippled and leaderless, reliant on criminal gangs for basic resources such as fuel. The game begins with a group of four characters—three of whom are entirely unknown and unexplained even to players of *KotOR*, including the protagonist—stranded on what appears to be an abandoned mining station. This initial lack of society not only adds an element of investigation to the game's plot structure, it also frees the narrative from the moral compass points of its predecessor, which begins with a space battle between Republic and Sith warships—an implicit suggestion for the player to *pick a side.*

The same can be said for the characters themselves. After the prologue, the first character the player encounters is Kreia, who even visually straddles the divide between the inherited expectations of good and evil in *Star Wars.* Her robe is reminiscent of Obi-Wan's on Tatooine in *Star Wars Episode IV: A New Hope* (1977), and yet something about her cowled head with no visible eyes, coupled with a subtle, somewhat Mephistophelean voice also evokes Darth Sidious of the Prequel films.[22] As the game progresses, even the eponymous

---

Switch," *Gamespot,* June 5, 2023, https://www.gamespot.com/articles/star-wars-kotor-2-restored-content-dlc-canceled-on-switch/1100-6514788/#:~:text=%22Sadly%2C%20today%20we're,for%20release%2C%22%20Aspyr%20said. The unofficial update remains available for the PC version of the game.

[20] The character Atton describes both Jedi and Sith as men and women with excessive power, fighting over religion. Chris Avellone, *Star Wars: Knights of the Old Republic II—The Sith Lords,* LucasArts, various platforms, 2004.

[21] David Brin, "Opening Statement for the Prosecution: I Accuse . . . Or Zola Meets Yoda ...," in *Star Wars on Trial,* ed. David Brin and Matthew Woodring Stover (Dallas, TX: BenBella Books, 2006), 22.

[22] Both are given as conscious references for the character in Matt London's "Interview with Chris Avellone, Game Designer, *Fallout: New Vegas,*" *LightSpeed,* Issue 6, (Nov, 2010),

Sith Lords are revealed to be if not sympathetic, then at least understandably damaged; Nihilus is a slave to the desperate, murderous hunger with which he was afflicted in a war not of his making and that will eventually consume him; Sion is literally held together by a hatred fueled by inescapable pain; both incarnations of Darth Traya are as guilty of self-betrayal and self-delusion as they are of any other moral failing. Similarly the Jedi, at the end, succumb to their fear and recalcitrant pride and are willing to lobotomize, metaphysically at least, the last real hope for the restitution of their order.

This undermining of the moral commonplaces of the *Star Wars* franchise itself emphasizes the importance of character choice in the narrative. This is perhaps unsurprising, since *KotOR2*'s lead designer and chief writer Chris Avellone previously worked in the same capacity on *Planescape*. Just as The Nameless One in *Planescape*, every character in *KotOR2* comes into the narrative based on the choices they have made in the past, and their capacity for action during the events of the game is informed and delineated by those choices. The protagonist, referred to within the game as the Exile, is so named because she was exiled from the Jedi, not simply because she chose to follow Revan to war against the Mandalorians but because she was the only Jedi who chose to return to them for judgment.[23]

In the 2006 essay collection *Star Wars on Trial*, co-editor David Brin makes the argument that the franchise, as it developed after *The Empire Strikes Back*, moved increasingly away from seeing the Force as the spiritual ally of the plucky egalitarian and towards it being the dominating root cause of a predestined, mystical aristocracy: "as the Übermensch Effect took over . . . the Force grew ever more elitist. You had to be born with it! No, not just born with it, you had to be a mutant! No, make that a fore-ordained by destiny, preselected long-ago, A bona fide Chosen One. A demigod."[24] Anakin is outstanding because he was the child of the Force; Luke and Leia are as well because they have inherited their Force-affinity from their messianic father. More recent entries in the canon might have gone some way to complicate this precedent, but even seemingly radical examples such as 2017's *Star Wars Episode VIII: The Last Jedi* are more concerned with the

---

https://www.lightspeedmagazine.com/nonfiction/feature-interview-chris-avellone-game-designer-fallout-new-vegas/.

[23] The gender of the Exile is decided by the player at the start of the game and itself has far-ranging consequences for the direction of the narrative, including which companion characters are available. The canonical representation of the Exile as female was established by Daniel Wallace in the (now Legends) *New Essential Guide to Droids* (2006). *Star Wars: The Old Republic* continues to honor this post-2014 de-canonization by Disney, though this source has so far not been included explicitly by the Lucasfilm Story Group in the new canon.

[24] Brin, "Opening Statement for the Prosecution," 35-36.

potential corruption or "failure" of the Force aristocracy, whose central figure is Luke Skywalker, than with offering alternatives to it.[25] The depiction of one's relationship to the Force in *KotOR2* is far more radical; except for the Handmaiden, whose parentage and indeed canonicity are ambiguous,[26] no character is exemplary because of some inherent advantage. In the original *KotOR*, the protagonist character might be introduced to the player as a tabula rasa on account of his wiped memory, but it is made clear as the game progresses that his former life as Revan has already established his innate capacity for greatness. In *KotOR2* however, the Exile is unique because she made the choice to turn away from the Force. This is initially described as a punishment inflicted upon her by the Jedi Council, but eventually this is proven incorrect—she did it to herself in the face of the mass destruction she unleashed at the Battle of Malachor V.[27] This is what leads to her pursuit by the Sith and her identification by Kreia. The entire narrative of the game may be viewed as an exploration of the potential consequences of that choice. As such, it is a dramatic exemplum of one of the defining features of the *Baldur's Gate* school of RPGs: the ability of the player to

---

[25] *Star Wars Episode IX: The Rise of Skywalker* (2019) effectively reverses even the tentative steps its predecessor makes away from Brin's "Übermensch Effect" by revealing that Rey was, after all, a descendant of Emperor Palpatine. Though Chris Kempshall argues that "*The Rise of Skywalker* presents a different interaction with history . . . [o]ne where the sins of fathers and grandfathers need not be the destiny of those who come after them," it still depicts the Force as a genetic inheritance which demarcates society. Kempshall, *The History and Politics of* Star Wars, 169.

[26] See note 23 regarding the question of canonicity. In the initial draft of the game, the Handmaiden was originally supposed to be part of a matriarchal clan led by the character who would eventually become Kreia, and the concept of her being Kreia's daughter might have persisted into later versions. The Handmaiden's mother is eventually named Arren Kae and there are various similarities between her backstory and that of Kreia, but final confirmation of the connection failed, as did so much else, to make the final cut. When asked explicitly about this connection for *Star Wars Knights* in 2007, Avellone responded "Can't comment, but good catch." Emperor Devon, "Interview with Chris Avellone."

[27] Cody Mejeur cites the Jedi Council's aversion to the Exile as evidence of what he calls "isolationism within the hyperdiegetic cycle," i.e. an attempt to repudiate the productive tension between the ever-expanding known and unknown within the evolving *Star Wars* franchise. Though often traumatic and violent, this cycle "has long-lasting effects and fundamentally changes the narrative universe by introducing new experiences, possibilities, and expectations for audiences." Effectively, the Exile represents a capacity for self-actualization with which the Council refuses to engage. Cody Mejeur, "Chasing Wild Space: Narrative Outsides and World-Building Frontiers in *Knights of the Old Republic* and *The Old Republic*," in *Star Wars and the History of Transmedia Storytelling*, ed. Sean Guynes and Dan Hassler-Forest (Amsterdam, Amsterdam University Press, 2018), 207-208.

affect the arc of their character through the narrative by making choices and having the consequences of those choices fuel that subsequent narrative.

Not the destination, the journey

The same holds true for the backstories of *KotOR2*'s companion characters. Each of their personal arcs sees them coming to terms with some major event in their past, whether that is Atton's sense of guilt and loss over the Jedi he tortured to death just as he fell in love with her (and through which his own Force sensitivity was revealed), Visas's betrayal of Nihilus as a means of processing the destruction she witnessed on her homeworld, or Mira's decision to spare Hanharr and tie him into the life-debt he finds so torturous. In each case, the character may be able, through an association with the player that manifests as a personal choice, not only to digest such past events but to capitalize on them. Here Force potential is depicted not as an inherent talent but as derived from experience—and especially trauma. When Kreia flippantly tells Atton that "the self-loathing that squirms within you gives you a curious strength,"[28] she is in fact highlighting his greatest potential advantage. This is of course another metaphor for the experience of playing this sort of video game; the fact that this story is told within an RPG adds a further level of complexity to it by rendering the player not as the passive recipient of the text but as a complicit agent within it. When Kreia declares that "it is only through interaction, through decision and choice, through confrontation, physical and mental, that the Force can grow within you,"[29] she not only summarizes her own doctrine but also makes an ironic meta-summary of the game's mechanics. The player progresses through the story by overcoming various challenges, receiving experience points from them, and using that experience to develop the statistics and powers of their character before continuing on to further challenges. As previously discussed, *KotOR2* sprang from a legacy of games that had pioneered not only the use of a morally neutral setting but also the capacity of the player to influence the narrative and to define the characters on their own terms. The order of the planets the protagonist visits, the degree to which the protagonist interacts with other characters, and the nature of the relationship they form with those characters are dictated to a greater or lesser degree by the player as they proceed through a narrative focused on exploring the consequences of individual choice. Kreia again observes as the game draws to a close, "all your decisions have brought you to this point."[30] This goes beyond mere ludonarrative consistency and into ludonarrative meta-representation.

---

[28] Avellone, *Star Wars: Knights of the Old Republic II—The Sith Lords.*

[29] Ibid.

[30] Ibid.

There are times at which the game goes further still to tie the game's mechanics into the philosophy of the narrative. In one of her pronouncements on the nature of the Force, Kreia instructs the player not to rely on their Force powers alone, arguing that there are other means of wielding power not derived from one's connection with the Force. She then goes on to list various skills such as piloting, mechanics, and medicine and ends with a reference to "the more subtle work of politics, persuasion."[31] Not only is this an overt reference to the precedent set by other *Star Wars* media (a note in the voiceover script that can still be found in the game files suggests reading the final sentence "a little quieter, referring to modern *Star Wars* canon"[32]), it also directly references the "skills" your character can develop mechanically during the game. Indeed, she follows this up by setting the player the task of improving the "skill" to which they have allocated the fewest "skill points" (received whenever they amass enough experience points to reach a new "level") and will only continue her conversation with the player once this has been done. This lesson from Kreia becomes increasingly significant as her views on the nature of the Force are gradually revealed. Here we see the mechanics of the game not only as compatible with its narrative but as narrative tools themselves.

This emphasis on choice, and on the way that the aggregate of choice creates both personal and narrative growth, is played out on a macro as well as an internal scale. For instance, Revan's war against the Republic, as established by *KotOR*, is recontextualized by its sequel's aversion to an unthinkingly evil Dark Side. Kreia's analysis, given early in the game, presents a very different vision of its inherited context:

> The Republic was never what was important—ever. It was but a shell that surrounds the Jedi—just as the teachings of the Jedi are a shell surrounding the heart of man. You see the war, the true war, has never been one waged by droids, or warships, or soldiers. They are but crude matter, obstacles against which we test ourselves. The true war is waged in the hearts of all living things, against our own natures, light or dark. That is what shapes and binds the galaxy, not these creations of man. You are the battleground.[33]

Here the events are no longer a stand-off between the paladins of righteousness and their blindly destructive foes, but rather a stage intended to amplify the

---

[31] Ibid.

[32] Voiceover script, Avellone, *Star Wars: Knights of the Old Republic II—The Sith Lords.*

[33] Avellone, *Star Wars: Knights of the Old Republic II—The Sith Lords.*

internalized conflict within the Jedi. Later she will argue that Revan's war was intended to convert the Jedi, not to the Dark Side, but into an amoral weapon to be wielded in defense of the very Republic they were fighting.[34] Such a recontextualization lends a premium to the choices made by the player in the first game, because it can encapsulate the divergent narrative paths that could have been chosen (whether Revan was redeemed for the Jedi or reverted to his Sith persona) rather than arbitrarily deeming one possible permutation to be "canonical." When viewed with the hindsight of *KotOR2*, the morally binary plot of *KotOR* becomes instead a cynical choice by Revan to sacrifice himself and his order for the sake of a bloodied but battle-hardened and thus more resilient Republic. Kreia tells the Exile that the teachings of a culture and its people's nature "achieve definition in conflict."[35]

Such cynicism is borne out by other elements of the game, such as GO-TO's mission to "save" the Republic, which it finds it can only achieve by disregarding the Republic's laws and becoming a crime lord. Chris Kempshall has argued that the Jedi of the Prequel films are manipulated into betraying their morality by their association with and desire to preserve the Republic.[36] GO-TO is similarly manipulated by his own programming; having been compelled by it to save the Republic, he is equally compelled to disregard any subordinate moral scruples in order to achieve this. GO-TO has no choice because he is being influenced by a force outside his control. Revan on the other hand, as interpreted by Kreia at least, abandons the doctrinal morality of the Jedi out of a calculated assessment of how best to preserve the institution the films would have us believe it is the Jedi's moral duty to champion.[37] Kreia argues that the Jedi Council could not understand or contemplate the possibility that Revan "never fell,"[38] but by her own assessment the reality is that in order to save the Republic—the institution the Jedi of the Prequels strive to preserve and in the Original Trilogy to revive—Revan *chooses* to fall.[39]

---

[34] The droid GO-TO also remarks that, though Revan inflicted crushing defeats on the Republic during the war, he made sure to leave its key infrastructure intact.
[35] Ibid.
[36] Kempshall, *The History and Politics of* Star Wars, 155-158.
[37] Compare Obi-Wan's repudiation of Anakin on Mustafar: "Anakin, my allegiance is to the Republic, to democracy!" *Star Wars Episode III: Revenge of the Sith*, directed by George Lucas (2005; Beverly Hills, CA: 20th Century Fox/Lucasfilm Ltd.), Disney+, https://www.disneyplus.com/movies/star-wars-revenge-of-the-sith-episode-iii/4WvbqLFumNvi.
[38] Avellone, *Star Wars: Knights of the Old Republic II—The Sith Lords.*
[39] Kempshall details a remarkably similar trajectory for the character of Jacen Solo in the *Legacy of the Force* series (2006-2008), though this comes several years after the release of *KotOR2*. See *The History and Politics of* Star Wars, 162-164. Unlike Revan in *KotOR2* however, the fate of Jacen Solo is portrayed as an unequivocally cautionary tale.

Pieces of a whole

Kreia's use of direct quotation from the original *Star Wars* trilogy (Yoda's "crude matter,"[40] Obi-Wan's "binds the galaxy"[41]) highlights the degree to which the internalized, choice-focused narrative of the game, as she articulates it, stands in contrast to the philosophy depicted in the films. Where Obi-Wan and Yoda declare trust in the Light Side of the Force both as the key to toppling the metaphysically reprehensible Empire and as the primary justification for doing so, *KotOR2* constantly presents and demands justification for choices made by its characters, the consequences of which often stand in contrast to their professed morality. At one point in the game, the Exile is approached by a beggar requesting money for food. The player is given a choice between giving the beggar five credits (a paltry sum) or threatening him until he runs away. If the money is given, Kreia immediately rebukes the Exile, not only for having robbed the beggar of the opportunity to work for his survival and thus become stronger for it, but also for making the beggar a target for the jealousy of his peers. Having not earned his resources, he is unable to defend them, and the player is shown a vision of the beggar being mugged for the money they received to salve the player's conscience and, by extension, the Exile's relationship with the mystical Light Side. Kreia sums this up with what could be a mantra for the entire narrative: "From such small things, from such critical points, the universe and its masses may be moved . . . that is why you must be careful in all that you do, and in every choice you make."[42]

This moral outlook contrasts starkly with the binary morality and one-to-one correlation of Good versus Evil = Jedi versus Sith in the main film series. Torill Mortensen argues that *KotOR2*'s successor, *Star Wars: The Old Republic*, attempts to undermine the assumption of moral certainty within the game by giving "Light Side" and "Dark Side" choices that can conflict with the player's understanding of the franchise's morality;[43] in *KotOR2* however, the question of whether the "Light Side" can occasionally be morally bad is less relevant than whether it is possible, within the conceit of the *Star Wars* universe, to

---

[40] *Star Wars Episode V: The Empire Strikes Back*, directed by Irvin Kerschner, 1980.

[41] *Star Wars Episode IV: A New Hope*, directed by George Lucas (1977; Beverly Hills, CA: 20th Century Fox/Lucasfilm Ltd.), Disney+, https://www.disneyplus.com/movies/star-wars-a-new-hope-episode-iv/12fVeZxD2fWJ.

[42] Avellone, *Star Wars: Knights of the Old Republic II—The Sith Lords.*

[43] Torill Elvira Mortensen, "Keeping the Balance—Morals at the Dark Side," in *The Dark Side of Game Play*, ed. by Torill Elvira Mortensen, Jonas Linderoth, and Ashley M. L. Brown (London: Taylor and Francis, 2015), chapter 10, https://www.perlego.com/book/1642776/the-dark-side-of-game-play-pdf.

step outside of the binary altogether and into a relativistic pragmatism based on the consequences, or "echoes" as the game describes them, of individual decisions. Its depiction of Revan's Jedi Civil War, for instance, stands in juxtaposition to the formation of the Clone Wars in *Star Wars Episode II: Attack of the Clones* (2002) and indeed seems to anticipate the more morally nuanced depiction of those wars in the *Star Wars: The Clone Wars* animated series (2008-2014, 2020). *KotOR2* establishes the precedent that the Jedi Civil War was designed to hone the Jedi into an effective military force whose morality is compromised by the realities and imperatives of conflict. As such, it articulates explicitly what is implicit in the climactic arrival of Yoda and his clone legions in *Attack of the Clones*: the "guardians of peace and justice in the galaxy"[44] transformed by machinations they can't detect into the generals of a clone army of what will all too apparently become stormtroopers. *Star Wars Episode III: Revenge of the Sith* (2005) was released after *KotOR2*, but retrospectively, the game's cynical vision adds weight to Palpatine's smear of the Jedi: at the end of the trilogy, he portrays the Jedi as having been forged into a weapon against the Republic by the very act of fighting in its defense.

The ethical consequence of this recontextualization of accepted *Star Wars* truths means the player is encouraged not only to think relativistically about their own decisions within the game, but also to look critically at the inherited ethics of *Star Wars* itself. Shanti Fader, for instance, has made an impassioned attempt to justify the multitude of flagrant untruths uttered by those Jedi (Yoda and Obi-Wan in particular) whom the narrative of the first two film trilogies would have us believe are moral paragons;[45] *KotOR2* is far less charitable; to quote Atton:

> Jedi lie. And they manipulate . . . The Jedi are pacifists . . . except in times of war. They're teachers . . . except when it comes to telling their students the truth.[46]

It is up to the player to decide whether such a track record is justifiable, and the game certainly does allow scope for that conclusion to be drawn, but it is nevertheless relentless in its mission to make the player pass judgment on their own terms, rather than based on assumptions inherited from other *Star Wars* media.

---

[44] *Star Wars Episode IV: A New Hope*, directed by George Lucas, 1977.

[45] Shanti Fader, "'A Certain Point of View: Lying Jedi, Honest Sith, and the Viewers Who Love Them," in *Star Wars and Philosophy*, ed. Kevin S. Decker and Jason T. Eberl (Chicago & La Salle, IL: Open Court, 2005), 192-204.

[46] Avellone, *Star Wars: Knights of the Old Republic II—The Sith Lords*.

Miguel Sicart argues that the original *KotOR* fails in its attempt to create either an "ethically deep game" or a "good game from an ethical perspective."[47] This is because, he says, "the player is bereft of her creative capacities, leaving a system that evaluates and labels her actions according to moral standards [ie. the Light and Dark sides of the Force] that are external to those the player has created."[48] He goes on:

> By embedding the morality of the players' actions in the game design and systematically evaluating them as "good" or "bad" actions, these games are taking away the player's moral responsibility, making the process of self-evaluation just another element in the game system and not a part of the moral interpretation of the game experienced by the player.[49]

KotOR2 inherits the Light/Dark spectrum mechanic for moral alignment of its predecessor (as described above) without any real adaptation on a system level, but due to the narrative, the ethical status of that mechanic is both undermined and recontextualized. Rather than representing an objective measure of "good" versus "evil" as it did in the first game, the alignment spectrum in *KotOR2* acts as a visual and mechanical representation of the way in which the Exile's (and thus the player's) relationship to the Force can be manipulated for its own sake. The player can decide to manipulate that relationship in line with their own sense of morality as the game presents them with choices, and if done honestly, this might not correspond consistently with moving their character towards the "Light" side of the Force. Alternatively, the player could choose to have their character make certain choices counter to their own sense of morality for the sake of some external incentive (whether narrative, such as an extra-moral judgment on the state of the Republic, or mechanical for the sake of some statistical benefit).[50] This is true for both games, but in *KotOR2* it is recognized by the narrative itself and reflected in the way other characters conduct themselves morally as well.

---

47 Miguel Sicart, *The Ethics of Computer Games* (Cambridge, MA: The MIT Press, 2009), 210.

48 Ibid, 212.

49 Ibid.

50 Chris Kempshall argues that later *Star Wars* games, in particular *Star Wars: The Force Unleashed* (2008), are evidence of a growing tendency in the franchise to break down the consequential link inherent in the use of "Dark Side" Force abilities seen in the *KotOR* games, both out of an acceptance of the player's desire to use them, and in the context of a perceived moral relativism incited by contemporary political events such as the War on Terror. Kempshall, *The History and Politics of* Star Wars, 161.

Further complicating the interpretation of the alignment spectrum is the introduction of a secondary mechanic of character "influence": the player is incentivized to push their character to one or the other extreme of the Light/Dark spectrum for the sake of various mechanical bonuses (increased ability statistics, cheaper use of certain Force powers, etc.), and the companion characters (apart from Kreia and the droids) are similarly pulled across the spectrum in the wake of the protagonist. Yet at the same time, the influence mechanic rewards the player with additional dialogue and other benefits by furthering the goals of their individual companions, and often the player is forced to choose between alignment points and influence points. This is different from the first game, in which the companions would be pleased or upset by specific choices in relation to their fixed place on the alignment spectrum. Indeed, there are several instances in which moving a particular companion towards the Light Side of the Force proves to be a painful and perhaps even a damaging experience for them, prompting the question of who really benefits from such influence.[51] Far from creating ludonarrative dissonance, this conflict of mechanical principles relegates alignment with the Force to just one of a series of priorities for the player. As such it epitomizes the narrative's argument that personal choices and responsibility for the consequences of those choices are what ultimately matter.

The knowledge of betrayal

This juxtaposition between the game and the films hints at the great revelation that forms the dramatic climax of *KotOR2*. Once both the Jedi and the Sith have been rooted out from their hiding places, it becomes apparent that Kreia herself has been manipulating events with the intention of honing the Exile into a weapon against the Force. In so doing, she radically repolarizes the power dynamic of the franchise. Early on in the narrative, she responds to the question of whether she is a Sith or a Jedi by saying that she is perhaps neither, and yet she holds them both "as what they are, pieces of a whole."[52] Once her true motivation becomes apparent, this self-definition changes—where before it seemed to say that Kreia was in the middle of that binary spectrum of Light and Dark inherent to the franchise and depicted mechanically in both *KotOR* games, now it serves to distinguish her from the spectrum altogether. Jedi and Sith are lumped together collectively as avatars

---

[51] Examples include cutting Visas off from her connection to Nihilus, encouraging Mira to experience the pain and suffering of the inhabitants of Nar Shaddaa, and in a comedic send-up of this theme, the attempted installation of the "pacifist package" into HK47.

[52] Avellone, *Star Wars: Knights of the Old Republic II—The Sith Lords.*

of the real tyrant of the narrative (for Kreia's character at least). Hearkening back to the pervasive theme of free choice once more, Kreia finally admits that her real enemy is the Force itself and specifically the fact that "it seems to have a will, [and] would control us to achieve some measure of balance, when countless lives are lost."[53]

Whereas the first game uses the character of Jolee Bindo as a means of showing that it was possible to interact with the Force without officially being a Jedi or Sith, in practice he exists within the same ethical system as the Jedi, notwithstanding a few objections to specific pieces of their dogma and the "formality" (as he describes it) of never having obtained the rank of Jedi Knight.[54] In Kreia we have a character who could have served merely as an analogue of Count Dooku from *Episode II: Attack of the Clones*: a historian of the Jedi and a mentor to some of its most notable members, whose eventual disillusionment led her to becoming its antithesis as a Sith Lord. And yet, having previously epitomized both ends of the binary spectrum, she does not end up in the middle of it but rejects it as a frame of reference altogether. The writing is subtle; that it does not actually admit the death of the Force is a real possibility highlights the fine line between the game's consistency with the *Star Wars* mythos and its radical challenge to the tenets of that mythos. Indeed, Avellone has described *KotOR2* and the character of Kreia in particular as constituting a mouthpiece for the "frustrations" he felt regarding the standard depiction of the Force.[55] Not only does the game encourage us to question the morality of our own choices outside of the Light/Dark binary, it also asks the same of the Force itself. As Marshall Honorof puts it, "only *KotOR2* stopped to question whether letting the Force control the galaxy's destiny was a good thing—and whether giving Jedi and Sith superhuman powers was itself a dangerous and undemocratic concept."[56]

---

[53] Ibid.

[54] There is a comic irony to his description of himself as "any other non-Jedi in our group, with a lightsaber, and Force powers." Drew Karpyshyn, *Star Wars: Knights of the Old Republic.*

[55] "As much as the nature of the Force frustrated me in some respects, Kreia was the personification of that frustration—the fact that some arbitrary force would feel the need to 'correct' the human species at times with mass slaughter in Episodes 1 through 3, and the hypocrisy of the Jedi that took place in IV and V. I've never really forgiven Ben Kenobi for his lies in Episodes IV and V, and Kreia definitely echoes that." Emperor Devon, "Interview with Chris Avellone."

[56] Marshall Honorof, "The best *Star Wars* game is *KotOR2*—and it's not even close," *tom's guide*, May 4, 2020, https://www.tomsguide.com/uk/opinion/star-wars-knights-of-the-old-republic-2.

Kreia herself is an undoubtedly tragic character, having been abandoned by her greatest Jedi apprentice (Revan) and betrayed by her Sith apprentices Sion and Nihilus. As such, she seeks revenge against both factions, consistently deceiving everyone until the game's final act. Yet her greatest betrayal and her greatest deceit are those she commits against herself. She sees in the Force something that robs sentience of its agency and Force-users of their capacity to affect the universe on their own terms. Where Qui-Gon Jinn in *Star Wars Episode I: The Phantom Menace* (1999) dissents from Jedi orthodoxy because he believes that his colleagues do not place *enough* faith in the will of the Force, Kreia sees both factions as unwitting tools of a metaphysical dictator. Worse, she considers those who submit themselves to the Force as infantilized by it. As she says to Atton: "Take the greatest Jedi Knight, strip away the Force, and what remains?" She argues they are more dependent upon the Force than even they realize, and without it, a Jedi is "nothing more than a woman—or a man. A child."[57] Yet she herself uses the Force, to such a degree in fact that she has lost the functionality of her eyes—she perceives the universe through the Force to the extent that they have atrophied from lack of use. Thus the whites of her pupil-less eyes, finally revealed towards the end of the narrative, serve to signify to the player both her reliance and her monomania: everything she does is mediated by the Force.

Kreia herself admits the dual nature of this relationship, saying she uses the Force as she would a poison, "and in the hope of understanding it, I will learn the way to kill it. But perhaps these are the excuses of an old woman who has grown to rely on a thing she despises."[58] She is the champion of action and of choice, and yet she spends her life in other people's shadows and in the greater shadow of the Force. In pulling the strings of everyone around her, Kreia becomes the personification of the very thing she is fighting against, and she knows it. From this perspective, the entire narrative may be read as Kreia's elaborate suicide—the desperate attempt of a wounded woman to exercise the limited agency she believes is available to her in defiance of a power she knows she cannot defeat.

The story of Kreia's failure would be tragically ironic in any medium but is especially relevant in the context of a computer game. As a playable element of the game, Kreia is directly manipulated by the player; they direct her movements, choose her equipment, command her abilities, and specify her statistical development. At the same time however she, as a character, manipulates the player both by driving the plot and, as the primary mouthpiece for both exposition and narrative commentary, by influencing

---

[57] Avellone, *Star Wars: Knights of the Old Republic II—The Sith Lords.*
[58] Ibid.

their interpretation of the characters and events they encounter. This driving of the plot in particular—the revelation that the player has been manipulated by Kreia where they thought they were making free choices—is ludonarratively consistent with the fact that, as a pre-scripted game, the player's capacity to affect the plot with their choices is also circumscribed.[59] Just as Kreia is bound by the will of the Force, however much she strives for agency within it, the player is bound by the necessary limitations of the game. That lack of a truly emergent narrative *KotOR* excuses by virtue of being set within the philosophical certainties of a "by the book" *Star Wars* story is equally the case for *KotOR2*, but here the fact is confronted head-on, using the questioning of those certainties to explore the creation of meaning within narrative gaming. At one point in the game, Kreia describes Atton as a pawn in a game of Dejarik, but she herself demonstrates that the roles of pawn and player are not mutually exclusive and that neither one may leave the board.

Conclusion

As part of a retrospective article on the history of *Star Wars* in gaming, Chris Thurston summarized the difference between the two *KotOR* games: "the former is an intelligent reconstruction of familiar *Star Wars* notions, while the latter is an intelligent *deconstruction* of them."[60] Mechanically *KotOR2* was not unique, and even where it did innovate, it stood firmly in an established tradition of choice-based RPGs. Equally, it is not the only piece of *Star Wars* media that attempts to challenge the generally unquestioned tenets of its own franchise (though in 2004 it was much more of an outlier in doing so). It is narratively flawed, admittedly rushed, long since bereft of canonicity, and has even been described as "not very good at being *Star Wars*."[61] Yet in the interaction of its critical approach to its source material and its status as a piece of inherently interactive media, *KotOR2* succeeds in creating a unique exploration of—and a compelling incitement to contemplate—the *consequences* of being *Star Wars*.

---

[59] Cf. also Esther MacCallum-Stewart and Justin Parsler's discussion of "illusory agency" as the "process of 'tricking' a reader into believing they have greater impact on and import within the game" in "Illusory Agency in *Vampire: The Masquerade—Bloodlines*," *Dichtung Digital. Journal für Kunst und Kultur digitaler Medien*. Nr. 37, 2007, 2.

[60] Samuel Roberts, Wes Fenlon, and Chris Thursten, "The Best Star Wars Games on PC," *PC Gamer*, May 4, 2020, https://www.pcgamer.com/the-best-star-wars-games-on-pc/.

[61] Ibid.

Bibliography

Avellone, Chris. *Star Wars: Knights of the Old Republic II—The Sith Lords.* LucasArts. Various platforms. 2004.

Barr, Matthew. "The Force Is Strong with This One (but Not That One): What Makes a Successful Star Wars Video Game Adaptation?" *Arts.* 2020; 9(4):131.

Bogost, Ian and Nick Montfort. *Racing the Beam: The Atari Video Computer System.* Cambridge, MA: The MIT Press, 2009.

Brin, David. "Opening Statement for the Prosecution: I Accuse . . . Or Zola Meets Yoda . . . ." In *Star Wars on Trial,* edited by David Brin and Matthew Woodring Stover, 17-48. Dallas, TX: BenBella Books, 2006.

Brooks, Dan. "Star Wars: Knights Of The Old Republic Strikes Back With New Remake." StarWars.com. September 9, 2021. https://www.starwars.com/news/knights-of-the-old-republic-remake.

Dahlen, Chris. "*Planescape: Torment.*" *The Escapist.* August 23, 2005. https://www.escapistmagazine.com/planescape-torment/.

Dees, Richard H. "Moral Ambiguity in a Black-and-White Universe." In *Star Wars and Philosophy,* edited by Kevin S. Decker and Jason T. Eberl, 39-53. Chicago & La Salle, IL: Open Court, 2005.

Devon, Emperor. "Interview: Chris Avellone, Obsidian Entertainment." *Star Wars Knights.* 2007. Accessed June 12, 2023. Archived at http://web.archive.org/web/20150924105808/http://www.starwarsknights.com/interview20070924.php.

Fader, Shanti. "A Certain Point of View: Lying Jedi, Honest Sith, and the Viewers Who Love Them." In *Star Wars and Philosophy,* edited by Kevin S. Decker and Jason T. Eberl, 192-204. Chicago & La Salle, IL: Open Court, 2005.

Gillen, Kieron. "Star Wars: Knights of the Old Republic." *Eurogamer.* September 17, 2003. https://www.eurogamer.net/r-starwarskotor-x.

Gordon, Rob. "Star Wars: Knights Of The Old Republic Switch Review—A Fantastic RPG." *ScreenRant.* November 17, 2021. https://screenrant.com/star-wars-knights-old-republic-switch-review.

Hocking, Clint. "Ludonarrative Dissonance in *Bioshock.*" Clicknothing Typepad. October 7, 2007. https://clicknothing.typepad.com/click_nothing/2007/10/ludonarrative-d.html.

Honorof, Marshall. "The best Star Wars game is KOTOR II—and it's not even close." *tom's guide.* May 4, 2020. https://www.tomsguide.com/uk/opinion/star-wars-knights-of-the-old-republic-2.

IGN Staff. "*Baldur's Gate II: Shadows of Amn*: Review." *IGN.* October 11, 2000. https://www.ign.com/articles/2000/10/10/baldurs-gate-ii-shadows-of-amn.

Karpyshyn, Drew. *Star Wars: Knights of the Old Republic.* LucasArts. Various platforms. 2003.

Kasavin, Greg. "*Planescape: Torment: Review.*" GameSpot. December 21, 1999. https://www.gamespot.com/reviews/planescape-torment-review/1900-2535119/.

Kempshall, Chris. *The History and Politics of Star Wars: Death Stars and Democracy.* London and New York: Routledge, 2023.

Kerschner, Irvin, dir. *Star Wars Episode V: The Empire Strikes Back.* 1980; Beverly Hills, CA: 20th Century Fox/Lucasfilm Ltd. Disney+. https://www.

disneyplus.com/movies/star-wars-the-empire-strikes-back-episode-v/iqtDTZAewwYl.

King, Brad and John Borland. *Dungeons and Dreamers: The Rise of Computer Game Culture from Geek to Chic*. Emeryville, CA: Mc-Graw-Hill, 2003.

London, Matt. "Interview: Chris Avellone, Game Designer, *Fallout: New Vegas.*" *LightSpeed*. Issue 6 (November 2010). https://www.lightspeedmagazine.com/nonfiction/feature-interview-chris-avellone-game-designer-fallout-new-vegas/.

Lucas, George, dir. *Star Wars Episode IV: A New Hope*. 1977; Beverly Hills, CA: 20th Century Fox/Lucasfilm Ltd. Disney+. https://www.disneyplus.com/movies/star-wars-a-new-hope-episode-iv/12fVeZxD2fWJ.

_______, dir. *Star Wars Episode III: Revenge of the Sith*. 2005; Beverly Hills, CA: 20th Century Fox/Lucasfilm Ltd. Disney+. https://www.disneyplus.com/movies/star-wars-revenge-of-the-sith-episode-iii/4WvbqLFumNvi.

MacCallum-Stewart, Esther and Justin Parsler. "Illusory Agency in *Vampire: The Masquerade – Bloodlines." Dichtung Digital. Journal für Kunst und Kultur digitaler Medien*. Nr. 37 (2007): 1-17.

Maison, Jordan. "Knights of the Old Republic II Developer Chris Avellone Discusses the Game's Impact 15 Years Later." Cinelinx. June 12, 2019. https://web.archive.org/web/20200611214227/https://www.cinelinx.com/news/culture/knights-of-the-old-republic-ii-developer-chris-avellone-discusses-the-games-impact-15-years-later/.

Mejeur, Cody. "Chasing Wild Space: Narrative Outsides and World-Building Frontiers in *Knights of the Old Republic and The Old Republic*." In *Star Wars and the History of Transmedia Storytelling*, edited by Sean Guynes and Dan Hassler-Forest, 199-209. Amsterdam, Amsterdam University Press, 2018.

Mortensen, Torill Elvira. "Keeping the Balance—Morals at the Dark Side." In *The Dark Side of Game Play*, edited by Torill Elvira Mortensen, Jonas Linderoth, and Ashley M. L. Brown, Chapter 10. London: Taylor and Francis, 2015. https://www.perlego.com/book/1642776/the-dark-side-of-game-play-pdf.

Roberts, Samuel, Wes Fenlon, and Chris Thursten. "The Best Star Wars Games on PC." *PC Gamer*. May 4, 2020. https://www.pcgamer.com/the-best-star-wars-games-on-pc/.

Seraphine, Frédéric. "Ludonarrative Dissonance: Is Storytelling About Reaching Harmony?" Academia.edu. Accessed June 8, 2022. https://www.academia.edu/28205876/Ludonarrative_Dissonance_Is_Storytelling_About_Reaching_Harmony.

Sicart, Miguel. *The Ethics of Computer Games*. Cambridge, MA: The MIT Press, 2009.

Williams, Demi. "Star Wars KOTOR 2 Restored Content DLC Canceled on Switch." *Gamespot*. June 5, 2023. https://www.gamespot.com/articles/star-wars-kotor-2-restored-content-dlc-canceled-on-switch/1100-6514788/#:~:text=%22Sadly%2C%20today%20we're,for%20release%2C%22%20Aspyr%20said.

Wilson, Jason. "The Dungeons & Dragons Effect." Game Spy. August 24, 2010. http://www.gamespy.com/articles/111/1115803p1.html.

Chapter 8

This is the Way: *The Mandalorian* and the Evolving Serial Medium

Paul Johnson

Abstract: The *Star Wars* films are serial films, operating as short bursts of narrative action that end with a cliffhanger before resuming with a new installment. George Lucas has often discussed the serial film and other similarly-styled influences in creating an episodic story, rich in world-building, using special and visual effects to fabricate locations, characters, and associated mise-en-scènes. Previously, *Star Wars* was cinematically based, but with *The Mandalorian* (2019-), the saga hit home television screens on streaming service Disney+ via weekly installments. Although the series builds its narrative akin to the preceding *Star Wars* films, its production and distribution more keenly identifies it with the serial format in vision and intent. In addition, *The Mandalorian* makes astute updates for the modern era, using technology and techniques including sophisticated video walls to create the series' world and remediating typical serial film principles, alongside distribution and exhibition, to create a modern interpretation of the serial medium. *The Mandalorian* demonstrates a reformulation of the episodic standard and highlights a means to understand how spectators connect with narratives in modern ways.

Keywords: Mandalorian, streaming, *Star Wars*, digital, world, technology, microcosmic, serial, *The Mandalorian*

***

As a film series, the *Star Wars* saga is well known as partially conceived upon the serial film: operating as short bursts of narrative action that end with cliffhangers, before resuming with a new installment. George Lucas has often discussed the serial film and other similarly styled influences, such as Alex Raymond's daily comic strip *Flash Gordon* (1934-1992), stating "I wanted to make a '*Flash Gordon*' movie, with all the trimmings, but I couldn't obtain the rights . . . So I began researching [and] found where Alex Raymond got his inspiration from."[1] In so doing, Lucas created an episodic story, rich in world-building, using special and visual effects (VFX) to fabricate the locations, characters, and associated mise-en-scènes.[2] As Brian Jay Jones writes of Lucas's drafting of the first film, "Lucas poured everything he had ever loved about the Saturday morning serials into his treatment, with plenty of chases, close scrapes, exotic creatures, and general derring-do."[3] Previously the series was primarily cinematically based, but with *The Mandalorian* (2019-), the saga not only hit home television screens, it did so on the streaming service Disney+ via weekly installments.[4] Regularly following its titular character through similarly serial exploits, escapades, fights, and death-defying moments, *The Mandalorian* is at once the past, the present, and peering towards the future. The following pages seek to highlight how streaming has updated *Star Wars* in ways that make Lucas's creation fitting for the modern era. This is a period where moving images—cinema, television, video games and so forth—are no longer confined to one defined and stable location so far as a platform is concerned, such as the movie theater, or even the conventional television screen. Theatrical cinema makes its way to DVD and Blu-ray discs and to Netflix, Disney+, and so on. As James E. Cutting relates "We used to go to the movies, we used to speak of flicks, even of flicking out,"[5] but he continues, "Now movies mostly come to us. Nothing flickers."[6] And not just movies, but pretty much all media, and that's changed how something like the *Star Wars* franchise operates, moving beyond the purely cinematic. Furthermore, the content is also viewable not just in different formats but also in different viewing spaces and in different temporal spans. Far from being anchored to the spot, both viewers and content move, and in addition our viewing spans stretch and condense here and there. We stop and start moving images at will and participate in the content in short bursts or longer stretches of time as we see fit. What follows demonstrates how *The Mandalorian* takes *Star Wars* and modifies it anew, creating a serial narrative for the streaming world.

---

[1] "Behind the Scenes of Star Wars," *American Cinematographer*, 2005, accessed November 22, 2021, https://theasc.com/magazine/starwars/index.html, 1.

[2] *Disney Gallery: Star Wars: The Mandalorian*, season 1, episode 4, "Technology," directed by Bradford Baruh, aired May 22, 2020, Disney+, https://www.disneyplus.com/video/8112cabc-5ed9-4176-b0f8-b4baa0ab15f1.

[3] Brian Jay Jones, *George Lucas: A Life* (London: Headline, 2016), 171.

[4] *The Mandalorian*, directed by Dave Filoni, Rick Famuyiwa, Deborah Chow, et al., written by Jon Favreau, Dave Filoni, et al., aired 2019- , Disney+, https://www.disneyplus.com/series/the-mandalorian/3jLIGMDYINqD.

[5] James E. Cutting, *Movies on Our Minds: The Evolution of Cinematic Engagement* (New York: Oxford University Press, 2021), 1.

[6] Ibid.

Episodes of this new show build to create a long-form story, like preceding *Star Wars* feature films, but their production and distribution simultaneously identify them as both appropriately reflecting the older serial format in vision and intent as well as current digital models. In addition, *The Mandalorian* makes other astute updates for the modern era, using technology and techniques including sophisticated video walls to create its content. This state-of-the-art technology allows quicker production of the series, but again its use looks back to the technologies of front and rear projection.

Most importantly, the series demonstrates techniques that are very much a part of the digital now. These draw the participant audience—who position themselves within streaming services as a part of the Internet and digital age and thus are more video game-oriented and enveloped within the digital world of media—into a *Star Wars* world of both the past and the present. *The Mandalorian* demonstrates the current and future of *Star Wars* and highlights how modern television production, distribution, exhibition, and reception operate and have reshaped *Star Wars* as moving picture entity. Episodes of *The Mandalorian*, as well as relevant scholarship surrounding this new entertainment landscape and antecedent serial media by authors including Gilder, Prince, Dixon, and Lahue, illustrate how audiences can quickly access the *Star Wars* worlds, experiencing a representative microcosm of digital technology that encapsulates and reflects both the titular science fiction world as well our current own.

Microcosms and volumes

In *Streaming: Movies, Media, and Instant Access*, Wheeler Winston Dixon says, "we live in a streaming world where everything . . . will be available like running water,"[7] highlighting how digital technology can be as plentiful as a natural resource. But Dixon also notes: "the rush to streaming creates many new ways to 'monetize' existing films, music, and books in a way that perpetuates the consumer's dependence on the supplier and ensures a constant revenue stream not only to access but also store, download, or view the works one has supposedly 'purchased,'"[8] and it's this latter remark that points out the lack of physicality to this technology that you never really own. Digital streams are ephemeral, nigh invisible, almost intangible, and gossamer-like, unlike previous digital media such as DVDs. Discs may house digital data, but like analog video tapes they still take up considerable space for the consumer and home viewer. Although streaming content is held

[7] Wheeler Winston Dixon, *Streaming: Movies, Media, and Instant Access* (Lexington, KY: University Press of Kentucky, 2013), Kobo Desktop.
[8] Ibid.

somewhere, it is spatially infinitesimal for the consumer and viewer beyond the perceived images and sound. This current digital world is therefore a development of the microcosm as discussed by George Gilder. Gilder's essential argument, which covers technological developments in computer chips and areas of quantum theory and how this engages with capitalism, is that the microcosm equals "the overthrow of matter."[9] Gilder's writing notes that microprocessor and chip technology take up limited space but, in its continued development, produces increasingly fast and powerful abilities to hold and harness data. This means, as Gilder says, "The smaller the space, the more the room."[10] No longer are we living in a world of hard physical science and its prescribed laws, but instead we frequent a landscape showing "a rich panoply of paradoxical sparks, comprising waves and particles that violate every principle of Newtonian solidity."[11] In this way, streaming television clearly demonstrates the microcosm as a metaphor for how we currently live: using technology such as mobile phones, tablets, and smart televisions. In each, we attend interconnected worlds of communication and streaming media that are instantly accessible and virtually invisible, aside from the screens we use to view them or the headphones through which we hear. And even these are becoming increasingly smaller, thinner, and almost impossible to detect.

In creating *The Mandalorian*, creator/executive producer/co-writer Jon Favreau and his co-workers demonstrate a prime example of this type of instantly attainable microcosmic media. They do so in the first instance by delivering a series that harks back to the serial pictures of yore but via cutting-edge techniques. Principally, *The Mandalorian* makes considerable use of video wall technology alongside game engine technology to produce virtual environments. Called StageCraft, the technique employs LED projectors and motion capture volumes, which in their original guise were large, enclosed stages festooned with sensors, alongside physical sets in the foreground.[12] Using a series of photographs taken at locations (known within the technique as scanning) alongside photogrammetry (where location photographs are mapped onto 3D objects), and lidar scanning (where lasers scan objects and measure the reflected distance to build objects, such as buildings) the volume is filled with locations where *The Mandalorian* characters' adventures take

---

[9] George Gilder, *Microcosm: The Quantum Revolution in Economics and Technology* (New York: Simon and Schuster, 1989), 12.
[10] Ibid., 37.
[11] Ibid., 12.
[12] "Stagecraft," *Industrial Light & Magic*, accessed March 23, 2022, https://www.ilm.com/stagecraft/.

place.[13] The marriage of game technology with these photographic techniques allowed the producers of *The Mandalorian* to composite visuals at a pace that enabled the rapid creation of a world in practical real-time on the volume sets. This is incredibly akin to entering a gaming world and (on set at least) moving about as if inhabiting said world's locales.

The ability to create this set outside of traditional cinema presets using the video wall technology enables high quality backgrounds of various types, creating immersive spaces for the action to take place. These spaces, such as star fields or other fantastic and exotic worlds distinct from our own, can then be combined in real time with the actors on set. Cast members can work to effect more credible performances, since they now have environments to react to and feel a part of. In addition, the techniques employed also enable VFX artists to set up shots for compositing with other elements more quickly. *American Cinematographer* notes of the process: "If the content was created in advance of the shoot, then photographing actors, props and set pieces in front of this wall could create final in-camera visual effects—or 'near' finals, with only technical fixes required, and with complete creative confidence in the composition and look of the shots."[14] Consequently, this makes production quicker and more streamlined. But more importantly, the interactive lighting involved, and especially the degree of detail within the screens, means the technology creates close to real-world environments—even when these worlds only really exist within the sphere of *Star Wars*. And although the series is live-action, *The Mandalorian* manages to evoke the now-dominant media form of video games, and as such it reflects the immersive and detailed world seen in *Star Wars Jedi: Fallen Order* (2019). The game used the same Unreal Engine technology from Epic Games used in the LED screens on the television show, which allowed a similarly realistic creation of worlds.[15] This crossover in technology, of the enveloping visuals of the show's LED screen and the game's 360-degree world, therefore shows analogous connectivity between video gaming and live action media. Using technology that situates both gamers into the *Fallen Order* world and viewers into the television show reveals how the microcosmic world of each—a vast, open *Star Wars* world—is brought together, perhaps as a means of helping to sell each form to the consumer and viewer.

---

[13] Jay Holben, *"The Mandalorian*: This Is the Way," *American Cinematographer*, February 6, 2020, https://ascmag.com/articles/the-mandalorian.

[14] Ibid.

[15] "Features," *Unreal Engine*, 2004-2022, accessed February 16, 2022, https://www.unrealengine.com/en-US/features.

In *American Cinematographer*'s article discussing Season One of the show, "This is the Way," Jay Holben writes about the production's deployment of the LED wall technology, noting that a Season 1 shot develops as follows:

> The shot starts with a low angle of Mando reading a sensor on the icy planet of Maldo Kreis; he stands on a long walkway that stretches out to a series of structures on the horizon. The skies are full of dark clouds, and a light snow swirls around. Mando walks along the trail toward the structures, and the camera booms up. All of this was captured in the Volume, in-camera and in real-time. Part of the walkway was a real, practical set, but the rest of the world was the virtual image on the LED screen, and the parallax as the camera boomed up matched perfectly with the real set. The effect of this system is seamless.[16]

The last words from Holben astutely underline how this *Star Wars* series manages to encapsulate the microcosmic digital world in which we now live. Essentially, almost the entirety of a world is very rapidly produced and integrated seamlessly into the real world of the set, and viewers perceive this seamlessly—just as in the aforementioned game, or indeed real life. Scenes such as the one described by Holben on Maldo Kreis, along with countless others, demonstrate a primary way in which *The Mandalorian* seeks to incorporate modern technology into an older media form. On one level the streaming show's production is cutting-edge, but it also shows a deference to the original *Star Wars* trilogy where Lucas tried to incorporate similar projection techniques. In the original 1977 *Star Wars* film, projection techniques were attempted for *Millennium Falcon* cockpit scenes, but technical issues saw them scrapped.[17] However, the goal to create an enveloping and immersive on-stage environment for the actors—and a contextually realistic scene for viewers—was realized for *Solo: A Star Wars Story* (2018)[18] and reached even greater heights in *The Mandalorian*.

The technology, which envelops and surrounds, creating a highly detailed digital world, is definitively microcosmic, allowing the vastness of the *Star Wars* world to be visualized in a realistic fashion in front of viewers' eyes. The production techniques echo past aspirations of *Star Wars* while manifesting up-to-the-minute and even futuristic ideas and scope. It develops what

---

[16] Holben, *"The Mandalorian."*

[17] J.W. Rinzler, *The Making of Star Wars* (London: Ebury Press, 2007), 212-213.

[18] "Rear projection on Solo: A Star Wars Story," *Foundry*, November 8, 2018, https://www.foundry.com/insights/film-tv/rear-projection-on-solo-a-star-wars-story.

George Lucas wished to attempt in his earliest endeavors in 1977, when his aim was to create a living, breathing, science fiction world; Lucas stated he was "trying to get a cohesive reality."[19] Use of the video wall technology, the detail of the photogrammetry, and scanning techniques produces—alongside the digital methodology of the LED projection—an updated, cohesive and more extensive sense of the universe and worlds used in the 1977 film. In *New Scientist*'s review, Bethan Ackerley relates how impressive the volume was in providing an enveloping but also realistic world to the show: "the volume accurately lights a scene while it is being filmed, so every scene our hero steps onto (in his gleaming beskar armor no less) feels like a real location."[20] Similarly, in Sean Nasuti's review for *The Disinsider* he notes how well the Unreal Engine is employed to evoke "some of the sharpest visuals from any *Star Wars* production to date . . . the visual effects work here is so seamless that you'd legitimately never notice."[21] Consequently, the use of the LED wall and the Unreal Engine technology showcase how *The Mandalorian* obtains "the seeming contradiction of strange graphics of fantasy combined with the feel of a documentary,"[22] seen in the original *Star Wars* films. Such technologies simultaneously produce an immersive and immense *Star Wars* world for the so-called smaller screens and worlds of home viewers.

The big and the small of it

Though many viewers will naturally watch *The Mandalorian* on now-conventional widescreen and HD screens while sitting on their couches in their living rooms, many will not. In this modern age, alongside smart televisions, people watch and consume media almost everywhere and through a variety of technologies. From mobile phones to tablets, laptops, and computers, the exhibition as well as the production has changed and morphed tremendously. In his book *Digital Cinema*, Stephen Prince highlights how big-screen filmmaking has now become ever more incorporated into the world at large. In Chapter 5, "Everywhere and Nowhere," his investigation argues cinematic production and exhibition no longer exist (like so many other media) as a strictly physical medium, but rather as an essentially digital construct.[23] Of watching cinema, Prince notes how it was previously an "experience like

[19] "Behind the Scenes of Star Wars," 2.

[20] Bethan Ackerley, "The Mandalorian review: How special effects made the Star Wars series," *New Scientist*, February 3, 2021, https://www.newscientist.com/article/mg24933202-300-the-mandalorian-review-how-special-effects-made-the-star-wars-series/.

[21] Sean Nasuti, "'The Mandalorian': Season One Spoiler Review," *The Disinsider*, October 28, 2020, https://thedisinsider.com/2020/10/28/the-mandalorian-season-1-spoilers-review/.

[22] "Behind the Scenes of Star Wars," *American Cinematographer*, 2.

[23] Stephen Prince, *Digital Cinema* (New Brunswick, NJ: Rutgers University Press, 2019), 136.

stepping into another reality," with theaters that were "epically spacious and grand."[24] Now that we watch films in a variety of spaces however, including at home and often on the move, the cinematic medium is "ambiguous" because of its portability. Prince's viewpoint sees cinematic exhibition's scale as reduced and instead returned to its origins as kinetoscope machines because of the abundance of close-ups (among other formal attributes).[25]

But his argument that cinema's evolution has seen a "shrinking [in the] size of its images,"[26] is perhaps misconstrued. As noted above, it is highly likely that some will watch films on smaller screens, but many, many films are still visually arresting and will be seen on the big screen. *Spider-Man: No Way Home* (2021), a film with spectacular scenes that use considerable amounts of VFX, was released solely in cinemas to critical acclaim.[27] Moreover, *No Way Home* grossed a huge amount at the box office and was not simultaneously released via streaming or sent to streaming platforms directly.[28] Although produced in association with Columbia pictures, the film's release went against the grain of other Marvel films, such as *Black Widow* (2021), which used Disney's own streaming service in conjunction with a limited cinema presentation because of the COVID-19 pandemic.[29] Although stymied by the pandemic, *No Way Home*'s first weekend domestic box office gross was considerably larger than *Widow*'s ($260,138,569[30] vs. $80,366,312[31]).

Furthermore, *The Mandalorian* represents productions that continue to be every bit as epic as previous large-screen productions, building on *Star Wars*'s previous cinematic outings. Richard Roeper says, in his review of *The Mandalorian*, "This is a visually stunning, consistently entertaining space-spaghetti-Western serial,"[32] and in hers, Kate Rife cites the "epic sweep" of

---

24 Ibid., 137.

25 Ibid., 139.

26 Ibid., 138.

27 "*Spider-Man: No Way Home*," Rotten Tomatoes, accessed February 26, 2022, https://www.rottentomatoes.com/m/spider_man_no_way_home.

28 "*Spider-Man: No Way Home*," The Numbers, accessed February 24, 2022, https://www.the-numbers.com/movie/Spider-Man-No-Way-Home-(2021)#tab=summary.

29 Anthony Dallesandro, "Disney Claims $215M+ WW Victory At The B.O. & Disney+ Premier With 'Black Widow' Weekend: Will Distrib Model Endanger A Movie's Life Cycle?—Update," *Deadline*, July 21, 2021, https://deadline.com/2021/07/black-widow-opening-weekend-box-office-1234789473/.

30 "*Spider-Man: No Way Home*," The Numbers.

31 "*Black Widow*," The Numbers, accessed February 28, 2022, https://www.the-numbers.com/movie/Black-Widow-(2021)#tab=summary.

32 Richard Roeper, "Thanksgiving weekend with Baby Yoda: Reviews of '*The Mandalorian*,' '*Servant*' and other shows for holiday streaming," *Chicago Sun-Times*, November 28,

the show's spaghetti-Western-inspired first episode.[33] These and others have asserted that the extravagance of *Star Wars*'s visual scope continues within the seemingly small-screen world.

In fact, critics have asserted that the distinction between film and television as forms is as ambiguous as its exhibition and distribution. In *Sight&Sound*'s 2017 films of the year list, David Lynch's cable television show *Twin Peaks: The Return* (2017) was listed at number two, and writer Michael Ewins noted in his overview that because "*Return's* narrative unravel[s] across several traversable planes [this] allows events to be rearranged, recontextualized or completely reversed over its duration."[34] This points to how a drama seen outside the cinema screen can be just as substantial, deep, and indeed spectacularly epic. Ewins marks out the quite astounding scene in Episode 8, wherein we see the Trinity Test of an atomic bomb refashioned in computer-generated (CG) imagery. The eleven-minute, digitally produced sequence takes audiences from a wide shot of the bomb exploding in black and white, then moves inside the blast; it is epic in both scope and duration, as well as thought-provoking. While *The Mandalorian* perhaps takes a less prosaic approach to its content, as with *Twin Peaks* it manages to play with the constraints of television to provide an extensive and epic narrative.

Like *Twin Peaks: The Return* and other shows, *The Mandalorian* uses a similarly sweeping, traversable, and long-form narrative with similarly constructed digital shots to transport its content to various screens for audiences to enjoy. Some viewers' screens are of smaller size, but many are not, with a growing trend in larger sized television screens of 65 inches in the USA dropping in price in 2019 when *The Mandalorian* started streaming.[35] More importantly, the contained shots, sequences, and the worlds envisioned are not shrinking. Rather, scenes and sequences like *Twin Peaks: The Return*'s Trinity Test sequence—and the many vistas and imaged worlds of *The Mandalorian* produced via massive video walls and real-time compositing effects—demonstrate that so-called televisual small screen worlds are growing much larger. These worlds and their aesthetics are built bigger and

---

2019, https://chicago.suntimes.com/2019/11/28/20982807/mandalorian-review-servant-klaus-merry-happy-whatever-noelle-netflix-appletvplus-amazon-disneyplus.

33 Kate Rife, "*The Mandalorian* brings Western sweep and Werner Herzog to the *Star Wars* universe," *AVClub*, November 12, 2019, https://www.avclub.com/the-mandalorian-brings-western-sweep-and-german-auteurs-1839814541.

34 Mark Ewins, "*Twin Peaks: The Return*," *Sight&Sound*, Vol. 28, Issue 1 (December 2017): 34.

35 Iris Hu, "TV Panel Prices Plunge in June, with No Signs of Stopping in July, Says TrendForce," *TRENDFORCE*, July 5, 2019, https://www.trendforce.com/presscenter/news/20190705-10159.html.

with more detail, distinctly connecting to the viewer in their own viewing space. Such practices and their presentation via streaming draw us into these vast worlds—appreciably so within those of the *Star Wars* universe.

The visual medium of streaming television is indeed ambiguous, but moreover ambivalent and amorphous, uncertain in its parameters for a variety of reasons, but in positive ways. Using the production techniques outlined above, *The Mandalorian* allows both the creators and the viewers to traverse worlds on a similar level to the characters in *Twin Peaks: The Return.* No longer are the parameters for creation and entry as concrete and solidified as before; instead, they are amorphous and ambiguous and perhaps shows and films are all the better for this. In the recent *Twin Peaks* show, characters such as Agent Cooper and his various doppelgangers traverse numerous spheres, crossing time and space and becoming wholly different people. The movement is often momentary, as we switch back and forth between characters in scenes throughout the show's episodes. As spectators, we inhabit these times and spaces fluidly as states we're already well accustomed to in recent years from enjoying such long-form shows. From a production perspective, the fluid movement across wide open spaces and timelines seen in narrative television serials and dramas is also demonstrated extraordinarily well within *The Mandalorian*'s techniques and technologies. A set of processes occur. The on-set personnel, including actors, frequent something approximating an integrated streaming visual world that envelops them; this is then finalized and made entirely harmonious for spectators. At both points, but unquestionably in the finalized and streamed form, we see the effect of Gilder's microcosmic sparks: particles and digital data reconvened from a variety of other digitized forms. The on-set space is exponentially expanded by introducing externally fabricated locations, creating a visually larger space within the confines of the volume, and the finished scenes' distribution to audiences across the world via streaming demonstrates the microcosm's small digital area creating a vast space for spectators to inhabit.

Going with the flow

In addition, this set of technologies and techniques allows a re-manifestation of the so-called "flow," a term used by David Arditi that echoes and condenses Dixon's previous water analogy in digital streaming. Indeed, Arditi notes the ways in which streaming is analogous to how water moves and is always ever-changing.[36] Highlighting the way modern television operates in terms of access and consumption, Arditi notes "we are no longer beholden to

---

[36] David Arditi, *Streaming Culture: Subscription Platforms and the Unending Consumption of Culture* (Bingley, UK: Emerald Publishing, 2021), 9.

broadcast schedules."[37] Previously, noting Raymond Williams's overview of the concept of the flow, we followed a set of sequential events that were "available in a single dimension and in a single operation."[38] However, we now follow new rules, allowing spectators to watch shows whenever they theoretically want to. And the viewing experience is an adjunct to the ways in which *The Mandalorian* is produced, which itself interrupted the flow of previous production techniques.

Alongside others, streaming shows like *The Mandalorian* operate in their own modern flow by allowing the spectator to watch an episode at their leisure. But interestingly, although this show appears via Disney+, and viewers do not have to watch it exactly when Disney releases it, there is an interesting and somewhat ironic complication to how the drama is streamed. While advertisements are currently not situated within the show, and there is no specific timetable of its screening within a television guide, only one new episode per week is released, akin to the antecedent flow of terrestrial television and indeed serial films. Therefore, unlike many other binge-watched shows, where the viewer can watch all episodes in a marathon single sitting, this cannot occur until all the episodes of the season have been released (or "dropped"). In this instance, despite the show being held, delivered, and partially produced in digital form, *The Mandalorian* rolls back the decades to echo early serial films. Period serial productions like *The Hazards of Helen* (1914-1917), which lasted 119 episodes over three years, and the 20 often-cliffhanging episodes of *The Perils of Pauline* (1914) both released their installments weekly. *The Mandalorian* accordingly went against the grain of many series released on streaming up to this point. Disney+ has used a similar strategy in delivering other *Star Wars* and Marvel series (such as *The Book of Boba Fett* [2021-] and *WandaVision* [2021]), but Netflix most especially (alongside others) has often dropped entire series worldwide simultaneously. Rather than flooding spectators with hours to watch immediately, viewers are placed back to a more traditional time, watching as antecedent spectators did—waiting several days to find out whether their favorite heroes would escape dangerous perils and threats. It might be argued that the use of weekly episodes enables Disney to retain subscribers over a longer period, allowing a greater suffusion of content to permeate the viewer's eyes and ears. But there seems to be a change developing in the wake of the Disney+ release strategy. As Daniel Frankel explained in February 2022:

> None of the six subscription streaming services that launched after November 1, 2019–Apple TV Plus, Disney Plus, Peacock, HBO Max,

---

[37] Ibid., 82.

[38] Raymond Williams, quoted in Arditi, *Streaming Culture*, 85.

> Discovery Plus and Paramount Plus–ended up adopting stacked, all-at-once releasing. In fact, with each of these services enduring their nascent stages amid hindered pandemic production environments, the production volume needed to sustain the strategy might not have even been feasible.[39]

And it is a strategy that continues outside those platforms mentioned, with Amazon using a hybrid model to release the third season of *The Boys* (2019-), releasing three episodes in one go with the rest arriving one per week thereafter.[40] This release pattern, like those seen on Disney+ and others, arguably shows that perhaps the established methods are still viable. *The Mandalorian* therefore invokes another strong sense of nostalgia, becoming the flagship for Disney+'s release pattern and demonstrating that a glance back to the past can be beneficial, even while forging ahead. And furthermore, with other streaming platforms following suit, the advantages of this yearning for the past in both television and film and release patterns seem bountiful to spectators and to fans, as well as to the platforms themselves.

Another interesting counterpoint to the seeming cultural norm of isolationist viewing habits in modern streaming media exists in the way watching *The Mandalorian* creates a communal space like the cinema. In *Streaming Culture*, Arditi initially highlights the changes in watching audio-visual media, such as television, stating that now families "can be gathered in one room with mom watching a broadcast show on the living room television, a daughter using a tablet to watch someone play Fortnite on Twitch, and a son watching Tik-Tok clips on his phone."[41] This, Arditi says, breaks up the structure of watching into an anarchic and disordered state.[42] This might be the expectation and convention for some, but interestingly, Arditi goes on to relate how watching streaming cinema, and by extension streaming television shows, affords the communal sensation of traditional cinema-going. Arditi calls the theatrical experience "collective effervescence—an electric feeling experienced by groups of people," and is

---

[39] Daniel Frankel, "Is the Binge Busted? All-at-Once Releasing of Streaming Series Could Be on Its Way Out," *NextTV*, February 10, 2022, https://www.nexttv.com/news/is-the-binge-busted-all-at-once-releasing-of-streaming-series-could-be-on-its-way-out.

[40] Ibid. Disney+ has since employed a similar hybrid model in its release of two 2022 streaming series: *Obi-Wan Kenobi* (two episodes released initially, four following weekly) and *Andor* (three episodes released initially, nine following weekly). However, it returned to the once-weekly formula with the third season of *The Mandalorian* and the singular release of the new season's first episode on March 1, 2023.

[41] Arditi, *Streaming Culture*, 13.

[42] Ibid.

adamant such a state is not achieved within the home.[43] Arditi does note however that something new arises when watching media in the home, where new social and communal formations are created surrounding shows. Indeed, writing during the COVID-19 pandemic, Arditi pinpoints how spectators frequented Zoom viewings with their friends, and although he does not feel a collective effervescence is created, he states "it does reinforce or form social bonds."[44]

In *The Mandalorian*'s case, Disney+ shrewdly added a "GroupWatch" feature for the second season that enabled just such social formations. Writing on the *BGR* website, Jacob Siegal reported the feature allows the invitation of up to six people to join and use emojis, such as "like," "scared," and "surprised."[45] In addition, those who join are synchronized in watching the episode, and members can pause, restart, and rewind in order to add emojis.[46] This allows viewers, as Disney+ put it in the accompanying image on the site, to "watch together, even when you're apart."[47] This may sound rather less-than-social for many spectators used to the traditions of analog cinema-going; for others, perhaps it even sounds like an abomination of social connectivity. But for the current generation of *Star Wars* fans, it surely matches their needs and arguably operates as their digital water cooler moment. The traditional water cooler moment, wherein work colleagues gather during spare moments or breaks and discuss last night's television, would be highly difficult to carry out in a pandemic. Moreover, younger generations and others are more likely to chat via WhatsApp or post their thoughts with images on Instagram, using emojis and shorter spellings of words to discuss and gossip. It therefore seems likely that such formats as Disney+'s GroupWatch feature may be used to continue digitally-based water cooler chat and, by extension, to enact similar *Star Wars* communal chatter and discussion. Consequently, viewing *The Mandalorian* allows spectators to carry out such social engagement in real time.

This is just part of how modern viewing can reorient the location and facilitation of discussion and enjoyment for fans of *Star Wars*. *The Mandalorian*,

---

[43] Ibid., 67.

[44] Ibid.

[45] Jacob Siegal, "Disney+ gets a watch party feature just in time for 'The Mandalorian' season 2," *BGR*, September 20, 2020, https://bgr.com/entertainment/disney-plus-groupwatch-feature-watch-party/.

[46] Daniel Furn, "Disney+ launches GroupWatch so you can watch with six friends," *Radio Times*, February 23, 2021, https://www.radiotimes.com/technology/disney-groupwatch-watchalong-friends/.

[47] Siegal, "Disney+ gets a watch party feature."

like so many other television shows, films, and other media, is readily discussed online in a variety of forums. Sites such as those found within the "Jedi Council forums" on TheForce.net enabled ongoing discussions of the first season in 2019.[48] More recently, a forum on The Cantina hosted by Starwarsnews.net set up its own watch party using Discord to enable viewers to join a live discussion for the second season in October 2020.[49] This and the aforementioned GroupWatch facility are arguably the natural progression of spectatorship and fandom, now a facet of modern media consumption. Of contemporary streaming habits, Dixon writes "Why go out when you can stay home? Why sit with a bunch of strangers in a dark, often dank auditorium when you can relax on your couch and watch the latest releases?"[50] Watching, enjoying, and interacting with *The Mandalorian* in these ways exemplifies how the world of streaming can be made microcosmic. The windows of viewers' laptops, tablets, or smart televisions open the depths of content within streaming platforms and the vast, multilayered worlds and narratives of the shows themselves, which viewers then enjoy and discuss. In this way, contemporary spectators begin to feel a similar effervescence to traditional cinema-going.

I have spoken

Writing about *Star Wars* (1977), Pauline Kael reflects on the film's constant return to the past, referencing nostalgia, noting a "return to childhood" and "old-movie ineptness."[51] Kael doesn't seem overly impressed by the first film, but she keenly highlights its position as based upon serial films, mentioning Republic Pictures and its "bad actors,"[52] which had made B movies and serials since the 1920s.[53] She also acknowledges the *Star Wars* films' utilization of comic books, which returns us to Raymond's *Flash Gordon*, a counterpart to pulp magazines and serialized science fiction. These included Edgar R. Burroughs's John Carter character in the

---

[48] Todd The Jedi, "The Mandalorian Season 1 Discussion (Spoilers Allowed)," Jedi Council Forums, October 29, 2019, https://boards.theforce.net/threads/the-mandalorian-season-1-discussion-spoilers-allowed.50052332/.

[49] DarthSnow, "EVENT: THE MANDALORIAN S2 LIVE WATCH PARTY [CANTINA+DISCORD]," The Cantina, December 4, 2020, https://thecantina.starwarsnewsnet.com/index.php?threads/the-mandalorian-s2-live-watch-party-cantina-discord.58165/.

[50] Dixon, *Streaming: Movies, Media, and Instant Access*, Kobo Desktop.

[51] Pauline Kael, "Contrasts," *When the Lights Go Down* (London: Marion Boyars, 1980), 291.

[52] Ibid.

[53] Republic Pictures was born in part via the merger of numerous studios, including Nat Levine's Mascot Pictures, which began in 1927 and made numerous serials until Republic's formation in 1935, as noted at "Nat Levine & Mascot Pictures," *The Old Corral b-westerns.com*, accessed March 10, 2022, https://www.b-westerns.com/levine.htm.

pulp fiction A *Princess of Mars*, serialized in *All-Story Magazine* (1912). Each of these media sees a development of the "space opera," those "colourful action-adventure stories of interplanetary or interstellar conflict,"[54] that *Star Wars* would so heavily pastiche and that *The Mandalorian* continues.

But as we've seen, although it reflects certain archetypal serial film attributes, *The Mandalorian* moves fluidly between the past and present. Writing about the silent serial film, Kalton Lahue remarks: "The silent serial is a part of a vanished America; an America that many of us look back at fondly and muse, 'Those were the good old days.' Others cry out that we do not have time to look behind us; we must forever face the future. To those people I can only say—you don't know what you've missed in life."[55] Lahue's writing, first published in 1968, is somewhat nostalgic, but also evocative and energizing. Lahue's remarks pinpoint how *Star Wars*, so fond of looking back to past halcyon days but also of casually critiquing the present, set out on a course of continual and thoughtful introspection. Like George Lucas's "original" film that amalgamated many sources, *Star Wars*—and within this *The Mandalorian* and other attendant series[56]—amalgamates the past with the present and the future. As before, the franchise creates an ever-growing microcosmic world for digital viewers to stream, permitting us to return to a galaxy far, far away. But in the streaming age, this world will also be available close at hand, available to enter at the click of a switch, without the need to leave our homes, or even our sofas or beds. Viewers will continue to attach to such stories with immediacy, demonstrating ever more ways of becoming ensconced within the blooming microcosmic world. For the evolving serial medium, "This is the Way."

Bibliography

Ackerley, Bethan. "The Mandalorian review: How special effects made the Star Wars series." *New Scientist.* February 3, 2021. https://www.newscientist.com/article/mg24933202-300-the-mandalorian-review-how-special-effects-made-the-star-wars-series/.

Arditi, David. *Streaming Culture: Subscription Platforms and the Unending Consumption of Culture.* Bingley, UK: Emerald Publishing, 2021.

Baruh, Bradford, dir. *Disney Gallery: Star Wars: The Mandalorian.* Season 1, episode 4, "Technology." Aired May 22, 2020. Disney+. https://www.disneyplus.com/video/8112cabc-5ed9-4176-b0f8-b4baa0ab15f1.

---

[54] "Space Opera," *SFE The Encyclopedia of Science Fiction*, last modified January, 13, 2020, https://sf-encyclopedia.com/entry/space_opera.

[55] Kalton C. Lahue, *Bound and Gagged: The Story of the Silent Serials* (New York: Castle Books, 1968), 12.

[56] These include the television shows *The Book of Boba Fett* (2021-), *Obi-Wan Kenobi* (2022-), and *Andor* (2022-).

"Behind the Scenes of Star Wars." *American Cinematographer.* 2005. Accessed November 22, 2021. https://theasc.com/magazine/starwars/index.html.

"*Black Widow.*" The Numbers. February 24, 2022. Accessed February 28, 2022. https://www.the-numbers.com/movie/Black-Widow-(2021)#tab=summary.

Cutting, James E. *Movies on Our Minds: The Evolution of Cinematic Engagement.* New York: Oxford University Press, 2021.

Dallesandro, Anthony. "Disney Claims $215M+ WW Victory At The B.O. & Disney+ Premier With 'Black Widow' Weekend: Will Distrib Model Endanger A Movie's Life Cycle? —Update." *Deadline.* July 21, 2021. https://deadline.com/2021/07/black-widow-opening-weekend-box-office-1234789473/.

DarthSnow. "EVENT: THE MANDALORIAN S2 LIVE WATCH PARTY [CANTINA+DISCORD]." The Cantina. December 4, 2020. https://thecantina.starwarsnewsnet.com/index.php?threads/the-mandalorian-s2-live-watch-party-cantina-discord.58165/.

Dixon, Wheeler Winston. *Streaming: Movies, Media, and Instant Access.* Lexington, KY: University Press of Kentucky, 2013. Kobo Desktop.

Ewins, Mark. "*Twin Peaks: The Return.*" *Sight&Sound*, Vol. 28, Issue 1 (December 2017): 33-36.

Favreau, Jon, Dave Filoni, et al., writers. *The Mandalorian.* Directed by Dave Filoni, Rick Famuyiwa, Deborah Chow et al. Aired 2019- . Disney+. https://www.disneyplus.com/series/the-mandalorian/3jLIGMDYINqD.

"Features." *Unreal Engine.* 2004-2022. Accessed February 16, 2022. https://www.unrealengine.com/en-US/features.

Frankel, Daniel. "Is the Binge Busted? All-at-Once Releasing of Streaming Series Could Be on Its Way Out." *NextTV.* February 10, 2022. https://www.nexttv.com/news/is-the-binge-busted-all-at-once-releasing-of-streaming-series-could-be-on-its-way-out.

Furn, Daniel. "Disney+ launches GroupWatch so you can watch with six friends." *Radio Times.* February 23, 2021. https://www.radiotimes.com/technology/disney-groupwatch-watchalong-friends/.

Gilder, George. *Microcosm: The Quantum Revolution in Economics and Technology.* New York: Simon and Schuster, 1989.

Holben, Jay. *"The Mandalorian*: This Is the Way." *American Cinematographer.* February 6, 2020. https://ascmag.com/articles/the-mandalorian.

Hu, Iris. "TV Panel Prices Plunge in June, with No Signs of Stopping in July, Says TrendForce." *TRENDFORCE.* July 5, 2019. https://www.trendforce.com/presscenter/news/20190705-10159.html.

Jones, Brian Jay. *George Lucas: A Life.* London: Headline, 2016.

Kael, Pauline. "Contrasts." *When the Lights Go Down*, 291-298. London: Marion Boyars, 1980.

Lahue, Kalton C. *Bound and Gagged: The Story of the Silent Serials.* New York: Castle Books, 1968.

Nasuti, Sean. "'The Mandalorian': Season One Spoiler Review." *The Disinsider.* October 28, 2020. https://thedisinsider.com/2020/10/28/the-mandalorian-season-1-spoilers-review/.

"Nat Levine & Mascot Pictures/The Old Corral." b-westerns.com. Accessed March 10, 2022. https://www.b-westerns.com/levine.htm.

Prince, Stephen. *Digital Cinema.* New Brunswick, NJ: Rutgers University Press, 2019.

"Rear projection on Solo: A Star Wars Story." *Foundry.* November 8, 2018. https://www.foundry.com/insights/film-tv/rear-projection-on-solo-a-star-wars-story.

Rife, Kate "*The Mandalorian* brings Western sweep and Werner Herzog to the *Star Wars* universe." *AVClub.* November 12, 2019. https://www.avclub.com/the-mandalorian-brings-western-sweep-and-german-auteurs-1839814541.

Rinzler, J.W. *The Making of Star Wars.* London: Ebury Press, 2007.

Roeper, Richard. "Thanksgiving weekend with Baby Yoda: Reviews of '*The Mandalorian,*' '*Servant*' and other shows for holiday streaming." *Chicago Sun-Times.* November 28, 2019. https://chicago.suntimes.com/2019/11/28/20982807/mandalorian-review-servant-klaus-merry-happy-whatever-noelle-netflix-appletvplus-amazon-disneyplus.

Siegal, Jacob. "Disney+ gets a watch party feature just in time for 'The Mandalorian' season 2." *BGR.* September 20, 2020. https://bgr.com/entertainment/disney-plus-groupwatch-feature-watch-party/.

"Space Opera." *SFE The Encyclopedia of Science Fiction.* Last modified January, 13, 2020. https://sf-encyclopedia.com/entry/space_opera.

"*Spider-Man: No Way Home.*" Rotten Tomatoes. Accessed February 26, 2022. https://www.rottentomatoes.com/m/spider_man_no_way_home.

"*Spider-Man: No Way Home.*" The Numbers. Accessed February 24, 2022. https://www.the-numbers.com/movie/Spider-Man-No-Way-Home-(2021)#tab=summary.

"Stagecraft." *Industrial Light & Magic.* Accessed March 23, 2022. https://www.ilm.com/stagecraft/.

Todd The Jedi. "The Mandalorian Season 1 Discussion (Spoilers Allowed)." Jedi Council Forums. October 29, 2019. https://boards.theforce.net/threads/the-mandalorian-season-1-discussion-spoilers-allowed.50052332/.

Watts, Jon dir. *Spider-Man: No Way Home.* 2021; Culver City, CA: Sony Pictures. Film.

Chapter 9

From "Utinni!" to "Aliit Ori'shya Tal'din":[1] The Glossopoeiac Journey of *Star Wars*

Andrew Higgins

Abstract: From *Star Wars Episode IV: A New Hope* (1977), in which Jawas squeal "Utinni," to *Star Wars Episode VI: Return of the Jedi* (1983) in which Princess Leia, disguised as a bounty hunter, threatens Jabba the Hutt with "Ei Yoto" while holding a thermal detonator, invented languages have helped develop and distinguish the peoples and cultures of a galaxy far, far away. This chapter explores how elements of these different languages were developed through sound design and went on to play an important part in *Star Wars* storytelling. The chapter focuses on sound designer Ben Burtt and his foundational *Star Wars: Galactic Phrase Book & Travel Guide* (2001), written in the diegetic context of the story-world, and some of the graphically-developed written scripts used to express its invented languages, especially Aurebesh and Sith. At the same time, the chapter acknowledges the problems of cultural misappropriation inherent in many of the ways in which the makers of *Star Wars* approached and executed the task of language invention for the franchise. Finally, it explores the current means of language invention in the franchise, especially how it has moved away from problematic practices of its past and embraced methods that actually increase diversity and representation in the franchise.

Keywords: *Star Wars*, George Lucas, invented languages, cultural appropriation, Huttese, Wookiee, Jawas, Jawa, Jawaese, Ewok, Ubese, Sith, Mando'a, Mandalorian, TSL, Tusken, science fiction, sound symbolism, phono-aesthetics

***

[1] The title of this chapter evokes one of the earliest languages invented for *Star Wars* (Jawaese) and one of the most recent (Mando'a, sometimes referred to as Mandalorian). More will be said about both phrases below.

A long time ago—there was sound

At the start of *Star Wars* (1977), after the opening narrative scroll and the breathtaking shots of a battle in space, audience members are introduced to two key point of view characters: the protocol droid C-3PO and his astromech droid companion R2-D2. In this opening scene aboard the fleeing *Tantive IV*, C-3PO in a panic turns to his companion and asks in English, "Did you hear that?" His companion responds to him not in English, but in a series of beeps the audience does not understand, though C-3PO clearly does.[2] Through this early, foundational scene of *Star Wars* storytelling, George Lucas lets the audience know that one of the key elements of his world-building will be the use of languages other than English, starting with the beeps of R2-D2. We later learn that the *Star Wars* universe is replete with different forms of communication when C-3PO boasts to Uncle Owen that, besides being able to assist in etiquette and protocol, he is "fluent in over six-million forms of communication."[3] Prior to this scene, audiences also experience another form of language from the diminutive, lisping junk dealers who capture the droids and sell them to Luke and his uncle: the Jawas, whose joyful exclamations of "Utinni"[4] as they capture the incapacitated R2-D2 are some of the first "foreign" words heard in the film. As the story unfolds, many more languages are spoken by the various species Luke and his companions encounter on their quest to find and save Princess Leia and battle the Empire.

The languages that appear in the three foundational *Star Wars* films, as well as those in the three Prequel movies that followed, each have a unique origin, invented as an integral act of the world-building of *Star Wars*. Unlike other invented or engineered languages for such worlds as Tolkien's Middle-earth and Roddenberry's *Star Trek*,[5] the foundational languages of *Star Wars* were invented through the recording and mixing of sounds. They were created not by a linguist, but by a sound engineer responsible for conjuring the entire aural landscape of the early *Star Wars* world—from the *wush* of Obi-Wan's lightsaber to the climactic sonic explosion of the Death Star. Therefore,

---

[2] *Star Wars Episode IV: A New Hope*, directed by George Lucas (1977; Beverly Hills, CA: 20th Century Fox/Lucasfilm Ltd.), Disney+, https://www.disneyplus.com/movies/star-wars-a-new-hope-episode-iv/12fVeZxD2fWJ.

[3] Ibid.

[4] An invented Jawa exclamation used several times in the *Star Wars* films; see Major Grin, "Jawas Utinni Compilation," YouTube, November 27, 2019, https://www.youtube.com/watch?v=0wkiHVWA98U.

[5] For more about the invented languages of *Star Trek*, see Andrew Higgins's chapter in the companion volume to this book, *Star Trek: Essays Exploring the Final Frontier*, ed. Amy H. Sturgis and Emily Strand (Wilmington, DE: Vernon Press, 2023).

languages for these early key texts were not built from a planned-out vocabulary and system of grammar; rather the "art" of the language invention was in the choosing, recording, and mixing of sounds into beeps, grunts, and spoken dialogue. Writer Ben Zimmer has characterized these acts as nothing more than the creation of a "sonic pastiche."[6] This chapter will explore the interesting and sometimes problematic origins of this "sonic pastiche" and how it grew into a nexus of invented languages spoken throughout the *Star Wars* story-world.

The Swiss linguist Ferdinand de Saussure (1857-1913) is known for the organizing principle of the arbitrary relationship in language between the signified (the object) and the signifier (the word). Saussure believed that this relationship was established only through common cultural agreement, and there was nothing inherent in a word that conveyed meaning.[7] However, alternative theories to this organizing principle, which explored the inherent relationship between the sound of a phoneme or word and its sound-sense, had been developed starting with Plato's *Cratylus* from the fifth century BCE, continuing through works of the Middle Ages and Renaissance.[8] In the early twentieth century, authors like T.S. Eliot, James Joyce, and Gertrude Stein explored these concepts in their works of prose and poetry. Writer, philologist, and language inventor J.R.R. Tolkien, in his "Essay on Phonetic Symbolism," suggested that certain sounds are more suited to express certain notions than others—in other words, that certain groups of notions tend to be expressed by sound groups having certain phonetic elements.[9] Lucas's decision to think of these alien languages as an element of sound design suggests possible influence from the thinking of Tolkien and others on language.[10] Far from a haphazard "sonic pastiche" then, the invented languages of *Star Wars,* in their sound-based creation, are rooted—if unwittingly—in such phono-aesthetic approaches to language. Regrettably, early *Star Wars* language invention also constituted acts of cultural misappropriation, and increased sensitivity to various cultures is also part of the story of the evolution of invented languages in *Star Wars.*

---

[6] Ben Zimmer, "The Languages of Star Wars: The Force Awakens," *The Wall Street Journal,* January 15, 2016, https://www.wsj.com/articles/the-languages-of-star-wars-the-force-awakens-1452892741 (paywall).

[7] Ferdinand Saussure, *Course in General Linguistics* (New York: Columbia University Press, 1958), 7-17.

[8] Margaret Magnus, "A History of Sound Symbolism," in *The Oxford Handbook of the History of the English Language,* ed. Keith Allen (Oxford: Oxford University Press, 2013), 191-208.

[9] J.R.R. Tolkien, *A Secret Vice: Tolkien on Invented Languages,* ed. Dr. Dimitra Fimi and Andrew Higgins (London: HarperCollins, 2016), 63-80.

[10] Tolkien's narrative influence on Lucas is widely noted. See Chris Taylor, *How Star Wars Conquered the Universe* (New York: Basic Books, 2014), 122-123.

Ben Burtt: the father of *Star Wars* language invention

If George Lucas is the father of *Star Wars* storytelling, then sound designer Ben Burtt is the father of the sounds of the languages created for the *Star Wars* story-world. Ben Burtt never intended to go into sound design and actually studied physics in college while having a real interest in filmmaking. After making some films for fun, he won a scholarship to go to film school. At University of Southern California's School of Cinema and Television, he completed a master's degree in production, and it was while working in this program that Burtt became interested in sound design for films. After he graduated in 1975, he met film producer Gary Kurtz who was assembling a crew for a new science fiction film that had been written and was to be directed by George Lucas. Kurtz asked Burtt if he wanted to work on the sound design for this new film, and Burtt started working at Lucasfilm in 1975 as sound designer for *Star Wars*. In addition to designing sound for the film, Lucas asked Burtt to come up with "voices" for his list of characters; this was considered a part of the sound design for the movie.[11] Burtt would later reflect on this process of language invention through the capturing of sounds to give the sensation of language and the phono-aesthetic nature of these languages and their relationship to meaning:

> Overall, the creation of alien languages has been the hardest task [of sound design]. A language, or more accurately, the *sensation* of language, has to satisfy the audience's most critical faculties. We are all experts at identifying the nuances of intonation. Whether we understand a given language or not, we certainly process the sound fully and attribute meaning—perhaps inaccurate—to the emotional and informational content of the speech. Our minds are trained to recognize and process dialogue. The task, therefore, of creating a language is all the more difficult because of the strength of the audience's perception.[12]

Burtt's process in this "invention" or "sound design" was through researching the source of the sounds and capturing them in a library that could be used to mix and construct the dialogue. To achieve this, Burtt broke down the languages needed from the *Star Wars* script into three general categories: languages to be composed and built from recorded animal sounds, those derived from human-produced sound by appropriating the sounds of various Indigenous languages, and those that were to be synthesized from acoustical

---

[11] Roadtrip Nation, "How sound designer Ben Burtt made Star Wars' iconic sound effects," YouTube, November 19, 2019, https://www.youtube.com/watch?v=WBKKXjNf1sE.
[12] Ben Burtt, *Star Wars: Galactic Phrase Book & Travel Guide* (New York: Del Rey, 2001), 122.

and electronic sounds. Thus the first phase of *Star Wars* language invention was made up of grunts, beeps, and strange words and phrases—strange to the average English-language speaker, that is—mixed together to convey a sense of meaning to the audience.[13] However, this first phase of *Star Wars* language invention also presents problematic elements from a cultural sensitivity viewpoint. Burt's appropriation of sounds and phrases from Indigenous languages as a source for dialogue in *Star Wars* may have seemed innocent and even resourceful in the 1970s, but it now represents an example of the misappropriation of culture for art—something today's inventors of art languages seek to avoid.

Bears, angry walruses, and braying mules: the sonic origins of Shyriiwook and Tusken

Audiences first encounter the Wookiee Chewbacca in *Star Wars Episode IV: A New Hope* in the Mos Eisley cantina, when Ben Kenobi approaches him at the bar. While audiences don't hear much of the dialogue, it is clear that Kenobi can understand the grunts of the Wookiee; after a ruffian loses his arm thanks to Kenobi's quick lightsaber work, the Jedi Knight informs a dazed Luke that Chewbacca is first mate on a ship that may suit their needs.[14] As the movie progresses, the audience hears Chewbacca's language, which sounds like a series of roars, yelps, and (in lighter moments) chortles. Other characters, especially the Wookiee's companion Han Solo, react to this language, clearly understanding what Chewbacca is saying. The sound of Chewbacca's language (later known as "Wookiee" or "Shyriiwook") derives from a combination of mixed and blended animal sounds. In pre-production, Lucas suggested to Burtt that, given the ursine look of Chewbacca, bear sounds might work for his language. Burtt went to various zoos and recorded the voices of bears, including a baby bear called Pooh. He mixed and augmented his collection of bear sounds by capturing the moans of walruses, apparently unhappy their pool in Long Beach, California was being drained, and other animals. Therefore Chewbacca speaks with a language that is part roaring of bears—to convey his anger and power, as when Han Solo warns the droids playing Dejarik with Chewie on the *Millennium Falcon*—and part groaning of upset walruses, as in Chewbacca's reaction to the smell of the garbage dump on the Death Star. Through these sounds, audiences get a sense of what Chewbacca is feeling. Thus this mixing of the particular sounds of bears and

---

[13] Daniel Bögre Udell, "May the Fourth Special: Where Star Wars Gets Linguistics Right," *Medium*, May 4, 2020, https://medium.com/wikitongues/may-the-fourth-special-where-star-wars-gets-linguistics-right-a00321a1d135.
[14] *Star Wars Episode IV: A New Hope*, directed by George Lucas, 1977.

walruses gives Chewbacca a sonic vocabulary that both matches the imposing look of the Wookiee and conveys his moods, even before other characters react to or translate what he is saying.[15]

A different set of animal sounds was used for the dialogue of the Sand People of Tatooine, later known as the Tusken Raiders. These sounds were inspired by the sounds of mules braying, which plagued the crew of the original *Star Wars* film while filming the initial Tatooine scenes in Tunisia. Mules were used to carry the tons of film equipment from different locations, and they would occasionally burst into barks and screeches during shooting, ruining takes. Burtt was interested in this sound, echoing off the canyon walls, and he recorded it and used it for the language of the Sand People.[16] The use of braying mules for the Sand People's sonic vocabulary conveyed to 1977 film audiences—just through sound—how alien and intimidating these people are; there was no need to know what they were actually saying. From these earliest braying sounds, a new and more humanizing *Star Wars* language would develop for the Tuskens, and we will return to the interesting evolution of these people and their language in more recent *Star Wars* storytelling below.

A problematic soup of voices

Burtt produced another group of languages for dialogue through the recording of human languages. One early idea he experimented with was "backward talking" where English dialogue would be recorded and then played backwards. This technique had been used in the 1940 serial *Flash Gordon Conquers the Universe* for the Rock Men on the planet Mongo.[17] Burtt tried this technique for these languages but found, given the familiar pattern of vowels and consonants in the English language, the dialogue for these characters did not sound alien enough. Then Burtt listened to various examples of real-world Indigenous languages, primarily through language lesson recordings and shortwave transmissions from all over the world.

The first time Burtt appropriated the sounds of an Indigenous language in this manner was for the language that would come to be called Huttese, first spoken by hit man Greedo as he confronts Han Solo in the Mos Eisley cantina. For this

---

[15] INDEPTH Sound Design, "Star Wars: A New Hope sound design explained by Ben Burtt," YouTube, April 2, 2019, https://www.youtube.com/watch?v=So0nmciiFJg (see especially 26:18-29:13).

[16] Ibid., see especially 13:37-14:20.

[17] See Norman Field, "Rock Men speaking normally; Flash Gordon serial 1940," YouTube, December 10, 2009, https://youtu.be/C9-ovXW69G0. The *Flash Gordon* serials were a noted influence on George Lucas for *Star Wars*.

dialogue, Burtt used elements of the ancient Indigenous language of Peru called Quechua. Burtt worked with a language student from Berkeley, Larry Ward, focusing on the sound of the language dialogue they were inventing.[18] According to Burtt, Lucas was originally going to have Greedo speak with an electronic insect-like sound, as the character resembled an insect with big bug eyes. Then he was going to speak in a "staccato 'oink-oink' language" created by Lucas and Burtt.[19] When Lucas heard the Quechua-inspired greeting invented by Burtt—"Koona t'chuta, Solo?"[20]—he was convinced, and it became the basis of Huttese, later to be spoken by the crime lord Jabba the Hutt in *Return of the Jedi.* It has since become one of the most extensively developed of the *Star Wars* languages. Given the pivotal nature of this scene towards building Han Solo's character, Lucas gave the audience subtitles to understand what Greedo was saying to Solo, while Solo understood the Huttese and, for the sake of the audience's understanding, responded in English. The result is a language that appropriates the sounds of Quechua, which Burtt perceived to sound "alien," but with a structure that makes it convincing as dialogue, with questions and statements. It is unclear as to whether any Native speakers of Quechua were consulted in this process. Unfortunately, this kind of cultural misappropriation in using an Indigenous language to create a language that sounds "alien" to Western ears has the unintentional but real effect of alienating or "Othering" those who speak Indigenous languages. For this reason, those who construct languages today avoid such potentially harmful practices.

For other languages in this category, Burtt went even further with what can, in retrospect, only be described as cultural misappropriation. For example, for the Jawas, Burtt not only used actual dialogue from several Indigenous African languages, including the Zulu language, but he also appropriated a perceived, generalized cultural marker of the Zulu people: their fierce bravery.[21] During recording, when Burtt asked one Zulu man to say the dialogue with fear in his voice, the man objected, stating that a Zulu warrior such as himself would not know any fear and therefore could not vocally express it in the sound of the Zulu language.[22] This anecdote became an assumption that all Zulus are brave, and this feature was instilled in not only

---

[18] INDEPTH Sound Design, "Star Wars: A New Hope sound design explained by Ben Burtt," see especially 18:56-20:44.
[19] Burtt, *Galactic Phrase Book*, 134.
[20] This phrase translates to, "Going somewhere, Solo?" INDEPTH Sound Design, "Star Wars: A New Hope sound design explained by Ben Burtt," see especially 18:56-20:44.
[21] Burtt, *Galactic Phrase Book*, 136.
[22] Ibid.

the sonic language for the Jawas, but in their character as well.[23] This fearless nature of the Jawas has persisted throughout *Star Wars* storytelling. In the most recent *Star Wars* television shows such as *The Book of Boba Fett* (2021-), the Jawas' brazen fearlessness is still apparent in their thieving of spare parts from the Pyke Syndicate, noted by the Mandalorian Din Djarin.[24] In the late 1970s, such cultural "borrowing" seemed innocent enough, and perhaps marking Jawas as brave was then considered a compliment to Zulu culture. Now, however, when Jawas are seen and heard in *Star Wars* storytelling, they act as witnesses to a darker aspect of *Star Wars*'s origins: the misappropriation of language and culture to invent languages.

Baby talk: giving R2-D2 a personality

Burtt considered the third form of early *Star Wars* language invention the biggest challenge, epitomized in the mechanical voice of R2-D2: droid speech. The real challenge of bringing R2-D2 to life was creating a sense of character, feeling, and intelligence using only nonverbal sounds. Burtt experimented with the synthesizers of the day, including the Moog and ARP (named for its creator, Alan Robert Pearlman). While these instruments created sounds, they did not convey emotion, and R2-D2 had to act alone—and credibly—in scenes with the great English actor Sir Alec Guinness. Burtt began adding mechanically generated sounds to the electronic beeps. During one session when he played this blending for Lucas, Lucas "began mimicking with his own voice a kind of baby babble, to illustrate a conversation between C-3PO and R2-D2."[25] Through this creative work, Burtt combined machine-generated beeps with a kind of baby talk. Burtt used this process to convert the very first lines of dialogue in the film: the aforementioned panicked conversation between C-3PO and R2-D2 on the fleeing *Tantive IV*. Burtt converted R2-D2's first response to C-3PO, scripted as "Don't blow your bolts, this battle's not over yet! . . . Let's head down to A deck for cover. Darn! They've sealed it off. We can't go this way,"[26] into the new droid talk, conveyed solely by the now-famous beeps of R2-D2. The sounds of the beeps blended with baby talk conveyed about R2 a sense of machine sturdiness yet endearing vulnerability, all without the audience even understanding R2's

---

[23] Ibid. Burtt comments that while Jawas are small, they are fearless in their scavenging of items to trade.

[24] *The Book of Boba Fett*, season 1, episode 5, "Return of the Mandalorian," directed by Bryce Dallas Howard, written by Jon Favreau, aired January 26, 2022, Disney+, https://www.disneyplus.com/video/0c9fad98-263c-401b-802d-bd697caccd89.

[25] INDEPTH Sound Design, "Star Wars: A New Hope sound design explained by Ben Burtt," see especially 3:32-7:57.

[26] Burtt, *Galactic Phrase Book*, 145-146.

share of the dialogue, which underscores the important role of invented sounds in conveying meaning. This sonic vocabulary of blended beeps and baby talk has made R2-D2 one of the most beloved and enduring characters in *Star Wars* storytelling, and a modified version of this "baby-beep" language can be heard in the sonic language of many other droids, especially the *Star Wars* Sequel films' endearing droid character BB-8.

"Yub Nub!": a problematic voice for the "little" people

For *Star Wars Episode VI: Return of the Jedi* (1983), Burtt returned to the appropriation of elements of Indigenous language to develop a new language for the furry, heroic Ewoks of the planet Endor. Their language needed to be distinct from the Huttese that Jabba and his minions speak in the opening sequence. Burtt looked for a sound that evoked the Ewoks' playfulness—something, he later remembers, "that was fun and interesting and kind of made you smile when you listened to it."[27] Burtt interviewed people who could recite folktales in their Indigenous languages with the belief that this type of recitation would reveal the aspects of the Ewoks he sought. With no real attention to the content of the folktales or respect for their role in Native cultures, this approach seems poised for biased misperception and alienation of Indigenous peoples and their cultures, and this chapter in the history of *Star Wars* invented languages is, from the perspective of cultural misappropriation, arguably the most problematic.

And the approach here is not even the most problematic aspect; the method, in at least one case, is worse. One of these interviews was with a refugee from Inner Mongolia, a woman in her seventies. "She had been really living in the wilderness—by comparative standards to us—all her life," Burtt said. "And [she] had just recently come over and immigrated and didn't speak any English. She would come in and speak for us and if she had a little vodka she was happy to do so,"[28] earning her the derogatory nickname "Grandma Vodka" among Burtt and his team. Unfortunately, Burtt does not document her real name, nor is the historic use of alcohol to disenfranchise Native peoples acknowledged in his account of her involvement in *Star Wars.*

This woman spoke the Indigenous Mongolian language Kalymk-Oriat in what Burtt perceived as a melodic kind of voice that he recorded and mixed with related Indigenous languages from Tibet and Sri Lanka. Thus Burtt

---

[27] Tami Katzoff, "'Return of the Jedi' Turns 30: Secrets of the Ewok Language Revealed!" *MTV News*, May 24, 2013, https://www.mtv.com/news/1708006/star-wars-return-jedi-ewok-language-secrets/.

[28] Ibid.

developed a sonic language for the Ewoks, which was then used to build the dialogue for the film. Again, the method and process of the language's development—for better or for worse—finds an echo in the narrative when C-3PO tells the "folktale" of the *Star Wars* story to the Ewoks in what the shooting script calls "the Ewok's squeaky native tongue."[29]

Another human-based language introduced in *Return of the Jedi* was Ubese, spoken briefly by the bounty hunter Boushh (really Princess Leia in disguise). Lucas wanted Ubese to have a scratchy, guttural monotone sound that would throw off the audience as to who was really behind the mask. For this short dialogue, Burtt recorded the raspy voice of actor Patricia Walsh speaking a language made up of several phrases with the same repeated words: "yatay" or "yotoh." Burtt met Walsh in a camera shop where he heard a rather slow and low-pitched voice talking with the clerk about a credit card. The source of this unusual voice was an elderly woman at the head of the line, and Burtt asked her if she would record dialogue in this language. This started a partnership that would culminate in Walsh's casting as the main voice for the alien E.T. in the 1982 film of the same name, directed by Steven Spielberg, for which Burtt provided sound design.[30]

However, Boushh's language, as invented by Burtt, caused future language inventor David J. Peterson, known today for his invention of languages for science fiction and fantasy works such as Dothraki and Valyrian for the HBO series *Game of Thrones* (2011-2019) some concern when he first encountered it. When Peterson re-watched the *Star Wars* films in the 1990s as a teen, just starting to explore languages, he sensed there was something wrong in the dialogue with this language as the invented Ubese word "yotoh" was used in the dialogue several times but, according to the sub-titles, appeared to have different meanings each time. Peterson started thinking about how this curious phenomenon could work within the context of the invented language, and this deepened his early interest in how invented languages are created and work.[31] While Boushh's language was sonically-derived and grammatically unsophisticated in its invention, it may have motivated other creators such as Peterson to take constructed languages to new levels.

---

[29] "Return of the Jedi," The Internet Movie Script Database, accessed November 10, 2022, https://imsdb.com/scripts/Star-Wars-Return-of-the-Jedi.html. Fortunately, the vodka was left out of the scene.

[30] INDEPTH Sound Design, "Star Wars: A New Hope sound design explained by Ben Burtt," see especially 6:45-8:44.

[31] David J. Peterson, *The Art of Language Invention: From Horse-Lords to Dark Elves to Sand Worms, the Words Behind World-Building* (New York: Penguin Books, 2015, 2021), 3-7.

The *Galactic Phrase Book & Travel Guide*

As the *Star Wars* franchise and story-world continued to expand through a vast collection of trans-medial texts, interest in Burtt's original albeit problematic sound-generated languages also grew, as viewers and fans wanted more information on these languages. This trajectory in *Star Wars* world-building and fan interaction is comparable with what occurred after Tolkien published the first two volumes of *The Lord of the Rings* trilogy in 1954; he immediately received letters from readers and early fans clamoring for more "information."[32] In the case of *Star Wars*, the growing fandom's interest in the various species presented in the films, attendant novelizations, and other paratexts caused Burtt to move from recording and mixing sounds for these languages to actually codifying them. He achieved this by applying a similar methodology employed by other language inventors through writing down the phonetics, vocabulary, and grammar of these languages from the now-established dialogue appearing in the movies. In doing this, Burtt also transferred the elements of cultural misappropriation of Indigenous languages and culture inherent in the language of the Jawas and the Ewoks into the written versions of these languages. This work culminated in a unique paratextual work, *Star Wars: Galactic Phrase Book & Travel Guide* (2001).

This book, in part, employs a framework that harks back to one of the earliest narrative structures authors have used to introduce invented languages into fictional works: the traveler's tale. In the traveler's tale, an explorer travels to a foreign land and encounters new peoples possessing different cultures and languages. The epitome of the traveler's tale is Jonathan Swift's 1726 political satire *Gulliver's Travels*, in which the surgeon-sailor Lemuel Gulliver travels to different islands and encounters strange creatures speaking different languages, about which, in the course of the narrative, he reports. In the *Galactic Phrase Book & Travel Guide*, the *Star Wars* equivalent of Swift's Lemuel Gulliver is Ebenn Q3 Baobab, a fictional author, traveler, humorist, adventurer, historian, and philologist. The introduction establishes the work as a guidebook for travelers in the post-Battle of Yavin period of the *Star Wars* narrative, offering an understanding of basic language elements for travel to different worlds and encounters with different species and cultures. In addition to practical information, Burtt's guide book also gives readers

[32] Tolkien expressed this in a letter to his publisher Rayner Unwin from 1955: "It is, I suppose, a tribute to the curious effect that a story has, when based on very elaborate and detailed workings, of geography, of chronology, and language, that so many should clamour for sheer 'information' or 'lore'." J.R.R. Tolkien, *The Letters of J.R.R. Tolkien*, ed. Humphrey Carpenter and Christopher Tolkien (London: HarperCollins, 1981), 210.

historical information (what Tolkien characterized as "lore"), creating a sense of historic and linguistic depth, as exemplified in this passage about the common origins of the languages of the Jawas and Tusken Raiders on Tatooine:

> The Jawa language seems to derive from a common ancestor to the Jawas and the Sand People, or Tusken Raiders, another Native life-form on ancient Tatooine. Baobab anthropologists have uncovered skulls of these ancient ancestors, which we have named the Kumumgah. There seems to have been a split in the once singular tribe, resulting in taller and shorter individuals, which led to insult, nomadic separation, and division of labor. . . . The ancient Kumumgah language developed into two different dialects with radically different sound textures.[33]

The publishing of Burtt's phrasebook led to several attempts by members of the *Star Wars* fan community to develop these languages through online websites. For example, *The Complete Wermo's Guide to Huttese*[34] built upon Burtt's expanded grammar and vocabulary for the language of the Hutts. Currently, *The Complete Wermo's Guide to Huttese* includes dictionaries of the language, a number chart, and graded lessons for learning the language of Greedo and Jabba the Hutt.

Current *Star Wars* world-building and language invention

In the ever-growing and expanding *Star Wars* story-world, with content delivered via many multimedia platforms, new *Star Wars* languages continue to appear as part of the building blocks of the franchise and as key markers distinguishing different peoples. These new languages have been invented using a blended approach, employing the sound design engineering of Ben Burtt while also employing development of vocabulary and grammar for more structured dialogue. These modern approaches have resulted in less cultural misappropriation and have even increased inclusion and representation in *Star Wars*.

Burtt's influence can be seen in the new languages invented for the conclusion of the Skywalker saga. For *Star Wars Episode VII: The Force Awakens* (2015), director J.J. Abrams hired Finnish singer and songwriter Sara Forsberg to invent several new languages. One of these languages is used by the Teedos, a species of reptilian scavengers native to the planet Jakku, where Rey starts her adventures. Forsberg was interested in ideas around what sense

33 Burtt, *Galactic Phrase Book*, 80.

34 "The Complete Wermo's Guide to Huttese," accessed on April 14, 2022, http://www.completewermosguide.com/index.html. "Wermo" is the Huttese word for "idiot."

unknown languages convey to the listener through their sounds. In 2014, she created a series of YouTube videos called "What Languages Sounds Like to Foreigners," exploring how the same phrases in different language inflections sound and what feelings the sounds convey when listeners do not know the meaning.[35] These videos went viral quite quickly and came to Abrams's attention. Forsberg was approached by Lucasfilm and thus developed the language of Teedospeak, focusing on the gruff sound of this reptilian species for its particular sound-sense. Forsberg's process for this language invention was similar to Burtt's for the Jawas and Ewoks.

> They asked me to listen to Euro-Asian languages, so I listened to Gujarati and Hindi and languages from different islands in Asia. I also watched YouTube videos of languages I didn't understand at all, and then I worked on creating words and structure so it would sound like a believable language. I didn't want it to sound like complete nonsense.[36]

But Forsberg's approach and the result is markedly different from Burtt's in significant ways. For example, Forsberg also invented a language for the Kanjiklub gang, who briefly face off against Han Solo and Chewbacca on a space freighter packed with slithery Rathtars. In this case, the sound of the language was inspired by those portraying the Kanjiklub gang, including Indonesian actors Iko Uwais, Yayan Ruhian, and Cecep Arif Rahman—all acclaimed martial arts film stars. So Forsberg listened to clips of Sundanese, from the actors' home region of western Java, and developed a language that sounded Indonesian.[37] Forsberg's use of Indigenous language for her language invention shows marked progress from Burtt's appropriation of Native languages, because the actors who spoke Forsberg's invented language in the film were actually from the culture that inspired the language. Their inclusion as live-action actors speaking a fictional language inspired by elements of their own language, while remaining distinct, shows a new approach to language invention in *Star Wars* that does not simply "grab" random cultural elements at will, but borrows intentionally and respectfully, increasing culturally diverse representation in the franchise.

---

[35] SAARA (Sara Forsberg), "What Languages Sound Like to Foreigners," YouTube, March 3, 2014, https://www.youtube.com/watch?v=ybcvlxivscw.

[36] Carita Rizzo, "'*Star Wars*': YouTube Star Creates New Language For Aliens," *Variety*, December 16, 2015, https://variety.com/2015/film/news/star-wars-sara-maria-forsberg-language-1201663521/.

[37] Ben Zimmer, "The Finn-donesian of 'The Force Awakens,'" *Language Log*, January 15, 2016, https://languagelog.ldc.upenn.edu/nll/?p=23527.

Currently, Wookieepedia lists over thirty known languages in both canon and, with the advent of the Disney era, "Legends" (or no-longer-canon) *Star Wars* texts.[38] In many of these narratives, a unifying lingua franca called "Galactic Basic Standard" (or "Basic") has become a shared form of communication of the many species and peoples across the galaxy and Outer Rim. The development of Basic suggests an attempt to point to an invented auxiliary language that explains the ease of communication among various species in the *Star Wars* universe. This attempt mirrors various attempts towards the end of the nineteenth century to invent what were termed auxiliary languages to aid communication among different peoples. Arguably the most well known but certainly not the only of these auxiliary languages is Esperanto, developed in the late nineteenth century by L.L. Zamenhof, a Polish linguist and physician who hoped to create a common language for the various European peoples to use for ease of communication and increased understanding.[39]

Linked to the expansion of *Star Wars* languages, several attendant writing systems have also been developed to phonetically and visually represent *Star Wars* languages.[40] One of the earliest of these (and most prominent) is Aurebesh, created by Stephen Crane for the 1994 West End Games books *Star Wars: Miniatures Battles Companion* and *Star Wars: The Role Playing Game* to visually and phonetically express Galactic Basic Standard.[41] Crane based Aurebesh on writing briefly seen in *Return of the Jedi* when Darth Vader's shuttle is transmitting codes to the second Death Star.[42] Since its publication, Aurebesh has appeared in such *Star Wars* texts as the Special Edition of *Star Wars Episode IV: A New Hope* (2004), where the instructions on the Death

---

[38] For more on the development of *Star Wars* canon and the relegation of pre-Disney texts to "Legends" or non-canonical status, see John Jackson Miller's chapter in this volume.

[39] Tolkien, *A Secret Vice*, 36.

[40] A defining document that analyzed the various histories and development of the writing systems of the *Star Wars* story-world appeared in 2010 on StarWars.com, written by *Star Wars* fan and writer John Hazlett. Called "The Written Word," Hazlett's piece offered the *Star Wars* fan community a comprehensive guide to these writing systems and their histories in both canon and legend. Although the article is no longer available on StarWars.com, a detailed summary can be found at "The Written Word," Wookieepedia, accessed April 15, 2022, https://starwars.fandom.com/wiki/The_Written_Word.

[41] The name Aurebesh comes from the first two letters of its alphabet, Aurek and Besh, and mirrors the word "alphabet," which is derived from the name of the first two letters "alpha" and "beta."

[42] *Star Wars Episode VI: Return of the Jedi*, directed by Richard Marquand (1983; Beverly Hills, CA: 20th Century Fox/Lucasfilm Ltd.), Disney+, https://www.disneyplus.com/movies/star-wars-return-of-the-jedi-episode-vi/6QGKo5mjDBS8.

Star's tractor beam now appear in Aurebesh script. The script has also appeared in myriad paratextual items including the *Star Wars* Monopoly game and even on a brand of sneakers.[43]

While the Aurebesh writing system was invented to express the lingua franca of Galactic Basic, the ancient Sith writing system expresses the arcane Sith language used in rituals to unleash the power of the Dark Side of the Force. The mention of a Sith language first appeared in the 1990s comic book series *Star Wars: Tales of the Jedi* and subsequently in several *Star Wars* video games such as 2004's *Star Wars: Knights of the Old Republic II—The Sith Lords.*[44] In 2010, author Ben Grossblatt, who holds a degree in linguistics, invented a constructed language (or conlang) for the Sith, featured in the paratextual work *Book of the Sith: Secrets from the Dark Side,*[45] including invented grammar, vocabulary, and a Sith runic script. Grossblatt elaborated on his Sith Language in a four-page article first published in the magazine *Star Wars Insider* 134 (2012), stating his goal in developing the language was "to create a plausible, linguistically sound language. Plausible in that it would sound and feel real—not like a cartoonish language for the bad guys to speak."[46] The Sith runic writing system has been used on various paratextual documents and on objects seen in such series as *Star Wars Rebels* (on a Sith Holocron).[47]

One key characteristic of the Sith Language as described in *Book of the Sith* is the power Sith words have in spells and incantations, the importance of

---

[43] "Pre-Order the new Aurebesh Sneakers from Po-Zu," *Jedi News,* accessed on April 14, 2022, https://www.jedinews.com/apparel/articles/pre-order-the-new-aurebesh-sneakers-from-po-zu/.

[44] For an in-depth analysis of the moral choices in *Star Wars: Knights of the Old Republic II,* see Aaron Masters's chapter in this volume.

[45] Daniel Wallace, *Book of the Sith: Secrets from the Dark Side* (New York: Titan Books, 2013; San Francisco, CA: Chronicle Books, 2020). *The Book of the Sith* is written as a collection of "dark texts" originally composed by such great Sith Lords as Darth Bane, Darth Plagueis, and his apprentice Darth Sidious. These "texts" were then annotated with handwritten notes by other Force users, including Darth Vader, Yoda, Mace Windu, and Luke Skywalker.

[46] Ben Grossblatt, "Speak Like a Sith," *Star Wars Insider* 134, June 12, 2012, 40.

[47] *Star Wars Rebels,* season 2, episodes 21 and 22, "Twilight of the Apprentice, Part I" and "Twilight of the Apprentice, Part II," directed by Dave Filoni, written by Dave Filoni, Simon Kinberg, and Steven Melching, aired March 31, 2016, on the Disney Channel, Disney+ https://www.disneyplus.com/video/bdb2a1e3-cd18-402d-8f68-750e21ef76b5 (Part I), https://www.disneyplus.com/video/7a2ad837-c828-4afe-9f5a-a5174171608b (Part II); *Star Wars Rebels,* season 3, episode 3, "Holocrons of Fate," directed by Steward Lee, written by Henry Gilroy, aired October 1, 2016, on the Disney Channel, Disney+, https://www.disneyplus.com/video/9036487e-2a1c-4856-8a10-ba7939480985.

pronouncing these words correctly, and the consequences of not producing the right sounds for the incantations.

> Sith spells that require vocalization are written in the Sith tongue, and consequently must be pronounced as such. Be aware that it is more than recitation! Your inflection must be both precise and passionate. Speak with hesitation, and the spell may hunt you instead! Most incantations have a specific meter and rhyme, and they can not be modified. The most complex incantations unleash spells of volcanic intensity.[48]

This focus on a language for arcane ritual with inherent power is redolent of a mysterious language called Aklo used by several authors in speculative literature. It was first cited by Arthur Machen in his 1889 short story "The White People" as a language used in a ritualistic game. The American writer H.P. Lovecraft admired this story and incorporated this ritualistic Aklo language, which had the power of summoning evil just by speaking it, into several of his eldritch stories, including "The Dunwich Horror" (1928) and "The Hunter in the Dark" (1935). Both the nature and sound of the Sith language suggest inspiration from the mysterious and deadly Aklo language.[49]

Another language has enjoyed recent development in *Star Wars*: Mando'a, also referred to as Mandalorian. It first appeared as a script seen in the controls of bounty hunter Jango Fett's ship in *Star Wars Episode II: Attack of the Clones* (2002).[50] It was then developed by *Star Wars* Expanded Universe content creators, especially author Karen Traviss for now-non-canonical works, namely the *Star Wars: Republic Commando* series (2004-2009).[51] It was first heard spoken in the (canon) animated television shows *Star Wars: The Clone Wars* (2008-2014, 2020), when Satine Kryze converses in a Mandalorian dialect with a Death Watch saboteur,[52] and in *Star Wars Rebels* by Mandalorian

---

[48] Wallace, *Book of the Sith*, 45. Interestingly, a contrasting, hand-written comment next to this passage by Jedi Master Mace Windu states, "The Jedi have no need for such rituals."

[49] Tim Conley and Stephen Cain, *Encyclopaedia of Fictional and Fantastic Languages* (London: Greenwood Press, 2000), 83.

[50] David West Reynolds, *Star Wars Episode II Attack of the Clones: The Visual Dictionary* (London: DK Publishing, Inc.: 2002), 43.

[51] "Mando'a/Canon," Wookieepedia, accessed January 7, 2023, https://starwars.fandom.com/wiki/Mando%27a.

[52] *Star Wars: The Clone Wars*, season 2, episode 12, "The Mandalore Plot," directed by Kyle Dunlevy, written by Melinda Hsu, aired January 29, 2010, on Cartoon Network, Disney+, https://www.disneyplus.com/video/91d2a7e2-8eb1-411d-941e-4bd8babe4e55.

Sabine Wren.[53] Mando'a script more recently appears in the Disney+ television show *The Mandalorian* (2019-), when Boba Fett shows Din Djarin the chain code for his armor, proving his legitimacy as its owner.[54] Spoken—or rather sung—Mando'a recently made the leap to live action in *The Book of Boba Fett* (2021-) with a phrase that features in this chapter's title, "Aliit ori'shya tal'din," meaning "Family is more than blood."[55] This phrase, which originally appeared in one of Traviss's now-Legends novels,[56] forms the lyrical focus of a chant-like song composed by Joseph Shirley and Ludwig Göransson for a tragic scene in *The Book of Boba Fett* in which Fett discovers his Tusken clan has been murdered. The phrase—as well as the scene—emphasizes the importance in Mandalorian culture of participation, either by birth or adoption, in a family or clan, declaring this bond is more sacred than blood. For a language that has only just begun to feature more prominently in *Star Wars* canon works, Mando'a has garnered much attention from fans who have participated in its development, adding vastly to the vocabulary and lore surrounding the language of this beloved race of armored warriors.[57]

Another recent innovation in *Star Wars* language invention dovetails interestingly with developments in how current *Star Wars* storytelling depicts and works with disability. Wilivaara has noted a progression in the ways in

---

[53] *Star Wars Rebels*, season 3, episode 16, "Legacy of Mandalore," directed by Mel Zwyer, written by Christopher Yost, aired February 18, 2017, on Disney XD, Disney+, https://www.disneyplus.com/video/45e7d38d-0534-428f-8a2c-bff5413903f1.

[54] *The Mandalorian*, season 2, episode 14, "The Tragedy," directed by Robert Rodriguez, written by Jon Favreau, aired December 4, 2020, Disney+, https://www.disneyplus.com/video/f0b3a47d-d833-4725-b46f-a2cf974271f6. Mando'a also appears in the third season of *The Mandalorian.*

[55] *The Book of Boba Fett*, season 1, episode 3, "The Streets of Mos Espa," directed by Robert Rodriguez, written by Jon Favreau, aired January 12, 2022, Disney+, https://www.disneyplus.com/video/b93d8ede-6b1b-4e10-aeec-5aeda1fe7c17. The song can be heard at "Aliit Ori'shya Tal'din," Lyrics Translate, accessed January 7, 2023, https://lyricstranslate.com/en/aliit-orishya-taldin-family-more-blood.html. Other Mando'a songs were previously composed by Jesse Harlin for a 2005 *Star Wars* video game; the game is now Legends. See Marv, "A History of Mando'a," *Numidian Prime* (blog), accessed January 7, 2023, https://numidianprime.wordpress.com/2022/01/25/a-history-of-mandoa/.

[56] Karen Traviss, *Star Wars Legacy of the Force: Bloodlines* (New York: Ballantine Books, 2006), 45.

[57] For instance, see this fan-created Mando'a database: "Dictionary," Mando'a, accessed January 7, 2023, http://mandoa.org/?fbclid=IwAR3XUVATnJPfKSNyZ3QEQbBRJVDbpK9hKltOo8tJCFRyanDrH-yBRxfOoKs; see also this fan-created Mando'a translator: "Mando'a-English Translator," Lingo Jam, accessed January 7, 2023, https://lingojam.com/Mandoa-EnglishTranslator?fbclid=IwAR2N8lh_DRVPjTNIux_0A5AF32FLBHiwZ-NlbKoVxlbiS0f5Bn-sZzDDGdE.

which disability is conceptualized in *Star Wars* storytelling. She explores, through the characters of Darth Vader and *Rogue One: A Star Wars Story* (2016)'s Chirrut Îmwe, how depictions of disabled characters have changed, moving from the isolation of Vader to the heroism of the blind Chirrut as a Guardian of the Whills.[58] This progression continues through an innovation in both invented languages and Deaf representation in the *Star Wars* world on the recent television shows *The Mandalorian* (2019-) and *The Book of Boba Fett* (2021-). In these shows, *Star Wars* storytelling returns to one of the first alien species seen in the original *Star Wars* film, the Sand People or Tusken Raiders, who become an important part of the storytelling for these two shows, both set, in whole or part, on Tatooine. In each show, the titular character must communicate with the isolated Tusken Raiders. This is achieved not simply through their strange, mule-inspired, braying, vocal language (though the Mandalorian seems proficient with it), but also by a system of hand signs and gestures.[59] For the first season of *The Mandalorian,* the Tusken Sign Language, as it has come to be known, was created by Oscar-winning actor, director, and writer Troy Kostur. A Deaf person, Kostur was brought on board by the suggestion of the production team to consult on the development of this new kind of sign language. Kostur said in developing this sign language his goal was to avoid ASL (American Sign Language) and to make sure Tusken Sign Language (TSL) was based on Tusken culture and environment.[60] For example, in Kostur's creation of the language, the sign for "Mandalorian" is based on his very prominent helmet and the letter "M" hand shape.[61]

---

[58] Josefine Walivaara, "Blind Warriors, Supercrips, and Techno-Marvels: Challenging Depictions of Disability in Star Wars," *The Journal of Popular Culture* Vol. 51, no 4, (2018): 1036-1056.

[59] Mars Garrett, "Geekery: Deaf Actor Created The Tusken Sign Language For 'The Mandalorian,'" *Bell of Lost Souls,* accessed April 15, 2022, https://www.belloflostsouls.net/2020/11/geekery-deaf-actor-created-the-tusken-sign-language-for-the-mandalorian.html.

[60] Josh Weiss, "Star Wars: The Mandalorian created a new form of Sign Language for the Tusken Raiders," *SYFY,* November 2, 2020, https://www.syfy.com/syfy-wire/the-mandalorian-tusken-raider-sign-language.

[61] Another possible source of inspiration for this hand language may be seen in the works of J.R.R. Tolkien, which, as previously mentioned, inspired some of the original *Star Wars* storytelling of George Lucas. Tolkien developed a "gesture language" achieved through hand-signs for his Dwarves, who spoke the strange, insular tongue Khuzdul. This dwarvish sign system was called Iglishmek, and Dwarfish children learned it simultaneously with the spoken language. For instance, the command to "Listen!" involved a slight raising of both forefingers simultaneously. The acknowledgment "I am listening" involved a slight raising of the right-hand forefinger, followed by a similar

Wilvaara's observations on the progression of the treatment and depiction of disability in *Star Wars* storytelling is corroborated by the development of TSL in at least three ways. First, the production team engaged with a Deaf person to invent the Tusken Sign Language, increasing disability representation among *Star Wars* creators. Secondly, Kostur went on to play one of the Tusken Raiders in the series, thus becoming the first Deaf person to play a role in *Star Wars*, marking a progression in Deaf representation in the *Star Wars* cast. Finally, the addition of this type of language to accompany the sonic braying of the Tusken Raiders also means greater Deaf representation in *Star Wars* narratives, as one father expressed on a Facebook page devoted to discussion of TSL: "I'm also a father to two deaf children. . . Seeing *The Mandalorian* series—and the Tusken Raiders, using a form of sign language in particular—really warmed my heart and excited my two children immensely!"[62]

In *The Book of Boba Fett* (2021-), the former bounty hunter Fett uses this same Tusken Sign Language in flashback scenes, showing how he gained the trust and alliance of the Tusken Raiders, partly through this shared system of communication. Kostur's invention has added both greater disability representation and a new dimension to *Star Wars* language invention with the addition of TSL—a form of communication viewers may well find in future *Star Wars* narratives.

Conclusion

A long time ago, in a galaxy not so far away, a sound designer was asked to go out and record various sounds to be mixed into the many voices that would make up the earliest elements of *Star Wars* glossopoesis. At this time, the use of invented languages in media such as film and television shows was very much in its infancy. Burtt's objective was not to "invent" structured language, as had been done in works of fiction going back to Classical times and more formally in works like Thomas More's *Utopia* (1516) and Jonathan Swift's *Gulliver's Travels* (1726), but to use sounds to invent dialogue. To achieve this, Burtt recorded and mixed some interesting and unexpected sounds. While his use of both sounds and dialogue from Indigenous peoples may have been considered benign and even resourceful at the time, they are problematic from a more modern vantage point—one that acknowledges the ravages of colonialism on Indigenous peoples, cultures, and languages. The bravery of

---

raising of the left-hand forefinger. See J.R.R. Tolkien, *The War of the Jewels: The History of Middle-earth Vol. 11* (London: HarperCollins, 2002), 395.

[62] Quoted in Mia Johnson, "A special form of sign language was created for Tusken Raiders in The Mandalorian," *Dork Side of the Force*, accessed April 15, 2022, https://dorksideoftheforce.com/2020/11/03/the-mandalorian-tusken-raider-sign-language/.

the Jawas and the playfulness of the Ewoks, indelible as they may be in *Star Wars* culture, have their origins in the misappropriation of perceived cultural characteristics from the peoples and languages from which Burtt took sounds and words, and this aspect of invented languages in *Star Wars* is important to acknowledge.

Despite these problematic elements, the unique nature of the genesis of *Star Wars* languages—using sound design to convey sound-sense to audiences—makes them both important and cautionary elements of study in the history of *Star Wars* storytelling and in language invention for fiction and world-building. These languages of grunts, brays, and beeps, later codified and developed by both *Star Wars* writers and the fan community, offer a unique perspective on how the sound of language communicates sense and how this sense can be built upon through a more structural process for inventing languages. Far from simplistic or haphazard, Burtt's pioneering sound gathering and sonic language invention gives *Star Wars* a complex—and at times problematic—heritage of communicated sounds that help create what Tolkien called the "inner consistency of reality."[63] Such consistency is particularly important within a linguistically vast and growing story-world containing, as C-3PO says, "six-million forms of communication": from the welcoming "Teeha Meechon nub hil vootak"[64] to the menacing "Chespo kutato kreesta krenko nyuaska!"[65]

Bibliography

"Aliit Ori'shya Tal'din." Lyrics Translate. Accessed January 7, 2023. https://lyricstranslate.com/en/aliit-orishya-taldin-family-more-blood.html.

Burtt, Ben. *Star Wars: Galactic Phrase Book & Travel Guide.* New York: Del Rey, 2001.

"The Complete Wermo's Guide to Huttese." Accessed on April 14, 2022. http://www.completewermosguide.com/index.html.

Conley, Tim and Stephen Cain. *Encyclopaedia of Fictional and Fantastic Languages.* London: Greenwood Press, 2000.

"Dictionary." Mando'a. Accessed January 7, 2023. http://mandoa.org/?fbclid=IwAR3XUVATnJPfKSNyZ3QEQbBRJVDbpK9hKltOo8tJCFRyanDrH-yBRxfOoKs.

Favreau, Jon, writer. *The Book of Boba Fett.* Season 1, episode 5, "Return of the Mandalorian." Directed by Bryce Dallas Howard. Aired January 26, 2022.

[63] J.R.R. Tolkien. *On Fairy-stories*, ed. Verlyn Flieger and Douglas A. Anderson (London: HarperCollins, 2008), 59.

[64] Ewok for "Thank You, I would like to visit your village." Burtt, *Galactic Phrase Book*, 50.

[65] The last line Greedo spoke in Huttese to Han Solo: "That's the idea, I've been looking forward to this for a long time." Solo follows with "I bet you have," and then someone shoots! Burtt, *Galactic Phrase Book*, 168.

Disney+. https://www.disneyplus.com/video/0c9fad98-263c-401b-802d-bd697caccd89.

_______, writer. *The Book of Boba Fett.* Season 1, episode 3, "The Streets of Mos Espa." Directed by Robert Rodriguez. Aired January 12, 2022. Disney+. https://www.disneyplus.com/video/b93d8ede-6b1b-4e10-aeec-5aeda1fe7c17.

_______, writer. *The Mandalorian.* Season 2, episode 14, "The Tragedy." Directed by Robert Rodriguez. Aired December 4, 2020. Disney+. https://www.disneyplus.com/video/f0b3a47d-d833-4725-b46f-a2cf974271f6.

Field, Norman. "Rock Men speaking normally; Flash Gordon serial 1940." YouTube. December 10, 2009. https://youtu.be/C9-ovXW69G0.

Filoni, Dave, Simon Kinberg, and Steven Melching, writers. *Star Wars Rebels.* Season 2, episodes 21 and 22, "Twilight of the Apprentice, Part I" and "Twilight of the Apprentice, Part II." Directed by Dave Filoni. Aired March 31, 2016, on the Disney Channel. Disney+. https://www.disneyplus.com/video/bdb2a1e3-cd18-402d-8f68-750e21ef76b5 (Part I), https://www.disneyplus.com/video/7a2ad837-c828-4afe-9f5a-a5174171608b (Part II).

Forsberg, Sarah. "What Languages Sound Like to Foreigners." YouTube. March 3, 2014. https://www.youtube.com/watch?v=ybcvlxivscw.

Garrett, Mars. "Geekery: Deaf Actor Created The Tusken Sign Language For 'The Mandalorian.'" *Bell of Lost Souls.* Accessed April 15, 2022. https://www.bellof lostsouls.net/2020/11/geekery-deaf-actor-created-the-tusken-sign-language-for-the-mandalorian.html.

Gilroy, Henry, writer. *Star Wars Rebels.* Season 3, episode 3, "Holocrons of Fate." Directed by Steward Lee. Aired October 1, 2016, on the Disney Channel. Disney+. https://www.disneyplus.com/video/9036487e-2a1c-4856-8a10-ba7939480985.

Grin, Major. "Jawas Utinni Compilation." YouTube. November 27, 2019. https://www.youtube.com/watch?v=0wkiHVWA98U.

Grossblatt, Ben. "Speak Like a Sith." *Star Wars Insider,* 134. 40-43.

Hsu, Melinda, writer. *Star Wars: The Clone Wars.* Season 2, episode 12, "The Mandalore Plot." Directed by Kyle Dunlevy. Aired January 29, 2010, on Cartoon Network. Disney+. https://www.disneyplus.com/video/91d2a7e2-8eb1-411d-941e-4bd8babe4e55.

INDEPTH Sound Design. "Star Wars: A New Hope sound design explained by Ben Burtt." YouTube. April 2, 2019. https://www.youtube.com/watch?v=So0nmciiFJg.

Johnson, Mia. "A special form of sign language was created for Tusken Raiders in The Mandalorian." *Dork Side of the Force.* Accessed April 15, 2022. https://dorksideoftheforce.com/2020/11/03/the-mandalorian-tusken-raider-sign-language/.

Katzoff, Tami. "Return of the Jedi Turns 30: Secrets of the Ewok Language Revealed." *MTV News.* May 24, 2013. https://www.mtv.com/news/1708006/star-wars-return-jedi-ewok-language-secrets/.

Lucas, George, dir. *Star Wars Episode IV: A New Hope.* 1977; Beverly Hills, CA: 20th Century Fox/Lucasfilm Ltd. Disney+. https://www.disneyplus.com/movies/star-wars-a-new-hope-episode-iv/12fVeZxD2fWJ.

Magnus, Margaret. "A History of Sound Symbolism." In *The Oxford Handbook of the History of the English Language*, edited by Keith Allen, 191-208. Oxford, UK: Oxford University Press, 2013.

"Mando'a/Canon." Wookieepedia. Accessed January 7, 2023. https://starwars.fandom.com/wiki/Mando%27a.

"Mando'a-English Translator." Lingo Jam. Accessed January 7, 2023. https://lingojam.com/Mandoa-EnglishTranslator?fbclid=IwAR2N8lh_DRVPjTNIux_0A5AF32FLBHiwZ-NlbKoVxlbiS0f5Bn-sZzDDGdE.

Marquand, Richard, dir. *Return of the Jedi.* 1983; Beverly Hills, CA: 20th Century Fox/Lucasfilm Ltd. Disney+. https://www.disneyplus.com/movies/star-wars-return-of-the-jedi-episode-vi/6QGKo5mjDBS8.

Marv. "A History of Mando'a." *Numidian Prime* (blog). Accessed January 7, 2023. https://numidianprime.wordpress.com/2022/01/25/a-history-of-mandoa/.

Peterson, David J. *The Art of Language Invention: From Horse-Lords to Dark Elves to Sand Worms, the Words Behind World-Building.* New York: Penguin Books, 2015, 2021.

"Pre-Order the new Aurebesh Sneakers from Po-Zu." *Jedi News.* Accessed on April 14, 2022. https://www.jedinews.com/apparel/articles/pre-order-the-new-aurebesh-sneakers-from-po-zu/.

"Return of the Jedi." The Internet Movie Script Database. Accessed November 10, 2022. https://imsdb.com/scripts/Star-Wars-Return-of-the-Jedi.html.

Reynolds, David West. *Star Wars Episode II Attack of the Clones: The Visual Dictionary.* London: DK Publishing, Inc.: 2002.

Rizzo, Carita. "'Star Wars': YouTube Star Creates New Language For Aliens." *Variety.* December 16, 2015. https://variety.com/2015/film/news/star-wars-sara-maria-forsberg-language-1201663521/.

Roadtrip Nation. "How sound designer Ben Burtt made Star Wars' iconic sound effects." YouTube. November 19, 2019. https://www.youtube.com/watch?v=WBKKXjNf1sE.

Saussure, Ferdinand. *Course in General Linguistics.* New York: Columbia University Press, 1958.

Taylor, Chris. *How Star Wars Conquered the Universe.* New York: Basic Books, 2014.

Tolkien, J.R.R. *A Secret Vice: Tolkien on Invented Languages,* edited by Dimitra Fimi and Andrew Higgins. London: HarperCollins, 2016.

———. *On Fairy-stories,* edited by Verlyn Flieger and Douglas A. Anderson. London: HarperCollins, 2008.

———. *The Letters of J.R.R. Tolkien,* edited by Humphrey Carpenter with the assistance of Christopher Tolkien. London: HarperCollins, 1981.

———. *The War of the Jewels: The History of Middle-earth Vol. 11.* London: HarperCollins, 2002.

Traviss, Karen. *Star Wars Legacy of the Force: Bloodlines.* New York: Ballantine Books, 2006.

Udell, Daniel B. "May the Fourth Special: Where Star Wars Gets Linguistics Right." *Medium.* May 5, 2020. https://medium.com/wikitongues/may-the-fourth-special-where-star-wars-gets-linguistics-right-a00321a1d135.

Walivaara, Josefine. "Blind Warriors, Supercrips, and Techno-Marvels: Challenging Depictions of Disability in Star Wars." *The Journal of Popular Culture* Vol. 51, no 4, (2018): 1036-1056.

Wallace, Daniel. *Book of the Sith: Secrets from the Dark Side.* New York: Titan Books, 2013; San Francisco, CA: Chronicle Books, 2020.

Weiss, Josh. "Star Wars: The Mandalorian created a new form of Sign Language for the Tusken Raiders." *SYFY.* November 2, 2020. https://www.syfy.com/syfy-wire/the-mandalorian-tusken-raider-sign-language.

"The Written Word." Wookieepedia. Accessed April 15, 2022. https://starwars.fandom.com/wiki/The_Written_Word.

Yost, Christopher, writer. *Star Wars Rebels.* Season 3, episode 16, "Legacy of Mandalore." Directed by Mel Zwyer. Aired February 18, 2017, on Disney XD. Disney+. https://www.disneyplus.com/video/45e7d38d-0534-428f-8a2c-bff5413903f1.

Zimmer, Ben. "The Finn-donesian of 'The Force Awakens.'" *Language Log.* January 15, 2016. https://languagelog.ldc.upenn.edu/nll/?p=23527.

_______. "The Languages of Star Wars: The Force Awakens." *Wall Street Journal.* January 15, 2016. https://www.wsj.com/articles/the-languages-of-star-wars-the-force-awakens-1452892741 (paywall).

Chapter 10

Expanding Universes: *Star Wars* and the Cultivation of Canon

John Jackson Miller

Abstract: *Star Wars* has brought more to storytelling than the hours of entertainment on screen; it transformed how media tie-in fiction, comics, and games are both created and perceived. For decades, licensed fiction was seen by the reading public—and certainly production studios and publishers—as just one more merchandise line, with no bearing whatsoever on the future of the parent property. But *Star Wars* breaks that mold, with Lucasfilm introducing a level of curation unseen before in spinoff storytelling. Shared-universe storytelling techniques imported from comics permitted unprecedented events, like 1996's *Shadows of the Empire*, tie-ins in a sense to a movie that did not exist. The 2010s saw a full maturation of this phenomenon, with Disney creating the Lucasfilm Story Group to manage story flow between projects in different media, allowing characters and concepts from films to be introduced in books, comics, and games. This chapter explores the evolution of tie-in fiction through the lens of *Star Wars*'s influential and evolving approach to multimedia storytelling.

Keywords: *Star Wars*, tie-in, fiction, comic, novel, Expanded Universe, Legends, canon, Lucasfilm, Disney, Lucasfilm Story Group, George Lucas, *Star Trek*

***

Well into its fifth decade, the body of storytelling licensed by the *Star Wars* franchise has grown enormous, encompassing a vast number of novels, comic books, gaming products, and stories in other media. Both in the fallow periods between movies and during the busier times of frequent *Star Wars* film and television show releases, these tie-ins have created a huge meta-story elaborating on—and sometimes feeding back into—the main property itself. The "Expanded Universe" or EU, as the collected contributions were known before 2014, had been said by many observers to have taken on a life of its own. But that was never the reality, as it was always developed in service of what *Star*

Wars creator George Lucas considered the official text: his movies and television work. The promotion of tie-in works to canonical status would happen later, due to Disney's purchase of Lucasfilm and *Star Wars* in 2013. Disney elevated the importance of future tie-in works, even as it reclassified stories of the past.

While never an employee of Lucasfilm, as a freelancer, I have written more than a hundred official comic books, short stories, game products, and novels for the *Star Wars* franchise since 2005. My perspective on the question of *Star Wars* and canon is unique; I wrote the first novel in association with the Lucasfilm Story Group, the body created by Disney in 2013 to streamline and coordinate narrative content across all media. Related to that, I worked with the company to publicize both the canonical status of new material as well as the rebranding of previous Expanded Universe works as "Legends."

Having written on both sides of that changeover—and also having worked with other franchises with their own burgeoning universes, including *Star Trek*,[1] Marvel, *Mass Effect*, and *Halo*—I had a good sense of what needed to be accomplished and why. Disney sought to create a canvas that could be filled in by creators working cooperatively in multiple different media, one that could be expanded as necessary to permit future growth. This required a new approach with new methods constituting, as will be seen, a distinct departure from what had come before.

Tying in

For much of the twentieth century, the licensed tie-in story, whether in prose or comics, existed for one purpose: to make money. By expanding the brand of the parent film, radio show, television program, or comic strip, tie-in stories provided the owners of properties with additional revenue streams parallel to what they took in from toy and apparel manufacturers. They were also practically interchangeable with those goods in many cases, with stories often produced with minimal studio oversight.

There were some exceptions even in the earliest days; *The Lone Ranger* radio creator Fran Striker wrote novels and the comic strip for the franchise.[2] The Edgar Rice Burroughs estate also maintained meticulous control over material

---

[1] I would like to gratefully acknowledge Alan J. Porter for participating in an interview for this essay.

For more about the multimedia storytelling of *Star Trek*, see John Jackson Miller's chapter in the companion volume to this book, *Star Trek: Essays Exploring the Final Frontier*, ed. Amy H. Sturgis and Emily Strand (Wilmington, DE: Vernon Press, 2023).

[2] "Fran Striker," *Radio Hall of Fame*, accessed April 19, 2022, https://www.radiohalloffame.com/fran-striker.

based on that author's Tarzan-related works—and Charles M. Schulz, who had full control of *Peanuts* licensed products, exercised care in deciding what appeared under that brand.[3] But quality control in many other cases left much to be desired. Licensed works were often seen as disposable—and the low public perception of comic books and paperback genre fiction only confirmed that impression.

With fandom getting more organized in the 1960s, demand grew for licensed merchandise of all kinds. Some in Hollywood recognized spinoff comics and novels as something that could help build a brand—or harm it, if they were poorly done. Gene Roddenberry moved to exercise more control over *Star Trek* products after some of its earliest licensed works strayed from the screen version in both tone and accuracy. And while *Star Trek*'s studio did not accept his recommendation to create an office of liaison for all literary licensed projects, his suggestion presaged corporate infrastructure that would later exist for both that franchise and for *Star Wars*.[4]

But while quality control improved, one thing remained the same: there was no expectation that what was on the tie-in page would ever feed back to the original property. Schulz oversaw, for example, the Dell *Peanuts* comic book series written and drawn by his assistants, but he hadn't imported ideas from it back into the parent comic strip. They were apocryphal "inspired-by" stories—another world. Richie Cunningham may have gotten engaged to Emma Watt in *Ready to Go Steady*, the first *Happy Days* novel in 1974, but there was no mention of Emma in the show, if producers were even aware of the book at all. Television shows were often doing their best just to maintain their own continuity without worrying about ancillary materials.[5]

Merchandising was central to George Lucas's hopes for profitability for his film, and he had reason to feel that way before the film's release. The first three *Planet of the Apes* movies had their network television debuts in consecutive weeks in September 1973, supercharging a collectible wave for that franchise. *The Six Million Dollar Man* launched in the same year, spinning off all manner of merchandise. And *Star Trek* fans regularly

---

[3] Associated Press, "Snoopy, Charlie Brown and Peanuts Gang Licensing Rights Sold," *Mass Live*, April 27, 2010, https://www.masslive.com/entertainment/2010/04/snoopy_charlie_brown_and_peanut.html.

[4] David Alexander, *Star Trek Creator: The Authorized Biography of Gene Roddenberry* (New York: Roc, 1995), 370.

[5] Exhibit A for *Happy Days* would be the vanished brother Chuck Cunningham, who incidentally does appear in the first novel, only to leave for the beach on page four, never to return. William Johnston, *Happy Days: Ready to Go Steady* (New York: Tempo Books, 1974), 4.

demonstrated their numbers by buying up everything connected to the franchise. In 1975, Franz Joseph's *Star Fleet* (sic) *Technical Manual* and *Star Trek Blueprints* both became *New York Times* bestsellers for Ballantine and their editor Judy-Lynn Del Rey, despite the latter product not being a book at all, but rather a bundle of fold-out sheets featuring *U.S.S. Enterprise*'s interior.

At Ballantine with her editor husband Lester, Del Rey would work with Lucas and his publicist Charlie Lippincott to bring the story of *Star Wars* to the printed page before the original movie came out. Meanwhile, Roy Thomas, former editor-in-chief at Marvel Comics, championed the idea of a comic book adaptation by that company. Lucasfilm saw both the comics and the Del Reys' novelization as advertising for the movie and insisted they release well before tickets went on sale. The first issue of the comics series came out two months before the film's release on May 25, 1977, while the prose novelization debuted even earlier, at the end of 1976. The gamble paid off for all involved. The resulting Del Rey line would be Lucasfilm's adult prose imprint for most of the years that followed. Meanwhile, Marvel's *Star Wars* #1, through its many reprints, was the first comic book to sell over a million copies since 1960. The hit helped to save the struggling publisher during a difficult decade for the comics industry.[6]

The two licensees also produced original storytelling within the *Star Wars* universe. In the Del Reys' case, it came right on the first page of their adaptation, which had been ghost-written under Lucas's name by Alan Dean Foster. Excerpted from an imaginary document called "The Journal of the Whills," Foster's brief prologue to *Star Wars* provided what was for many years the only history of the Old Republic, and it also identified the Emperor by his name, Palpatine.[7]

When the comics adaptation of the film completed its run, Marvel followed it with new stories set in the universe. Continuations of previous science fiction films had fared poorly for the company, with 1977 seeing the cancellations of *Logan's Run, Planet of the Apes,* and *2001: A Space* Odyssey, but the demand for new *Star Wars* material was insatiable. Uncertain of how to follow the blockbuster, Thomas delivered four issues that played on movie themes. The first dealt with the prejudice against "non-organics." But other elements were tonally off, including a *Magnificent Seven* take-off that included Hedji—a porcupine man—and, infamously, Jaxxon, a seven-foot tall green rabbit, which Thomas said that Lucas particularly disliked. "I had

---

[6] Jim Shooter, "Roy Thomas Saved Marvel," *JimShooter.com*, July 5, 2011, http://jimshooter.com/2011/07/roy-thomas-saved-marve.html.

[7] Alan Dean Foster, *Star Wars* (New York: Del Rey, 1976), 1.

figured my 'green rabbit' Jaxxon wasn't really much weirder than a Wookiee," Thomas wrote in 2007, "but obviously George, as the creator of the Star Wars mythos, felt differently."[8] As in the *Star Trek* case earlier, the licensor ensured that later comics writers would tack back to Lucas's vision—but the continuing off-screen story of *Star Wars* was off and running, developing many new supporting characters.

In the spring of 1978, the first original prose novel released: *Splinter of the Mind's Eye,* written by Foster in part as a possible low-budget sequel to *Star Wars,* had the original movie failed. It included a duel between Darth Vader and both Luke Skywalker and Leia Organa; Han Solo was notably absent, as Harrison Ford had yet not been contracted for later films. As with Thomas's comics, the novel had tonal inconsistencies with the film, but it did add Mimban, a location that would appear in many later stories, as would the Kaiburr Crystal, which Foster brought in from an early draft of the *Star Wars* screenplay.[9]

With a comic strip joining the comics and novels in 1979, a burgeoning story had already developed for *Star Wars* before *Star Wars Episode V: The Empire Strikes Back* reached theaters in the following year. At Marvel, the new film required writer Archie Goodwin to write a story undoing one of his developments in earlier comics. In *Star Wars* #28 from 1979, Han Solo strikes a bargain with Jabba—or, rather, the mandrill-like character that Marvel had been depicting as Jabba since its movie adaptation in 1977—to remove the bounty from his head. As writer of the upcoming *Empire* comics adaptation, Goodwin knew that no longer worked, and so *Star Wars* #37 in early 1980 features a two-page coda in which Jabba restores the bounty.[10]

Yet Goodwin told a different story about "that bounty hunter on Ord Mantell"[11] in the *Star Wars* comic strip he was also writing. Close transmedia coordination still lay years in the future. Lucasfilm's early interactions with tie-ins had more of a preventative nature, keeping authors from colliding with what was planned on screen. The biggest example came when comics writer David Michelinie trod upon *Return of the Jedi*'s plot with a story that would have seen the construction of a second Death Star. Lucasfilm communicated

---

[8] Roy Thomas, "Star Wars: The Comic Book that Saved Marvel," in *Alter Ego* #68 (Raleigh, NC: TwoMorrows, May 2007), 75.

[9] Pablo Hidalgo, *Star Wars: The Essential Reader's Companion* (New York: Del Rey, 2012), 227-228.

[10] Archie Goodwin, *Star Wars* #37 (New York: Marvel, 1980), 29-30.

[11] *Star Wars Episode V: The Empire Strikes Back,* directed by Irvin Kerschner (1980; Beverly Hills, CA: 20th Century Fox/Lucasfilm Ltd.), Disney+, https://www.disneyplus.com/movies/star-wars-the-empire-strikes-back-episode-v/iqtDTZAewwYl.

through the series editor that it would rather not do that, Michelinie told me in a 1997 interview. "They didn't say specifically that they'd be doing a Death Star in the next movie, but we had to assume it would be something similar." Alterations were made, and the story that appeared in *Star Wars* #51-52 in 1981 was instead about an attempt to rebuild just the space station's laser cannon.[12]

In early 1983, Michelinie's successor Jo Duffy also was required to make changes to her story about the Lahsbees, a cuddly diminutive species that too much resembled the Ewoks. But Lucasfilm did allow her to make her main comics story arc about the pursuit of secret cargo. After the movie had been out for several months, she was able to reveal that the cargo was secret information tapes smuggled by Bothan spies, with the implication that they were plans for the second Death Star.[13] The studio wasn't ready to let a comic book tip such information *before* the movie, Duffy told me, but the episode suggests that new transmedia storytelling possibilities could have come along for *Star Wars*.[14] They might have, were it not for one minor inconvenience: the Rebellion won.

Galaxy, interrupted

After *Return of the Jedi*'s release in 1983, *Star Wars* publishing slowly wound down, with the Marvel comic book ending in 1986. The standard-bearer for external *Star Wars* storytelling after that would come not from comics or prose but the gaming world. West End Games obtained the license for *Star Wars: The Roleplaying Game* in 1987, beginning a line that would, over the next dozen years, generate dozens of books—and many ideas that would cross back not just into other fiction and comics, but onto the screen.

That's in large measure because when Lucasfilm took a renewed interest in licensed fiction at the start of the new decade and engaged author Timothy Zahn to write a trilogy for Ballantine set after *Return of the Jedi*, it saw that he received a stack of books from the role-playing game as a resource.[15] Eventually, there would be West End gaming volumes about Zahn's *Heir to the Empire* trilogy—with comics adaptations as well from new licensee Dark Horse Comics. With licensees building on one another's works, the Expanded Universe was officially underway.

---

[12] David Michelinie, interview by John Jackson Miller, February 1997.

[13] Jo Duffy, *Star Wars* #80 (New York: Marvel, 1980).

[14] Jo Duffy, interview by John Jackson Miller, February 1997.

[15] Timothy Zahn, "Foreword" in *Star Wars: The Roleplaying Game: The Thrawn Trilogy Sourcebook*, Bill Slavicsek and Eric S. Trautmann (New York: West End Games, 1996), 4.

As Lucas prepared to return to the screen with his Special Edition releases and the Prequel Trilogy, his company's licensees were brought together to collaborate on something unprecedented in tie-in fiction. There was no movie called *Shadows of the Empire* taking place between *Empire* and *Jedi*—but in 1996, the participating firms acted as if there were, telling a story that involved novels, comics, and games, and that spun off its own action figures as if it *had* been a film. It was a proof-of-concept for more interconnected works in the future.

In 2000, Lucasfilm created the office of continuity database manager, appointing Leland Chee, formerly an employee of its video game arm LucasArts, to keep track of all the characters, worlds, species, and other details developed over the years. Later officially dubbed "The Keeper of the Holocron," Chee became part of the workflow for fiction and other licensed works, doing continuity checks and advising when conflicts arose. Chee also played a role in reducing sprawl in the story universe by encouraging economical uses of what already existed. One of the earlier pieces of advice I received on being hired as a writer of licensed *Star Wars* stories in 2004 came from Chee in the form of a suggestion to try to reuse existing planets for settings when practical, as the database already held thousands of named planets. The position—similar to what Roddenberry had first recommended for *Star Trek* in the late 1960s—spoke of a commitment to universe management, and this set the stage for further growth.

While it was home to various expansions of the timeline ranging from the literal *Dawn of the Jedi* to my own *Knight Errant* novel and comics, the period following 2005's *Star Wars Episode III: Revenge of the Sith* release wasn't the same kind of fallow period that existed in the late 1980s. New official content came from Lucas in the form of *The Clone Wars* (2008-2014, 2020) animated television series. Along the way, the series introduced some new conflicts for the tie-in literature to navigate, particularly surrounding the portrayal of the Mandalorians. Author Karen Traviss, who had developed the Mandalorians in tie-in novels, withdrew from a sequel to her *Imperial Commando: 501st* novel in 2010—and while she said the differences with the television show were a secondary issue to other concerns, she also said she had no discussions with the team creating *The Clone Wars*, noting "that's common practice for the tie-in industry."[16]

---

[16] Quoted in Charlie Jane Anders, "Is It Too Late to Save the Imperial Commandos?" *IO9.com*, February 12, 2010, archived at https://web.archive.org/web/20200603012620/https://io9.gizmodo.com/is-it-too-late-to-save-the-imperial-commandos-5466313.

A rare episode, this stood as a reminder that, while Lucas had drawn some elements from the Expanded Universe into his films—from locations like Coruscant to characters like Aayla Secura—he had never considered himself beholden to it. “There’s my world, which is the movies,” Lucas told *Cinescape* magazine in 2002, “and there’s this other world that has been created, which I say is the parallel universe—the licensing world of the books, games and comic books. They don’t intrude on my world, which is a select period of time, [but] they do intrude in between the movies. I don’t get too involved in the parallel universe.”[17] Chee’s codes from his Holocron database expressing these distinctions came to be well-known in fandom. In Chee’s taxonomy, “G-canon” meant materials from George Lucas’s films, “T-canon” covered television, and “C-canon” was the continuity from comics, novels, and games—with other categories for materials only tangential or irrelevant to storytelling.

A new owner—and a new challenge

When Disney purchased *Star Wars* and its associated properties from George Lucas on October 30, 2012, it immediately announced the production of sequel films set after *Return of the Jedi.*[18] The event called many observers to question what would happen to the Expanded Universe stories set in that timeframe, which by that point had come to encompass the 21-volume *New Jedi Order* project and several major character life events—not to mention an important death.

The marriage of Han and Leia, later shown in Dave Wolverton’s *The Courtship of Princess Leia* novel in 1994, had already been assumed to have happened as of Zahn’s initial trilogy; twins Jacen and Jaina were born in 1993’s *Heir* finale, *The Last Command.* A third child, Anakin Solo, followed as a result of a contemporaneously published story set at a different time: Leia had been depicted as expecting in 1992’s *Dark Empire* #5 comic book from Dark Horse. Later, Luke married the *Heir* character Mara Jade in Michael Stackpole’s *Union* comics miniseries in 2000, with the birth of their son Ben following in 2001. The children grew older and took part in the adventures, eventually becoming main characters in novels of their own right. They lived, fought, and also died. Anakin Solo died in an adventure in 2001; Jacen, having fallen to the Dark Side, was killed by sister Jaina in 2008. And one screen character had died: Chewbacca.

---

[17] “Jedi Master,” *Cinescape* #62 (Venice, CA: Mania Entertainment, July 2002).
[18] The Walt Disney Company, “Disney to Acquire Lucasfilm Ltd.,” press release, October 30, 2012, https://thewaltdisneycompany.com/disney-to-acquire-lucasfilm-ltd/.

The 1999 *New Jedi Order* novel *Vector Prime* told the story of Chewbacca's heroic death while trying to help residents of Sernpidal escape from their planet's collision with its moon. Author R.A. Salvatore depicted the controversial death while under instructions to do so: the publishing arm had sought a chance to show there were real stakes, and as Leland Chee put it, the challenges of writing Chewbacca in novels made him the prime candidate.[19] All of this posed an intractable problem for Lucasfilm in the time before J.J. Abrams's *Episode VII* approached. Billion-dollar movie franchises seldom circumscribe their creators to that degree; it was unrealistic to expect a film seen by tens of millions to hew to a history previously known to hundreds of thousands at most.

Worse, the EU had left Abrams with a series of downbeat moments. The opening crawl of *Star Wars Episode VII: The Force Awakens* (2015) could no more say that Chewbacca was already dead than it could say that Han and Leia had raised two sons and a daughter, but that the sons were already dead, one killed by his twin sister. "There's no way that I'd want to do an *Episode VII* that didn't have Chewbacca in it and have to explain that Chewbacca had a moon fall on his head," Chee said. "And if we were going to overturn a monumental decision like that, everything else was really just minor in comparison."[20]

Possible paths: *Star Trek* and James Bond

J.J. Abrams's other relaunched film franchise, *Star Trek*, had found a way to allow its new 2009 iteration to coexist with past film and television continuity thanks to something that already existed in that universe: time travel. With alternate realities and timelines a familiar part of *Star Trek* for decades, Abrams was able to make a major plot point of it, bringing back Leonard Nimoy as Spock from the "Prime Universe." *Star Wars*, by contrast, had no time travel in 2014.

What *Star Wars* crossovers there had been came from Force tricks like "flow-walking" or visions, as seen in the "Vector" crossover Dark Horse did in 2008, which allowed Luke Skywalker to appear in the same sequence with far-future descendant Cade Skywalker and ancient-era character Zayne Carrick. Alternate realities also were not a characteristic of *Star Wars* storytelling. Dark Horse had done "Infinities" stories—its version of Marvel's *What If?* series and DC's *Elseworlds* line—and several stories in *Star Wars: Tales* that were

---

[19] Jordan Zakarin, "Inside Lucasfilm's Top Secret Star Wars Database," *SyFy.com Fandom Files*, January 15, 2018, archived at https://web.archive.org/web/20200811080527/ https://www.syfy.com/syfywire/inside-lucasfilm%E2%80%99s-top-secret-star-wars-database-fandom-files-13.

[20] Ibid.

designated as unofficial. But there was no crossing between worlds at all. No multiverse existed.

At the same time, many franchises over the years had been able to negotiate major changes without a word, trusting in fans' willingness to make their own explanations and to see past conflicting information. As an outsider with no vote and no knowledge of the internal workings at Lucasfilm, my particular preference was for what I called "the *Skyfall* option" when I mentioned it to Chee in the summer of 2013: to wit, every previous story happened, and none of them happened. In the 2012 James Bond entry *Skyfall*, viewers saw the Aston Martin DB5 that Bond drove in 1964's *Goldfinger*. It appeared with no explanation and made no sense from a continuity perspective.

But that's a feature endemic to the franchise, explained Bond expert Alan J. Porter: "No matter how you look at it, the legacy of Bond is one where the idea of a tight continuity doesn't work, despite recent efforts by the filmmakers; there is no such thing in Bond as a tight 'expanded universe' or closely connected stories as we've come to expect from properties such as *Star Trek*, *Star Wars*, etc."[21] Much of that owes, Porter said, to the source material: like Arthur Conan Doyle, Ian Fleming wrote the Bond stories at different times and not always with an eye to consistency. This exists to an even greater degree in the ancillary material, where Porter and his co-writer identified 28 different incarnations of Bond as of 2021, each with their own chronology and continuity. Some stories are set in the Cold War, others in the modern day.

Bond as a franchise, then, is already one in which cognitive dissonance is called for regularly. There's no *Doctor Who*-like mechanism for handling actor changes. Viewers are just expected to go with it. There is no literal confirmation in *Skyfall* that Daniel Craig's 007 met Oddjob's gold-loving employer at some point in the past, but even in the in-jokiest Easter egg there's an invitation for longtime fans to imagine that *something* like that might have happened. The invocation says that the stories they invested in still mean something. "It doesn't really matter where the Aston Martin in *Skyfall* came from," Porter said. "We should just enjoy the fact that it was there."[22]

The *Skyfall* option, then, offers an "all accounts are true, except when they aren't" freedom, a canon-of-the-moment that allows creators to pick and choose bits of continuity. It's something Marvel and DC comics writers have employed forever, and viewers have grown more accustomed to it as multiple

---

[21] Alan J. Porter and Gillian J. Porter, *The James Bond Lexicon* (Lexington, KY: White Rocket Books, 2021), 6-7.
[22] Ibid., 7.

versions of franchises have proliferated over the years. And so, even as Lucasfilm under Disney decided to go for a tight "everything counts" continuity when it came to new materials released starting in September 2014, the earlier content seems to have wound up in a similar kind of zone: not part of canon, but yielding up material for it with regularity.[23]

Dawn of a new day

In late 2013, I began writing a tie-in prequel novel for the *Star Wars Rebels* series, which was to debut in the fall of 2014 on the Disney XD network. Previously, comics, games, and novels I had written went through their licensed publishers to Lucasfilm's fiction editor for approval and also to Chee for a continuity check. In the case of the *Rebels* prequel, as the television show debut was a year away, my story proposals also went to the executive producers, Dave Filoni, Simon Kinberg, and Greg Weisman, all three of whom provided comments. Furthermore, in addition to my previous workflow, I participated in a conference call with a new body called the Lucasfilm Story Group.

The group included participants from various parts of the *Star Wars* storytelling engine, bringing in principals on projects when needed. In my case, series co-creator Dave Filoni attended to offer further advice on what to write and how to approach the characters. The group, as I was given to understand, was intended not so much as an additional layer of approvals but as an enhancement of what transpired before, with its members tasked with more than simply handling air-traffic control for fictional characters. The Story Group focused on both the larger meta-story of *Star Wars*, as well as the individual components, and they worked to improve the flow of concepts between them. Through its work, film and television creators could use tie-in media to more easily tease clues about their works well in advance of their release dates—and original concepts appearing in books, comics, and video games could more easily make the jump to other media.

In March 2014, with the *Rebels* novel—still under my unofficial title *Loose Cannons*—two-thirds complete, I was informed that novels, comics, games, and other products featuring narrative would henceforth be considered canonical, thanks to the involvement of the Story Group. Further, previous works in the Expanded Universe were to be rebranded as "Legends." As my novel was the first released under the new policy, I was invited to Lucasfilm to

---

[23] Dominic J. Nardi, "Canonical Legends: How the Expanded Universe (Selectively) Lives On TV," in *The Transmedia Franchise of Star Wars TV*, ed. Dominic J. Nardi and Derek R. Sweet (London: Palgrave Macmillan, 2020), 175-199.

appear in a video making the announcement—as was Timothy Zahn, who had relaunched *Star Wars* prose fiction in 1991.

It was with this new understanding that I completed the novel, which we called *A New Dawn* as an indicator of what was now its triple role: launching the Rebellion, the *Rebels* storyline, and the new era of storytelling all at once. The fact that most of the novel took place on a planet tidally locked to its sun—where witnessing an actual dawn would have been fatal—was a fun bit of irony, as was the fact that thorilide, the elusive substance the Empire was chasing throughout the book, was something it used for cannon maintenance. (There's a further canon-related matter for thorilide, as will be seen in a section below.)

The move to canonical licensed works, the creation of the Legends classification, and the *A New Dawn* novel were all announced by Lucasfilm on April 25, 2014; it released our video the same day. Beyond the benefits of networking elements together, the release announced the other rationale for the change. As suggested above, "to give maximum creative freedom to the filmmakers and also preserve an element of surprise and discovery for the audience," the Sequel Trilogy could not follow the events of the post-*Return of the Jedi* Expanded Universe.[24]

The announcement generated intense attention—as well as opposition—from many fans right from the start. Some opponents mistakenly assumed the Expanded Universe had previously been canonical, when what licensees were really doing was working to keep things consistent, always understanding that Lucas could go his own way. Lucasfilm's press release that day made clear that the filmmaker had never considered himself beholden to any licensed works and that the six *Star Wars* episodes and the content he developed and produced in *The Clone Wars* were "the immovable objects of *Star Wars* history, the characters and events to which all other tales must align."[25]

Others seemed to miss the nuances of the studio's message. Previous works weren't being discarded, but rather would provide ideas and inspiration for the films, television shows, and new fiction to come. Lucasfilm's release said that explicitly, adding examples of things that would be appearing in *Rebels*, including the Inquisitor, the Imperial Security Bureau, and Sienar Fleet Systems, all concepts that dated back to the West End roleplaying game.

---

24 "The Legendary Star Wars Universe Turns a New Page," StarWars.com, April 25, 2014, https://www.starwars.com/news/the-legendary-star-wars-expanded-universe-turns-a-new-page.
25 Ibid.

Before the show aired, *A New Dawn* would provide even more proof, as the prized substance everyone in the story was chasing, thorilide, had come from my *Knights of the Old Republic* comics, now deemed Legends. Its chemical properties fit the story need I had, so there was no need for something new. And using it didn't mean that everything about the previous story it had appeared in was suddenly canonical, any more than the mention of planets and species from the Expanded Universe made canonical previous stories involving them.

The tweet is no longer available, but I recall it was Lucasfilm's Pablo Hidalgo who said in those days something to the effect that legends can be true in part, in whole, or not at all. Tales of Robin Hood and King Arthur aren't histories, but there are bits and pieces in the lore that have real origins. I felt that summed up the approach for previous works. In the prologue to *A New Dawn*, Obi-Wan Kenobi tells young Jedi students, "There are truths, and there are legends touched with truth, and all can teach you something."[26] To my recollection, that line—or one like it—from me predated my knowledge of the major change, but it certainly fit both the in-story situation and also that of the real world. The Ahsoka character would say a similar line later in the *Rebels* series.[27]

A New Dawn was released on September 2, 2014, marking the beginning of the canon era for *Star Wars* ancillary works. (A comics mini-series, *Darth Maul: Son of Dathomir*, had released in the summer, based on an unproduced *The Clone Wars* episode with attendant claims that Lucas and Filoni considered its story canonical,[28] but it had been announced before the Legends changeover and in fact has appeared with the Legends banner in foreign editions.) Filoni provided the foreword for *A New Dawn*, explaining the Story Group's mission:

> More than at any other time in its existence, more *Star Wars* stories are being told every day. More importantly, the old concept of what is canon and what isn't is gone, and from this point forward, all our stories and characters exist in the same universe; the key creatives who work on the

---

[26] John Jackson Miller, *Star Wars: A New Dawn* (New York: Del Rey, 2014), 6.

[27] *Star Wars Rebels*, season 2, episode 20, "The Mystery of Chopper Base," written by Steven Melching, directed by Bosco Ng, aired March 23, 2016, on Disney XD, Disney+, https://www.disneyplus.com/video/011fcd55-95a2-4ef7-8850-200f23c53caf.

[28] "Sam Witwer talks The Clone Wars, Siege of Mandalore, Maul, and Honoring George Lucas' Legacy," *SW Holocron*, April 17, 2020, https://www.swholocron.blog/2020/04/17/exclusive-interview-part-1-sam-witwer-talks-the-clone-wars-siege-of-mandalore-maul-and-honoring-george-lucas-legacy/.

> films, television, comic books, video games, and novels are all connected creatively for the first time in the history of the *Star Wars* universe.[29]

Meanwhile, my own acknowledgments directly addressed the strong feelings that had been—and would continue to be—expressed by the fans of the older material: "The stories we love may not always fit neatly into a single timeline, but they will always matter."[30]

Aftermaths

While some fans organized online to voice their feelings, *A New Dawn* benefited, I believe, from two facts. First, I had put in nearly a decade conversing with fans in their own spaces, regularly contributing to TheForce.net's boards and appearing on many podcasts. People who engaged with me directly were civil. The bigger happenstance is that *A New Dawn* took place in what has been called the "Dark Times" era, between Episodes III and IV. While not devoid of EU content, it had been relatively underutilized, and nothing I did in *A New Dawn* overwrote anything.

My fellow author Chuck Wendig didn't have that luxury when he was tasked with writing *Aftermath*, a trilogy set after the end of *Return of the Jedi*. Now, finally, the timeline with the New Jedi Order and expansions to the Skywalker and Solo families began to be overwritten. The first installment came out on "Force Friday" in September 2015 with the first wave of merchandise for *Star Wars Episode VII: The Force Awakens*, which was due out three months later. It was a smashing sales success, landing on the *New York Times* bestseller list four weeks in a row despite—and to some degree because of—backlash among certain readers.[31]

Aftermath also included an element that showed off some of what was possible in the Story Group era. During that March 2014 visit, I had recommended that one of my novel characters, the Imperial Captain Rae Sloane, might serve as a good character to export into other media. A woman and a person of color, Sloane was a canny professional who believed in the Empire's aims while not yet being aware of its evils. It was easy enough to

---

[29] Dave Filoni, "Foreword," to Miller, *A New Dawn*, xiv.

[30] Miller, *A New Dawn*, vii.

[31] The first novel was struck by "review bombing," a tactic previously used against video games and later commonplace for movies. Amazon's algorithm appears to have read the negative responses as a high level of public interest, elevating the book's profile in its automated promotions. Wendig discusses the review bombing at Chuck Wendig, "In Which I Am Fired from Marvel," *Chuck Wendig: Terribleminds*, October 12, 2018, http://terribleminds.com/ramble/2018/10/12/in-which-i-am-fired-from-marvel/.

imagine her as an Imperial equivalent to C.S. Forester's Horatio Hornblower, who readers got to see at many points in his career.

Before *Aftermath*'s release, a short story of mine about Sloane as a cadet appeared in *Star Wars Insider* magazine. Wendig depicted her much later, serving as Grand Admiral of what remained of the Imperial fleet. She next appeared in an issue of the *Star Wars: Kanan* comics series—and would eventually have an on-screen role in the *Star Wars Squadrons* video game. Sloane remains a popular character among fans and stands as an early example of the kind of cross-media storytelling synergy the Story Group was working toward.

More significantly, Lucasfilm demonstrated its willingness to bring Legends characters into canon with Timothy Zahn's Thrawn character. Introduced in 1991 in *Heir to the Empire*, Thrawn was given a role in the *Rebels* television series, in two new series of novels, a mention in the second season of *The Mandalorian* (2019-), and is a featured character in the new Disney+ streaming series *Ahsoka* (2023).

The positive fan response to Thrawn's return—without all the baggage of the stories he had previously appeared in—served as evidence of something I had come to believe in my interactions with fans. Many had demanded resolutions for the EU's post-*Return of the Jedi* character arcs, going so far as to campaign for the release of *Sword of the Jedi*, a trilogy by Christie Golden that had been announced before the changeover. There was nothing to release, however, and it was not conceived of as a story wrapping up continuity in any event.

The cry was heard, interestingly, a universe away. When the events of the streaming series *Star Trek: Picard* overwrote events of two decades of novels, three *Star Trek* authors cited the *Star Wars* experience in creating a finale for those stories. Ironically, that series, *Star Trek: Coda*, found its most vocal opponents in the fans most devoted to the previous literature, according to David Mack, who wrote the last installment.[32]

What the Thrawn experience suggests, by contrast, is that many fans of characters whose storylines have been made inoperative are seeking not resolutions, but rather simply more stories in which they appear. In many open-ended franchises, "final stories" tend not to appear in any event—or if they do, they're set in an alternate reality, as is the case with Marvel's "The End" line of comics depicting the imagined last adventures for specific characters.

---

[32] David Mack, interview by John Jackson Miller, December 16, 2021.

New territory

The internet and the streaming age created new opportunities for *Star Wars* licensed storytelling but also new challenges. The projects that started its comics and literature lines, film adaptations, had grown more difficult to produce in the digital era; a great deal of what's going to be on the screen simply isn't present in the script. And while spoiler culture had been a concern as far back as 1983's comics adaptation of *Return of the Jedi*,[33] by the late 2010s it could threaten a film opening financially.

Alan Dean Foster's *Star Wars* novelization came out five months before the movie, but by the 2010s, security concerns were such that the print version of his *The Force Awakens* adaptation didn't release until three weeks after the film. Its e-book did release simultaneously with the film. The printed edition still became one of the best-selling novels for the franchise in years.

The novelizations for *Star Wars Episode VIII: The Last Jedi* (2017) and *Star Wars Episode IX: The Rise of Skywalker* (2019) released in all formats three months after their films, and they were offered and marketed as expanded editions as a means of attracting interest. Comics adaptations were scheduled to release even later, with *The Last Jedi* #1 appearing five months after the film. *The Rise of Skywalker* comics adaptation was slated for June 2020, *six* months after its film release, only to be taken off the schedule indefinitely due to the COVID-19 pandemic.

Original works could still be crafted to tie into films before their releases: *Catalyst* by James Luceno (November 15, 2016) set up *Rogue One* (December 16, 2016), and *Canto Bight* (December 5, 2017), an anthology with novellas by Saladin Ahmed, Rae Carson, Mira Grant, and myself, dealt just with the casino world from *The Last Jedi* (December 15, 2017) and its background patrons. Those characters appeared in the movie, but their histories came from another as-then unpublished resource, *Star Wars The Last Jedi: The Visual Dictionary* (December 15, 2017). Going by order of release, the consumer might well have assumed the dictionary was drawing upon material from *Canto Bight*, rather than the other way around—and both were drawing on a mid-production understanding of what was in the film.

The streaming world offered something new for *Star Wars*: multiple live-action mini-movies, as opposed to the animated series that had come before. *Star Wars*

---

33 When *Marvel Super Special* #27, adapting *Return of the Jedi*, hit comics shops a month before the film release, none other than comics fan Mark Hamill alerted Lucasfilm about the problem. Marvel dispatched its sales team—including Peter David, later a novelist and comics writer—to get as many copies as possible off the stands. Peter David, "But I Digress," *Comics Buyer's Guide* #1296 (August 7, 1998), 62.

Celebration: Chicago in April 2019 spotlighted the cast of the upcoming *The Mandalorian* series for Disney+ and also teased the creation of something new for licensed comics and fiction: Project Luminous, which turned out to be a new fiction setting, The High Republic. While multiple licensees working to elaborate on a corner of the distant past of the *Star Wars* universe had already occurred with the *Knights of the Old Republic* video game, comics, and fiction, The High Republic was something new: a dedicated preserve, in a sense, which comics creators and novelists could develop without colliding with anything upcoming on screen. It succeeded at that, with a "Phase II" running in 2022 and a "Phase III" set to begin in late 2023.

What readers didn't see were novels and comics based directly on *The Mandalorian.* A comics series announced in June 2020[34] didn't release until July 2022,[35] and was a direct adaptation rather than an original story; the same was true of the junior novelizations that appeared on the prose side. An original adult novel tying into the series had been slated for late 2020 and then delayed, until Del Rey canceled it "due to the ever-expanding world of *The Mandalorian* . . . as the story continues to unfold on screen."[36] Whether or not a well-publicized cast change[37] the month before was responsible, this underscores that ongoing television series in particular are fast-moving vehicles, and tying into them is particularly challenging. In light of that, settings like The High Republic offer licensees more control.

Still expanding

As 2022 dawned, *The Book of Boba Fett* (2021-) Disney+ streaming series was drawing on content from tie-in materials Lucasfilm considered canon—as well as ones it had deemed Legends. Black Krrsantan, a Wookiee bounty hunter who first appeared in February 2015's *Darth Vader* #1, debuted on television in the second episode of *Boba Fett.* The same episode has yet another Legends-era deep cut: a crate of sansanna spice, a substance that first appeared in Marvel's *Star Wars Annual* #2 in 1982. And my own 2013 *Star Wars: Kenobi* novel—one of the first books to be reprinted with the Legends branding—saw one of its major

---

34 "The Mandalorian Publishing Program Revealed," June 30, 2020, StarWars.com, https://www.starwars.com/news/the-mandalorian-publishing-program-revealed-exclusive.

35 "Marvel Finally Announces a Mandalorian Comic, But There's a Catch," IGN.com, May 19, 2022, https://www.ign.com/articles/star-wars-mandalorian-marvel-comics-adaptation.

36 Star Wars Books (@DelReyStarWars), "Due to the ever-expanding . . .," Twitter, March 9, 2021, 12:01pm, https://twitter.com/DelReyStarWars/status/1369332524288212997.

37 Daniel Holloway, "Lucasfilm, UTA Drop 'Mandalorian' Star Gina Carano Following Offensive Social Media Posts," *Variety,* February 10, 2021, https://variety.com/2021/tv/news/mandalorian-gina-carano-1234905589/.

plot points reappear in the *Obi-Wan Kenobi* streaming series later in 2022: the fact that Qui-Gon Jinn had not responded to Obi-Wan's attempts to communicate through the Force. Ewan McGregor described having read the novel in one of his press interviews[38] for the series, and Del Rey released the novel in a new edition in advance of the show's launch.

I've often compared writing for a licensed universe to visiting a national park: you use what's there to create enjoyment and try not to leave the place worse than you found it. Disney, which runs literal amusement parks drawing on content from its universe, has crafted a situation in which the borders of its own conceptual *Star Wars* park can continue to grow, serving up more ideas for future works in all media. Licensed content began as a method for exploiting properties commercially, with the understanding that ideas flowed only one way in the hierarchy, from the parent work to everything else. *Star Wars* may have done more to change that than any other franchise.

Bibliography

Alexander, David. *Star Trek Creator: The Authorized Biography of Gene Roddenberry.* New York: Roc, 1995.

Anders, Charlie Jane. "Is It Too Late to Save the Imperial Commandos?" *IO9.com.* February 12, 2010. Accessed from the archived original on January 17, 2022. https://web.archive.org/web/20200603012620/https://io9.gizmodo.com/is-it-too-late-to-save-the-imperial-commandos-5466313.

Associated Press. "Snoopy, Charlie Brown and Peanuts Gang Licensing Rights Sold." April 27, 2010. *Mass Live.* https://www.masslive.com/entertainment/2010/04/snoopy_charlie_brown_and_peanut.html.

David, Peter. "But I Digress." *Comics Buyer's Guide* #1296 (August 7, 1998): 62.

Duffy, Jo. Interview by John Jackson Miller. February 1997.

_______. *Star Wars* #80. New York: Marvel, 1980.

Filoni, Dave. "Foreword." In *Star Wars: A New Dawn*, xiii-xiv. New York: Del Rey, 2014.

Foster, Alan Dean. *Star Wars.* New York: Del Rey, 1976.

"Fran Striker." Radio Hall of Fame. Accessed April 19, 2022. https://www.radiohalloffame.com/fran-striker.

Goodwin, Archie. *Star Wars* #37. New York: Marvel, 1980.

Hidalgo, Pablo. *Star Wars: The Essential Reader's Companion.* New York: Del Rey, 2012.

Holloway, Daniel. "Lucasfilm, UTA Drop 'Mandalorian' Star Gina Carano Following Offensive Social Media Posts." *Variety.* February 10, 2021. https://variety.com/2021/tv/news/mandalorian-gina-carano-1234905589/.

[38] Screen Rant (@screenrant), "Interview with Ewan McGregor," Twitter, May 27, 2022, 12:48pm, https://twitter.com/screenrant/status/1530229369569951744.

"Jedi Master." *Cinescape* #62. Venice, CA: Mania Entertainment, July 2002.

Johnston, William. *Happy Days: Ready to Go Steady.* New York: Tempo Books, 1974.

Kerschner, Irvin, dir. *Star Wars Episode V: The Empire Strikes Back.* 1980; Beverly Hills, CA: 20th Century Fox/Lucasfilm Ltd. Disney+. https://www.disneyplus.com/movies/star-wars-the-empire-strikes-back-episode-v/iqtDTZAewwYl.

Mack, David. Interview by John Jackson Miller. December 16, 2021.

"Marvel Finally Announces a Mandalorian Comic, But There's a Catch." IGN.com. May 19, 2022. https://www.ign.com/articles/star-wars-mandalorian-marvel-comics-adaptation.

Melching, Steven, writer. *Star Wars Rebels.* Season 2, episode 20, "The Mystery of Chopper Base." Directed by Bosco Ng. Aired March 23, 2016, on Disney XD. Disney+. https://www.disneyplus.com/video/011fcd55-95a2-4ef7-8850-200f23c53caf.

Michelinie, David. Interview by John Jackson Miller. February 1997.

Miller, John Jackson. *Star Wars: A New Dawn.* New York: Del Rey, 2014.

Nardi, Dominic J. "Canonical Legends: How the Expanded Universe (Selectively) Lives On TV." In *The Transmedia Franchise of Star Wars TV,* edited by Dominic J. Nardi and Derek R. Sweet, 175-199. London: Palgrave Macmillan, 2020.

Porter, Alan J. and Gillian J. Porter. *The James Bond Lexicon.* Lexington, KY: White Rocket Books, 2021.

"Sam Witwer talks The Clone Wars, Siege of Mandalore, Maul, and Honoring George Lucas' Legacy." *SW Holocron.* April 17, 2020. https://www.swholocron.blog/2020/04/17/exclusive-interview-part-1-sam-witwer-talks-the-clone-wars-siege-of-mandalore-maul-and-honoring-george-lucas-legacy/.

Screen Rant (@screenrant). Twitter post, May 27, 2022, 11:48 a.m. https://twitter.com/screenrant/status/1530229369569951744.

Shooter, Jim. "Roy Thomas Saved Marvel." *JimShooter.com.* July 5, 2011. http://jimshooter.com/2011/07/roy-thomas-saved-marve.html.

Star Wars Books (@DelReyStarWars). Twitter post, March 9, 2021, 12:01p.m. https://twitter.com/DelReyStarWars/status/1369332524288212997.

"The Legendary Star Wars Universe Turns a New Page." StarWars.com. April 25, 2014. https://www.starwars.com/news/the-legendary-star-wars-expanded-universe-turns-a-new-page.

"The Mandalorian Publishing Program Revealed." StarWars.com. June 30, 2020. https://www.starwars.com/news/the-mandalorian-publishing-program-revealed-exclusive.

Thomas, Roy. "Star Wars: The Comic Book that Saved Marvel." *Alter Ego* #68. Raleigh, NC: TwoMorrows, May 2007: 63-78.

Walt Disney Company, The. "Disney to Acquire Lucasfilm Ltd." Press release. October 30, 2012. https://thewaltdisneycompany.com/disney-to-acquire-lucasfilm-ltd/.

Wendig, Chuck. "In Which I am Fired from Marvel." *Chuck Wendig: Terribleminds.* October 12, 2018. http://terribleminds.com/ramble/2018/10/12/in-which-i-am-fired-from-marvel/.

Zahn, Timothy. “Foreword.” In Bill Slavicsek and Eric S. Trautmann, *Star Wars: The Roleplaying Game: The Thrawn Trilogy Sourcebook*, 4. New York: West End Games, 1996.

Zakarin, Jordan. “Inside Lucasfilm’s Top Secret Star Wars Database.” *SyFy.com Fandom Files*. January 15, 2018. Archived at https://web.archive.org/web/20200811080527/https://www.syfy.com/syfywire/inside-lucasfilm%E2%80%99s-top-secret-star-wars-database-fandom-files-13.

Contributors

Emily Austin is an artist and graphic designer working primarily in watercolor, digital media, and photography. Born and raised in Hawaii, she currently lives in northern Indiana. Her work seeks to honor the beauty of the natural world and also to capture the delight found in well-loved books. In particular, J.R.R. Tolkien's Middle-earth has provided a consistent source of landscapes for her imagination to explore, and Emily is featured alongside four other illustrators in the HarperCollins Tolkien Calendar for 2023. She has also contributed to several book covers and illustration projects for Tolkien and Inklings-related publications. Visit www.emilyaustindesign.com to view Emily's portfolio, visit her online store, or connect with her on social media.

Ian Doescher is the *New York Times* bestselling author of fifteen books published by Quirk Books, including the William Shakespeare *Star Wars* series and the Pop Shakespeare series, and five self-published books. In 2020, Ian established the Shakespeare 2020 Project, a public read-through of Shakespeare's works that attracted 6,000 participants in its first year and continues today. Ian has a B.A. in Music from Yale University, a Master of Divinity from Yale Divinity School, and a Ph.D. from Union Theological Seminary. Ian is a Portland, Oregon native and lives in Portland with his spouse Jennifer. Visit Ian online at iandoescher.com.

Dr. Andrew Higgins received a Ph.D. in 2015 from Cardiff Metropolitan University. His thesis, "The Genesis of Tolkien's Mythology," explored *The Book of Lost Tales* materials with a specific emphasis on the interrelated nature of myth and language in Tolkien's earliest world-building. With Dr. Dimitra Fimi, he co-edited *A Secret Vice: Tolkien on Invented Languages* (HarperCollins, 2016) and has published Tolkien- and language-related papers in *A Wilderness of Dragons: Essays in Honour of Verlyn Flieger* (2018) and *Sub-Creating Arda: World-Building in J.R.R. Tolkien's Work, Its Precursors, and Its Legacies* (2019). He published the essay "The Gothic World Building of *Dark Shadows*" in *Exploring Imaginary Worlds: Essays on Media, Structure, and Subcreation* (2020) and has given Tolkien-related papers at The International Medieval Congresses at Kalamazoo and Leeds, The Enchanted Edwardians Conference in Bristol, and for the UK Tolkien Society. He has contributed articles and book reviews to *Tolkien Studies*, *The Journal of Tolkien Research*, *Mallorn*, and *Mythlore* and has taught an online course on language invention at Mythgard Institute/Signum University. Andy is the Director of Development at the Imperial War Museums in the UK.

Paul Johnson is an independent academic researcher engaging in the investigation of film, television, and media forms, with particular emphasis on modern cinema and the position of digital technology therein, most especially the use of digital visual effects. He also continues to explore the wider position of cinema in cultural history, examining Hollywood and other cinematic production bases from early cinema to the present. He has written about directors Steven Spielberg, James Cameron, Robert Zemeckis, and Stanley Kubrick as well the position of digital visual effects and violence in films.

Aaron Masters received a B.A. in Classics from Emmanuel College, Cambridge University, for which he wrote a thesis on the cultural impact of the Library of Alexandria. He then moved on to an M.A. in English Language and Literature from Signum University, which culminated in a thesis assessing the association between J.R.R. Tolkien's *The Lord of the Rings* and Gothic fiction. It was at Signum that he first studied *Star Wars* under Amy H. Sturgis, who convinced him that it might actually stand up to being taken seriously. He lives in Cambridge, UK and works for local government, largely in pursuance of the needs and whims of his cat. His interests are broadly academic.

Kathryn N. McDaniel is McCoy Professor of History and Chair of the Department of History, Philosophy, Religion, and Gender and Sexuality Studies at Marietta College in Marietta, Ohio. She has her B.A. from Davidson College and M.A. and Ph.D. degrees from Vanderbilt University. A British historian specializing in the intersections of history and popular culture, she has published and presented on travel literature, historical themes in fantasy fiction, and pedagogy. She is editor of *Virtual Dark Tourism: Ghost Roads* (Palgrave) and co-editor of *Potterversity: Essays Exploring the World of Harry Potter* (McFarland) and *Harry Potter for Nerds II* (Unlocking Press). She also hosts the Potter Studies podcast *Potterversity* (formerly *Reading, Writing, Rowling*) on MuggleNet.com.

John Jackson Miller (M.A. Louisiana State University, Comparative Politics, 1992; B.S. Journalism, University of Tennessee, 1990) is a *New York Times* bestselling author. A three-time winner of the Scribe Award for best Media Tie-In Novel—Speculative Fiction, his *Star Wars* novels include *A New Dawn,*

Kenobi, Knight Errant, Lost Tribe of the Sith, and the *Knights of the Old Republic* comics. His *Star Trek* novels include the hardcover novel *Picard—Rogue Elements,* the *Discovery* novels *Die Standing* and *The Enterprise War,* the *Prey* trilogy, *Takedown,* and *Star Trek: Strange New Worlds—The High Country.* He has written comics and prose for *Battlestar Galactica, Halo, Iron Man, The Simpsons, Conan, Planet of the Apes,* and *Mass Effect.* An authority on comic-book circulation history, he runs Comichron (comichron.com), the world's largest public collection of comic-book sales figures. His fiction website is farawaypress.com.

Amy Richau writes about *Star Wars,* pop culture, and history. She's the author of several non-fiction *Star Wars* books including *Star Wars Timelines* and *Star Wars: I Love You. I Know.* Her work has also appeared at StarWars.com, *Star Wars Insider,* StarTrek.com, and in the documentary *Looking for Leia.* Amy received a Film Studies degree from University of California Santa Barbara and studied film preservation at the George Eastman house. She lives outside Boulder, Colorado, with her husband, two children, and several pets.

Jennifer Russell-Long (M.A. English Composition and Literature, Indiana University of Pennsylvania, 2020; B.A. Individual and Family Studies, Minor Women's Studies, Pennsylvania State University, 1987) is an English Teacher at Renaissance Academy in the Virginia Beach City Schools. She earned IUP's Outstanding Scholarship Award for her Mid-Atlantic Popular Arts and Culture Association conference presentation on Jane Webb Loudon's 1827 novel, *The Mummy! A Tale of the Twenty-Second Century,* a futuristic science fiction novel demonstrating the earliest roots of the Steampunk genre. She is currently a Ph.D. English Literature and Criticism student working towards the dissertation process, having completed her coursework. A few of her wide-ranging specialties include nineteenth century to the present Gothic, Horror, Science Fiction and African American literature and film, Play Studies, and Video Games as Literature. She is a USA swimming coach at the Coastal Virginia Aquatic Club whose philosophy centers on her term of "Swim-enrichment" to support swimmers' understanding of the sport through educational facets of STEM and Humanities. She has three sons and lives in Bayview Beach-Ocean View, Virginia with her husband. Connect on Instagram @dolphingram7 to learn about her upcoming *Prin-Sass '77* podcast.

Emily Strand, M.A. has taught religion at the collegiate level for more than 20 years; since 2015 she has instructed nursing students in world religions and cultural competence at Mount Carmel College in Columbus, Ohio. She is author of two books on Catholicism and several essays on religious and literary themes in popular culture in peer-reviewed publications. Strand co-edited the scholarly anthologies *Star Trek: Essay Exploring the Final Frontier* (Vernon Press) and *Potterversity: Essays Exploring the World of Harry Potter* (McFarland). She co-hosts the podcasts *Potterversity* and *Meet Father Rivers*, writes the blog *LiturgyandLife.com*, and is a proud member of the 501st and Rebel Legions, international *Star Wars* costuming associations. Her official website is emilystrand.com.

Amy H. Sturgis holds a Ph.D. from Vanderbilt University and focuses on the intellectual history of speculative fiction. She teaches at Lenoir-Rhyne University and Signum University and regularly offers both undergraduate and graduate courses devoted to *Star Wars*. Sturgis has authored four books, edited/co-edited ten others, and published more than sixty essays, many on topics related to the intersection of science fiction and history. She has been interviewed as a genre expert by *LIFE Magazine*, *The Huffington Post*, and NPR's "Talk of the Nation," among other media outlets. Sturgis also contributes the "Looking Back on Genre History" segment to the Hugo Award-winning podcast *StarShipSofa*. Her official website is amyhsturgis.com.

Vikki C. Terrile is an Assistant Professor at Queensborough Community College, the City University of New York (CUNY), where she serves as the Public Services and Assessment Librarian and Co-Coordinator of Information Literacy. She has a B.A. in English from Wells College, an M.S. in library science from Long Island University, an M.A. in urban affairs from Queens College (CUNY), and a Ph.D. in education from SUNY, the University at Buffalo. Her research has explored how librarians understand their work with families experiencing homelessness, the information practices of Renaissance Faire performers and artisans, how community college faculty teach about housing deprivation and homelessness, and how temporary housing providers receive library services. Vikki's Ph.D. dissertation research explored how symbolic understandings of libraries and homelessness by youth services librarians in the US impact library services for families experiencing homelessness.

Éloïse Thompson-Tremblay has been fascinated with representation of women and queer people in films and media, particularly in science fiction and dance films, since she started studying films in 2015. She holds a Bachelor of Fine Arts, majoring in Film Studies and Art History, from Concordia University and graduated from New York University Master's program in Cinema Studies in 2019. Since then, she has worked in the visual effects industry in her home town of Montréal and has strived to keep original takes about gender in films and media. Her favorite *Star Wars* character, unoriginally yet unapologetically, is Leia, though she has a soft spot for Han Solo.

Index

K

L

M

N

O

T

V

W

Y

Z

Ingram Content Group UK Ltd.
Milton Keynes UK
UKHW020113140723
425100UK00001B/5/J

9 781648 896712